CONEtrolled

How we've lost our freedom and how to reclaim it

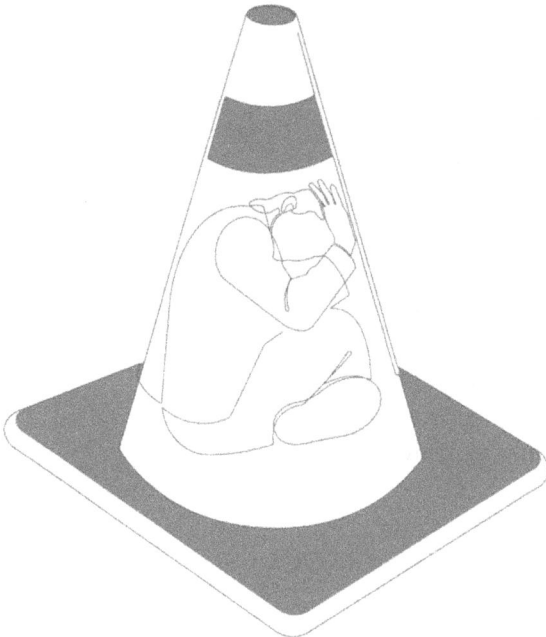

Nava Israel, PhD

PerpetuaLight Publishing
9350 Yonge St
PO Box 61585 Hillcrest Mall
Richmond Hill, Ontario L4C 0C9
Canada
perpetualight.ca

Nava Israel
CONEtrolled, How we've lost our freedom and how to reclaim it
First edition: June 2024

Includes bibliographical references.

Cover artwork by Ryan Prakoso
Cover and book design by Edunjobi Oluwaseun

ISBN: 978-1-7771057-5-4 (print)

Printed in Canada

You are welcome to visit Nava's website: www.navainc.ca

To all who feel we can and should do better for
ourselves and for our world.

Contents

How It All began 9

... where I tell you a tiny bit about myself, how I came up with the Cone Model, and what it's all about. It's also where I provide disclaimers and warn you about potential triggers.

PART 1: The Answers to Our Problems 19

CHAPTER 1: The Things We Know to Be True 20

... where we explore the nature of Core Certainties, their origins, how they influence our reality, and how they transform.

CHAPTER 2: From Problems to Needs 54

... where we explore the deeper meaning of Problems, the confusing path from Problems to Needs, and how profiteers manufacture them for us.

CHAPTER 3: From Needs to Solutions 87

... where we examine our winding paths of Solution-finding and the many forces that drive creativity and innovation.

CHAPTER 4: Obstacles to great Solutions 99

... where we examine the obstacles we face on our way to great Solutions, and why the best ones can get thrown away.

CHAPTER 5: From Solutions to Systems 120

... where we explore how Systems are born, charm us, and become self-conscious.

CHAPTER 6: Dogma, the one true Solution 131

... where we get a bird's-eye view on how Systems morph into Dogma, and what Cones are all about.

PART 2: How Cones are built 141

CHAPTER 7: The Cone Master emerges 142

... where we behold the creation of "The One" who will befriend, shepherd, dazzle, rile, and save us from ourselves.

CHAPTER 8: Picking the low-hanging fruits 156

... where we discover how Cone Builders sniff out our vulnerabilities, pull on our heartstrings, and lure us into their Cones.

CHAPTER 9: Building Cone foundations 186

... where we discover how Cone Builders establish their power, find their recruits, and create a magical role reversal.

PART 3: The Cones gain control 200

CHAPTER 10: Stupefying us 201

... where we discover how Cone Masters manage to stupefy us all the way into their Cones.

CHAPTER 11: Dividing and isolating 212

... where we witness how Cone Masters manage to unleash the very worst in us by dividing us.

CHAPTER 12: Mind control by a thousand cuts 235

... where we discover how Cone Masters manage to control us by invading our minds and legitimizing our darkest desires.

PART 4: How Cones operate 270

CHAPTER 13: A Cone by any other name 271

... where we explore the many Cone variants and the ways they differ.

CHAPTER 14: The corrupting power of power 283

... where we discover how monsters are made and what they do with their power and wealth.

CHAPTER 15: Cone legalities and enforcement 295

... where we discover what makes one a criminal, how Cones come up with their laws, and how they enforce their Dogma.

CHAPTER 16: Belly of the beast 321

... where we discover how Cone Systems devolve into sluggish bureaucracies while expanding their power and reach.

PART 5: How Cones fall... and come back........................ **344**

CHAPTER 17: Trouble in paradise........................... **345**
... where we discover how Cone Masters deal with sticky
situations.

CHAPTER 18: The emptying Cone......................... **362**
... where we discover how Cones collapse, and what Cone Masters
do when that happens.

CHAPTER 19: Cones die... and reincarnate........................**379**
... where we discover what happens to Cone Subjects once their
Cone collapses, and how and why Cones are reborn.

PART 6: A better future within our reach........................ **403**

CHAPTER 20: The light at the end of this tunnel............... **404**
... where we expose the BS of "there's no other way," agree we
can't continue this way, and reclaim our freedom. It's also where
we explore better alternatives and our role in shaping the future.

References.. **437**

Index.. **446**

List of Figures

Fig. 1: The cycle of Core Certainties, Problems, Needs, and Solutions.22

Fig. 2: Core Certainty—Planet Earth is a spherical, inanimate rock 24

Fig. 3: Core Certainty—Planet Earth is a living, sentient being 26

Fig. 4: The Basic Model of Cultural Dimensions 29

Fig. 5: How Cultural Dimensions affect Core Certainties, Needs, and Solutions...32

Fig. 6: Maslow's Hierarchy of Needs (basic categories)..............39

Fig. 7: Blackfoot (Siksika) motivational model 40

Fig. 8: How Core Certainties affect Need definitions and Solutions 46

Fig. 9: Augmenting or manufacturing Need 82

Fig. 10: Intersecting Problems lead to common Needs 106

Fig. 11: Intersecting Needs lead to common Solutions 107

Fig. 12: Self-serving Needs overtaking Solutions 108

Fig. 13: From Solution to System 122

Fig. 14: Major differentiators between System and Dogma 133

Fig. 15: Major milestones for Cone Builders 137

Fig. 16: Easy recruits—the successful, and the failed repeats 161

Fig. 17: Easy recruits—the domineering, and the obedient and insec. ... 167

Fig. 18: Easy recruits—the hopeless pessimists and the relentless optimists 169

Fig. 19: Easy recruits—the entitled and the wannabes 171

Fig. 20: Easy recruits—the immoral and the righteous................ 175

Fig. 21: Easy recruits—the envious and vengeful, and the perpetual victims 180

Fig. 22: Easy recruits—the wilfully ignorant, and the naïve 184

Fig. 23: The anatomy of a Cone—driving forces and Cone Masters 195

Fig. 24: The anatomy of a Cone—types of Subjects and Cone Masters197

Fig. 25: Major variants of divide-and-conquer.................................214

Fig. 26: Major motivations Cone Builders exploit to divide and conquer218

Fig. 27: Common othering mechanisms.................................. 220

Fig. 28: The sum of our Cones is much of who we are and what we believe in 272

Fig. 29: Example of mini- and mega-Cones intersecting in a "free" society.................................279

Fig. 30: Example of mini- and mega-Cones stacking in a theocratic society.................................. 282

Fig. 31: Cone Masters' finances................................. 288

Fig. 32: Major types of crimes................................. 296

Fig. 33: The many causes of criminal activity 297

Fig. 34: Power relations and enforcement vectors in the KKK 314

Fig. 35: Cone enforcement—a cult. of oppressors and sub-oppressors 317

Fig. 36: Cone expanding through recruitment.................................334

Fig. 37: Cone expanding through colonization.................................334

Fig. 38: The U-turn of the emptying Cone.................................367

Fig. 39: When a Cone starts falling apart 377

Fig. 40: Cone fallout 380

Fig. 41: The paths to re-Coning 383

Fig. 42: Example of circular re-Coning.................................385

Fig. 43: Example of a political pendulum re-Coning.................................394

Fig. 44: Example of spiral re-Coning 398

Fig. 45: The five stages of a growing Cone.................................400

Fig. 46: A typical life cycle of Cones 402

How It All began

... where I tell you a tiny bit about myself, how I came up with the Cone Model, and what it's all about. It's also where I provide disclaimers and warn you about potential triggers.

Your life is a mirror image
Stitched by the silk of your thoughts.
It takes every shape and colour
Even those you have never sought.

~ Marina Fedak, a friend and a gifted poet, 2021

Riddle me this... Why is religion like communism, sports clubs like modern medicine, and organized crime like the beauty industry?

This riddle may sound like the one from Alice's Adventures in Wonderland: "Why is a raven like a writing desk?" Unlike Carroll's question, however, mine is not whimsical. There is, in fact, a pattern that applies to each of the listed fields in a consistent and predictable manner.

I admit, I'm a sucker for patterns. Ever since I can remember, patterns presented themselves everywhere I looked. Predictable rhythms were all around. The waterline of my favourite Mediterranean beach advanced and retreated in a never-ending cycle. If you arrived at the beach around noon and didn't plan to stay long, you could put your towel near the waterline. But if you lost track of time, the tide would swipe your stuff into its department of lost-and-never-found. And it wasn't only nature displaying patterns and rhythms. Observing behaviours of living beings revealed a whole slew of fascinating, repeating forms. Large dogs strutted the streets as if they owned the city, while their miniature versions barked their heads off at the slightest provocation. A few mean hens would team up and bully the shy ones. The bullies would end up getting most of the food and the best spots in the coop, proving our belief that "crime doesn't pay" sometimes comes down to wishful thinking.

I found the same patterns in people. The strong and confident walk upon this earth with silent poise, while the emotionally injured and insecure make all the noise and inflict their pain on others. A single, charismatic person can lead an entire flock, sometimes in their millions, all the way to their demise. A few mean bullies can dominate a whole yard and get away with it—at least for a while. Patterns were everywhere. Intriguing, beautiful, inspiring, infuriating, and yes, sometimes plain stupid. To counteract the cruelty around me, I looked for acts of kindness and generosity. I saw animals taking care of their young and mourning the death of a family member for days on end. Living beings formed alliances with others, even across species, to keep everyone safe. It had occurred to me we humans displayed nearly identical behavioural patterns at any scale, be it as individuals, family members, sports fans, students in the schoolyard, corporate employees, or prisoners of war in death camps. Human behaviour became my new pattern-seeking fascination.

I sought a profession that would allow me to realize my desire to understand and heal people of their pains and ailments. So I pursued a career in clinical nutrition. In the early days, this supplied me with the trifecta I desired most: science, people, and healing. Unlike many of my colleagues, I couldn't care less about foods or calories. It was the health and pathology components that fascinated me, though not nearly as much as human behaviour. Working with multidisciplinary teams and conducting research expanded my perspectives on life and sharpened my observations. For my PhD, I chose epidemiology that allowed me to translate qualitative observations into quantitative, statistical data on my clients' behavioural patterns. Curious, irrational, yet uncannily predictable.

One pattern that stood out and tormented me since childhood was that of oppression and social injustice. It started with my experience of antisemitism under an oppressive communist regime, having spent my formative years in communist Soviet Union, now Ukraine. Though the government officially forbade all religions, its loathing attitude toward Jews resulted in rampant persecution, systemic discrimination, mass incarcerations, and a colossal loss of life. Just before I turned eight, my parents and I were able to break through the Iron Curtain at great peril and immigrate to Israel—our ancient motherland. The one place in the world where we were supposed to be welcomed with open arms. Alas, human nature harbours predictable patterns no matter the context. Being an outsider in a new country made for a rough journey that had revealed to me a plethora of patterns, from the cruel to the benevolent.

Later in life, I immigrated again, this time as an adult with my own children. We moved to the friendliest country in the world known for its peaceful nature and abundant use of "sorry." Nonetheless, being welcomed with open arms is rarely the experience of immigrants, even in a country like Canada. Xenophobia and the sense of superiority over outsiders are two of the many patterns etched in most of our cultures.

My need to make sense of people, the world, and the universe made me an insatiable learner. I dabbled in psychology, quantum theory, medicine, string theory, fractals, education, economic models, business, anthropology, philosophy, spirituality, and every other scientific and metaphysical area that held the promise of expanding my understanding of life. Recurring patterns were everywhere, crossing lines between animate and inanimate, physical and psychological, scientific and spiritual. I have learned that even chaos exhibits patterns, and an elaborate physical and ethereal tapestry connects everything and everyone. That's when the Cone pattern had revealed itself to me. Incredibly consistent, relentless, and destructive. Suddenly, wherever I looked, there it was in every area of our lives and on every scale.

Distinct as each of us may seem when examined superficially, we are much more alike, more predictable, and more unified than our separatist cultures and doctrines make us believe. Contrary to popular opinion, people aren't either cruel or kind, wise or stupid, idle or productive, generous or greedy, biased or objective. Let's not kid ourselves. We are all capable of everything and anything, given the right circumstances and persistent mind manipulation. This flexibility is both our strength and our weakness. Despite our differences, we all experience the same basic fears, needs, fragilities, pains, desires, hopes, and joys, something that is also known as the human condition. It is from this understanding and lifelong observations that I have developed *The Cone Model*—a recurring pattern that explains how and why we start with brilliant solutions to our problems yet end up with controlling and destructive life systems.

What is the Cone Model?

The Cone Model describes rigid dogmas that not only rob us of our freedoms, but also fail to address our problems. The problem-to-dogma process forms a cone that grows from the base up. Its wide base represents our view of the world and the many possibilities available to us. Its gradual narrowing through each stage reflects the narrowing of our choices and freedoms. The reason it is a three-dimensional cone and not a triangle is because this construct contains and encloses its followers.

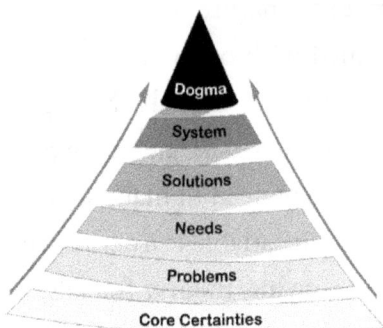

Almost everything in our lives starts with the way we see the world. Our view of reality is based on the sum of our beliefs, upheld values, experiences, and personal traits. These Core Certainties are the unquestionable base assumptions we feel "every child should know." Our Core Certainties inform how we define Problems, and there's never a shortage of those. It can be anything from our fear of dying to being bored out of our minds on a Saturday night. Problems, big or small, lead to Needs. However, Problems and Needs aren't always what they seem. Not only do we view them through a whole stack of Core Certainties, but we are influenced by a myriad of profiteers who will warp our reality, manipulate us, manufacture, or augment our Problems and Needs, and then offer us their quick fixes.

True or false, eventually we require Solutions, which we devise, collaborate on, try out, fight over, try something else, and refine until we get a few tried-and-true Solutions. These might not be the be-all and end-all, but they address our identified Need and resolve at least part of our Problem. In the early days of these Solutions, everyone knows they aren't perfect, but they are still much better than nothing (or at least better than the "old" Solutions). In the months, years, or generations to come, we narrow our selection, sometimes to a handful of Solutions, and they become part of our lives and our regular operations. We come to rely on them, speak their praise, and distribute them outside our immediate circle.

Once one of the "winning" Solutions becomes widespread and deeply rooted in our daily lives, we develop structures to support its distribution, access, and delivery. As all systems go, this Solution narrows still through tighter control and implementation. Having a solid answer means fewer new ideas and greater caution with new approaches. If the new idea isn't aligned with our Solution, we are quicker to dismiss it. This is the System stage, where we no longer ask too many troublesome questions about our Solution or justify its use. Give it some more time and leave it in the hands of Solution zealots and self-serving interests, and it becomes "The One Solution," further narrowing our options. This is where the System becomes more important than the Problems and Needs it is supposed to address. Power and means are no longer equally distributed. At this stage, we find ourselves locked inside the very narrow tip of the Cone. This is where dogma lives. This is where freedom dies, and oppression thrives. At the Dogma stage, we lose our Solution-related freedom of thought, speech, and action, whether or not we are aware of it.

The upholders of "The One Solution" become our oppressors, and we their willing or unwilling Subjects.

A cult is one basic example of a typical Cone. People who feel lost and isolated can be manipulated by a charismatic leader who preys on their vulnerabilities. This leader, who is usually a megalomaniac or a stone-cold exploiter seeking power and means, draws them into the Solution (the cult) with the promise to solve all their problems. What starts with a sense of purpose and unity gradually morphs into something hyper-controlling and abusive, stripping members of their identities and free will. Once the benevolent ruse is no longer required, the leader isolates cult members from the outside world, turns them into cult zealots through mind-controlling manipulation, and enacts harsh enforcement and penalties to make sure "true believers" don't stray from the righteous path. Not all Cones are as obvious and harsh as a cult. In fact, most Cones are much more covert, coming across as "the normal way to be." Nonetheless, they are structured and operate in the exact same way, with the main nuance being their visibility.

Why does it keep happening?

You might be tempted to believe that only naïve idiots buy into an oppressive system and that you are immune to such folly or that these things only happen in fringe groups, but you will be wrong. It happens everywhere and to all of us because we all experience the same basic fears, needs, fragilities, pains, desires, hopes, and joys. We are indoctrinated into and grow up inside many Cone Systems that confine us and control our behaviour, and we are all vulnerable to unhealthy coping mechanisms and shrewd propaganda. This model is easy to grasp because we all experience Cones in almost every area of our lives.

Cones are never accidental. We don't simply slip on a banana peel and fall into an oppressive dogma. Cones are driven by two powerful forces—the well-intended and the self-serving agendas. Like the proverbial angel on one shoulder and devil on the other, almost everything in our lives results from a tug-of-war between givers and exploiters, kindness and cruelty, or darkness and light. The Cone pattern doesn't exist because we have studied its premise and are now applying it widely. Quite the opposite. We are applying it widely because we fail to recognize the recurring pattern and therefore never learn from our mistakes.

Going back to my riddle: Why is religion like communism, sports clubs like modern medicine, and organized crime like the beauty industry? The answer is simple—they are all Cones. Though, on the surface, one couldn't be more different than the other, they all abide by the same rules and operate using nearly identical systems on different scales.

The good news is that while Cones make us believe they are eternal and indestructible, they eventually crumble from within like every other unsustainable system. It may take weeks, months, years, or centuries, but eventually every oppressive Cone topples. The bad news is that we tend to erect new Cones on the ashes of the old ones. So long as we are unaware of the coning process, we keep falling into the same traps that yield the same oppressive systems under new management. On the bright side, once we understand how Cones work, we can no longer unsee them. Understanding the bowels of the Cone beast can help us seek alternative ways to come up with Solutions we choose to embrace.

Why this book matters

The Cone Model has a triple purpose: to make us aware of the many mind prisons (Cone Solutions) we are trapped in; help us rescue ourselves from them; and guide us toward better ways to address our Problems and Needs. Once we break free, we can lead more sustainable lives as individuals, members of our communities, residents of our planet, and integral elements of our universe.

In writing *CONEtrolled*, I aim to lay healthy foundations to open-minded, inclusive, and enlightened debates, and to communities driven by a positive and constructive mindset. None of this can happen so long as multiple Cones imprison us and keep us in endless cycles of mindless obedience. Our Cones dictate to us who we are or aren't; which thoughts we should cultivate or suppress; which choices we should make or be ashamed of; which ideas we can express or withhold; which laws are "God-given" or "of the devil"; which people we should trust or fear; and whom we must protect or annihilate.

Throughout this book, we will journey through the endless cycles of dogmatic patterns that govern our lives and our thought patterns in every major area, from the frivolous to the profound. We will uncover the mechanisms behind this pernicious coning process and conduct an unabashed analysis of what we believe "every child knows." Eventually, we will touch on alternative strategies we can all use to rescue ourselves from those nasty mind prisons so we can build a better future.

Despite the many oppressive dogmas that surround us, we mustn't be bogged down by anger, despair, or hatred because these are the motivations that build the next Cone in line. The Cone Model does not intend to feed baseless conspiracy theories or spread fear and distrust. My goal is to see past the oppressive Cones and empower people to build better futures for themselves, for their communities, and the rest of the world. Though our reality is a far cry from the utopia we wish it to be, there is yet hope for us. Yes, we are predictable and tend to repeat mistakes, but most of us are also mutable, well meaning, and ever evolving.

A few words akin to a disclaimer

Spelling and capitalizing

I wrote this book in Canadian English; therefore, words such as centre, colour, favour, or neighbour aren't misspelled. If you think they are, it's probably because you're not a Canadian. That's okay, nobody's perfect. If you find other brutally misspelled words that defy Canadian spelling standards, that's on me. As for capitalization, this model includes several terms I have coined to describe processes, role-holders, and states of being such as Cone, Problem, User, or Subject. Since I borrowed these words from everyday language, I have capitalized them. Therefore, when Need is capitalized, it refers to the particular construct within the Cone Model, as opposed to the *need* to read this book in one sitting.

Terminology

Terminology is ever evolving. From the time this book first hits the shelves to the moment you get the pleasure of reading it, many of the terms I've used may have been retired and rebranded. Do you say Western, advanced, industrialized, more economically developed, or First World countries? Is it queer, LGBTQ, or LGBTQ2SIA+? Is it a foreigner, an immigrant, or a newcomer? Should we say BIPOC, racialized, black, or people of colour? Each of us will have preferences and sensitivities, and each generation will define the proper way of saying something it considers sensitive and condone the old as profane. The terms I used were all considered respectful when I wrote them, but by the time this book gets into your hands, who the hell knows? I urge you not to get stuck on specific terms and phrases. The principles I'm describing in this book and the general message I'm trying to convey are far more timeless and important than a vocabulary that will inevitably become outdated.

Accuracy

I wish I could say that I am completely objective, categorically bias-free, or that I know divine truths others don't. I am a fallible human being who strives to see the naked truth and not shy away from it, even when it shatters my understanding of reality; even when it is embarrassing or painful. I am a work in progress and all I wish for you is to be your own work in progress. I hope that, despite the discomfort, you will choose freedom and well-being over a cozy but limiting comfort zone.

In writing this book, I did my best to rigorously research every piece of included information. If I have misrepresented, made an error, or provided incorrect data, I apologize. It is likely the result of living in a world where truth is a rare commodity often buried under many layers of misguided beliefs, rewritten history, and intentional misinformation. I welcome you to provide me with any data you feel was omitted or misrepresented along with corresponding evidence. Corroborated evidence please; the fake evidence I can find by myself. I encourage you to contribute to this narrative and promise to check inputs and include verified facts on my website (www.navainc.ca).

Potential triggers

This book includes mentionings of and outrage with patriarchy, homophobia, transphobia, anti-indigenous sentiment, Islamophobia, hate crimes, assault, state-sanctioned violence, police brutality, domestic violence, mental health stigma, ableism, antisemitism, sexism, racism, narcissism, cancer, violence, death, genocide, anti-homelessness stigma/hate, indoctrination, religious trauma, starvation, abuse, misogyny, cults, classism, wealth inequality, imperialism, colonization, trauma, dogfighting, child abuse, white supremacy, xenophobia, exploitation, school shootings, suicide, and war.

Part 1:
The answers to our problems

↓

Part 2:
How Cones are built

↓

Part 3:
How Cones gain control

↓

Part 4:
How Cones operate

↓

Part 5:
How Cones fall… and come back

↓

Part 6:
A better future within our reach

CHAPTER 1:

The Things We Know to Be True

... where we explore the nature of Core Certainties, their origins, how they influence our reality, and how they transform.

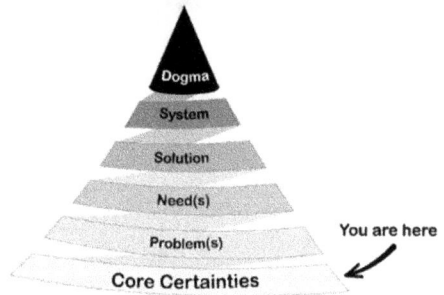

Core Certainties pyramid: Dogma, System, Solution, Need(s), Problem(s), Core Certainties. You are here.

here is a famous urban legend about a mother instructing her daughter on the best way to cook a pot roast:

Mother: "First, get yourself a nice brisket. Before you season it, cut and discard its two edges."

Daughter: "Why cut the edges? What's wrong with them?"

Mother: "That's how grandma taught me to make it. I'm not sure why, but my pot roast always comes out great, right?"

Unsatisfied with her mother's explanation, the daughter goes to her grandmother with the same question, only to receive the same answer. In a last act of inquiry, she asks her great-grandmother:

Great-grandmother: "Why cut the edges? Because back in my day we didn't have large pots like you have today, so we had to make the brisket smaller to fit it into the pot."

Save for natural disasters, not much in this world is as powerful as our Core Certainties—those things in which we thoughtlessly believe. Like a mighty tree, we are rooted in a rich soil made of all our perceptions, beliefs, values, personality traits, and experiences, as illustrated in Figure 1. Everything we think and do draws from this soil for us to make sense of ourselves, other people, and the world around us. We are all born into multiple social constructs that exist simply because we believe in them.

Almost anything you can think of that guides your actions and rules your life is based on constructs our societies have come up with and agreed upon: Countries, borders, and nationalities that separate people; regional and ethnic cultures that define "wrongs and rights"; money as the way to exchange goods and accumulate assets and power; racial differences that separate Us from Them; beauty standards that assign personal value; concepts of crimes and models of punishments; gender identities and gender roles; corporates as legal entities; marriage and family structure; and religions. These and many others are all social constructs we came up with, and they only exist because we believe they do.

Our social constructs are based on historical events that shaped the lives of many generations and created shared stories, lessons, and trauma. This "soil" is further fertilized by our personal traits, childhood, and life experiences. It is the foundation upon which our joys, hopes, dreams, and difficulties grow, both as individuals and societies. I coined the term Core Certainties instead of using "beliefs" to eliminate confusion around the potency of this state of mind. When we say, "I believe I should cut the edges off the brisket," it may leave room for debate, as opposed to, "I am absolutely certain I must cut the edges off the brisket." Our Core Certainties are far more potent than casual beliefs, to the point of being untouchable.

The many Core Certainties that create our reality guide the way we frame our Problems as one thing or another, leading to particular takes on our Needs and the Solutions we come up with. Using our pot roast example, if our Core Certainty is that there are only small pots in existence, we will consider an oversized brisket to be a Problem, which leads to a Need to reshape the slab of meat to fit into a small pot, which leads to a Solution of cutting the edges. Beyond cooking principles, our Core Certainties shape the types of education our kids get, how we treat the natural world, how we define health and which healing methods we apply, the technologies we favour, and the spiritual practices we uphold. Since our chosen Solutions will be based on our Core Certainties, they will act in a feedback loop, further strengthening our worldview. Solutions that we have abandoned, or that have evolved, will challenge, and eventually change our Core Certainties.

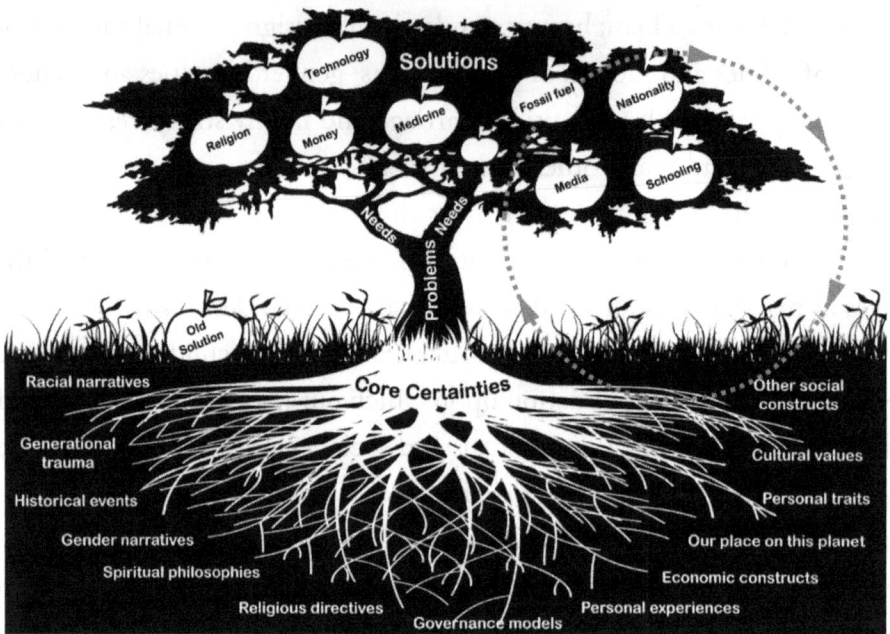

Figure 1: The cycle of Core Certainties, Problems, Needs, and Solutions

Even the way we see our planet is based on our Core Certainties. Figure 2 illustrates one set of Core Certainties that lead to the determination that Earth is a spherical, inanimate rock. This unquestionable assumption is based on layers of other unquestionables, which in themselves are a fusion of more basic Core Certainties. If we believe we are limited to our five senses, that we can rely on our superior brain to perform logical data analysis, and we consider religious or spiritual beliefs to be irrelevant in this scientific day and age, we will be assured that we are rational beings living in a purely physical world. From there, we will assume that, since we can rely on our senses, there is nothing beyond what we physically experience. Therefore, we must be able to measure everything with physical tools. The tools we develop help us get to that single, objective truth about the world.[1] Since our tools and five senses cannot measure or prove religious or spiritual beliefs, we consider them bogus. These beliefs will create a Core Certainty that rational people rely on science alone.

This will be the foundation for the next set of certainties, such as, "All scientific evidence indicates a physical, spherical, rock planet that orbits around the sun along with our fellow planets in the solar system." We will also be certain that whatever we determine to be "living things" must be like us: organic and capable of reproducing. We will believe that all non-scientific claims about our planet and other forms of non-physical life or intelligence are superstitions. This will feed into a Core Certainty that planet Earth is an inanimate rock we happen to inhabit. Such scientific purism will become the bedrock of our definition of Problems and Needs and the development of proper Solutions. Being at the top of the food chain and highly impressed with our own intellect, we will be certain that the purpose of this big rock and everything on it is to sustain us. Based on these Earth-objectifying Core Certainties, we will develop measurement tools along with irresponsible waste dumping and environmentally destructive, resource-exploiting industries. In time, these Solutions will feed and reinforce our Core Certainties on the subject. Since all our mechanical Solutions only measure our planet's physical properties, we will grow increasingly certain that there is nothing beyond these qualities.

---

[1] Note that even the belief in the existence of a single, objective truth is a Core Certainty.

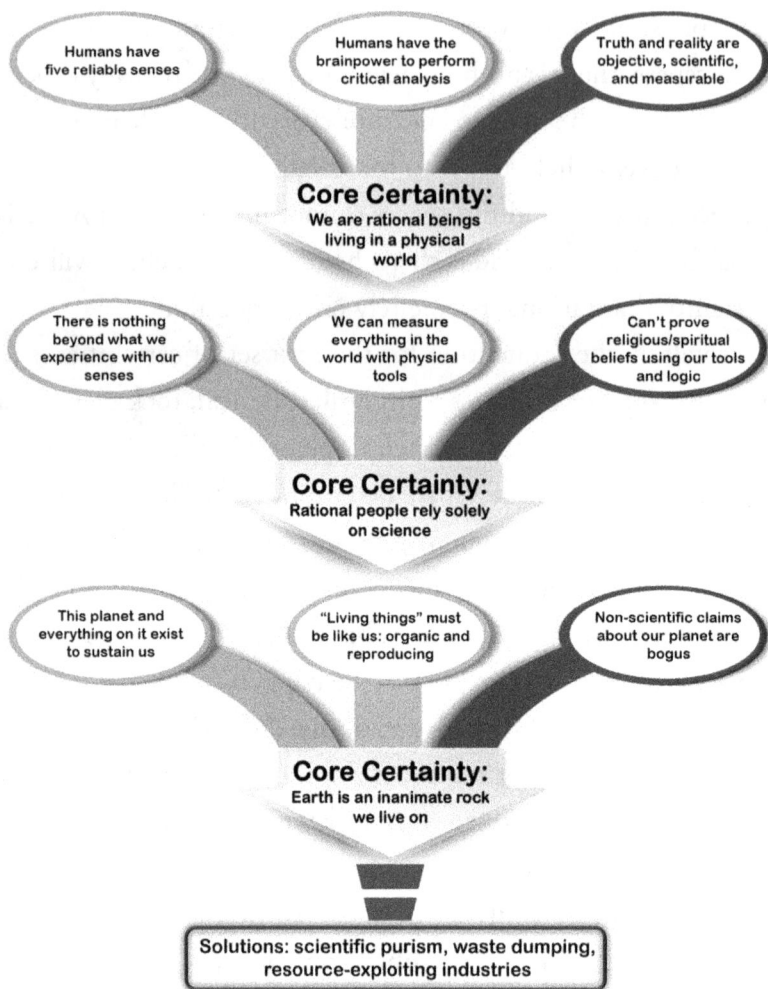

Figure 2: Core Certainty—Planet Earth is a spherical, inanimate rock

Changing a few major Core Certainties will lead us to a completely different understanding of life, as illustrated in Figure 3. Our base assumptions may claim that our five senses are limited. Therefore, they can deceive us and hinder any attempt at a truly objective, critical data analysis, and what we call "objective truth and reality" is a subjective and illusive concept. These views will create a Core Certainty of us as limited beings with much that is beyond our comprehension. This is not to say we are incapable of rationalizing anything; it is simply a more intellectually humbling worldview.

With that in mind, we may be more likely to accept religious or spiritual beliefs. Since we live in a world we cannot ever fully understand, measuring it with physical tools may be helpful for daily life and science may still be valuable, but deducing profound insights based on such limiting methods and placing ourselves in the centre of it all will be seen as a meaningless, ego-driven exercise. This set of beliefs will form a Core Certainty that we are an integral part of a grand, mystery-filled universe. Since nothing is as it seems to our restricted minds, we must heed to our intuition and attune to higher sources for deeper levels of reality. These will reveal to us that—contrary to the information we perceive with our limited senses—everything around us is alive. All this will in turn mean that our role is to sustain this planet and everything on it because, just like us, Earth is a living, sentient being.

This Core Certainty will generate very different Need definitions and Solutions than the ones we develop when we believe ourselves to be the chance and supreme inhabitants of a spherical, inanimate object. Recognizing that life and consciousness exist everywhere, we will be more inclined to develop ecosystem-preservation methods, sustainable-living modes, and creative ways to communicate with our host planet. In time, these Solutions will further reinforce our Core Certainties, or whatever it is we believe "every child knows."

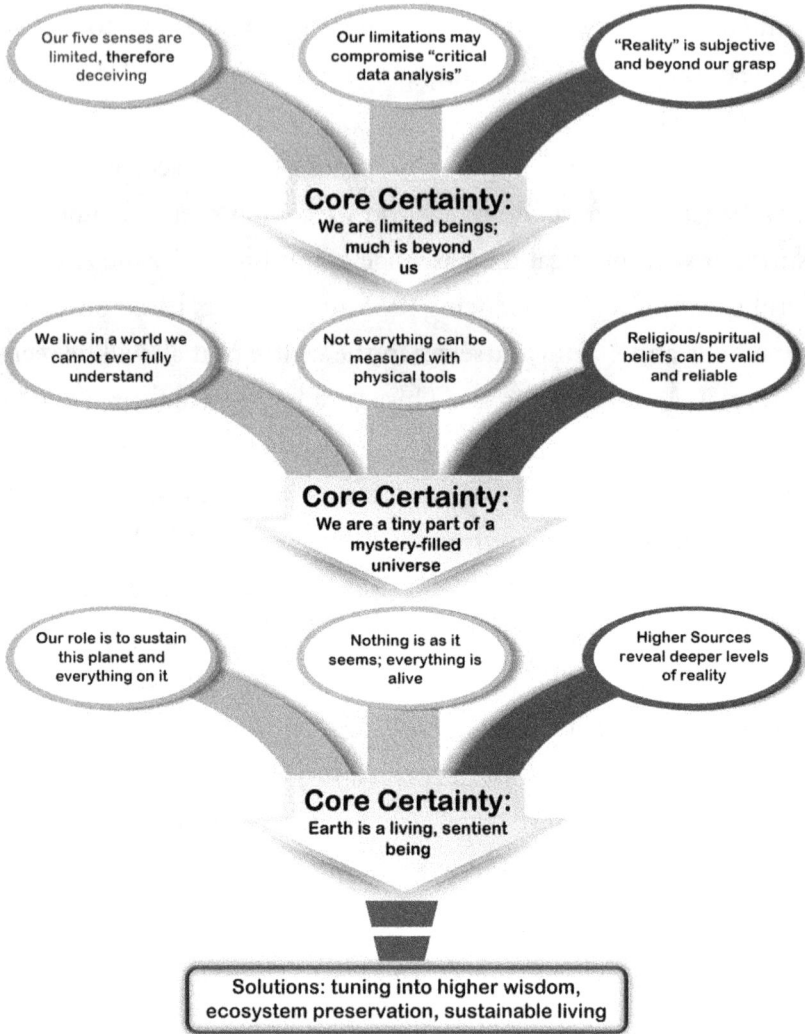

Figure 3: Core Certainty—Planet Earth is a living, sentient being

The sources of our Core Certainties

Everything we are and everything we do is a medley of internal traits and external experiences and circumstances. Our age alone affects the way we see life. The level of our cognitive maturity and our life events will make us different people who hold different worldviews at various stages. The quality of nurturing or the severity of neglect and abuse we experienced in our childhood will affect the way we function throughout life, how we relate to other people, and what we are certain of. So does our sex, race, gender identity, social standing, socioeconomic status, religious beliefs, multi-generational history, the season of the year, natural disasters, plagues, or war.

Most if not all the facts we consider "every child knows" are just that—whatever it is we were told as children based on old belief systems. Our Core Certainties are never absolute or even true—as far as truth can be verified. Therefore, we should develop the habit of adding an asterisk to each of our beliefs with a notation, "conditions may apply."

No matter how much we want straightforward answers, there really is no such thing as a single, objective reality. Our life as we know it is merely a reflection of our perceptions and interpretations of the world around us. What one person will consider a wonderful opportunity, for another it will be an existential threat. What one will regard as success, another will see as failure based on their Core Certainties. If "every child knows" rainy days are troublesome because rain drenches clothes and stalls traffic, our Need will be to stay dry and avoid busy roads at all costs. This will result in the creation of Solutions such as umbrellas, raincoats, boots, video calls, and indoor playgrounds. If "every child knows" rainy days are a blessing because they bring much desired water, our Need will be to "seize the rain." This will lead to the development of rain-summoning rituals and rain festivals.

If you are made to believe from the day you were born that a person must justify their right to live by working, making money, and becoming successful, that is how you will see the world and your place in it. Everything you will do throughout your life will aim for that "deservedness" and you will keep measuring yourself against this yardstick. If that society finds you wanting, it will regard you as a failure and a disappointment (or a traitor). It might even consider you undeserving of life. In other, mainly indigenous societies, people grow up knowing that we exist and are part of nature, just like the rocks, plants, and animals. The concept of "earning your right to exist" makes no sense in these cultures. Their focus is simply on living in full communion with people and with the land as nature intended.

Sometimes we may embrace opposing beliefs and accept that rain can be both bothersome and wonderful, depending on the context. We may accept that group members should be productive for everyone's benefit while having the freedom to decide what "productive" means to them. Mostly, however, our Core Certainties will be quite binary, defining one as absolutely right, and the other as totally wrong. This type of absolute polarity is often driven by our personalities and life experiences, working in tandem with our societal Core Certainties. Holding on to extreme certainties can also be the handiwork of profiteers, who will persuade us of one point of view over another, depending on what product they wish to sell us or what mindset they wish to impose upon us.

Just like the roots of a tree hidden beneath the ground, most of us are unaware of our Core Certainties. We rarely, if ever, revisit what "every child knows." We only become aware of them when we encounter other people's Core Certainties that we disagree with, because they will trigger strong emotional responses, such as ridicule, contempt, fear, or hatred. When reading through the examples on planet Earth earlier, you may have nodded at one worldview as being obvious, while scoffing at the contradicting one, thinking to yourself, "I can't believe those people." In fact, one of the primary sources of both personal and global conflict is that "the other guy" feels exactly the same about you and your Core Certainties.

Cultural Core Certainties

There are numerous definitions of culture. Here is mine: It is everything I and the group I am affiliated with consider true and normal. Most people intuitively relate cultures to nations or societies, but as few as two people can share a culture. A couple, a friendship, a family, a neighbourhood, a workplace, a gender, a sport, a profession, and a street gang each have a culture. These mini cultures operate within incrementally larger ones that dictate their own set of Core Certainties.

One of the most common opposing forces is our complicated relationship with other members of our species. As social animals, we feel compelled to survive with each other despite each other. Multiple factors we learn from infancy affect the way we maintain kinship or enact hostility. Cultural Core Certainties skew our perception of people and events without us having to weigh the evidence and make well-informed decisions. Geert Hofstede (1), a Dutch social psychologist, researched and developed several distinct Cultural Dimensions to support more effective cross-cultural communication. Our Cultural Dimensions spell out our most revered Core Certainties. These guide the ways we interpret and interact with the world, what governance systems we build, how we behave and treat others, and how we communicate. Despite the many revisions to his findings, Hofstede's work still serves as the bedrock of the Core Certainties each culture holds dear, as described in Figure 4.

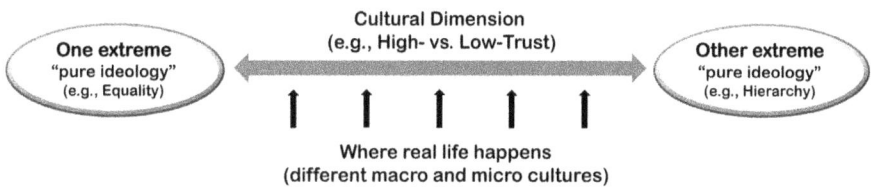

Figure 4: The Basic Model of Cultural Dimensions

Hofstede described national cultures along several dimensions, such as high- vs. low-power distance, individualism vs. collectivism, or high- vs. low-trust. Knowing a nation's place on the continuum of one Cultural Dimension or another may provide insights into some characteristics for sizeable groups. Yet there is absolutely no way of predicting what a single person out of that group will be like. The dominant culture of a certain country may be low-trust, but a single individual from that country can be anywhere on this dimension's continuum. It is at least one reason we should refrain from profiling entire nations and societies using prescribed cultural profiles. For one, individuals are not their societies. Second, societies and nations are far more nuanced than to be defined by six, eight, or even twenty Cultural Dimensions. Every large group of people is a mosaic of multiple sub-cultures that cannot be reduced into a simple average, not to mention the multitude of individual personality variations. The third reason to avoid cultural stereotyping is that cultures are not perpetual. They are ever evolving. The combination of these three factors forbids a stagnant view and stereotyping of any kind.

Rather than tagging people by their societal or group affiliations (e.g., all Americans are… all doctors are… all men are… all Buddhists are…), Cultural Dimensions can help us broaden our understanding of diversity of thought and behaviours, because we will find these variations in every society. Understanding these diverse outlooks on life makes us less judgmental, tempers our ethnocentric ego, and opens our minds to learning a thing or ten from others. Without stereotyping anyone, Cultural Dimensions have a great impact on our Core Certainties, and therefore the way we define Problems, Needs, and Solutions. One such dimension, as described in Figure 5, refers to power distribution within a group, with *Ultimate Equality* on one far side and *Extreme Hierarchy* on the other, with varying levels in between. To better understand how it works, let's explore the lives of two people.

Asger was born and raised in Denmark on his parents' small farm where they taught him that just like in nature, everyone had equal worth regardless of individual differences. This was also the core message during his schooling years and throughout his adult life. He had seen that when anyone wasn't being treated equally or justly, people considered it unacceptable. Asger grew up to value human rights above all. He knows that denying individual, human, employee, or client rights is not only unacceptable but also illegal. Therefore, he expects everyone to treat him fairly and as an equal and makes sure to do the same with others. Asger speaks freely of his personal beliefs and values, even when his opinions aren't aligned with the common social narrative. Some people might not like what he's saying, but they will respect his freedom of speech. Being a creative person, Asger shares his innovative ideas at work where he is appreciated for being an independent thinker. He developed friendships with many of his co-workers and managers, and often goes out with them after work for drinks.

Jawahar was born and raised in a small village in India. In his caste-based society, he is the bottom of the barrel—an "Untouchable" that is considered impure and less than human. Jawahar was taught by his family that just like in nature, everyone is different, and therefore must be treated by their level of importance in the world. Jawahar never went to school, because it was far from his village and limited to higher caste children. He never learned to read or write, being assured that all someone like him needed to know was how to keep his head down, obey his elders and higher-ups, and do his duties without making trouble. Everything he saw around him confirmed these teachings. Being abused by people of higher castes was part of normal life, as these kinds of behaviours were the prerogatives of his betters. Jawahar would never, under any circumstance, consider sharing his thoughts or even trying to hold a conversation with those above him. Such brazen actions might not only get him thrown out of his meagre job, but it might actually get him killed. For Jawahar, the hope of getting promoted or moving up in the world is beyond fantasy.

The differences between the extreme poles of this Cultural Dimension are immense. The foundation for all Solutions in equality-based groups and societies will be maximizing benefits to all while maintaining the rights and safety of each member. This approach applies on any scale, from an equitable partnering relationship, through communal groups, to social-democratic governance where, ideally, multiple social and financial systems secure everyone's well-being and human rights.

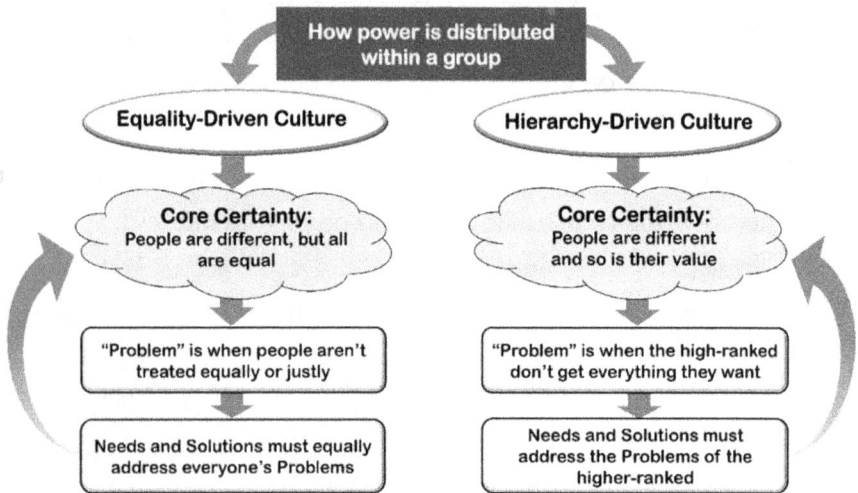

How power is distributed within a group

Equality-Driven Culture

Core Certainty: People are different, but all are equal

"Problem" is when people aren't treated equally or justly

Needs and Solutions must equally address everyone's Problems

Hierarchy-Driven Culture

Core Certainty: People are different and so is their value

"Problem" is when the high-ranked don't get everything they want

Needs and Solutions must address the Problems of the higher-ranked

Figure 5: How Cultural Dimensions affect Core Certainties, Needs, and Solutions

In highly hierarchical societies, the personal value of an individual is ranked from zero to hero, and each has to know their place. Authoritarian families, traditional or cult-like communities, or nations that rank individuals from the sub-human to the entitled and powerful elite operate based on values of hierarchy. As illustrated in Figure 5, Problems and Needs focus on the higher-ranked members of the group and are based on the premise that life is better when the lower-ranked serve the Needs of the higher ranked. Subsequently, formal Solutions will focus only on the privileged.

Another example of a Cultural Dimension that affects our Core Certainties relates to how we identify ourselves within our group. One side of this dimension is Individualism, with Collectivism on the opposing side. Like in the previous dimension, let's use two imaginary people living in very real societies to demonstrate each extreme.

Gunter lives in Munich, Germany. He was raised with the knowledge that his life is entirely in his hands. "If you want something," he was always told by his parents and teachers, "go ahead and get it, because no one will get it for you." Though both his parents were professionals who wished him to follow in their footsteps, Gunter chose to become a mechanic. He moved out of his parents' house after graduation, as is expected in his culture, and settled in another city. Throughout the years, he made sure to show his employers how good he was at his job and fought hard for promotion. Gunter was always friendly with his co-workers, but none of them ever considered the others to be friends. When a better opportunity came up, he left his job and took the new one because it was a smart career move. Outside of work, Gunter enjoyed meeting his childhood friends and led heated debates about politics and religion. He and his girlfriend decided not to have children and a traditional marriage because they rather focus on their own journey as a couple without unnecessary formalities and constraints.

Emma lives in a small, rural Amish community in the American Midwest. She was raised with the knowledge that her life is entirely bound and intertwined with the lives of her community members. She was always told by her parents and teachers that "the whole of our collective is far greater than the sum of its individuals. Those who stand apart lose their very being." Emma grew to trust unreservedly the leaders and members of her community while being cautioned about the perils of "outsiders." She was designated by the elders to work in the community dairy farm. If asked, she would have picked any other vocation, but the decision wasn't hers to make or dispute. Emma was matched with the neighbour's son, got married, and moved out of her parent's home. A year into her marriage, she gave birth to her first child, one of many to come. Emma wasn't always happy with the way her life turned out, but she kept being assured this is the natural order of things, and the will of God. She never spoke of her grievances, as it was seen as being ungrateful and a betrayal of the community.

In individualistic environments, people are raised on the Core Certainty that, like cars on the road, each person is separate from and unrelated to all others. Though some may "drive" closer to us, such as family and friends, they have little impact on our autonomy. The more extreme the individualistic group, the more it will focus on personal choices and freedoms vs. other peoples' rights. Extreme individualistic groups are often uncaring and oppressive toward their more vulnerable members. The operative pronoun in highly individualistic groups and societies is "I." A Problem emerges when a person doesn't get what they feel they deserve, and the most abundant definitions of Need focus on independence of action and thought, and on personal gains before everything and everyone.

In highly collectivist environments, every person is a train car hitched in a long line of other train cars, all pulled and navigated by the engine. Unlike a car on the road, a train car is part of a greater machine. In the same way a train car only has purpose, value, and meaning while hitched to the train, so does a person who is embedded within their collective. The operative pronoun in these societies is "we," sometimes to the point of self-denial. Issues that affect the whole collective are the ones considered as Problems, and the most common Need focuses on uncompromising unity and collective gain above all.

Trust is another Cultural Dimension that affects people's perceived Problems and Needs. One side of this dimension is high-trust, with low-trust on the opposite side with varying levels in between. In high-trust societies, the main Core Certainty is that "people and governing systems are trustworthy and are on my side." On the low-trust end of this dimension, people believe that "other people and governing systems are against me and can never be trusted." Figuring out the nature and the intentions of other people and of governing systems is at the core of our survival.

When we see a tiger and a rabbit coming at us, it is easy to figure out which one might make us their next meal. Not so when we observe two people approaching. Each may turn out to be an ally, a friend, an indifferent passerby, a menace, or a killer. A reckless high level of trust might end up getting us killed, and unwarranted lack of trust might end up isolating us. While isolation sounds like a better outcome than being killed, it isn't a great outcome for a social being. At the very least, it will have us miss out on great opportunities to create favourable alliances and synergies.

Living in communal settings means we must build relationships and provide mutual supports. But is everyone trustworthy, especially when we might not have enough food, water, or mating partners to go around? How then do we determine the right level of trust? The two big factors at play when it comes to trust is the combination of predictability of behaviours and the rule of law.[2] The more predictable the behaviours of group members, and the more stable and supportive their governing organizations, the more high-trust their culture. Though we will find corruption wherever we find human beings, we will find less of it in high-trust than

---

[2] The rule of law is the principle by which, (1) all group/society members must have full access to all the laws, regulations, and processes, (2) no one can change laws, regulations, and processes without a transparent and legal process, and (3) all members of the group/society (including leaders and those in government) are considered equal under these laws.

in low-trust groups. It happens because high-trust members will consider it shameful, and their strong rule of law will restrict such opportunities. In high-trust cultures, whatever the Problem, the Solution must be law-abiding and protect all members of the group/society.

On the other side of this dimension, the more unpredictable the group members, and the more inconsistent their governing organizations, the more low-trust their culture. Members in these groups are never sure what norms and rules they must follow. Being overtly self-serving, trampling others without remorse, double-crossing, and snitching is common in these cultures, making it difficult to predict or trust people. These are also the groups that experience high levels of systemic corruption and inequality. On this distrustful side of surviving with-and-despite-each-other, Core Certainties dictate that people and systems are untrustworthy. The common belief is that everyone is out to get everyone else, or to compete with them over limited resources. This low-trust framework is common in societies where racism, sexism, and homophobia may not only be acceptable, but also embedded in law. It is also common in groups that idealize individualism to the extreme, upholding the motto of "me, myself, and I above others" (e.g., highly competitive workplaces), or in tyrannical societies where people have no voice (e.g., dictatorships or crime organizations).

In low-trust groups, the "official" Problems and Needs will be defined by and for the powerful. Individuals living under the heavy boot of their oppressors will come up with "alternative Needs" that will focus on self-preservation, such as "keep everyone intimidated to ensure my supremacy," or "do whatever I need to survive while keeping it under wraps," or "take care of myself, the hell with others." Some of the resulting Solutions will serve the powerful. Other, more covert Solutions will serve the oppressed or the self-interested. In these societies, a single Solution could never serve such opposing perspectives.

As I've mentioned earlier, up to the age of eight, I grew up behind the Iron Curtain, then known as the USSR. Unfortunately, the pure and humanitarian ideology of communism, which speaks to social justice and equality, was never made into reality. Instead, power hungry people bastardized it into a highly oppressive regime. Fear, rampant corruption, and ridiculous inefficiencies plagued the USSR, leading to severe shortages of every essential commodity. Though boasting with values of ultimate equality, the regime ranked people based on their position in the communist party. The closer one got to the proverbial plate, the greater their freedoms, their financial benefits, and their ability to fill an actual plate. George Orwell's book *Animal Farm* provided an astoundingly accurate depiction of the daily realities behind the Iron Curtain, not only in the USSR, but in other countries burdened by that same corrupt version of communism.

Under these low-trust conditions, people had to obey the system and live in deep poverty or be cunning and resourceful to improve their lot. The monthly wages in the mid-1960s were barely enough to keep a small family afloat for a week. At the same time, taking on a second job or opening a business to supplement income were illegal options. This reality drove my parents and grandparents to take part in a black-market shoe-making operation, for which many of their less lucky friends ended up in prison. By day, my grandfather worked in a shoe-making factory, my father in a glass-blowing factory, and my mother at a hair salon. My grandmother took care of the household, took care of the grandchildren, yours truly included, and smuggled leather she bought on the black market using creative clandestine methods. By night, they all made shoes on the kitchen table and sold their products to their commodity-starved community, while having the local police officer look the other way for a few pairs of shoes. Occasionally, my grandfather "confiscated" equipment from his government-owned factory to help with their domestic production line.

For all intents and purposes, my family members were criminals. I once asked my grandfather whether the scissors he brought home weren't, in fact, stolen. He explained that since we lived in an unfair system, where the government was the biggest thief, all bets were off. This meant that our Need to survive superseded the state's draconian definitions of the law, therefore, stealing from those government muggers was a downright mitzvah (a charitable deed). Translating my grandfather's explanation into my model looks like this:

Problem:	Relying on legal income sources alone cannot sustain my family.
Core Certainties:	The government is corrupt; my situation is their fault; if I don't take care of myself, no one will.
Need:	Find ways to supplement my income by every means possible without being caught.
Solution:	Contraband and illegal manufacturing.

There is no shortage of instances, now and in the past, where the lens of distrust of "the system" is at play—illegal freedom movements that rebel against tyrannical regimes, unionized workers that strike to fight exploitation, the Underground Railroad that smuggled runaway enslaved folks to slavery-free zones throughout the nineteenth century, families who were hiding persecuted Jews during World War II, or organizations that illegally liberate girls subjected to child-marriages in countries where the law allows it. Not all low-trust, stick-it-to-the-man Core Certainties are noble. Some are driven by greed, such as a myriad of pyramid schemes and vast operations of narcotics and human trafficking. These endeavours profit the few while costing dearly all others.

There are many more Cultural Dimensions and they all make a sizeable impact on the way we perceive reality, define Problems and Needs, and conceive Solutions. Each Cultural Dimension, and the Core Certainties it creates, is part of a grander kaleidoscope that defines our "normal." Comparing Maslow's Hierarchy of Needs (2) and the motivational model of indigenous people (3) shows how our cultures can radically shape our understanding of life (Figures 6 and 7). Abraham Maslow first introduced his concept of a hierarchy of needs in 1943. Expanded and refined, it has become a broadly accepted model (i.e., a set of Core Certainties) that classifies the universal needs of all humans.

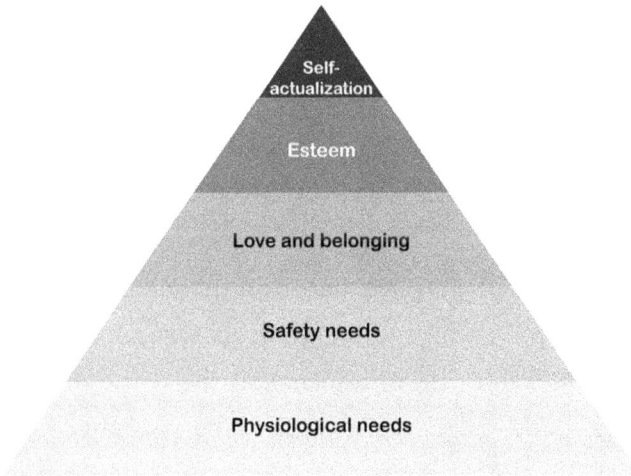

Figure 6: Maslow's Hierarchy of Needs (basic categories)

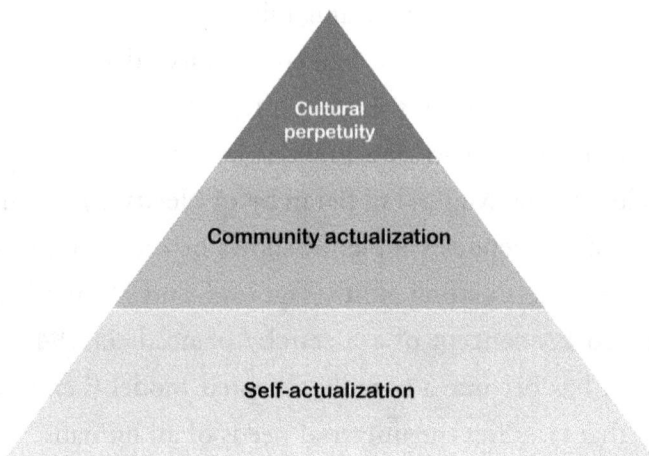

Figure 7: Blackfoot (Siksika) motivational model

According to Maslow, the most basic physical needs, such as air, nourishment, hydration, shelter, warmth, rest, clothing, and sex form the foundation of the pyramid upon which every other need is built. The next level is safety, both physical and emotional. The higher we go in Maslow's pyramid, the less corporeal it becomes, and therefore perceived to be less critical—the need to belong and be loved; achieve accomplishments and be respected by self and others; understand the world around us; attain esthetics, beauty, and balance; realize personal potential and experience self-fulfillment. Finally, at the top of the pyramid where the truly "nice to have but okay if you don't" lives, is our need to transcend beyond the personal self (e.g., mystical experiences, connection with nature, joys of service to others, pursuit of science, religious faith, etc.).

Though Maslow admitted that the model was imperfect, the pyramid emerged as a cornerstone in Western psychology, sociology, management training, economy, policy making, and our personal understanding of how we should handle life. Those who make their priorities using this model, will place love and belonging, self-actualization, and connection with nature at the very bottom of their list. This is the cultural "normal" or the Core Certainty in societies that focus on basic physical survival and all but ignore the higher tiers of this pyramid.

For many indigenous peoples, such as the Blackfoot Nation (Siksika), the motivational model is very different. The first and most fundamental tier is self-actualization, which is the feeling of reaching one's potential, completeness, and comfort with oneself. The second tier is community actualization—the opposite of individualism, which is the most common framework in many Western/so-called developed societies. This model maintains that for any member to survive, all members must act as one to ensure the group's self-sufficiency, and everyone must care for all community members. It also refers to maintaining traditions and embracing new ideas that sustain the community. The third and final tier is cultural perpetuity. As long as the first two tiers are fully realized, people can sustain their culture forever through multi-generational preservation.

Five years prior to publishing his model, Maslow learned about the Blackfoot Nation motivational model when he took part in a Canadian anthropological expedition. In his unpublished paper (4) Maslow described life views that puzzled him:

"Children are not humiliated by their parents as they are in our society. Women are not humiliated by men. Inferior men are not humiliated by superior men, nor are the poor humiliated by the rich. (Security is) evidenced by dignity and friendliness, (and by) little insecurity, suspicion, envy, jealousy, antagonism and hostility or anxiety. The Blackfoot character has little drive for power, not seek ascendancy over other people. A leader… does not use (their position) to dominate. The Blackfoot are clearly a society in which those in power are expected to help those who have given them their power; power involves reciprocal duties to the society that bestowed it."

Despite his observations, Maslow saw no relevance of this radically different perspective on life to his own Core Certainties. Moreover, when he published his model, he never mentioned that it only applies to

Western, individualistic, and capitalistic societies, not to all mankind. Such is the power of Core Certainties. Or peer pressure.

Core Certainties and the way we are

Our Core Certainties don't stem from culture alone; they are both external and internal. Like in basketball, Cultural Dimensions provide us with the rules of the game and their potential rewards and penalties. Yet they cannot determine our aptitude, playing style, or even our level of adherence to the rules. That's where our inner world comes into play. Our fascination with human nature is probably prehistoric. It spans thousands of years and was discussed by the scholars of Kemet (ancient Egypt), the authors of the Vedas (ancient India), Socrates and Plato (ancient Greece), and Confucius (ancient China), through to the more recent Freud, Lacan, and Jung (Europe). Contemporary Western approaches boiled down our mysterious inner workings into concepts such as personality traits and behavioural styles (personality is what you are born with, and behavioural style is what you have learned and can modify). No matter which definitions we favour, figuring out and predicting people help us function in society.

Our personality, or the way we are wired to operate and interact with the world, will determine how open we are to people and ideas, how honest we are, how prone we are to get ahead by trampling on or manipulating other people, how comfortable we are with getting ourselves out there in the presence of other people, how agreeable we are in our relationships with other people, how optimistic we are in times of uncertainty, or how neurotic we get when we find ourselves outside our comfort zone. These and many other personality traits and facets make up at least part of our individual operating systems. They affect our level of adherence with our group's Core Certainties, and the way we define our Problems and Needs. Just like Cultural Dimensions, we can lay out our personalities and behaviours along spectrums with opposing extremes. Our place on each of these dimensions will add to our Core Certainties. Just like Cultural Dimensions, our brain-wiring and behaviours aren't stagnant. Rather, they are ever evolving.[3]

Take for example the continuum of relation to other people, with hostility and aggression on one extreme and inclusivity and peace seeking on the other. One of the oldest philosophical questions deals with the question, "Are we innately good or bad?" Are we born as kind, nonviolent beings later corrupted by our surroundings, or are we malevolent from the get-go? Some scientists and theorists, such as the proponents of Kropotkin (5), see humans as a naturally peaceful and unaggressive species that society has distorted through cultural novelties, such as territorial living, patriarchal ideology, and lethal technology.

On the opposite end of this spectrum, the followers of Huxley (6) reject the idea of the "noble savage" and claim that we have always been a violent species. According to them, our steep dominance hierarchies[4] and the many millions killed by our own hands are proof that humans do not differ from some of the aggressive primates. This approach states that the only thing that keeps us alive is our cultural constraints on violence (e.g., strong leaderships that control and enforce order). In other words, humans are a naturally aggressive species civilized by society. As in all polar theories, the truth probably lives somewhere in between with the dial shifting based on timing and context. We are neither saints that are driven to evil, nor evil beings kept in righteous cages. Most if not all of us can be

---

[3] This statement is a generalization that doesn't apply equally to individuals with cognitive and/or developmental disabilities.

[4] Dominance hierarchies refer to societies that are arranged by people's levels of importance. Lower ranked groups and individuals are expected to show great deference to power and authority, as opposed to egalitarian societies that intentionally blur the power distinction.

both peace seekers and aggressors, depending on our cultural Core Certainties, goals, lived experience, impulse control, and circumstances.

The range between hyper-competitiveness on one extreme and hyper-collaboration on the other is another mindset or personality trait that affects and intersects with our Core Certainties. Our desire to compete and triumph over others sits on one side of the spectrum, and our desire to collaborate and ensure everyone's success sits on the other. Groups with a Core Certainty that "life is all about competition because it's a jungle out there," will define Problems and Needs through a lens of "there isn't enough for everyone, therefore I need to grab it before others do." This is also known as scarcity mindset. On the other side of the spectrum is the Core Certainty that collaboration is the key to the good life. These types of societies will define Problems and Needs through a perspective of "there is enough for everyone if we collaborate and share resources," also known as abundance mindset.

As with aggression, the opposing Core Certainties of competition vs. collaboration (or scarcity vs. abundance) can be contextual. In a simple world, people are either highly collaborative, somewhat collaborative, somewhat competitive, or highly competitive. Regrettably, our muddled reality does not fit into the categories used in questionnaires. We know ruthless competitors can become incredibly collaborative, and benevolent collaborators can become fierce competitors under the right circumstances. We have seen runners who had dedicated their lives to winning and yet stopped mid-race to help a rival who had fallen, thus forfeiting their own chance of winning. We have also witnessed collaborative, service-oriented people exhibiting ruthless behaviours when it suits them, such as heads of charity organizations sabotaging fellow charities when competing over limited funding.

Pessimism vs. optimism is another certainty-producing spectrum. Pessimism is a mindset that triggers fear and pulls us into the darkest corners of our minds. It is a lens that paints mental pictures of every negative outcome and potential catastrophe, sometimes realistically, but most times based on very little evidence. Besides making us tentative about the world around us, pessimism is also the attitude that keeps us vigilant in a world that isn't always safe for us. Pessimism drives us to find Solutions that will keep us alive. A pessimistic lens will create a Core Certainty that states: "Whatever can go wrong surely will, therefore it is always wise to avoid, suspect, or take every precaution."

On the other side of this spectrum, optimism fills us with joy, paints our world in brighter colours, and lifts us up from the daily grind. It is a mindset that pushes past our fears and allows for risk taking, shedding old traditions, and trying new and exciting Solutions. An optimistic mindset will create a Core Certainty that states: "Why worry about something that hasn't happened yet? Life is about seizing the day and trying something new." While some people and communities are more optimistic or more pessimistic by nature or tradition, these certainties are not constant. They may be affected by circumstances, the passage of time, and many other intersecting factors.

There are many other traits and factors that feed into our Core Certainties, inform our Problems and Needs, and guide our Solutions, such as in the example provided in Figure 8, describing two very different individuals. Juan grew up in a highly collectivist community where everyone trusts and helps everyone else. He has always been a very curious and logical person who takes his time to explore and examine evidence, and then deliberate on possible consequences. Juan is a great believer in equality and human rights, and he is a relentless optimist who sees the best in people.

Karen grew up in an affluent neighbourhood where each family kept to themselves unless they were comparing their new cars. She was taught by her parents and close friends that this world is a dangerous place, with so many "outsiders" that want to take over their country and ruin their way of life. As a woman living in a hostile reality, she relies on her gut feelings to keep herself safe. She expects things to always go wrong, and for people to always pose a risk. Especially those dangerous "Others."

When Juan and Karen encounter rumours of a malicious conspiracy, each will view reality through their Core Certainties. Juan will investigate the threat in depth and make a calculated estimation of the actual risk. If the risk isn't real, his Solution will focus on restoring trust within his community. Karen, on the other hand, will perceive this rumour as a confirmation of everything she already believes about the world. Her Need will be to protect herself from the threat, and then come up with Solutions that identify offenders and use force.

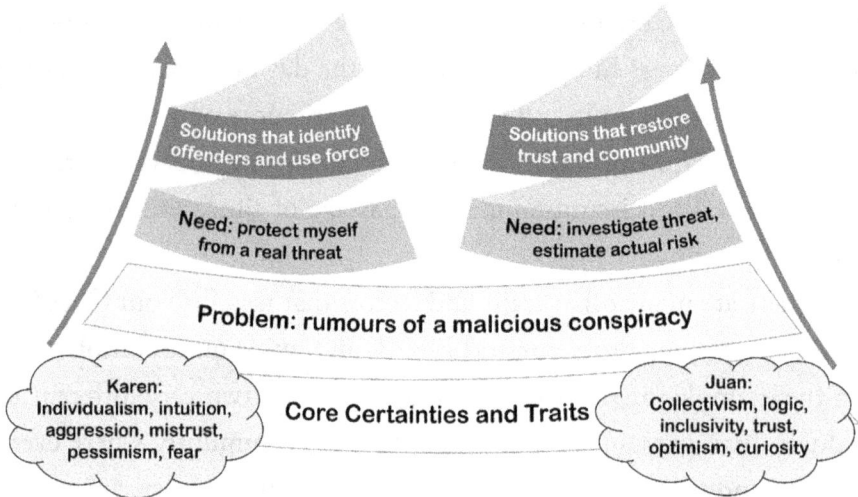

Figure 8: How Core Certainties affect Need definitions and Solutions

Upon a quick examination of this example, one may conclude that we can assign value to Core Certainties where some are good, and others are bad. Under this assumption, we should try to avoid the bad ones. While it is advisable to always aspire to peace, love, and harmony, there is something to be said for the equilibrium between opposing forces. It is the combination of optimism and pessimism, trust and distrust, logic and instinct, or competition and collaboration that enables us to push forward, innovate, and survive. It is the balance that helps us discover the most practical, helpful, and elegant Solutions while taking all the precautions that keep us alive long enough to reap the fruit of our labour. Alas, maintaining these polar qualities in just the right proportions is a trick most of us haven't yet mastered. This is, at least in part, the reason we often use our brilliantly construed Solutions against each other or to the detriment of our planet.

Core Certainties and the nature of reality

Have you ever noticed that when something happens to you or becomes important to you, suddenly that's all you see around you? I remember when I was pregnant with my first child; suddenly all the women I saw on the street were pregnant. When I got my first pair of glasses, everyone around me suddenly wore glasses. It was truly uncanny. Had my pregnancy and my failing eyesight become contagious or awarded me magical powers? Nope. My skewed perception of my surroundings simply reminded me I was not immune to cognitive biases, and that what I may see as "reality" is not, well… real.

We are raised to believe that reality is something singular and objective.[5] We are taught that since the world around us is "real," we can be purely objective about everything. If we only put our minds to it, we should all witness the one true reality. We are also told that being subjective results from poor character or a weak and undisciplined mind. Our history, life experiences, and ample research show otherwise. In reality (pardon the pun) our mind is a much more psychedelic place than most of us realize. We don't need hallucinogenic drugs to paint life in

---

[5] This is particularly true in what we refer to as "modern Western societies." Many other societies around the world hold a more expansive view and interpretation of reality, and greater openness to the infinite possibilities beyond our superficial perception of events, the passage of time, and life as a whole.

imaginary colours or to warp "reality" beyond recognition. We are perfectly capable of doing it ourselves, thank you very much, and we do so every waking moment. Psychedelic drugs merely amplify our mundane illusions and open new mind-bending channels.

Thousands of books and research articles have been written on the matter of our perception of reality, malleable mind, and cognitive biases with but a single point of agreement: each of us processes information differently and creates our unique versions of reality, no matter our age, gender, experience, or education. The illusion of subjectivity grows from a basic gut feeling that relies on our five senses. Based on these senses, "reality" must be a simple compendium of what we see, hear, smell, taste, and touch. But is it truly a simple compendium?

Imagine getting a box that contains one thousand pieces of a jigsaw puzzle. There are no instructions on what the final picture should look like, and every piece fits with every other piece any way you place them together. Naturally, each of us will use preconceived methods (or Core Certainties) when building such a puzzle. Some will believe they must divide pieces by colours and cluster each with their own colour. Some really like rainbows and will assemble them with whatever colourful pieces they have. There will be those who will start with the large pieces and leave the small ones to be placed later, or to be discarded altogether. Many will start the puzzle from the outside and build inward, and others will start from what they believe to be the heart of the picture and build outward. Others yet will be weary of building puzzles and will simply hand the pieces over to people they consider master-builders and then accept whatever picture that was assembled for them.

What are the chances of two people ending up with an identical image? Slim to none. That is unless someone else who has their own picture in mind has assembled it for everyone else. Even the same person will build different images from the same set of pieces depending on their mood, time, and peer pressure. Now imagine getting ten thousand of these boxes every day. Can you blame our brain for going for shortcuts and using predefined Core Certainties? Or for deferring to other people who seem confident about the nature of reality to build these pictures for us? Be honest, now.

We all share a limited and imperfect "operational system" that is riddled with a multitude of preconceived certainties. Having an enormous influx of information moment to moment, we cannot possibly be purely objective or see reality "for what it truly is." In short, our reality is whatever we think it is. Therefore, no two realities are identical, and "pure objectivity" is wishful thinking.

Ten family members attending a holiday dinner will each end up with a unique experience of that reality. For one, it will be the joyful pinnacle of their otherwise solitary life. For another, it will be a colossal bore. For the black sheep of the family, the reality of the event will be punitive and filled with shame and guilt, whereas the patriarch's reality will be the shining proof of his superiority. Subsequently, each will develop a unique narrative about the event. Each of these narrated realities may differ to such an extent that you wouldn't believe they attended the same event. What, then, if we tried to force objectivity into the description of the family event? What if we transcribed the conversations and recounted the actions that took place on a precisely measured timeline? No matter how much hard data we will collect, there will be too many individual interpretations to compose an event report everyone will agree on. Ergo, multiple realities.

One may argue that some things can be objective. For instance, machine or instrument-based measurements must be objective, right? Not necessarily. Reality will depend on the context and purpose of the measurement, and on the relevance of the measuring method to the reality we are trying to observe. Measuring a person's body weight may sound like irrefutable reality. But even if we use the most precise scale, the "real" weight will still rely on variables, such as local gravity that changes with altitude, the calibration of the tool, the person's hydration, or the last time they went to the bathroom. Beyond the weighing exercise, there is the question of data interpretation. How objective can it truly be? Will we base it on cultural norms of beauty or on medical research related to ideal body weight? On a foundational, twenty-year-old research or the revolutionary newly released one? Or perhaps on wrestling weight categories?

How about an even more precise and objective description of reality? Can we get any more precise and objective than in physics and mathematics? If you are a science enthusiast, you will have heard about Schrödinger's cat thought experiment where the cat can be both alive and dead. Or perhaps the double-slits experiment where particles behave one way when we aren't looking at them, and another way when we are. In fact, there is growing belief among hard-core scientists we may be living in a multidimensional universe (i.e., multiple, concurrent realities) or in a simulation. So much for a single, objective, and true reality.

Our ability to bend and restructure reality is not a random fluke in our programming. Being remarkably good at adapting to changing environments and circumstances, we want to make unfamiliar things seem "normal" as quickly as possible. This mental flexibility is crucial for our mental well-being and sometimes our very survival. Like every other mechanism that can help us survive, this mental flexibility can also sabotage us because our perceived reality is what we consider being our truth. In the same way there is no single, objective reality, there is no single, objective truth in existence. At least not in our earthly, three-dimensional state of being. And yet, most of us swear by our Core Certainties and our truths, and many of us will get into heated arguments, break ties with those who see different realities, and even kill or die for what we believe to be true. This is the extraordinary illusory power of Core Certainties in our psychedelic mind.

Can we change our Core Certainties?

The short answer is yes, but it's a tricky ordeal. Despite the uncompromising nature of our Core Certainties, we can evolve and even radically change them, sometimes without even admitting to the change. This is the magic of a bias known as cognitive dissonance. When our Core Certainties don't match the changing reality around us, the conflict between "what is" and "what it's supposed to be" can become terribly uncomfortable. Some will ignore this mismatch and stick to their Core Certainties. Others will end up changing their Certainties to align with the new information. The latter is a healthy process that helps us maintain a sense of internal consistency while keeping us with the times.

Nonetheless, changing our Core Certainties can be very disturbing because what it really means is that we were profoundly wrong, stupid, or really bad. And who wants that? Our cognitive dissonance helps us forget, deny, or downplay our old Certainties and behaviours to protect our self-image and maintain a positive view of ourselves. This irrational behaviour usually happens on an unconscious level. Which is why we may genuinely believe that we have always held our current Core Certainty and never believed in the previous one, even if evidence suggests otherwise. How many times have you heard people say, "What do you mean I used to say/think that way? You must be confused!"

Though cognitive dissonance can affect anyone, there are factors that can make people more vulnerable to it or make it more difficult for them to resolve the discomfort of change. One such factor is how important the belief is to us. When a Core Certainty is an inseparable part of our identity, we will be much more distressed when facing conflicting information or alternative viewpoints. We will struggle to accept the new reality and might fight it tooth and nail no matter how strong the evidence is against it. Men who grow up in highly patriarchal societies have their very identity entangled with their superior status and dominance over women. These men find it nearly impossible to embrace gender equality because it shatters everything they are as human beings. The same goes for loyal members of religious congregations, cults, or extreme hate groups where the members' identity is defined as "devout believers." Doubting such powerful Core Certainties is no different from doubting your very identity as a human being.

Another factor that can affect our unwillingness to change Core Certainties is our level of investment in them. If we have put in a significant amount of time, effort, or resources into a particular Core Certainty, we may have a stronger urge to justify our previous choices. We can see this type of stubbornness in people from all walks of life. Even the highly intelligent and educated can sometimes refuse to abandon an outdated scientific Core Certainty despite ample new evidence against it. When Charles Darwin came up with his theory of evolution and natural selection, it took decades for many scientists to warm up to the idea. You might consider this opposition understandable in the context of mid-1800s when creationism was still an inseparable part of most people's worldviews, including many scientists. However, this behaviour can as easily be found in modern-day science. For example, the distinguished biologist, Lynn Margulis, formulated a theory of cell evolution in the 1960s with ample proof of a process now known as symbiogenesis where different types of microbes combine to form a single cell while retaining their own DNA. The combination of the two results in a much more sophisticated cell. For example, in each of our cells, we have an external partner—the mitochondria, which is responsible for our cell metabolism. In plants, the chloroplast is the symbiont partner that is responsible for the photosynthesis function. While Margulis's theory and supporting evidence were irrefutable, she had to endure nearly twenty years of antagonistic rejection from her peers.

Regardless of one's level of education, people who are mostly open-minded, confident, and receptive to new ideas will be more willing to confront cognitive dissonance and adopt new Core Certainties in the face of change. Their counterparts who are more closed-minded, insecure, or resistant to change will hold on to their old Core Certainties for dear life.

And then, of course, there is the power of the crowd and of manipulative profiteers. Breaking free from old Core Certainties will be more difficult for people immersed in powerful and punitive cultural norms and are exposed to all forms of propaganda and indoctrination[6]. If a person's certainties align strongly with the views heralded by the bandwagon, they will feel pressured to maintain consistency and resist conflicting information no matter what.

---

[6] Indoctrination, or undue influence, is any act of persuasion that overcomes the other person's free will and judgment by means of deception, coercion, and other mind-controlling means.

CHAPTER 2:

From Problems to Needs

... where we explore the deeper meaning of Problems, the confusing path from Problems to Needs, and how profiteers manufacture them for us.

Problems here, there, and everywhere

The second tier of the Cone Model is "Problems." Nowadays, using this term is often frowned upon. We consider it outdated and negative compared to "challenges," which creates a hopeful mindset. When we say, "The mountain blocking our path is a problem," it makes us feel that the mountain is insurmountable and creates a defeatist mindset. But when we rephrase to, "The mountain blocking our path is a challenge," at least some of us may get excited with the opportunity to climb it.

Though I would normally agree with this constructive approach, using a positive term would misrepresent a Cone Model related Problem. A challenge is often a situation that offers us a choice to either rise to the occasion, leave it to someone else to grapple with, or simply let it be. A Problem is much more insistent. It pains us enough to seek Solutions. A Problem won't go away just because we refuse to deal with it. Exciting challenges are less likely to end up as dogmatic Solutions, whereas painful Problems usually do.

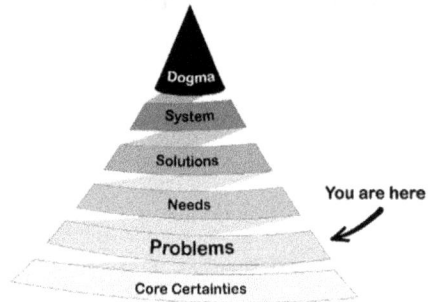

We all have Problems, no matter how positive our outlook on life. And while we may think our Problems are obvious, they rarely are. Try it yourself. What are some common difficulties you face? Take a minute for silent contemplation and make a list. Think of the things that pain you. Those you wouldn't want to deal with if you had a choice on the matter. Identifying danger is part of our survival mechanism, which should make this exercise a simple task. Much easier than if I asked you to make a list of all the wonderful things in your life that you are grateful for. That one takes much more effort for our ancient, risk-focused brain.

How is your list of Problems going? Here are a few examples you may have come up with (feel free to add your own):

My health is failing.
Public speaking terrifies me.
I don't get the respect I deserve.
I'm not attractive enough to be loved.
My life has no meaning.
I'm not rich and powerful enough.
I feel like I can't go on.
My life is boring.
I struggle with addictions.
I have lost my faith in God.
I'm gay and struggling to hide it.
I'm never good enough.
My boss is out to get me.
My favourite sports team keeps losing.
My life is in danger.
The world is coming to an end.
I'm lonely.
I suffer from racism every single day.

Traffic drives me nuts.

I don't know where my next meal will come from.

I can't keep up with the latest fashion.

I don't get enough likes on my posts.

I have tons of energy and nowhere to put it.

If you go through it, you may observe that the list lacks any organization by topic, severity, political agenda, urgency, or even alphabetic order. This is not because of an editorial lapse of judgment. Just like beauty, the severity and the urgency of Problems are in the eye of the beholder. Our perception of a situation and the subsequent decision of what makes a Problem are highly subjective. It might seem that something like "My life is in danger" surpasses by a mile a complaint as trivial as "I don't get enough likes on my posts," until you consider all the people who succumb to social media blues by comparing their ordinary existence to another's play-pretend glorious life. A problem such as "The world is coming to an end" sounds quite dire, and yet, for many people, the fear of public speaking is so great they'd rather get bitten by a venomous snake than get up on stage. And while "I feel like I can't go on" sounds alarmingly serious, there have been more than enough fatalities attributed to "Traffic drives me nuts," or to "My sports team keeps losing," and many heinous crimes committed on the grounds of "My life is boring."

All that to say that Problems are abundant, everyone encounters them, and they are as severe or as insignificant as their owner deems them to be. Nonetheless, as members of the same species, we share some core Problems. Every single problem you can think of, from "I can't keep up with the latest fashion" to "I don't know where my next meal will come from" can be traced back to our fear of dying, fear of social isolation, fear of pain and suffering, or to actual pain and suffering. The only variations on the subject are the specific elements we consider being deadly to us, the elements that isolate us, the sources of our pain and suffering, and how acutely we experience each of those.

For starters, just like in Shakespearean plays and contemporary horror movies, we all die in the end. The main difference is how each of us deals with this reality. Some are continually horrified by the idea of dying. Others don't think much about it until it stares them in the face. Others yet live peacefully with the idea, especially if they have positive perspectives on an afterlife. But even the latter may find dying itself disturbing. In the words of the renowned sci-fi author Isaac Asimov, "Life is pleasant. Death is peaceful. It's the transition that's troublesome." Even if you aren't afraid of ending up dead, the thought of the suffering that might lead to dying can be haunting. Also, most of us don't want to die prematurely—including those who believe in a glorious afterlife.

The famous joke about survival mechanisms in nature is that snakes hatch with a venomous bite, antelopes are born to run from day one, alligators are born with teeth, and humans are born cute. When it comes to survival in nature, our cuteness is pretty much the only thing going for us as babies. All we have is the hope for good caregivers and either an actual or a proverbial village to raise us. It isn't difficult to see why fear and self preservation form our most easily triggered instinct.

Emotional pain is another survival mechanism—one that, in itself, can be the death of us if it gets out of hand. We are wired to suffer emotionally when we fail to meet our Needs, however we define them. Compared to our fear of death, emotional pain may sound like a soft incentive to resolve Problems, but it is nothing of the sort. In many cultures, people are taught to bury emotional pain and hide it from the public eye because it is disruptive, feminine, and a sign of weakness. This is especially true for men living in patriarchal societies (i.e., most societies around the world, to one degree or another), where masculine composure and "face" are everything. It is also true for women in these societies where strong emotional expressions mark them as feeble and hysterical. Buried emotional pain is like toxic waste. You can stash it away, but it will always leak and end up poisoning you and others around you in ways you don't anticipate and cannot prevent.

No matter our background, our fears and survival struggles provide fertile ground for Problems to propagate. Even the mechanisms that are supposed to alert us of Problems can quickly become Problems of their own.

The bumpy road from Problems to Needs

Needs are not uniquely human. Everything living has Needs, be it a tiny virus, a whale, or a forest. A Need can be at the level of a basic impulse, such as an amoeba having to ooze toward a food source, or at a cognitive awareness level where we make complex decisions. Whichever it is, we gear our Needs toward whatever sustains and helps us thrive. Our most basic Need definition is: "I need the Problem to be gone."

Sometimes, a single, straight line connects a Problem with the corresponding Need. When we experience loneliness, we need companionship. Pain requires relief. Hunger begs for sustenance. Fear demands safety. It may sound like straightforward deduction, but it rarely is. As we have already seen in the previous chapter, our Need definitions are heavily affected by our Core Certainties, individual personalities, traits, and emotional responses. No matter the issue, what we usually seek is a sense of relief or satisfaction, which won't always address the Problem.

One challenge with identifying the correct Need is that we don't always experience our Problems in their purest forms. Sometimes they are second-hand emotions.

Try this one:

Problem:	I have a headache.
Need:	I need it to go away right now.

Or this one:

Problem:	Traffic is driving me nuts.
Need:	I need to avoid heavy traffic at all costs.

Correct? Not necessarily.

One reason so many Problems remain unresolved is our tendency to confuse them with their symptoms. This confusion leads to a misguided definition of our Needs and therefore to all the wrong Solutions. Take the simple example of your garden-variety headache. If you define your Problem as having pain, you will perceive the pain itself as the Problem, therefore easing it would be the logical Need definition. If you go that route, you will seek Solutions that will relieve your headache, such as pain medication. Once the headache subsides, you have addressed your Need and solved your Problem. Pretty straightforward. Except for being useless at addressing the real Problem.

How about this one: You are the captain of a ship, sailing across the Pacific. Suddenly your first officer bursts into your cabin while you are having your morning coffee. Flushed and breathless, he reports the lower deck is starting to fill with water. You rush to follow the man to the lower deck where sea water splashes your pants. With the right level of calm and authority, you instruct the crew to employ all available water pumps to flush the water out. You ask your first officer to provide you with an update when the water has all been pumped out and then you go back to your cabin. Sipping on your lukewarm coffee, you may feel you have handled the situation well. But have you? Is the water in the lower deck the actual Problem or a symptom of another Problem altogether?

If your boat sprang a leak, pumping the water out should not be your first step, unless you're about to go under. A more wisely defined Need would be: "Find how the water is coming in." If it's a hole, your Solution should be to seal it to stop the leak. Then go ahead and pump away. If the leak is severe, engage the pump at the same time. If you're a good captain, this will not be the end of this incident. You will investigate the core Problem once the emergency has passed. Is the hole the actual Problem or is it a symptom indicative of another one? After all, a breach doesn't just happen for no reason. Are you neglecting the maintenance of your ship? Are you navigating your ship through dangerous reefs while ignoring the risks? Did someone sabotage it? Is the quality of your ship not as advertised?

Each of these will reveal a core Problem and an actual Need that will lead to more effective Solutions. Only once you have resolved these questions can you truly address the Problem. If you remain oblivious to the core issue and focus on solving symptoms, you might end up investing all your resources in purchasing top-of-the-line water pumps and life-saving equipment. While these aren't bad to have onboard your ship, they cannot prevent the next leak or even resolve the existing one.

One of the funniest stories I read in my childhood that exemplifies confusing a Problem with its symptom is a tale found in *The Wise Men of Chelm*.[7] In this one story, the village of Chelm grew to sprawl over two mountains with a suspended bridge connecting them. Since building new dwellings drained most of the villagers' funds, little remained for the maintenance of the bridge. Years down the road, some of the rotten

---

[7] *The Wise Men of Chelm* is a collection of Eastern European Jewish folktales. The name of the village appears in different English versions ("Chelm" in the Polish and Khelem in the Yiddish and Hebrew pronunciations).

planks made for a perilous crossing. Inevitably, some villagers would fall into the valley to their death or sustain severe injuries. By the time the villagers found and hauled the injured to the hospital on the mountain, most would perish. The wise men of Chelm were forced to address the problem only after one of the richest men in the village had fallen off the bridge. After seven days and seven nights of exhaustive deliberation, they came up with a brilliant solution. They organized a big fundraiser and built a state-of-the-art hospital down in the valley to ensure they could dispense treatment as quickly as possible. Then they proceeded to collect data to justify their investment. To their delight, they found a significant increase in the survival rate among the injured.

While we can all agree that the Chelmites' Need definition and their subsequent Solution were foolish, how does it differ from treating a headache with pain relief medication? Just like the Chelmites, we are quick to assume that the pain itself is the Problem. Moreover, if we conduct research on painkillers like the research done in the story, we will get similar results. We will find that a significant number of people who use pain medications do indeed experience relief from their headaches about fifteen to thirty minutes after taking the drug. Unfortunately, since the medication treats a symptom, not a core Problem, the pain is likely to come back time and again and require more medication, just as the Chelm hospital will continue treating the influx of injured villagers, and the leaking ship will continue to require the use of the water pump. As in the more obvious examples, a headache doesn't occur for no reason. It will always have an underlying Problem, ranging anywhere from stress through dehydration to a tumour, none of which will be solved by pain meds.

Though less obvious, the same goes for the common problem of "Traffic is driving me nuts." Our misguided instinct will identify our Need as "avoiding heavy traffic at all costs," leading us to Solutions such as working from home, conducting phone meetings while in traffic, or the more common one: raging over the maddening traffic lights and incompetent drivers. While traffic jams can be a serious menace, not everyone stuck in traffic is driven to road rage. In these cases, the actual Problem is our unmanaged stress and anxiety, and our inability to regulate anger. Our Need will therefore be "manage stress and anxiety," with a yet deeper Need of "recognize and treat sources of stress and anxiety," and "improve emotional regulation." Once we identify the correct Problem and subsequent Need, we can find better Solutions, such as meditation, psychotherapy or, at the very least, "don't go off your medications before going into traffic."

Another example of confusing problems with symptoms starts with: "My supervisor is out to get me." Alex works as a project manager at a big, manufacturing company. It has been a year since his old supervisor has retired and was replaced by Natalia. Ever since she took on the role, Alex has been miserable. He sees her as a bully hellbent on "putting him in his place." He has a hard time understanding what she expects of him, and her feedback always offends his. All Alex needed was for Natalia to stop harassing him. He kept complaining about her to his co-workers, who kept telling him this was a conversation he should be holding with her, not them. Being uncomfortable confronting Natalia, Alex considered issuing a formal harassment complaint, or leaving his job. Unfortunately, his strained financial situation and the risk of losing his job made these Solutions unrealistic. As time went by, Alex decided he needed to find a way to live with it. It wasn't as easy as he thought. To soothe his anger, he started drinking and inflicting his pain on his partner.

It is true that some people in a supervisory position abuse their power and mistreat their supervisees. However, this scenario can also be the result of subjective perceptions. Alex's sense of being bullied and harassed may be a symptom of one or more completely different Problems. For example:

- **Personality clash.** Alex and Natalia may have very different personalities, resulting in different working and communication styles and, eventually, unintentional miscommunication and misunderstandings. His actual Need here will be: "Find ways to acknowledge, accept, and reconcile our different styles."

- **Insecurity in own value and capabilities.** Insecurity often leads to hypersensitivity to feedback, small and insignificant as it may be. Alex's actual Need here will be: "Acknowledge my insecurities and learn to overcome them."

- **Lack of respect for the supervisor.** If Alex feels Natalia is incompetent, he may be resentful to any form of feedback from her. Moreover, he might treat her disrespectfully, effectively inviting the negative feedback. His Need here may be: "Overcome resentment and focus on my own job;" "Learn to keep my disrespectful behaviour at bay;" or, "Examine my perception for bias."

- **Sense of entitlement.** Alex may believe that he deserves recognition and constant praise simply because of who he is, regardless of how he performs. As a result, his wonderful, perfect, deserving self will categorically reject and be deeply offended by any form of criticism. His true Need will be: "Recognize my sense of entitlement and eliminate it." Realistically, most entitled people will define their Need as: "Make Natalia understand I'm too good for her," or, "Move to another employer who values my natural wonderfulness."

If these are truly some of Alex's core Problems, none of his Solutions when assuming it is Natalia's fault will do the trick. If anything, they will augment the actual Problem. This type of Problem investigation barely scratches the surface. Insecurity, entitlement, or a lack of respect for his supervisor are certainly problematic, but they might not be Alex's deepest Problems. They, too, are symptoms. To figure out the core Problem, he will have to understand what makes him feel insecure, or believe he is entitled to constant praise without having to earn it.

No matter how small or serious the Problem, it's important to get it right, lest we spend precious time and resources on developing pointless Solutions. Despite the potential complexities of unpacking our core Problems, it will benefit us if handled correctly. Even if we buried the problem way-back-when for a reason, nothing good will ever come from keeping it in our mental catacomb. Just like an untreated wound, these hidden Problems fester into multiple symptoms that make us miserable and deceive us into seeking all the wrong and useless Solutions. And here's the bigger problem: in using the wrong Solutions, both our Problems and symptoms will grow and multiply, and we will feel even worse about ourselves and our lives. Misdiagnosing Needs and leaving Problems unattended will make us more susceptible to self-deception and leave us wide open to manipulation by profiteers who will happily offer their Solutions—those that serve them, not us.

Although we are prone to confusing Problems with their symptoms, it is very much possible for us to get it right. Sometimes it may take years of errors and poor consequences, until we start getting the results we seek. One fine example of differentiation between Problems and symptoms is the concept of Social Determinants of Health.[8] In our not-so-distant past, the medical establishment attributed most ailments, both physical and mental, to the patient. If you were sick, it was because you had a weak constitution. Perhaps you were a female and therefore fundamentally flawed. Or you were cursed, bewitched, or a heretic. Because you came

---

[8] The World Health Organization (WHO) definition of Social Determinants of Health are available at: https://www.who.int/health-topics/social-determinants-of-health#tab=tab_1

from a family with an inferior heritage of disease. Because you were poor and filthy to your core or of a racial background that was afflicted by uncivilized diseases, or any combination of the above.

The few who had escaped this supposition were those who had fallen ill in widespread epidemics such as the influenza or the smallpox. Even then, the disease mostly affected the poor, who lived in sub-par conditions. It justified the claim they were the spreaders of the disease to people of higher social standing, who obviously, didn't deserve to be sick. As medical science progressed, blame-casting became less socially acceptable. Instead of being eliminated, victim-blaming was clad in scientific sophistication. On one hand, we could now attribute many of our problems to microorganisms and our flawed DNA—neither our fault. On the other, we have discovered the connection between our health and our misbehaviours, such as faulty hygiene, smoking, poor eating habits, lack of physical activity, or substance abuse. These modern-era studies created alleged proof that we brought diseases upon ourselves, since poor life choices were totally our fault.

Until recently, and still today in many old-school medical circles, the perception of illness has been: "The patient is the Problem," or the more advanced view, "The disease is the Problem." These two defined the Need as: "Teach them to stop misbehaving" and "Cure the disease." This patient-blaming, symptom-driven approach was the platform upon which modern medicine grew and is still growing. It wasn't until the early 2000s that this approach started shifting toward a more systemic view, driven by social concepts of equity, equality, and human rights. European and Canadian teams conducted massive research with very different Core Certainties in mind. They gradually built new understandings of health and disease which, hopefully, will grow into the next generation of medical Solutions. Social Determinants of Health acknowledge that we do not exist in a vacuum. Rather, the environments in which we grow up and spend our lives have a significant impact on our choices, health, and well-being.

Let's take two people who happen to live in the same city as examples:

Ryan is in his mid thirties. He is a Caucasian, able-bodied cis male[9] born to an affluent family. He grew up as an only child in a loving home with two highly educated, functional, and involved parents. Ryan studied in one of the most prestigious private schools in the city, completed degrees in business and economics, and now works as a financial advisor. His employer pays well and provides comprehensive health insurance. He owns a spacious apartment and a car—both bought for him by his parents. Ryan meets with his childhood and university friends over weekends when he isn't playing golf with his co-workers. He frequents the gym at least three times a week and buys organic food.

Loretta, who was abandoned by her mother at the age of three, is in her mid-thirties. She never knew her father. Loretta is a transgender[10] woman of colour. Growing up in foster care, she experienced repeated neglect and abuse. Her schooling effectively ended in Grade 9 because she had to work two jobs to sustain herself. Having no formal education, she could only find low-paying employment without job security or health insurance. Throughout her life, Loretta experienced homelessness, racial discrimination, gender-related discrimination and abuse, sexual abuse, and untreated injuries and health conditions because of a lack of access to health services. She smokes, uses street drugs, eats mostly cheap fast food when she can afford it, and has no friends or other support systems. Her

---

[9] Cis is a short form of the term cisgender. It refers to a person who was assigned a specific gender at birth, and grew up to identify as that gender (e.g., identified as male at birth, grew up to identify as a man).

[10] Transgender refers to a person who doesn't identify with the gender they were assigned at birth. In this example, though Loretta was assigned a male gender at birth, she identifies as female, regardless of her male organs.

social isolation is further aggravated by depression, anxiety, and severe trust issues.

None of Ryan's or Loretta's life circumstances or outcomes were up to them. Ryan won a birth lottery, entering a near perfect world that allowed full access to all that life has to offer without ever earning it. Loretta received the short end of the stick in every possible way without ever deserving it. All Ryan must do to remain healthy is to not screw up really badly. But what of Loretta? What are her realistic chances of maintaining good health or making the "responsible" health-related decisions?

According to Social Determinants of Health, many factors outside of our bodies and our control have a far greater cumulative impact on our health than our DNA. These may include our living conditions, the quality of our early childhood care, education, access to housing, working conditions, level and security of income, the extent of supportive social circles that are available to us, the quality and availability of food and drinking water, the quality of our environmental conditions, our access to healthcare services, our sexual identity and orientation, and our experiences of racism, oppression, and discrimination. In fact, genes and biology can only account for 10 to 15 percent of our health condition, while about 30 percent can be attributed to our behaviours or "life choices." The remaining 60 percent or so are affected by our social conditions. Moreover, those 30 percent that are defined as our "personal life choices" are often no choices at all. It is often an illusion of choice that is available to the privileged members of society, but much less so to the disadvantaged, as in the cases of Ryan and Loretta.

Social Determinants of Health help us sort out symptoms from Problems. They help us look deeper into the core Problems that cause disease. They show we can only achieve good health and wellness for all when we live within a supportive system that provides us with health-promoting environments that enable us to make better life choices. Then, and only then, will medicine evolve into a more effective Solution.

According to this progressive model, the disease-related Problem is: "Society isn't creating sufficiently favourable conditions for the person to be healthy." The corresponding Need: "to be collectively responsible for creating conditions that will allow every person to be healthy." Quite a bit of difference from the current predominant medical definition of Need, which is: "Teach them to stop misbehaving," and "Cure the disease."

Confusing Problems with symptoms is more common than we may think. It can result from a simple judgment error, a lack of awareness of emotional undercurrents, cultural Core Certainties with "blind spots" to certain issues, or a nearsighted approach to problem solving. However, more often than not, this confusion is intentional and is driven by those who profit from such misdiagnoses.

Natural vs. manufactured Problems and Needs

Some of our Problems are naturally occurring. Should a draught hit our land, water will become in short supply. If a volcano erupts near our hometown, our lives will be in danger. If we contract an infectious disease, it might kill us. However, not all our Problems are naturally occurring. Many were framed as such or caused by people that have a vested interest in us having Problems and Needs. Go back to the list of problems you have created for yourself, or the one I provided on page 58. Separate the Problems that are a natural part of being human from the ones that have been created for us to enrich someone with means and power. Even if we examine our basic physical Needs, which can cause real Problems, the devil is in the details. Here is how the same Need can be genuine or manufactured.

Basic Need: Air

Natural Need:	I need constant availability of clean, breathable air.
Manufactured Needs:	I need a constant supply of purified, filtered, ionized air or pure oxygen.

Basic Need: Food

Natural Need:	I need a consistent supply of food in sufficient quantity, quality, and variety to sustain myself.
Manufactured Needs:	I need specialized, brand, gourmet, religiously acceptable food. I need an endless selection of foods, fast food, and super-sized portions available to me at all times of night and day.

Basic Need: Water

Natural Need:	I need a consistent supply of clean water in sufficient quantity to sustain myself.
Manufactured Needs:	I need designer water, bottled water, brand beverages, soft drinks, alcoholic drinks.

Basic Need: Shelter

Natural Need:	I need a durable or portable structure that suffices to shelter me from the elements and from external hazards, and close enough to vital resources (e.g., water, food sources).

Manufactured Needs:	I need a big house (as big as I can get, bigger than the neighbours'); a house in a socially popular/exclusive area; several houses in different locations; a "smart home."

Basic Need: Warmth

Natural Need:	I need consistent access to sufficient warmth to prevent freezing, or cooling to prevent heat stroke.
Manufactured Needs:	I need brand cooling and heating systems and constantly cooled and heated environments (both in private and public areas) set to exact temperature and humidity levels for optimal comfort at all times.

Basic Need: Rest

Natural Need:	I need to replenish my energy so I can perform my daily activities (e.g., sleep, rest, nature walk).
Manufactured Needs:	I need specialized and/or designer sleeping gear, spa treatments, and expensive overseas vacations. I need to work harder to justify my right to rest. I need to show I'm strong and don't need rest.

Basic Need: Clothing

Natural Need:	I need sufficient and adequate clothing to protect me from the elements.
Manufactured Needs:	I need brand clothing. I need to keep up with changing fashion and own a wide variety and quantity of clothes, shoes, and accessories that show affluence.

Basic Need: Sex

Natural Need:	I need sufficient access to sex partner(s) to satisfy my sexual needs and my desire to procreate.
Manufactured Needs:	I need abundant sex to prove my status and my personal worth. I need sex as part of my pastime. I need to be sexy to be valued. I need to be ashamed of or abstain from sex to conform to my religious system.

Reviewing these examples, you may argue that many of the things I call manufactured Needs represent progress. Why house twenty people with their farm animals in a crowded straw house, when we can build a sturdy dwelling large enough for ourselves and keep our farm animals in a separate structure? And what's wrong with air conditioning, abundant sex, spending a day in the spa, or travelling the world as more advanced approaches to our basic Needs?

Absolutely nothing is wrong with progress. On the contrary—it makes us who we are as a species. The problem emerges when progress falls into the wrong hands with self-serving agendas that create unnecessary and unfavourable new Needs. Wasteful, unsustainable, polluting, divisive, socially destructive, and oppressive Needs.

Whereas there is nothing wrong with building a dwelling that is big enough for its inhabitants, I trust we can agree that a 10,000 square-foot (about a 930 square-metre) house for two people serves no progressive purpose. It is both wasteful and oppressive to people who cannot afford housing due to an artificially inflated housing market. And while it's wonderful to have a variety of foods available to us, creating a lifestyle that requires ridiculously oversized portions that go to waste doesn't do justice to the diners, the environment, or starving members of society. Similarly, making us believe that a perfectly good outfit is an embarrassment to its owner because it was worn for more than one public appearance is unrelated to progress.

In the 1921 film *The Kid*, Charlie Chaplin, who plays a glazier, sends a kid into town to throw stones and break windows. Shortly after, the glazier just happens to pass by the vandalized property and offer the owner to repair the broken glass. I always found it to be a brilliantly concise depiction of a widespread and often complex phenomenon of manufactured Needs that isn't always this obvious. Artificial Needs add new and unnecessary Problems into our already difficult lives, and yet we are mostly unaware of the forces that generate them. As opposed to natural causes, manufactured Needs are man-made. Industrious profiteers excel at recognizing our exploitable weaknesses, and then act on them in many creative ways.

The augmenters

Members of many earthly species, from sapiens to simpler life forms, seek beauty in their mating partners (1). Those with extreme visible defects are suspected of bringing inferior genetic traits to the table. Most species destroy or abandon esthetically flawed offspring. Those who survive face mistreatment and slim pickings of willing mates. Therefore, it is fair to say that the matter of beauty is a naturally occurring Problem for those who lack the desired qualities. Our primal preference for beauty is no different from many other ancient human instincts we no longer entertain. When there is no interference of profiteers, we can root out harsh beauty-related judgments. We can achieve it through good education, proper legislation, and cultural values of respect, love, compassion, and inclusion. It is very much possible to raise our children to see that external beauty is both meaningless and transient, and what we ought to cherish are people's inner qualities.

But that is not our reality. From a very young age, society bombards us with both explicit and subliminal messaging that glorifies physical perfection and shames those who don't meet the minimum standard. Profiteers inflate our primal Need by creating beauty standards that are not only unrealistic, but are increasingly unnatural. The high-speed train of commercial propaganda systematically runs over our self confidence and self value. Ample research has shown that the media can cause body dissatisfaction, low self-esteem, and disordered eating. This is especially true among girls, particularly of non-white ethnicities, who experience poor representation and frequent shaming in white-washed media.

Women in many societies are constantly being subjected to unattainable standards of beauty and youth. Marketing companies manipulate the appearance of female celebrities by photoshopping them to their standard of "perfection." They erase any blemishes in their skin and modify their body shape to either make them look more prepubescent or more voluptuous, depending on what they advertise. Filters on social media platforms "improve" our images to ridiculous, unnatural levels. Extreme slimness, eternal youth, whiteness, or unnatural body proportions used as desirable standards, deliberately set up billions of women to feel unattractive. In most societies, every women's magazine is a combination of "how to lose those extra pounds, flatten your belly, get rid of those arm flaps, tighten your ass, and hide those ugly wrinkles," alongside "how to prepare scrumptious cakes in less than twenty minutes." Speaking of the glazier sending their faithful agent to break windows.

Darker skin tone is an alleged "aesthetic affliction" for which people are judged and discriminated against in many countries around the world, especially the colonized ones. From the early days of the agricultural revolution, affluent families remained indoors while the commoners worked in the fields, thus gaining a darker skin hue. Later on, enslavers imported enslaved people, often from tropical areas where people had darker skin, perpetuating the connection between skin colour and perceived social class, power, and beauty. Predatory chemists who saw the opportunity developed skin-whitening products. To promote their sales, they augmented an existing prejudiced Core Certainty through nasty commercials and shaming tactics, especially that of dark-skinned women.

Our body weight is another easy target for profiteers. Numerous studies have consistently shown that the dieting industry fails to achieve long-term weight loss, quality of life, or health benefits. In fact, a growing body of research shows that repeated dieting may cause us to gain more weight (2), harm our health (3), and compromise our mental health (4). And yet it is an empire on a continuous growth curve, persistently inflating our Need for slimness even if it kills us. The leaders of these industries invest not only in perpetuating unrealistic body standards, but also in medical research on the subject, particularly the kind that supports their products.

No matter how harsh, unreasonable, or unsustainable the dieting regime, those who adhere to it for a while will lose weight. That's just how our body works under stress and caloric deficit. Maintaining the weight loss, however, is a whole different story. The magnets of the dieting industry know it and yet they keep promoting their twelve-week research-based spectacular successes while withholding the truth on their post- twelve -week remarkable failures.

Contrary to common wisdom and well-crafted promises made by the Need augmenters, the beauty and commercial dieting industries are not here to make us feel beautiful. The only way profiteers can continuously line their pockets is by making us feel we will never be beautiful, young, light-skinned, or slim enough to be worthy of love and respect. If we just inject the next serum, undergo the next surgery, apply the next lotion, whiten our skin, or go on the new diet and exercise regimen, maybe, just maybe.

Like race dogs chasing a fake rabbit tied to a rail, close enough to tantalize but forever out of reach, so the beauty industry has us ride on a cruel asymptote. They make sure we never reach our desired destination, no matter how close we get to it. That is the evil genius of augmented Problems and Needs. When the results of their Solutions fail to meet the promised outcomes, it is the consumer's fault for not doing it right, or simply for being innately insufficient. No worries—they will tell you— the next product is sure to solve all your Problems.

Since resolving the augmented Need will mean a reduced consumption of products and services, profiteers rarely design these Solutions to provide lasting effects. It is, in fact, in their best interest to make sure we keep coming back for more. If, by some miracle, their Solution solves our Problem, the profiteers will shift the dial on the beauty standard to create the next Problem that will generate the next Need.

The magicians

Another way to manufacture Problems and Needs is by creating them out of thin air. Like a magician pulling a rabbit out of an empty hat, so do profiteers find original ways to produce Problems and Needs where they never existed. Like the augmenters, the "magicians" harp on our fears and insecurities and promise their Solution will make us safe, loved, and whole. But what if their Solution meets no existing fear or insecurity? To reel us in, they will intentionally invoke in us those powerful emotions by using one or more creative tools, such as shaming, creation of calculated misery, and fantasy-building.

Creating Problems and Needs through shaming

You may be familiar with Listerine as one of the oldest mouthwash brands. Developed in the late nineteenth century for floor disinfection in medical facilities, its producers were looking to break out of their small niche and penetrate larger markets. They went on promoting Listerine as a treatment for itchy scalp, and even a cheap cure for gonorrhea (don't try it at home). Some time later, its manufacturers discovered it could also kill oral bacteria that causes bad breath. The problem they faced was that bad breath wasn't perceived as an issue. It was seen as a natural phenomenon, and no one fretted about it. How does one carve out a new mega market that doesn't consider bad breath as a Problem? You do it by calling it a Problem and shaming the afflicted. In a brilliant marketing stunt, the producers of Listerine labelled bad breath as "halitosis." Once it had a clinical name, it was easy to frame it as a terrible condition and a colossal Problem, for which they just happened to have the cure. Following a well-executed campaign, the world has become acutely aware of halitosis.

Unlike most clinical conditions that were of a private nature, halitosis was marketed as the leading cause of social humiliation. Even something as embarrassing as gonorrhea one could hide from society. Not so the devastating affliction of bad breath. Listerine's early ads featured a woman sitting, shoulders drooping, and a gruff man standing over her. The wording: "Halitosis makes you unpopular. It is inexcusable... can be instantly remedied." Another ad depicted a mother attempting to kiss her child, who is turned away with evident disgust. The wording: "Don't fool yourself... Are you unpopular with your own children?" It was such a brilliant move that "the halitosis appeal" was coined as a term used to this day to describe advertisers inventing Problems that force consumers to buy their Solutions.

In the past, growing old was a sign of distinction, and being an elder awarded people with significant social points (still does in more traditional societies). In recent decades, one of the most profitable strategies of the beauty industry has become shaming people who grow old, or at least those who allow themselves to look their age. Sagging body parts, wrinkles, and grey hair are portrayed as devastating conditions that rob us of our social capital. We are told these are signs of self-neglect and deterioration rather than a natural progression of life. As a result, a plethora of anti-aging and age-concealing products and treatments have grown into sizeable money-making industries on the back of our manufactured shame.

A more detrimental manufactured Problem can be found in Cambodia. A well-orchestrated campaign by multiple baby formula companies convinced women that only negligent mothers would feed their babies with unclean and unhealthy breast milk when they could, instead, use "superior" factory-made products. Though all scientific research in the field proved the superiority of breast to powdered milk, their blatant lies worked like a charm. By 2014, there were 113 different milk-powder formulas available on the market in Phnom Penh alone (5), with not even one adhering to the government's legislation on quality assurance. Throughout this campaign, five times the number of women had switched from natural breastfeeding to formula (6).

Creating Problems and Needs through fantasy-building

Though "fantasy" may ring like a world of dreamy positivity, in this context, it is another word for "I can't believe you don't have it," and the glorified sibling of "you're not enough," and "shame on you."

Consumerism is one mammoth manufactured fantasy. Prior to the nineteenth century, social status wasn't nuanced. If you were born wealthy, your biggest fantasies were to have more assets than other wealthy families, or to possess as much power as the rulers of your society. But these applied to less than 0.1 percent of the population. If you were one of the other 99.9 percent who were born poor, you worked in servitude for scraps or lived on a farm, grew your own food, and wore homespun clothes. No one in your social circles would have any delusions of ever becoming wealthy and powerful. Much has changed since, especially in developed countries.

Though marketing is as old as trade and overlords, it was traditionally limited to smaller geographic areas and wealthy niche clients. It wasn't until the mid-nineteenth century, when the industrial revolution made commodities more affordable to all. New ways to transport products brought them even to remote areas. People could suddenly imagine themselves buying more goods and climbing the social ladder. Profiteers quickly cultivated a new Need, bringing fantasy worlds to the burgeoning middle classes, also known as "keeping up with the Joneses."[11] The development of widely distributed print communication systems such as newspapers and catalogues, along with a rising level of public literacy, made fantasy-building even easier. This was the cradle of modern marketing campaigns. The invention of radio and television further broadened opportunities to build fantasy worlds for us. Nowadays, the rapid evolution of personalized internet has reached a level of intravenous infusion of fantasies every online moment.

One of the most pernicious Problem- and Need-producing fantasies connects our happiness with owning possessions and commodities. This

---

[11] Keeping up with the Joneses is an idiom referring to people's desire to compare their possessions and social status to the more affluent and successful members of their community. People who fail to "keep up with the Joneses" are thus considered inferior.

mega-fiction is the proud birth parent of consumerism—an economic and social ideology that encourages us to keep consuming and purchasing goods and services whether we need them or not. The underlying message of this manufactured fantasy is the pursuit of "the good life." The key here is excess. We are constantly pressured to purchase and consume much more than we need with the promise of true happiness. The fantasy goes on to claim that we must engage in endless consumption, not only for our own benefit, but also for the state of our economy.

A consumerist society barrages us with messages of what this "good life" should look and feel like, of what we should aspire to, and therefore what we lack. This alleged shortage is the reason we are unhappy. Advertisements, discounts, product launches, and product giveaways reinforce these messages, encouraging constant spending on goods and services. To further enforce the fantasy, we are immersed in cultural messages that tie the receiving of services and the owning of possessions to our personal value and social status. As previously shown in the comparison of natural with manufactured Needs, we are being persuaded by profiteers that we are not only what we eat, but also what we wear, drive, do for a living, where we live, and where we take our vacations. Consumerism is a bottomless pit of fantasy Needs because there is always the next new thing to buy, and always someone who has more than you, and therefore puts you to shame.

Profiteers often build a fantasy of ideal living by using entertainment icons and other celebrities to promote everything from overpriced knickknacks to political parties and social ideologies. They use celebrities to show us how desperately we need to buy a certain brand of clothes, drink a certain type of alcoholic beverage, drive that luxury car, or vote for that handsome candidate. They make us believe that emulating celebrities will elevate us by making us as beautiful, exceptional, worthy, popular, or loved as them. But these profiteers are not there to elevate us. They want to us compare ourselves to social icons and realize we ain't it.

The real goal of fantasy-builders using celebrities is not only to make us excited with the fantasy and believe in it, but also to make us feel insufficient without it. In our heart of hearts, we may know that we will never reach the heights of our celebrity idol, them being so perfect, desirable and all, and us being so flawed by comparison. But if we could only follow their example and use those products, or follow the cause they are promoting, we will surely climb to higher ground, where our famous demigods live.

Using celebrities isn't the only way to build profitable fantasies. Many profiteers promote their Solutions by fabricating a picture-perfect world to which we must all aspire. Politicians who claim to stand for "family values" feed us with a fantasy of the perfect family. A typical ad will portray one handsome cis male, one attractive cis female (preferably a "domesticated" one—slim, feminine, and unthreatening), two joyful children, and an optional dog. They all look delighted with their perfect life while posing in front of a nice house in a nice neighbourhood. They will usually be white, unless the profiteer targets different demographics.

On the surface, these ads set a standard to aspire to and make target followers fantasize about the perfect world this politician or religious leader will create for them. Underneath the perfect veneer, there is shaming and a manufactured sense of insufficiency for all those who don't meet this standard, which is pretty much everyone. Because even if you happen to be white, straight, married, beautiful, have a nice house and two kids, who on earth is always so carefree and happy? If you already have all that but aren't as gleeful all the time, something is missing in your life. The more sophisticated profiteers will allude to who is to blame for your insufficiencies or who might take this perfect life away from you (the opposing party, minorities, immigrants, heretics, your sins, etc.). Luckily, the Solution for their followers' sorry situation is at hand.

Though women have always been a target for fantasy-building that shatters self-confidence and warps body image, men aren't exempt from this manipulative approach. All a profiteer has to do is build insecurities about manhood. Marlboro built its appeal to men by showing what a real man looks like—a handsome, manly cowboy lighting up a Marlboro cigarette. The man every woman (or man) will fantasize about. The advertisers of Tipalet cigarettes went all the way on the scale of nasty. In their ad, a man blows a lungful of smoke into the face of an enamoured woman who looks eager to inhale it. To make sure this not-so-subtle insinuation of ultimate male dominance wasn't lost on the simpleminded, the slogan says: "Blow in her face and she'll follow you anywhere." I kid you not. In recent decades, men have been increasingly exposed to the pressure of unrealistic beauty standards. The contemporary ideal man is trim, has no body hair, boasts a full mane, and shows zero signs of ageing, all brought to you by the beauty industry through movies, shows, advertisements, and influencers. Those who wish to be "real men" are pressured to purchase hair trimmers, dye their hair, undergo plastic surgeries and hair implants, and commit to the dieting and exercising industry.

While these fantasies pretend to empower men, they aim for the exact opposite. By showcasing what a real man looks like and the level of control he is expected to have over women, these profiteers implicitly highlight their clients' shortcomings. Luckily, their super-manly brand or ingenious product can rectify these shortcomings.

Sometimes exploiters can contaminate even the most positive traditions by transforming hope into Need-generating fantasies. Anne Helen Petersen, author of *Culture Study*, writes in her blog (7) about the tradition of "New Year's Resolution." She speaks of the ills of staging every New Year as a potential life changer, which pretends to be a hope-building tradition while making us feel like losers. Because the real meaning of these "resolutions" is an admission of our past and present failures.

Failures we can solve by subscribing to something, buying something, or many, many somethings.

Profiteers thrive on this manufactured fantasy of "bettering ourselves this coming year." They target our fear of failure, and then place their magic Solution wherever we shop, live, work, play, and browse. They will offer the Solutions to each of our Problems, for the right price. Alternatively, they will offer us the very temptation that will blast our resolution out of the water (a luxury car ad right next to an article on how to save for retirement). This will ensure the cycle of shame, guilt, fantasy, and the Need to consume keeps spinning.

Figure 9 illustrates a typical process profiteers use to augment or manufacture Need. Let's take a fundamental shared Problem—the fear of social isolation. Three different people will approach this Problem in three different ways based on their personal traits and Core Certainties about the world. Consequently, each will respond differently to manipulation.

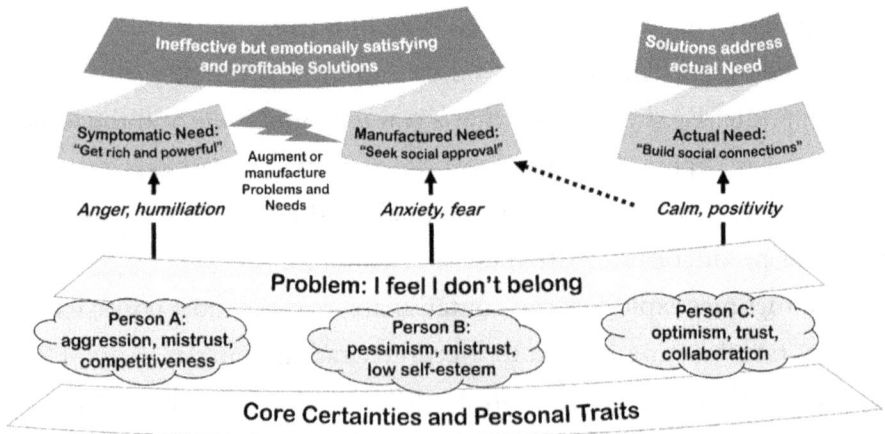

Figure 9: Augmenting or manufacturing Need

Person A, who is extremely competitive, doesn't trust other people, and uses aggression to deal with the world, will develop anger and a sense of humiliation in response to their fear of isolation. These powerful emotions will lead to person A's perceived Need for becoming rich and powerful, which will supposedly make them admired and desired. This is a typical confusion of core Problems with superficial symptoms. By focusing on soothing their anger and humiliation, person A will fail to address the source of these emotions—likely related to cultural pressures and unresolved trauma.

To achieve their desired wealth and power, person A will invest in augmenting or manufacturing Problems and Needs for their potential buyers or followers. They will promote their Solution as the saviour from the horrors of social rejection and isolation. They will play on people's fear and anxiety, alluding to the fact they simply aren't good enough to belong with society without this Solution.

Person B, who holds a pessimistic view on life, doesn't really trust other people, and lives with deep-seated insecurities and low self-esteem, will develop anxiety and fear of social isolation. In seeking Solutions for their insufferable emotions, they will be highly vulnerable to false promises and manipulation. Person A will easily persuade them that the proposed Solution will buy them the social approval they need so badly.

Person C, who holds an optimistic view of life, trusts other people, and believes in the value of collaboration, will be more positive about their prospects of social belonging. They will identify their Need as "Build social connections," and will trust in their ability to do so. They will be much less likely to fall for the profiteer's manipulation. That said, even person C might not be completely immune to the profiteer's propaganda. Given time and persistence, they, too, might succumb to believing that without that magical Solution, they will never achieve their desired level of social belonging.

Manipulating individuals to make the wrong choices isn't the only way to manufacture Problems from thin air. Planned obsolescence is another ingenious form of Problem generating. Some time ago our twenty-six-year-old washing machine broke, and as these things usually happen in pairs or trios, so did our old dryer. When the technician arrived, I asked if he thought fixing the old machines was even worth it. That's when I learned that, following a quick and simple repair, our old machines are sure to outlast any of the new ones by three lifetimes. In his many years as a technician, he had learned that the more recent the machine, the shorter its lifespan and the less likely it is to be fixable. As if to prove his point, the following day, our seven-year-old dishwasher broke down and couldn't be salvaged.

This story goes beyond my personal woes with house appliances. Most household appliances produced throughout the twentieth century are still functioning unless people replaced them for novelty. Not so the ones made in the last few decades. Not only do they break earlier and more frequently, but most companies also make it almost as expensive to fix them as to buy new ones. Apple, Microsoft, Amazon, Google, Tesla, General Electric, and several other companies invest billions lobbying against right-to-repair laws. These laws protect our right to fix our stuff and use it for as long as we can. But if we are allowed to fix our stuff, how will the big companies keep making money on their merchandise? They solve it by intentionally designing products to have a short lifespan (also known as planned obsolescence) and then preventing us from fixing them when they break. However we try to go about it, our only option is to keep buying new products. To top it off, profiteers invest in marketing campaigns and culture changes that instill in us constant hunger for "the next shiny thing." This growing demand incentivises companies to produce faster than they can, which leads to shortcuts and feeds back into product obsolescence.

Creating Problems and Needs through calculated misery

There is an old joke about a woman going to a plastic surgeon to get a quote on breast augmentation. Following a full examination, the surgeon provides her with the quote. When she nods in agreement, he adds, "That's the price for one breast." When she nods again, he says, "Not including the implants." Every time the woman accepts the quote without arguing, the surgeon moves another item from the previous all-in total and adds it under "extras."

Tim Wu, a Columbia University professor, dubbed this method of generating a profit by creating new problems where they hadn't already existed: "calculated misery." If you're old enough, you'll remember the days when you could fly with any airline without having to pay extra for your seat of choice, meal, leg room, boarding time, or luggage. Over time, airlines started making it deliberately more inconvenient to travel, unless you were willing to pay for a level of comfort you used to get for free. Wu writes in an article (8): "Basic service, without fees, must be sufficiently degraded to make people want to pay to escape it. And that's where the suffering begins." In 2022, this method of inflicting calculated misery on travellers earned eight major US airlines $4.2 billion on assigned seat fees (9). Twenty global airlines raked in $29 billion on baggage fees (10) on top of their revenue from ticket sales. That is a lot of money gained by artificially imposing misery on their customers.

Calculated misery isn't limited to airlines and greedy plastic surgeons. Tech companies have good financial reasons to intentionally slow down and compromise electronic devices through software updates, creating unnecessary problems for their users. This calculated misery is also known as "performance throttling." Apple paid a fine of $113 million (11) for deliberately slowing down the performance of older iPhones (though they never acknowledged any wrongdoing as part of the settlement agreement). But what is $113 million for a company that made $192 billion in revenue from the sales of iPhones in 2021 (12)? It is less than 6 percent—a very modest cost of doing business.

Calculated misery is also applied to our online experience as a money milking strategy by profiteers. In the early days of most online platforms, everyone had free and equitable access. That is until we got hooked. Then we started seeing a steady increase in ads and all forms of interruptions that worsened our experience. They made sure to make us more and more miserable unless we pay for upgrades and premium memberships.

Many of the manufactured Problems and Needs are so well strewn into our lives, and the lies are so well hidden, that we take them for granted without ever second-guessing the impure motives behind them. Many of us spend our lives within manufactured realities or intentionally fostered ignorance. To unravel manufactured Problems and Needs, we must dig deeper to find the actual Problem and Need, and then follow the power and money to find who pulls our strings.

CHAPTER 3:

From Needs to Solutions

... where we examine our winding paths of Solution-finding and the many forces that drive creativity and innovation.

We are a creative bunch

Humans are creative beings if nothing else. What was it that enabled us to become who and what we are today? In his book, *Sapiens* (1), Yuval Noah Harari takes us on a journey through three major developmental breakthroughs that shaped the course of our history. As far as we know, the Cognitive Revolution kick-started the rapid evolution of our creative capacity about seventy thousand years ago, which is less than a blink of an eye in this planet's lifespan. The Agricultural Revolution that took place as recently as twelve thousand years ago in major regions of the world further sped our development and made history worth documenting beat-by-beat. And, finally, the Scientific Revolution, which got underway only five hundred years ago, sped up by leaps and bounds in the last fifty years, is now reaching an exponential rate we can barely keep up with.

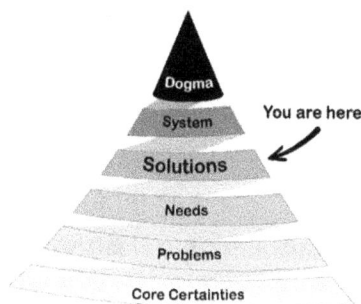

What were the secret ingredients in our evolutionary recipe that catapulted our development as a species? What equips us to come up with so many creative Solutions to our Problems? One life-changing Solution we came up with was wielding fire, which became a major differentiator in our early days of food-chain hopefuls. The other was proficient tool building. Though these two were essential to our development as a species, it was the power of our imagination that had made humans an exceptional species. The concept of imagination is much more profound than spinning tails on cute unicorns riding rainbows. Imagination allows us to be elsewhere while our body stays put. It enables us to play out full and complex scenarios and predict many possible outcomes without ever leaving our campfire or moving a piece on a chessboard. It allows us to come up with multiple options for creative Solutions to our Problems, play them out in our minds, try them out, fail, reimagine, and try again. As Michelangelo once said, "The sculpture is already complete within the marble block before I start my work. It is already there; I just have to chisel away the superfluous material."

Our imaginative creativity helps us generate new Solutions. But it wouldn't do us much good if we weren't able to somehow communicate ideas, successes, and failures to other members of society, and across generations. Communication is not a human invention. Though no other life forms speak or write, at least not on our watch, many are adept at multiple elaborate forms of communication. That said, we are unique in our more supple and sophisticated communication. Human speech allowed us to connect a few sounds to produce an infinite number of words that could be strained into an infinite number of sentences to convey an unlimited scope of information and ideas. Later, we applied that same principle to symbol-based and then to written communication.

Our ability to imagine options and our advanced methods of sharing information allowed us to collaborate, develop alliances, and enhance Solution-finding. Cooperation, like communication and tool building, is not unique to humans. Even simpler life forms such as ants and bees have extraordinary levels of collaboration based on drone-like, biological programming. Yet it is narrow in scope and only allows for a handful of potential actions with no room for creativity. More advanced species can calculate their chances of catching prey, outrunning a predator, finding water by going in a certain direction, and overcoming the alpha male. Many forms of collaboration even happen between species. These collaborative abilities are impressive, but they focus on immediate outcomes. Apes come the closest to the complexity levels of human cooperation and creativity. But even they cannot plan for the long term, forge large-scale alliances, or imagine something out of nothing.

Humans are unique in that way, at least on this planet. For one, we recognize our individuality even when we are part of a group. We can reflect on our personal desires and agendas, identify other people's agendas, and understand what it might mean for us. Using a combination of rational and emotional motivations, we may choose to compete, avoid action, or cooperate with others. We choose to do it even when the conditions are less than ideal, because we can weigh pros and cons and then calculate possible short-term and long-term outcomes of our actions. Collaboration is a daily reality in almost everything we do. We collaborate on the production and distribution of goods and resources; we cooperate with our governing systems; agree on driving on the same side of the road within a geographic area, or on lining up in an orderly fashion at the grocery store checkout. We support others in need, whether by helping them cross the street, donating money for charity, or rallying up to rescue people we've never met following a natural disaster.

It isn't very difficult to achieve collaboration in small, organized groups. Apes do it every day. But how do we achieve super-cooperation when in large numbers? There is only so much that shared language can do. What made us into what we are today was the ability to envision and then transmit information about things that are not seen, heard, or even existing. At an unknown point in our ancient history, we have developed the capability to spin and share myths such as creation stories, invisible gods, and tribal spirits. Those who subscribe to spiritual teaching would say that we can tap into our higher selves or into a higher form of intelligence and communicate its wisdom with one another. Either way, being able to share a belief in invisible forces was the key to pulling together great numbers of people who had never met each other, or even spoke the same language. In more modern times, we have woven a vast volume of myths such as religions, nations, laws, and corporates; myths we consider unquestionable Core Certainties.

Shared myths gave humans the unprecedented ability to cooperate in large numbers across space and time, bridging all forms of distance and differences. Two devout Muslims who live on separate continents, have never met, speak different languages, relate to different nationalities, identify as different genders, subscribe to different cultures, and belong to different age groups, can contribute funds toward building a hospital or a school somewhere else in the world. They will do it because they share a belief that Allah is the creator and Muhammad is His prophet, and that benevolent deeds for those in need are a divine directive. Be it mere fiction or Allah's honest truth, so long as it feels true to these two individuals, they will collaborate toward a shared goal, regardless of all other differentiators.

The concepts of nations, laws, and corporates are no different, even though they feel real to us. What is it that makes our "nation" and, by extension, our "nationality"? It would stand to reason that a nation ties itself to the land on which it sits, often known as the motherland. Except that it isn't. Many nations around the world and throughout history have lost their land to conquerors or natural disasters, and yet maintained their nationality even when displaced. In today's global village, millions of people relocate for work or for personal reasons, yet most keep their original national identity. If it isn't land, perhaps our nationality lives within our flag or our national symbols? Not that either. Flags and symbols change, yet our nationality remains intact. Is our government synonymous with our nationality? Not even remotely. Governments and governing systems rise and fall, while national identities remain.

What is it then that keeps nationality alive through time and space despite every kind of change and catastrophe? Our nationality exists in our collective imagination and nowhere else. It is not a tangible object. It is not a scientifically proven fact or phenomenon. The only reason it is real to us is because we believe in its existence. This is one of our Core Certainties. If tomorrow we decide to unite and become "children of planet Earth," all current nationalities will cease to exist, simply because we will no longer believe in their existence.

The same is true for our borders, laws, religions, cultures, and most other concepts and institutions that govern our lives. They are all Solutions based on shared myths to which our creative minds breathe life. The advantage of such powerful myths is that they build vast and long-lasting mega-collaborations. These are critical to our development as a species because there are only so many Solutions we can generate on our own or in small, isolated groups. The downside of these myths is that they are hard to kill, even when they become obsolete and even harmful.

Driving forces for creativity and innovation

Before we address the creative process, we should agree on the meaning of creativity and innovation. Creativity is our tendency and ability to generate novel ideas. It is the proverbial lightbulb that lights up when we seek Solutions. Sometimes it even happens when we're doing nothing special, just going about our day, when a flash of genius hits us. Or at least a flash of what seems like a great idea. Unlike creativity, innovation had different meanings throughout history. In the thirteenth century, "novation" described a new version of something that had already existed, like a renewal of a legal contract. Three hundred years down the road, the Christian religious establishment tied the concept of innovation with people who had dared to doubt or rewrite religious texts. "Innovators" were jailed and even executed.

The industrial revolution redeemed innovators from the depths of notoriety. Scientists and inventors of new machinery that produced goods became the popular kids on the block. Nowadays, we define innovation as our ability to use our creative thoughts and transform them into something tangible, practical, and marketable. Or as Steve Jobs once said: "Innovation is creativity that ships."

Though creativity may be a constant human ability, innovation has had its ups and downs. Throughout recorded history, we have seen periods with incredible spurts of innovation followed by eras of stagnation before the next spur of open creativity and innovation. Our ability to make good on creative ideas doesn't simply disappear for centuries and then magically reappear. Local incentives and penalties can easily stifle or boost both creativity and innovation. This explains why, even within the same period in human history, we witness different levels of innovation in different regions of the world.

The more a group or a society adheres to tradition and strict religion, the less it will reward and the more it will penalize creativity and innovation. In highly traditional, autocratic, and religious groups, some forms of innovation are as blasphemous today as they were in sixteenth-century Europe. The more a group or a society rejects tradition and seeks new grounds and opportunities, the more it is likely to reward their creative members, and the more innovation materializes.

Creativity for its own sake

Our creativity is not always constrained by practical Needs. As children, we scout our surroundings, find all sorts of stuff, and then try to use them or build something, either with or without premeditated purpose. We also come up with a variety of social interactions such as games, art creations, plays, and competitions. This allegedly purposeless childhood build-a-thing, play-a-game prepares us to deal with more serious life situations that will require physical and social Solutions. The greatest creatives among us never lose their childlike playfulness.

Our thirst for exploration may have originated from practical survival Needs, such as finding water, food, or mating opportunities, but it grew into a Need of its own. We all share the desire to explore, albeit at different levels of urgency and daring. Our ancestors stood curiously at the mouths of caves and wondered what was in there. We saw uninviting mountain ridges and decided to climb them for the opportunity to see beyond. We faced enormous and capricious bodies of water, and dared sail them at great peril for the chance to find out what's out there. Mix curiosity with imagination and creativity and bam! We're exploring the galaxy for no other practical purpose than discovery.

Stumbling upon Solutions

Alexander Fleming was a Scottish physician and microbiologist. Serving throughout World War I in battlefield hospitals, Fleming saw too many soldiers dying from infected wounds. He noticed that the standard use of antiseptics often worsened the injuries and brought the injured closer to death than recovery. Returning from the war, Fleming picked up his work on bacterial cultures with renewed gusto to find antibacterial, life-saving substances. Though he was a brilliant scientist, he was also quite the slob. His workstation was often messy, with chemical reagents and lunch leftovers competing over his lab table's real estate. Slowly but surely, his abandoned food crumbs grew mould. A stray draft blew some of these moulded crumbs on a petri dish where Fleming was growing bacteria, creating sterile circles of dead bacteria. That's how he stumbled upon penicillin (mould from the genus *Penicillium*), dawning a new era of life-saving antibiotics.

The story of penicillin is but one of many instances where we stumble upon a Solution and then find the Problem it will solve. This reverse creativity is also common to newfound resources, such as discovering the many uses of fossil oil. Petroleum is not new to us. Many civilizations have come across it throughout the ages. For some, it was a pesky pool of pungent substance in the middle of the desert where they would much rather find water. For others it was a byproduct they had to get rid of while mining for salt. By mid-nineteenth century, people found a way to distill crude oil and use it to illuminate dark nights and enclosed spaces with kerosene lamps. This innovative use of a byproduct created the first oil rush. Suddenly, an undesirable substance became a commodity in high demand. By the end of the nineteenth century, the invention of an internal combustion engine used in cars further spiked the demand for petroleum products around the world. And the rest is, unfortunately, history.

Problems and Needs begging for Solutions

Beyond random creativity and accidental Solution-finding, the most common motive for innovation stems from our many Problems and Needs that result from our never-ending interactions with the world and its residents. The way it usually happens goes like this: we have a Problem, a Need for a Solution, and off we go. We try, and then try again until we figure things out. Examining some of the things we eat provides enough proof for us to realize that, at some distant point in our collective past, an unknown number of courageous souls experimented with everything they came across that looked even remotely nourishing. Some took on a hostile cactus and turned it into an edible or drinkable item. Some saw unsavoury looking snails, bugs, and jellyfish and thought, "I wonder what that would taste like? What if I roast, salt, dry, ferment, or rot it?" Others found berries and mushrooms of all sorts and risked deadly consequences until they figured out a safe selection. Others yet used tree barks and herbs for healing purposes. How many cycles of trials and fatal errors have we gone through until we got it right? That quality alone is a testament to human persistence and insatiable curiosity. We are surely the poster kids of the proverb: If at first you don't succeed, try, try again (even if it kills you).

Adversity is another powerful driver for Solution-finding. Different people respond in different ways to potential danger. Give children Barbie dolls and you'll find that some will use it for interactive make-belief scenarios, while others will use the emaciated plastic figures as swords to stab their playmates. In a world of grownups, one group of scientists will develop an incredibly efficient energy production system, while another will convert it into a weapon of mass destruction. It is said that, as a species, we are too young for our brains. We are intelligent enough to build a chainsaw, but far too reckless to be running around with one.

Solution-finding from a place of fear and distrust can translate into anything from a mild "I will find ways to avoid trading or interacting with other tribes" to "I will find ways to kill all foreigners that approach my borders." Either way, few things in life get our creative juices flowing like fear of others as it triggers our most primal Problem—our impending mortality. Life-threatening conditions require the kind of creativity that will help you outrun, outgun, or outsmart your opponent. Wars and pre-emptive measures against wars have fuelled incredible technological leaps. As a species, we have allocated more talent, resources, and budgets to warfare Solutions throughout our history than perhaps to most other human Needs put together.

Beyond being well resourced and funded, like a deadly virus, war-related innovations propagate. During the early days of World War II, Sir Robert Watson-Watt developed the first practical radar that was used by the British to detect enemy movement. Based on the principle of "one man's military Solution becomes another man's Problem," this invention required new warfare strategies that evaded the radar. That's how stealth aircraft technology came to be. The invention of explosives drove the invention of bigger and more lethal explosives. The invention of missiles drove the invention of armours, that drove the invention of armour-piercing missiles. Computer viruses led to the invention of firewalls, that led to more advanced viruses, hacking, and so on.

Small people, big egos

Unchecked ego is another powerful driver for innovation and Solution-finding. Some may believe that a person with an inflated ego possesses admirable self confidence and even a grandeur of sorts, but it is merely a facade. Like a balloon, people with super-sized egos behave in ways that inflate their outer persona to conceal unmanaged insecurities. Low self-confidence may lead people in different directions. Some will let it crush them, some will live with or overcome it, and others will create an illusion of overflowing confidence and self-importance to hide their fragility. In extreme cases of overgrown ego, people can develop delusions of grandeur, where they start believing in their own fantasies. Toxic ego (usually a masculine one) has caused enormous conflicts throughout history and spearheaded much Solution-finding to match.

On a small scale, ego drives a variety of interpersonal "pissing competitions," such as who has the most enviable car in the neighbourhood or the coolest gadgets. The Need to feed this ego-generated competition pushes the development of advanced engines, car designs, and wearables. On a larger scale, ego wars can lead to patterns akin to an arms race. One of many such examples is space travel. Our desire to explore the unknown and "go where no man has gone before," per Gene Roddenberry, was but a fraction of what drove the Space Race in the mid-twentieth century. The urgency and the budgets allocated to this race hardly had anything to do with space exploration. It was mostly a grand who-has-the-biggest competition between two major Cold War rivals—the Soviet Union and the United States.

World War II taught the communist USSR and the capitalist USA that whoever could fly the highest would have greater military supremacy. In their battle for world domination, the two superpowers competed over having the greatest number of outer-space platforms, as the winner would control global firepower. The moon was not necessarily a romantic or scientific mystery these governments desired to reveal. It was a military sky advantage. Each pushed to be the first to achieve spaceflight capability with no other practical justification save for national ego and military advantage. Having the US flag as the first one to be mounted on the moon was promoted to the American people as a scientific achievement and a source of national pride. In a less public arena, it was a grand triumph over their adversaries and a symbol of military superiority.

Making the best out of a bad situation

Luckily for humanity, we also possess more positive and less arrogant driving forces for Solution-finding, and enough fertile minds that repurpose tools of destruction into Solutions for our daily Needs. A metal processing method[12] the Romans invented to reinforce their arms and armour is used to this day to build sturdy bridges, high-rising constructions, and durable metal tools. The invention of military radar led not only to stealth aircraft but also to another invention we can now find in most kitchens. It all started one fine day when Percy L. Spencer, a self-taught scientist, was standing near a magnetron[13] while sporting a chocolate bar in his pocket. When the bar began to melt for no apparent reason, intrigued Spencer decided to examine what sort of invisible energy got a hold of his chocolate. Some time later, the first microwave oven hit the market.

---

[12] This process is called carburization, in which iron or steel is made harder by absorbing carbon when the metal is heated.

[13] Magnetron is a device that powers the radar, not one of the Transformers.

The same goes for multiple innovations originally funded and developed for space travel. Artificial muscle systems, robotic sensors, diamond-joint coatings, and temper foam originally developed for space vehicles were repurposed for artificial human prosthetics, making those more functional, durable, comfortable, and lifelike. The Need for battery-powered tools for drilling and extracting rock samples in space was transformed to the domestic hand-held cordless vacuum cleaner. The Need to power spacecraft off-planet enabled the development and the consistent improvement of solar cells, now used for a sustainable and pollution-free energy source right here on earth.

Other spurs of creativity during wartime contributed to the advancement of medicine. Severe, multiple wounds in combination with field conditions required new Solutions. Up to the mid-nineteenth century, there was no way to ease the raw pain of surgeries and amputations conducted on fully lucid and very unhappy soldiers. Physicians measured their excellence by how quickly they could amputate a limb, preferably before their patient had died from the excruciating pain. It was during the American Civil War that the use of anaesthesia became widely used, though it had only been discovered less than fifteen years earlier. The use of anaesthesia has progressed since, enabling significant surgical advances, on and off the battlefield.

At the risk of sounding condescending, I believe we truly are a creative bunch capable of greatness. We have come a long way since we've climbed down trees and wielded fire. Considering the pace of innovation we've hit in the last few decades, it is difficult to predict or even imagine just how far we are yet to go. That said, we are facing major obstacles to true greatness—the kind that elevates and benefits us all while harming no living being, planet included. Unfortunately, we face great obstacles to good Solutions; obstacles driven by greed for power and means.

CHAPTER 4:

Obstacles to great Solutions

... where we examine the obstacles we face on our way to great Solutions, and why the best ones can get thrown away.

Our perfect imperfections

Have you ever presented indisputable facts and logic to prove your point, believing it was impossible for the other person to reject your perfectly reasoned claim or proposal? How stunned were you when that person wasn't swayed by your logic and refused to budge, even though their own rationale was laughable, at best? I'm guessing this happened to you more than once. The state of our emotions is one of the many reasons we often come up with faulty Solutions. Much as we would like to believe that we analyze situations and decide based on logic, our responses to the world are by far more emotional than rational. Logic and analysis may be vital components of any Solution, but our state of mind gets the final say on all decisions and actions.

Though we take pride in our reasoned planning and analytical thinking, we encounter irrationality everywhere we look. We may believe that all it takes to persuade someone is presenting bulletproof facts and logic, but it rarely works. Though it boggles the mind, it is much easier to persuade people by using a few catchy slogans that play to their emotions while completely ignoring facts and reality. Sometimes to the point of absurdity. The more facts and logic thrown on the table to counter the charlatans, the more people will dig their heels in and refuse to budge. Baffling and counterintuitive as it may be, it is perfectly natural.

In the 1980s, the neuroscientist Antonio Damasio (1) studied a patient who had lost a portion of his brain's frontal lobe in a surgery to remove a tumour. Having lost the part that generates emotions, the man could no longer experience any emotions. Though he still had a very high IQ, he had lost not only his ability to feel happiness, sadness, or love, but also his ability to make decisions. He could describe what he should logically do, but when it came to finalizing even simple decisions, such as what to eat, the man struggled. Damasio concluded that although logic is part of our reasoning process, emotions play a critical role in our final decision-making.

While it sounds like a flaw in our design, much research in neuroscience and psychology has shown that there are good reasons for emotions being a crucial part of reasoning. When we are bombarded by information, it's our emotions that screen, organize, and prioritize our decisions and actions (2). They help us decide what convinces us and what sticks in our memories. Integrating emotions into reasoning and decision may make us fallible and easier to manipulate, but it also makes us empathetic, sociable, and all-around human. Be as it may, marketers and lobbyists thrive on our emotional soft spots. Commercial and power-seeking bodies often use a strategy called Emotional Marketing, cleverly making us notice, remember, share, buy, or believe in their products and rhetoric. Emotional Marketing is the type of campaign that "helps people decide with their hearts," which is a vernacular for "helps people ignore reason." It typically harps on a singular emotion, such as happiness, sadness, anger, guilt, shame, or fear, depending on the product, the audience, and the profiteer's end goal.

Though we're looking at practicalities, our Solutions must also satisfy our fears, anxieties, self-esteem issues, sense of meaning, or our Need to belong with our social group. Our cognitive process, or what we call "thinking things through," often reminds me of the game Snakes and

Ladders.[14] Just like in the game, we believe that our progression over the gameboard is dictated by impartial dice. If you get three on your dice, you take three steps forward. Steady, logical, and rule based. That is until we encounter a situation that triggers the irrational forces lurking in our minds and divert us from our path. Much like the ladders on the gameboard that produce an unexpected positive effect, and the snakes that pull us down and away from our original Needs, logic be damned. Our emotions, far more than our logic, guide what we eat, buy, and produce, who we socialize with, believe in, vote for, or reject. And profiteers know it all too well.

It's a complicated world

Another major culprit for faulty Solutions is complexity. Things may have been easier for us if life was simple. Bacteria grown in a petri dish under optimal conditions may have to deal with a single Problem—how to multiply as quickly as possible. We have no such luxury, being complex beings living in a complex system. Our Problems do not exist in a pampering petri dish. Rather, they are the products of multiple internal and external realities, struggles, and circumstances that intersect and interact. Every decision we make triggers a domino effect in multiple directions, some less predictable than others.

Even if we overcome biases, emotions, manipulative profiteers, and inflated egos, and set aside the many false Core Certainties that shape our reality, our Solutions might suffer because life is too complicated for our limited cognitive capacity. In his book, *The Logic of Failure* (3), Dietrich Dörner shows that effective planning and decision-making are more

---

[14] Snakes and Ladders is a Westernized version of an ancient Indian board game known as Moksha Patam. It is played on a game board with numbered, gridded squares and a set of dice. An assortment of drawn ladders has the player move up the game and closer to the finish line, whereas drawn snakes force the player down and away from the finish line.

difficult than we may think, because most of the problems we currently face are interrelated.

In our not-too-far past, we have dealt with problems on an ad hoc basis. Our most complex tasks were to gather firewood, drive a herd of bison off a cliff, or build a trap for wild horses. These tasks had no significance beyond themselves. The amount of firewood collected by a Stone Age tribe was of no threat to the sustainability of the forest. Though some of their hunting activities were wasteful (killing an entire herd for the one animal they could consume), being so few, they posed no real threat to global wildlife populations or other tribes across the globe. Our prehistoric ancestors rarely had to stop and analyze a problem within the context of many other factors and future timelines. This is no longer our world. Our reality is made up of countless intersecting subsystems that require us to process multidimensional and multivariable types of data. Every decision we make and every action we take become entangled with countless other decisions, actions, and unanticipated outcomes.

Pope Gregory IX must have been a staunch dog person because he considered cats to be the incarnation of Satan. His decree led to a mass killing of cats as part of an allegedly divine directive meant to guard us from evil. True to the idiom, "When the cat's away, the mice will play," the rat population went out of control and eventually quickened the spread of the Black Death that killed about one third of the European population.

In 1930 the US government passed the Smoot–Hawley Tariff Act[15] in response to the alarming number of business failures during that period. The intention behind this high tax on imports was to encourage consumption of local goods and support US industry and farming. Makes perfect sense, right? While the intention was good, this Solution backfired

---

[15] The US Smoot–Hawley Tariff Act of 1930 was a law that implemented a tax on goods and services imported from other countries.

in a big way. Seeing the United States thwarting their exports, European countries went for the tried-and-true political move known as, "Oh yeah? Hold my beer!" They retaliated by raising their own tariffs on American goods and reducing their purchases of American-made products. This tariff battle created an economic decline all around. With no export on either side, the production workers were let go, and the farmers went bankrupt. Instead of protecting the workers in each of the countries involved, these tariffs further contributed to the economic decline now known as the Great Depression.

Mao Zedong was another leader who failed to account for complex systems. In 1958, Chairman Mao declared sparrows the number one enemy of Chinese agriculture. He ordered the annihilation of all these winged nemeses that were eating grain and supposedly compromising food supply. His obedient (and fearful) citizens went into a hunting frenzy, all but eliminating the population of sparrows in China. Turned out that without sparrows eating insects, grain-eating critters had a blast. Locust swarms of biblical proportions flooded the countryside and ate all the crops. Within three years, Mao Zedong's near-sighted view on nature's delicate balance caused severe famine and the death of 36 million of his people (for comparison—the total population of Canada in 2020). By the time he had realized his mistake and stopped the sparrowcide campaign, it was too late. The population of birds had declined so drastically, China had to ask the Soviet Union for sparrows. Despite the rushed bird import, it took decades for the farming industry to recover.

You may think, "Well, such outlandish Solutions dictated by tyrants, backward thinkers, and inflammatory politicians are bound to fail. What we need is the big thinkers—the scientists and engineers." But has all scientific progress benefitted humanity? Let's set aside the glaring horrors of the atom bomb and use a more human-friendly invention—the steam engine. Coal is not a new energy source. Even our ancient cave-dwelling ancestors used it to sustain their fire pits. Prior to the brilliant invention of the steam engine, mining for coal was not only one of the hardest, back-breaking jobs, it was also extremely dangerous.

The invention of the steam engine propelled a true revolution on many fronts. It allowed miners to use machinery to do much of the manual work they had done previously, and it improved worker safety and longevity. This engineering progress also allowed for the extraction of much more coal per worker. You would think that this much improved mining process would solve the societal Need for coal. Yet it had the exact opposite effect. Making coal more widely available increased the demand for steam engines to make work easier and more efficient for other industries. Since the steam engine itself required coal to heat the water into steam, this growth increased the demand for coal. More demand meant more burning coal, more mining, further industrial growth, and further demand for coal. This spiral phenomenon of new efficiency that creates greater demand is known as the "rebound effect." No matter how brilliant the people who came up with the Solution, when we get caught in this rebound, instead of solving our original Problem, we make it bigger.

In the past two hundred years, we have seen a phenomenal growth in rational and free thinking, and in engineering and scientific innovation. And yet we find ourselves in a time where overhunting, over-logging, and polluting our planet are no longer as impactless as they used to be in the Bronze Age. The scale on which our so-called progressive actions take place is so vast that we have already caused mass extinction of plants and animals and an alarming rise in Earth's temperatures. How is it possible that the more educated and technologically sophisticated we are, the more destructive we become within our complex life system? The rebound effect is merely one reason. According to Dörner, a person's IQ is not necessarily a good predictor of their ability to make good decisions within complex systems. A person can be highly educated and intelligent and yet make fatal judgment calls.

The predictors for such mistakes include, but certainly aren't limited to, factors such as one's tendency to walk away from difficult problems or delegating them to be solved by others; getting easily distracted by new information that may be completely irrelevant to the problem; addressing the problems they can solve rather than the ones they are supposed to solve; refusing to recognize their own helplessness and failures; and turning away from the unknown in favour of their comfort zone. The most likely people to come up with good Solutions for complex problems aren't necessarily the most intelligent ones among us; rather, these are the ones who aren't full of themselves and who feel comfortable with uncertainty and self-scrutiny. The problem is that people who aren't full of themselves rarely accumulate power or make it into decision-making positions.

Cultural Core Certainties add another irrational layer that affects the quality of our Solutions. Our cultures determine our priorities, guide our decision-making, and tell us how to deal with the damage we cause. The physicists who worked to develop deadly nuclear weapons were neither stupid nor evil. They simply operated within the cultural parameters of modern science that empowered and rewarded them for brilliant discoveries no matter their impact within a complex, global system. They also operated within the broader national governance Dogma that prioritized military achievements over life on earth.

The road from Problems to proper Solutions is often winding and paved with all forms of landmines that throw us off the right track. This is why many of our Solutions may seem and sound wonderful but are essentially useless or harmful. Then there are the self-serving forces that take every good Solution and corrupt it for their personal benefit.

The good of the few on the backs of the many

This is a story about two friends. Chun is a high-energy woman who sometimes feels her life is lacking purpose. It often fills her with frustration and nervous energy. Though she has a few friends, she feels lonely. Then there's Enzo who has been sick for a while. Though they still have hope for recovery, Enzo feels it would take a miracle to find the right cure for their ailment. They are often filled with dread about dying young, and their state of mind distances them from their friends. Though Chun and Enzo are very different people with seemingly different problems, apart from their friendship they share many similarities when it comes to their Needs, as described in Figure 10. Both have the Need for social and emotional support to overcome stress and pain; the Need for physical action of some sort to release energy, build connections, and possibly find purpose; and the Need for all forms of "cures" to eliminate disease, distress, and premature death.

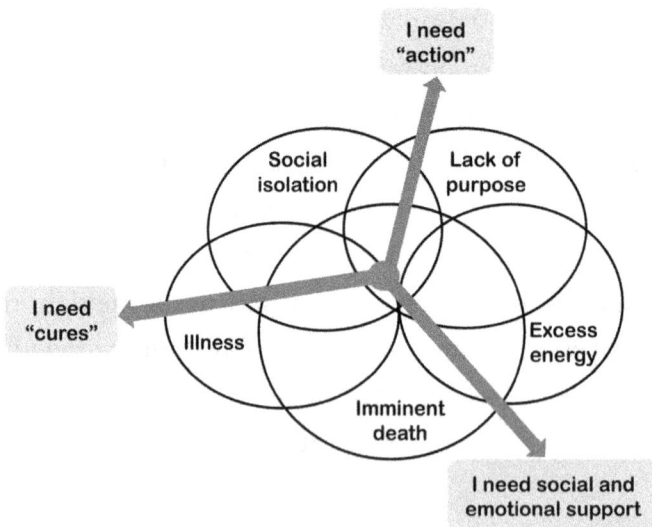

Figure 10: Intersecting Problems lead to common Needs

Enzo's and Chun's overlapping Needs may be served by a range of good Solutions, as illustrated in Figure 11. Both can benefit from various and individualized healing methods for their physical and emotional ailments. Both can enjoy individual and collective physical activities that will help them release stress, build social bonds, and improve mental and physical health. Both can also benefit from engaging with faiths and spiritual practices, which can provide a sense of meaning, alleviate emotional pain, and possibly help find a purpose.

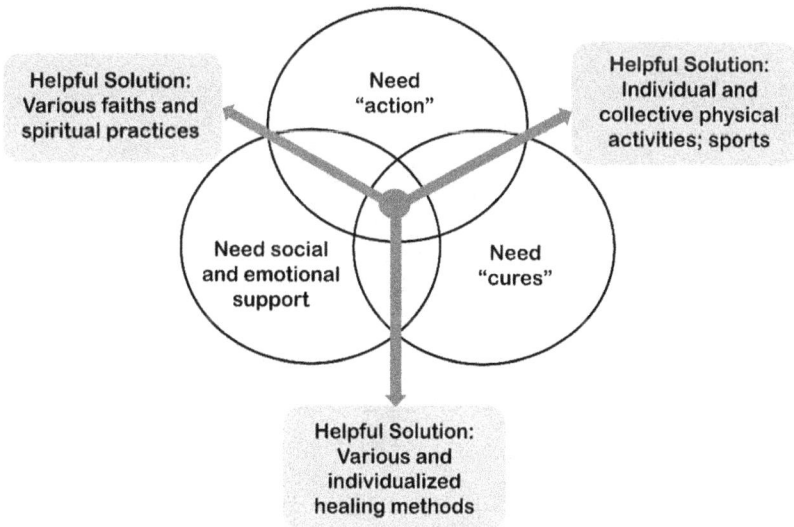

Figure 11: Intersecting Needs lead to common Solutions

When self-serving groups and individuals interfere with Solution-finding, they infuse their own agendas. Their Need for power and means takes over most other Needs, as shown in Figure 12. Pursuing faith and spirituality for a sense of wholeness, wellness, and unity can transform into rigid, organized religions where the head organizers (clergy, "church") gain ultimate power over their believers. Engaging in physical activity for a sense of joy, comradery, and release, transforms into professional sports that serve the organizers' desire for profits, status, and power. Finally, a wide range of individualized healing methods for healthy living transform into a single, one-fits-all, medication-based treatment path, allowing profiteers to dominate the healthcare market and make sizeable profits.

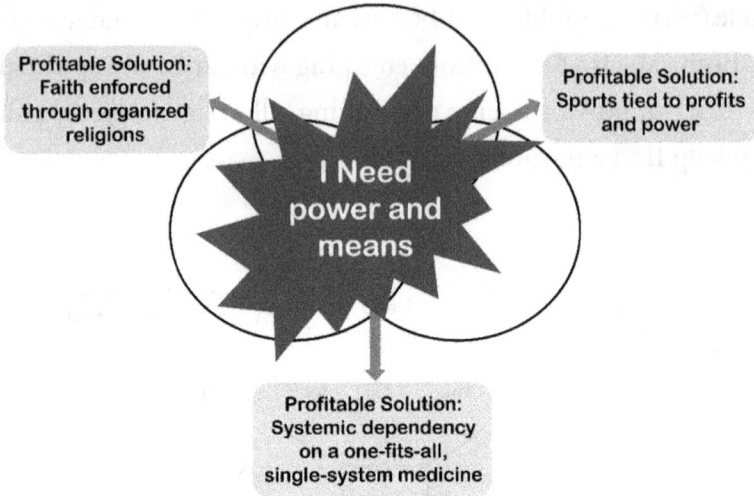

Figure 12: Self-serving Needs overtaking Solutions

The enormity of the desire for power and means and its destructive impact on us and on our planet is unmistakeable. I dare say there is not a single element in our lives and not a single bio-system that has escaped the dire consequences of this dynamic. Our search for energy sources is one such example. Much has been said and written about the ills of mining and the use of fossil fuels. Land degradation and its devastating effect on natural landscapes and precious ecosystems. Water pollution caused by the seepage of toxic fluids from fracking and coal processing, and from massive oil spills during extraction or transport. Air pollution from toxic emissions. Ocean acidification. Drastic and unprecedented rise in CO_2 levels in our atmosphere. Drastic climate change and global warming. Mass extinction of flora and fauna.

Anyone who wishes to preserve our home planet for future generations can tell that further use of fossil fuels is a creeping global suicide. And yet we are still far from putting our weight behind environment-sustaining energy production systems. Many decision-makers and industry representatives claim that, until recently, we weren't aware of its devastating effects. Those who make such proclamations, and those who still deny global climate change, are wilfully ignorant or downright lying. When the industrial revolution started booming in the mid-nineteenth century, we had little understanding of the massive impact fossil fuels and coal burning would have on the environment. In fact, the whole concept of humanity having a role in preserving the environment is fairly recent in what we call the Western world, despite being a basic tenet for time immemorial for indigenous people around the world. Yet even in the West, there were clear indications difficult to ignore.

Acid rain resulting from the release of human-produced sulphur and nitrogen compounds into the atmosphere was shown to cause measurable damage to plants, fish, soil, and forests in the early twentieth century. In 1948, severe industrial air pollution created a deadly smog that killed twenty people in Donora, Pennsylvania, and made seven thousand very sick. In 1952, pollutants from factories and home fireplaces mixed with air condensation killed at least four thousand people in London within several days. In the late 1950s, the geochemist Charles Keeling developed The Keeling Curve, which revealed a steady rise in CO_2 levels that can lead to climate change.

Despite lagging by a few thousands of years behind indigenous wisdom, in the 1960s some Westerners had finally acknowledged our responsibility to preserve our planet and our role in its destruction. Environmental movements began to emerge, seeking to curb the tide of pollutants flowing into the planet's ecosystems. They gained more power to act following a few more disastrous incidents around the world that had proven a clear connection between pollution, the safety of our environment, and human death tolls.

By the 1980s, computer models showed that a doubling of CO_2 could cause global temperatures to rise by 2.6°F (1.5°C) within the next century. Twenty-some years into this century, we are already nearing this number. Though in the last eight hundred thousand years, CO_2 levels rose and fell in natural cycles, since 1850 human activities have raised its atmospheric concentrations by nearly 49 percent. This is more than what had happened naturally over a twenty-thousand-year period (4). The last time atmospheric CO_2 amounts were this high was over three million years ago, when the temperature was 3.6°F–5.4°F (2°C–3°C) higher than during the pre-industrial era, and sea level was fifty to eighty feet (fifteen to twenty metres) higher than today.

All that to say, we have had more than enough information in the past seventy to eighty years on the devastating effects of fossil fuels and the perils of nuclear power. Therefore, we cannot use the "I never knew" and "I never thought" arguments in all earnest. Clearly, these destructive Solutions are being upheld and protected by those who stand to lose power and means should we adopt other energy Solutions.

Another argument industry representatives use in their defence is that sustainable, environmental energy sources have always been scarce, so we are forced to use what has been available to us. That, too, is a convenient lie. Though it is little known, the first electric car was launched to replace the horse and carriage as early as 1835 by Robert Anderson. It was crude and took another few decades to refine, but by 1899 it became popular with urban residents, being quiet, easy to drive, and non-polluting.[16] In the early days of the twentieth century, around a third of all

---

[16] This refers to local pollution within urban centres. It is important to note that the electricity for these cars was produced mostly from coal burning. However, given time and targeted investment, alternate sources could have been developed much earlier.

vehicles on the road in the U.S. were electric. And yet, more than a hundred years later, their presence on our roads is negligible. In 2024 only about 14 percent of global passenger vehicle sales were electric or hybrid cars.

What happened? The discovery of vast oil fields in Texas and in the Middle East in the early 1900s is what happened. Within a few years, thousands of oil companies were chartered, and oil became the dominant fuel of the twentieth century around the world. This, and the rise in the gasoline-powered Model-T Ford car were the beginning of the end for electric vehicles and all other more environmentally friendly energy sources. Not because fossil fuel was a better source, but because it was more profitable and created opportunities for gaining political power. This greed for power and money boosted the mass production of gasoline-based vehicles, sabotaged investment in further development of electric cars and in public transportation, and changed the North American take on urban planning.

Our addiction to the gasoline-run automobile wasn't the result of personal preference. In his book *Fighting Traffic* (5), the historian Peter Norton chronicled the ways the newly emerging car industry, supported by the oil companies, had recreated cities into car-dominated geographies. They organized opposition against attempts to enforce speed limits, expanded highways, and forcefully (and illegally) replaced electric streetcar lines in cities across the United States with gasoline-run buses. They attacked critics like Ralph Nader, ignored known vehicular defects, and lobbied against and evaded environmental regulations. But the automobile and gasoline industries didn't stop there. To ensure their car-per-person vision, they had to create urban environments that forced us into complete reliance on private cars. For that to happen, they lobbied heavily and invested much money and effort in changing urban planning. These two industries practically invented the North American suburbs, as we know them today.

According to Matt Huber, a geographer, and author of *Lifeblood* (6), the suburbs were mostly a post-World War II creation. For that to happen, the purchasing power of upcoming suburban homeowners started much earlier. Between the early 1930s and mid-1950s a series of legislative initiatives in the United States enabled white workers and soldiers to buy a home and a car. In 1956, following years of aggressive lobbying by the automotive industry, the Federal Aid Highway Act allocated tens of billions of dollars to construct the interstate highway system. This was done on the backs of communities of colour, whose houses were demolished to make way for the new roads.

Canada followed suit. Geographer Owen Toews describes in his book, *Stolen City* (7) how Winnipeg's chamber of commerce convinced the municipal government to construct a network of new roads to facilitate suburban development, based on the same premise that suburbanization was inescapable. Similarly to the United States, Canadian legislation heavily subsidized suburban homeownership, leaving the working-class with little choice but to buy in the suburbs. A life outside the city, where bus services were intentionally sparse to non-existent, necessitated the ownership of cars. This is an excellent example of the tail wagging the dog, or the profitable Solution driving the Problem and Need, instead of the other way around.

Fossil fuels and the car industry are but few of countless ways we allowed self-serving Needs to override our genuine Need for safe and effective Solutions. Greed and thirst for power often lead us in all the wrong directions, resulting in harmful, if not deadly, Solutions for the benefit of the few and the detriment of the many.

The diminishing sphere of Solutions

I used a Cone for the shape of my model because it illustrates the narrowing of each tier as it appears above the one below it. Our perspectives and definitions of Problems are informed by the broad spectrum of our Core Certainties, as shown in the lower tier. The second tier of the Cone narrows into very few or a single identified Problem, which further narrows based on limited or skewed Need definitions. The next tier shrinks as we distil many creative options to a narrow band of acceptable Solutions. As the Cone tiers progress from base to tip, not only do options narrow, but freedoms narrow as well.

We all know that a single Solution, no matter how ingenious, is unlikely to resolve profound Problems such as "I don't feel loved," or even simpler ones such as, "I'm constantly late for work." These sort of be-all-and-end-all Solutions usually belong in fantasies and deceitful propaganda. Being incredibly creative, we can easily come up with abundant Solutions that will address any one Problem from every angle. And yet, something happens on the path from creative thinking to applied innovation. Our finalized Solutions narrow to such extent they fail to address the entirety or even a portion of our Problems and Needs. One common reason is the quick-fix trap.

Let's face it, who doesn't love quick fixes? Even when we have a range of Solutions that could fully address our Problem, we are not built to draw from a deep pool of options. Here is a simple proof: when you use a web search engine to find an answer to your question, how many pages of results do you normally review? According to 2020 web stats, the first page of Google captures nearly 95 percent of search traffic clicks, even though most search results offer thousands of pages of valuable information. Most people don't even bother scrolling to the bottom of the first page. In fact, with the rise of Artificial Intelligence (AI), most of us won't even bother using traditional search engines. We will simply ask the AI engine to produce the quickest and shortest answer possible, and then won't even bother to corroborate the AI-generated response.

The average adult living in an industrialized society makes roughly thirty-five thousand decisions every day. Many of these decisions are basic, such as how much milk to add to your coffee, or which shirt you will wear, and then which arm will be the first to push into a sleeve. For some of us, decisions come easily. Others may have fewer of them, having chosen to lead a simpler life. But for most of us, decision-making is exhausting. Living in a fast-paced world requires a multitude of decisions that often result in one of two evils. One is decision fatigue, where the more time we spend on decision-making, the lower the quality and rationality of our decisions. The other is a paradox of choice, where too many options paralyze us from deciding at all. Decision fatigue is now understood as one cause of irrational decision-making, and none of us is immune to it regardless of our education, intellect, or intent. Being stuck in a paradox of choice isn't much better, since it grinds to a halt everything that should be moving forward.

Our evolution in a simpler world wired us to pursue quick fixes for immediate Needs. What we really want is a single Solution or a tiny cluster of Solutions that responds to our Needs instantly and solves at least part of our Problem. Try it yourself. Identify your go-to Solutions for each of the Problems you have listed in our exercise in Chapter 2. Review your list and answer honestly—are you using true Solutions that resolve your core Problems or are these quick and convenient patches that resolve symptoms or soothe emotional unease? Let's examine a few of the Problems some of us may grapple with. For each, you will find a few commonly used quick-fix Solutions, as well as Solutions that provide more comprehensive and effective responses.

Identified Problem: I'm not attractive enough to be loved.

Common Solutions: Apply makeup, work those abs, get plastic surgery, compromise.

More effective Solutions: Acknowledge that physical appearance isn't a condition to being loved; learn to love and accept yourself; know you are enough; stay away from people who judge or shame you for your looks; create or join groups of like-minded people; do things you are passionate about; etc.

Identified Problem: I am depressed.

Common Solutions: Go on antidepressants, think positively.

More effective Solutions: Use antidepressants if this is a good solution for you, but don't stop there; acknowledge your emotions, don't fear them; seek professional therapy; meditate; surround yourself with people who love you unconditionally; stay away from people who judge or tell you to "get over it"; get enough sleep; eat a balanced diet; go out in nature; do something meaningful to you that fills you with joy; etc.

Identified Problem: My phone is only a year old and it's already obsolete.

Common Solutions: Get a new phone (quickly, before they run out).

More effective Solutions: Acknowledge this is a manufactured Problem and choose not to fall into the consumerism trap; decide that so long as your phone still works, no need to replace it.

Identified Problem: My child isn't doing well at school.

Common Solutions: Scold the child for being lazy, get a tutor, medicate the child.

More effective Solutions: Withhold judgment; have a heart-to-heart with your child and actually listen; explore the deeper issues without assigning blame; collaborate on finding strategies your child is able and willing to try; accept that the educational system is "one-fits-all" and might not meet your child's needs; seek alternative educational or extracurricular support systems; understand neurodivergence and seek effective approaches; accept that not everyone can or should go "academic"; help your child find their strengths and thrive on them; etc.

The listed quick fixes are among the most widely used, yet they are not very likely to solve these Problem in full, if at all, and most of us know it. And yet, these are our common go-to approaches. Why is that? For one, seeking and using a full range of Solutions is much too exhausting. Most of us will sacrifice quality and efficacy for speed and simplicity. One may argue that quick fixes have merit in our busy lives. If you're in the middle of your workday and you develop a splitting headache, you can't always take the time to reconnect with the emotions that may have brought it about. You may also not be up for meditation, or a long nature walk. In truth, most of us will say, "Just give me them pills." It makes perfect sense in the moment. The problem is that these moments accumulate and end up making up our entire lives.

One of the many challenges of overcoming our desire for quick fixes is that it has become the benchmark of modern life. We expect to have resolutions right now, preferably yesterday. Technological advances, worldwide communication networks, fast food, same-day delivery, online purchases, and social media, among many other factors, made us into a rather impatient bunch. If a video takes longer than a nanosecond to upload, we feel cheated out of our precious time and move on to something else. If food takes longer than two minutes to prepare, we will opt for a processed, pre-cooked meal. If an app takes more than two clicks to get results, we will vote it down. A posting longer than two sentences will be skipped in favour of images with a single, usually shallow, or meaningless statement.

Not only do we love quick-fix Solutions, we love it even more when a single quick Solution rids us of many Problems in one fell swoop. Who wants to carry around an enormous tool bag when you can get a Swiss Army knife embedded with multiple items and fitting right in the palm of your hand? It would be a terrible waste if we were to limit our use of fire to scented candles, or laser to fancy lighting in night clubs. Obviously, we want to fully capitalize on every Solution we come up with. Unfortunately, this very trait also makes us susceptible to believing that bottled snake oil can save us from hair loss, diabetes, erectile dysfunction, gout, upset stomach, and bad weather. This preference for multi-purpose marvels often makes us loyal to Solutions that overpromise and underdeliver, while hindering the search for better alternatives.

Another trap that leads us to develop faulty Solutions is our aversion to change which, paradoxically, coexists with our thirst for exploration and discovery. The term cookie-cutter solution[17] is the signature of the uninspired, boring technocrats who are unable to "think outside the box." The problem is that we don't always mean what we say. Even when we think we want "out-of-the-box" Solutions, we include terms and conditions in the small print section. This is especially true when these original Solutions require us to change.

---

[17] A cookie cutter is used to cut dough into shapes before baking the cookies. A cookie-cutter approach refers to the use of the exact same method in different situations without considering individual differences.

Children—the ultimate out-of-the-box thinkers—may enjoy using cookie-cutters when given the opportunity to bake cookies as part of their discovery process. But most will quickly move to forming their creations (unless you went ahead and spoiled it by telling them this isn't how it's done). During a social gathering, close friends and family members will be delighted with the oddly shaped cookies and consider them adorable. However, if you were the one who had created the "artistic" cookies, even your close family members might not find them endearing. Most people will consider you an attention seeker. The same goes for what we wear, where we live, the people we befriend, the ideas we express, and nearly every other aspect of life we are supposed to conform with.

Where, then, is our pride in out-of-the-box thinking? Though we claim to encourage unabridged creativity, most of us are uncomfortable with anything that lives outside our mental boxes. The hidden small print says: "We encourage you to think outside your own box so long as you remain inside our collective, agreed-upon box." Critical thinking, like creativity, suffers the same fate. Established systems, employers, and even innovative research institutions will tell you they encourage, nay, they *expect* you to show critical thinking. That is until you do. That's when the fine print is pulled out to let you know, "When we say critical thinking, we mean thinking like us." Despite public statements that encourage innovation, the constraints of the quick fix, and the orthodox cookie-cutter thinking, stifle creativity. These limitations narrow the Solutions we come up with.

That said, our lazy ways and orthodox minds aren't the only culprits for insufficient Solutions. Look again at the examples provided earlier. Can you identify a fundamental difference that isn't related to our impatience, short-sightedness, or aversion to change? Here's a clue: follow the money. As described in the previous section, ulterior motives are a major reason for a narrowing scope of Solutions. The most popular ones usually line someone's pockets. Some Solution providers design Solutions not only to generate wealth but also to help them accumulate power, status, and influence. These people invest much time, resources, and energy in promoting their Solutions to us, all while silencing, publicly shaming, discrediting, or downright eliminating those who come up with alternatives. Every Cone will have a unique blend of causes for a narrowed Solution. No matter the reason, a finalized Solution will almost inevitably be partial at best, if not useless or harmful.

CHAPTER 5:

From Solutions to Systems

... where we explore how Systems are born, charm us, and become self-conscious.

A System is born

Think of a typical morning in an average family (whatever that is) getting organized to send their young kids to school. Every functional family will have its own systematic procedures. Wake the kids up, check that they're up, make sure they brushed their teeth and dressed properly for the weather, make them breakfast, prepare their lunch for school, ensure they didn't forget anything before leaving the house, get them to the bus or drive them to school, kiss goodbye and wish them well, then get back to the rest of your morning activities. Every school-day morning will look more or less the same, with minor variations of mood or mishaps. Well-functioning families are not rigid, but they are systematic, following consistent and predictable processes. Having a functioning school system to send the kids to that prescribes instructional content and mandates schooling for a fixed number of years is systemic.

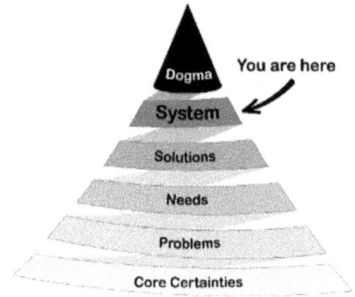

For a Solution to become commonplace, it must grow into a System, and a functional System must be at least systematic. The bigger it is, the more it is likely to become systemic as well.

In the past (and still in many regions around the world), we grew our own food and produced whatever goods we were skilled to produce. Everything else, we sourced from other members of our local community. When wandering from one farm to the next to obtain necessities proved inefficient, we have created a better Solution: the weekly or biweekly market where we could offer our goods and easily access everyone else's. It was a far better Solution, but not the best one possible. Since no single community had the skills and resources to produce and address every possible necessity, we still had to schlep to other, more distant markets. It also didn't solve our Need to access goods outside market days. The invention of grocery stores that were constantly open and sourced goods from both local and distant regions addressed these Needs. These stores were budding Systems that operated systematically to ensure a steady supply of goods, and often expanded into other regions.

Once this System caught on, it was only a matter of time until supermarkets and megastores took hold in larger urban centres. Though you could still access local farmers' markets and grocery stores, the mega-systems gained purchasing power and created well monitored and standardized supply chains that competed with, and sometimes took over, local enterprises. While their stated purpose was to provide communities with goods, another purpose emerged: self preservation. The bigger the System grew, the more it needed to preserve itself as an operational and profitable business.

When an idea transforms from Solution to System, several factors evolve from "free range" to systemic and systematic structures, as described in Figure 13. The first step is for the Solution to evolve from anecdotal to formal. In the early life of a Solution, it is experimental and adopted by a small number of people. As time goes by and it either proves itself useful or fervently promoted by profiteers, the Solution becomes more stabilized, less flexible, and more widely adopted. Eventually, it becomes the most popular of all similar Solutions and the common go-to.

Solution   System

	Solution		System
Stage of the Solution	Experimental; limited adoption	▷	Well tested and/or widely adopted
Exposure to Solution	Through word of mouth, informal, local	▷	Deliberate and systematic distribution of the Solution
Knowledge and Expertise	Transferred via ad hoc, local sharing	▷	Distributed broadly via structured sharing
Access and Delivery	Sporadic or local via improvised system	▷	Widespread, systematic, systemic
Innovation	Multiple new options tested and tried; openness to other approaches	▷	Less solution-seeking; must meet "standards" and require systemic approval
Leadership	Casual and sporadic; individual or small group	▷	True believers or profiteers

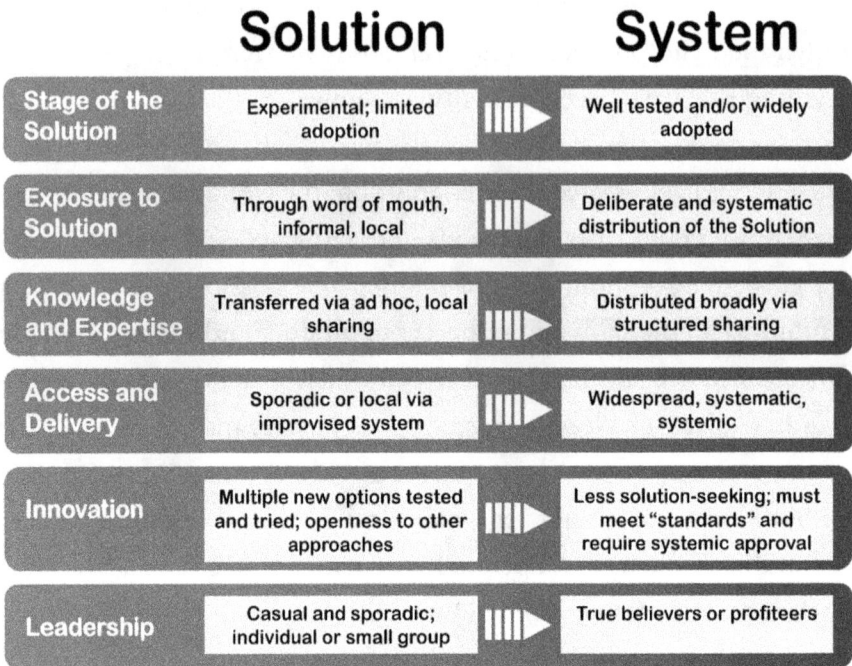

Figure 13: From Solution to System

Once the Solution is well-formed and accepted, interested parties (e.g., developers, profiteers, great believers in the Solution) develop reliable systems to get it out there. It may start with knowledge sharing within small circles. Given time, resources, and motivation, the Solution Leadership will build an organized information transfer. They may use storytellers, celebrities, ads, lectures, scheduled gatherings, promotional campaigns, and product distribution systems, depending on the type of the Solution and its intended Users. One very effective way to educate target audiences on the Solution is by putting it in writing. The written word has been a double-edged sword ever since its inception. On the one hand, it allowed us to share valuable information and ideas on a much larger scale than any spoken word ever could. It enabled us to capture thoughts, events, and instructions, and to preserve them beyond any single lifetime. Even more importantly, writing allowed us to express and share our artistic creations with the world.

On the downside, once an idea or a piece of information is put down in writing, it quickly becomes "the undeniable truth" simply because it's written. Worse still, it often becomes sanctified and untouchable, thus holding us hostage with no expiration date on concepts that have gone stale a long time ago. Even the best-intended documents, such as spiritual writings and national constitutions, can and do become obsolete with time. And yet, once they are documented, they become written in stone, despite the idiomatic claim that nothing is.

For that reason, sturdy Systems rely on comprehensive formal documentation, be it written, electronic, recorded, or filmed. In aboriginal societies, multi-generational story telling and retelling are used to transfer Systems. The advantage of this method is that it allows for the evolution of the narrative—something that doesn't happen much with written records. Formal records rid the Solution from the need to prove itself worthy. All we have to do is refer to "what has been written" in user manuals, processes and procedures, patents, contracts, laws, or scriptures. Unlike the Solution stage, where everything is debatable, once it has turned the corner into a well-documented System, it becomes the reality as we know it.

Creating and using formal expertise is another way to protect the System from loss, destruction, or rogue ideas. At this stage, it isn't enough for the original creators of the Solution to profess its value and merit, or even to document it. What a System needs is a combination of widespread expertise on the Solution, and a way for the System to qualify this expertise. Formal, standardized training, education, or certification create formal authority structures (e.g., expert, technician, licensed practitioner, ordained clergy, appointed witch hunter). The combination of documentation and Solution-approved expertise builds a stronghold for the Solution System.

The next crucial evolutionary stage is the development of effective access and delivery systems. In the early Solution stage, Users access it locally or via improvised distribution systems such as word of mouth, the occasional travelling salesperson, or "Solution disciples." Gradually, this sporadic outreach grows into a widespread, organized distribution, and then gets imbedded in the System. People who have a Problem that the Solution can address will be referred to those who have the authority to deliver or dispense it. Those who are qualified to deliver it will offer the Solution in a structured manner.

The System not only serves its Users but also actively supports the Solution in various ways, including funding, endorsements, or making it the default choice. If you are the developer of a new scientific theory, you will first want to have it reviewed, approved, and acknowledged by the scientific community. Once this is done, you will go on some form of a campaign to speak its praise through interviews, articles, and conferences. For better results, target not only the scientific community but also lay-people, albeit in simpler and more practical terms. You will use appealing catchphrases and translate them into "why it's good for us" or "this is the issue we're addressing." You will then need to integrate your theory into educational materials, courses, and research protocols. Next, you will train scientists on the proper use of your theory, and then qualify them to train others in ways that ensure correct and effective distribution of knowledge. You can start these steps on your own, but eventually you will require a system to support you—a commercial sponsor, professional association, regulatory body, or a government ministry.

Once the System is in place, it will methodically promote the implementation of your theory as a standard in all relevant scientific applications. The System will include your theory in all educational materials aimed at students to ensure they grow up with this vital knowledge. It will monitor the use of your theory to make sure irresponsible individuals don't corrupt it. The System will expand and distribute this knowledge to the rest of the world.

Another role of the Solution System is monitoring and scrutinizing alternative and competing ideas. In the early stages of the Solution, creativity and innovation are only limited by the developers' imagination and prevailing Core Certainties. New Solutions come and go, and multiple new options are tried and tested. Once a System develops, it will restrict much of this freedom. First, having a well-established Solution—whether it solves the Problem or only makes people believe it does—reduces the sense of urgency to come up with more Solutions. Our comfort and confidence in resolving our Problem (or the illusion of resolution) will lead us to generate fewer new ideas and show less interest in anything that isn't "ours." We will invest much more in refining and improving the existing Solution than in seeking better ones.

Second, the System is a guardian of the Solution and its Users. It may run mandatory quality control of products, monitor service providers to limit potential damage to Solution Users (e.g., clients, patients), or ensure no one compromises its foundational ideology. The System will develop standards and benchmarks that all new Solutions for that Problem will have to meet. Every new idea will require the System's approval, which will inevitably limit that "out-of-the-box thinking" we so desire. New Solutions will not only have to prove they work but also fight for their right to exist. Having new "out-of-our-box" Solutions to completely replace the existing one will be an uphill battle, because they will face a well-established mechanism that will put up a fight against the change.

Then there's the matter of leadership. In the early stages, its developers and close supporters will lead the Solution. As it grows into a System, those who have the power to govern systemic Solutions will take over. System Leaders don't have to be experts on the Solution itself; it is more important for them to be able to manage a System. The CEO of a hospital may or may not be a healthcare professional by training, but for the hospital to survive, they will require superior organizational and leadership skills.

The traitorous charms of the System

At the System stage, we no longer feel that we should be questioning the base assumption that can be prefixed with "every child knows." We all want to predict, control, and explain our reality, and have clear answers to our Problems and Needs. Solution Systems help us move to higher grounds by creating a practical and intellectual staircase. Every newly gained System is another predictable stair for us to climb up with confidence, furthering our understanding of life, and our ability to deal with it. Imagine you had to reinvent the staircase each time you wanted to climb from the basement to the ground floor, where you now spend most of your life. How convenient it is to have the stairs already in place so that you may ascend higher and further explore the mysteries of the second floor. How convenient it is to know without a doubt that one and one make two, two times three make six, and which way is north. How else would we be able to advance to higher forms of mathematics, engineering, science, and literature?

A structured Solution System provides us with powerful assurance. It sets the way we think about the realities of our world and shapes our Core Certainties. Systems help us make sense of everything around us. They make this blunder we call life more bearable. And yet, they can hold us back as readily as getting us further ahead. By offering us a sense of resolution and the emotional comfort we so desire, Systems lull the very thing our curious mind is designed to do. Even though Solutions in the System stage are not compulsory, very few of us choose to dispute the assumptions upon which our lives are built. One has to be a philosopher at heart or a born rebel to question that which "every child knows." Even in the most advanced societies, doubting Systems as more than an intellectual exercise in a classroom or over cocktails may put people in an uncomfortable position with their System-upholding circles.

Not only do Systems steer us away from the thrill of invention, but consider this: What if we built some of our stairs in the wrong direction? We would constantly follow in the wrong direction without even realizing it. Think of the two examples of the true nature of planet Earth. Each set of Core Certainties and their related Systems will lead us in a completely different direction while eliminating alternatives.

Though Solutions tend to grow into Systems, not every Solution ends up as one. An idea must meet several criteria to take hold. A Solution must, first and foremost, be grounded in our Core Certainties. Ideologically divergent Solutions are the first to be kicked out at the stage of conceptualization, because they threaten to undermine everything we believe in. A Solution must be at least partially satisfactory as well as practical, or else it will not be scalable enough to become widely used. It must offer a quick fix since we will rarely bother with ongoing effort or lengthy and complex adoption. Even though our emotions produce symptoms that confuse us, a Solution must address them, no matter how much it compromises practical approaches. Irrational as this emotional driver may be, we won't grow a Solution into a System unless it soothes and comforts us. And, last, a Solution that profits someone will also be more likely to be adopted, because those who stand to profit will invest in its development, execution, and distribution. Having at least some of these prerequisites at play often establishes Systems that protect useless or partial Solutions.

These requirements also tend to intersect and reinforce each other. For example, profiteers will promote their quick-fix Solution, make sure we can easily access, purchase, and use it, and then manipulate our fears and anxieties by showing how their Solution heals our souls. Despite their shortcomings, we embrace many of the Systems that govern our lives because they serve our less-than-rational, misguided, or manipulated psyche.

Self-preservation above all

Once we establish a System, many agendas and less-than-noble driving forces come to the forefront. This corrupting effect isn't surprising for Solutions that were conceived out of deceit and manipulation. Unfortunately, it happens even when it was the brainchild of the best of intentions. For one, most Systems require people to lead and maintain them. These people gain expertise, prestige, connections, power, and means. Even if it is a charity organization that supports a noble Solution for a humanitarian cause, once established, the System itself becomes a cause we must protect. Sometimes at the cost of its original mission.

Let's take a theoretical scenario. Nabila is a brilliant and resourceful woman who desires to change the world for the better, or as she says, "To leave the world in better shape than I found it." After much groundwork, fundraising and campaigning, she establishes a charity organization that aims to end water shortage in developing countries. The Solution this organization offers is installing wells in desolate areas. These wells, equipped with a mechanical pumping system, will help villagers access clean water without having to haul heavy buckets for miles from a distant or polluted water source.

Nabila recruited staff, made rent deposits for office space, and then renovated and furnished it. She was able to purchase equipment, train professionals, contract vendors, build trusting relationships with local authorities in the destination countries, and send teams to install the equipment. Nabila was happy. She was finally realizing her life's dream. Once data from the sites started streaming in, she publicized their achievements and continued to raise funds to keep up the good work. Some time later, the organization started receiving disturbing reports from the field. The water pumps frequently broke down, there were no parts to be found locally, and no domestic skilled installers to fix them. The cost of sending a crew overseas to replace every broken well quickly became unsustainable.

Nabila was distraught. Though well intended, her Solution was proving to be useless and wasteful. However, she now had forty-five employees in the charity whose livelihoods depended on ongoing operations. She had just renewed the contract for the office space for the next five years, and signed an irrevocable three-year contract with equipment suppliers. On top of that, her organization is accountable for government funding that would be clawed back should the operations be terminated before the end of the funding period. Recently Nabila was able to generate social hype around her mission, and her work has just earned her a nomination for a national award.

It isn't difficult to see why even the best-intended Systems may disregard faulty Solutions. Sometimes the cost of change is simply too steep for a System and its leaders to bear. Though Nabila may feel terrible about perpetuating a dysfunctional Solution, her decision-making will not be an obvious one. At least some people in her position will choose to conceal their failures as much and for as long as possible or go for flimsy fixes that will sustain the organization.

Even the most conscientious individuals like Nabila who find themselves stuck with faulty System Solutions often respond to the situation with two major fallacies. One is cognitive dissonance, which makes us wilfully ignore the truth if it might ruin everything we believe in and live by. It is that mental condition where we won't allow facts to ruin our cozy theories. Charities will claim their contribution is irrefutable. Scientists will cling to their theories while trying to discredit and silence their opponents. And partners of deceitful individuals will never read the signs of infidelity, no matter how large the writing is on the proverbial wall. The other reason for this irrational response is the sunk cost fallacy. It has us follow through with whatever we have already invested time, effort, or money into, even when we discover the costs outweigh the benefits. It's the classic, "I've already done/invested so much, so I might as well keep going."

The bigger, more organized, and more deeply embedded the System, the more self-conscious it becomes, like a living being with a strong survival instinct. It may be strange to attribute consciousness to something which is supposedly inanimate or abstract, until we realize Systems are human-made, and are therefore "made in our image." Everything we have created, be it a gadget or a concept, is run by humans. Every formalized System becomes an extension of our individual and collective consciousness. That's why even the best-intended Solution Systems can end up prioritizing their own survival over their original purposes. Ignoring the dangers of self-conscious Systems paves a highway to dogmatic coning.

The evolution from Solution to System works for all types of Solutions, be it a product, a method, a relationship, or an ideology. Traditionally, it took years, if not generations, to transform a Solution into a System. Nowadays, our communication technologies and social media significantly shorten this transformation, sometimes to a matter of weeks.

Limitations and disadvantages notwithstanding, we need Systems. Life would be very difficult without having us rely on Solutions that we already know and don't have to rethink every time we need them. We must accept some assumptions at face value to be able to function but there are better ways to manage Systems (as will be further discussed in the last chapter of this book). The genuine danger of Systems is that they have a way of outgrowing us and developing into restricting dogmas. When a Solution slips into the final Dogma stage, we lose not only our itch for critical analysis and creativity but also our freedom of thought, speech, and action.

CHAPTER 6:

Dogma, the one true Solution

... where we get a bird's-eye view on how Systems morph into Dogma, and what Cones are all about.

A Cone is born

E very Dogma has humble beginnings. It all starts when we inherit Core Certainties from our caregivers and communities, and form new ones throughout our lives. These Core Certainties frame our view of Problems and Needs, which drive the types of existing Solutions we will choose to use and the new ones we will come up with. As time goes by and our Solutions become more consistent, we develop a Need for these Solutions to be more stable, reliable, and widely accessible. That's when we turn them into operational Systems. The Solution System presents boundaries, whereas the Dogma stage creates impenetrable walls. According to the *Oxford Dictionary*, dogma is a principle or set of principles laid down by an authority as undeniably true. It is the ultimate my-way-or-the-highway.

Once a System grows into the Dogma stage, a clear division of roles comes into place. As described in Figure 14, the tightening of a System into Dogma permeates all the model tiers. First, System Leaders become Cone Masters and the only ones calling all the shots, while Solution Users become Cone Subjects whose role is to follow and obey. This change can happen abruptly and violently through coups and hostile takeovers, or it can transform subtly through a creeping, nearly undetectable change. Think of the urban legend of the frog that sits in a pot of slowly warming water, eventually being boiled alive without ever jumping out of the pot. These Leaders gradually change the System into their dominion, until there is no way out.

At the System stage, we believe the Problem is unfortunate but natural. Once it morphs into Dogma, the narrative changes. The Problem usually becomes someone's fault. It can be those in-house subversives branded as Internal Traitors, or those external, dangerous Others who brought this Problem upon you. It could also be your own fault because of your insufficiencies. Luckily for you, once you properly align yourself with the Cone Dogma and distance yourself or eliminate Internal Traitors and Others, your Problem is sure to go away.

This shift extends into the definition of Need. At the System stage, we assume that since our general Need is to solve the Problem through the Solution, our specific Need is building good Systems to deliver it. At the Dogma stage, the Need is no longer directly tied to solving the Problem or addressing the Cone Subjects' Needs. Either the official or the unstated new Need requires everyone to fully align and comply with the prescribed Dogma and obey their Cone Masters. The premise is that by doing so, the Problem and Need will be resolved by virtue of our belonging with the Cone.

When it comes to the Solution, the difference between System and Dogma is even more profound. At the System stage, the induction and the use of the Solution are optional. While the general sentiment is, "We don't really need other Solutions now that we have a good one," no one will force you to use it. The System will not actively encourage seeking new Solutions and it will scrutinize them more rigorously, but it still allows innovation.

System   Dogma

	System		Dogma
Leadership	• Appointed, democratic	▶	• Takeover, autocratic, pretend-democratic
Problem	• The problem is unfortunate but natural	▶	• The problem is someone's fault (yours, Internal Traitors, Others)
Need	• Need to create a system for the Solution to address the Problem	▶	• Need Subjects to comply with the Solution and obey the Cone Masters
Solution	• Systemic induction and optional use of Solution • Managed by Solution Leaders, serving Solution Users • Power divided between Leaders and Users • "Don't really need other Solutions" • Other Solutions allowed but scrutinized using "standards"	▶	• Systemic indoctrination, mandatory use of Solution • Cone Masters govern; Solution Subjects obey them • True power resides only with Cone Masters • Seeking other Solutions "dangerous or prohibited" • Using other Solutions forbidden and punishable; harsh enforcement

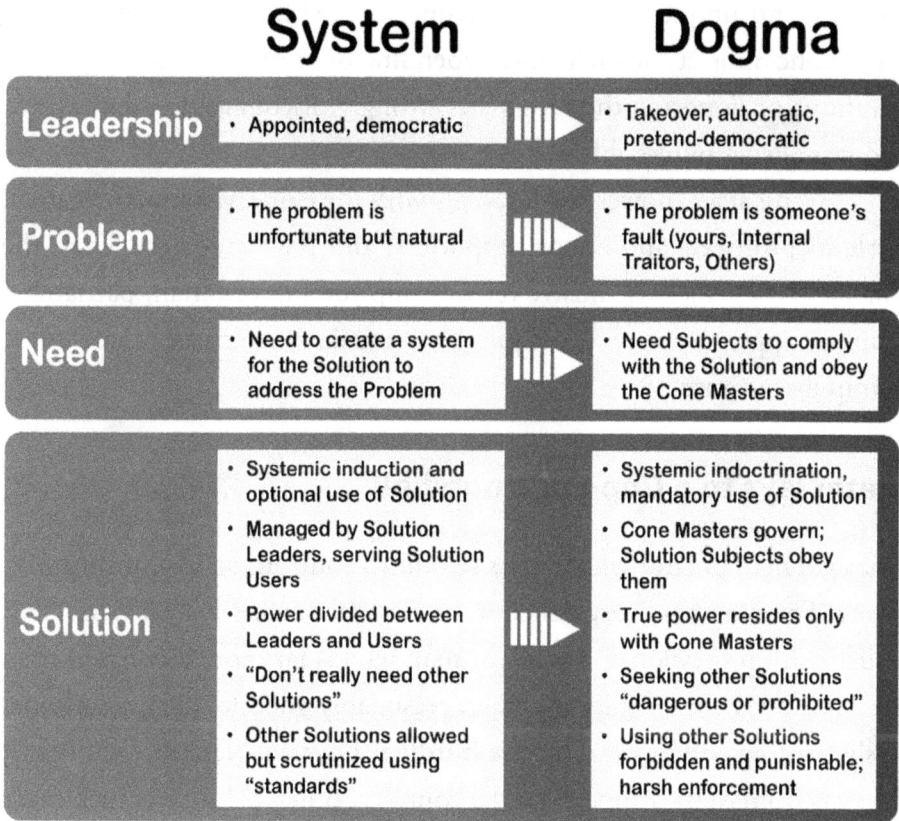

Figure 14: Major differentiators between System and Dogma

Once the System turns into Dogma, the induction and the use of the Solution become mandatory (or as close to it as possible). Cone Masters establish systemic indoctrination into the Solution on all levels. They will craft origin stories, rewrite histories, control information outlets, install Dogma-focused educational systems, and use consistent propaganda. Cone Masters will also invest in enforcement systems, apply a variety of punishments for transgressors (Internal Traitors), and take harsh measures against those Others.

In the Dogma stage, the use of "The One True Solution" is no longer optional and all other "divergent Solutions" are improper, shameful, or downright prohibited. Compliance with the Dogma must be absolute and unquestioning for anyone who wishes to be considered a loyal Cone Subject (or a live one, depending on the Cone). Seeking other Solutions or doubting the Dogma is strongly discouraged or forbidden, and it is always punishable.

At this stage, power resides solely with the Cone Masters, their small circle of profiteers and zealot supporters, and their enforcers. Even the smaller Cones, such as abusive relationships or authoritarian, patriarchal families, apply the same principles on a smaller scale or in more subtle, manipulative ways.

Pathways to a Cone in a nutshell

Erica is a manipulator who desires to build a controlling relationship with Mark. The man has every delicious quality that makes her salivate. He is a successful professional, a brilliant man who is far more intelligent than her, a beloved community member, reasonably good looking, and hopelessly trusting and naïve. The one hurdle is his wife, Neelam. Not that it detracts from Mark's appeal; on the contrary. It makes him so much more desirable. Before she approaches Mark, Erica must first understand his relationship with Neelam. She inserts herself into their social circles, befriends their friends and a few key family members, and investigates the couple's social media. Bit by bit, she builds a detailed profile of Mark and Neelam and finds every weakness and vulnerability. Erica discovers the couple had a few past conflicts, and that Mark's mother isn't sure Neelam is good enough for her son.

Once Erica is ready to make her move, she joins Neelam's gym and befriends her. They start meeting for lunches, where Erica gently navigates conversations to Neelam's marriage. She cleverly starts planting seeds of doubt and suspicion in the woman's mind about Mark's character and loyalty. She might have seen him with another woman but can't be sure. He might be a great husband, but does he really listen? At the same time, she builds a closer bond with Mark's mother, and plants similar seeds of doubt about Neelam. There's no one like a dissatisfied mother-in-law to be your ally in a conquest campaign. Someone who can help poison your victim against your opponent.

Erica is ready for her final move. She finds a way to befriend Mark and make him feel "finally seen and heard." She bombs him with unconditional love and uses his vulnerabilities to drive a wedge between him and his wife. Shortly after, she manages to seduce him into an intimate relationship. While at it, she gathers evidence on his infidelity and leaks it anonymously to Neelam. From here on, Erica has a clear and easy path to her final destination. She will make Mark dependent on her conditional love, gaslight him to lose his confidence, isolate him from his friends and family, and take charge of his life.

Aspiring Cone Builders can either form a Cone from the ground up, or latch onto an existing System, Erica style, and convert it into their own Dogma. When starting from scratch, Cone Builders will have a few more steps to cover, but it doesn't always translate into more time and effort than taking over an existing System. It all depends on their position within it, their aptitude as Cone Builders, and the type of their Solution (e.g., a fan club, commodity market, cult, crime cartel, government, religion, or world domination). Some Cones can be built within weeks, others will take years. The largest ones take generations. Still, one must start somewhere.

To clarify, not every bully is a Cone Master and not every failing System is a Cone. A family or an organization can be dysfunctional. A thug can harass peers to display power and steal their lunch money for personal gain. But for them to be Cones their leaders will require sophistication and intentional control systems. A thug, a patriarch, or a CEO who wish to become Cone Masters will not rely solely on brute force. They will add emotional and psychological manipulation into the mix to create loyal followers. They will divide insiders from outsiders, create penalties for those who dare question them, blame others for their own mistakes, and establish systems that enforce their dominance. Figure 15 describes the major milestones Cone Builders follow on their way to mastering a Cone.

When a Cone Builder has a Solution in mind, they will have to figure out where they stand. If no one recognizes the Problem or the Need for their Solution, they will use all the tricks described in the previous chapters to initiate their enterprise. Once they have created the Need for their Solution, they find ways to glorify it and convince everyone this is *The* Solution they've all been waiting for. At the same time, they keep an eye on competitors and critics, and eliminate them as quickly as possible. Depending on the Solution, they may go for discrediting, shaming, splitting, alienating, dehumanizing, demonizing, or even physically eliminating such threats.

The next step is presenting their persona as The One and starting recruitment of potential Subjects. The Cone Builder must create a persona that attracts their target audience, whether it is the trusted partner, enviable superstar, parental shepherd, courageous rebel and truth teller, or heroic saviour.

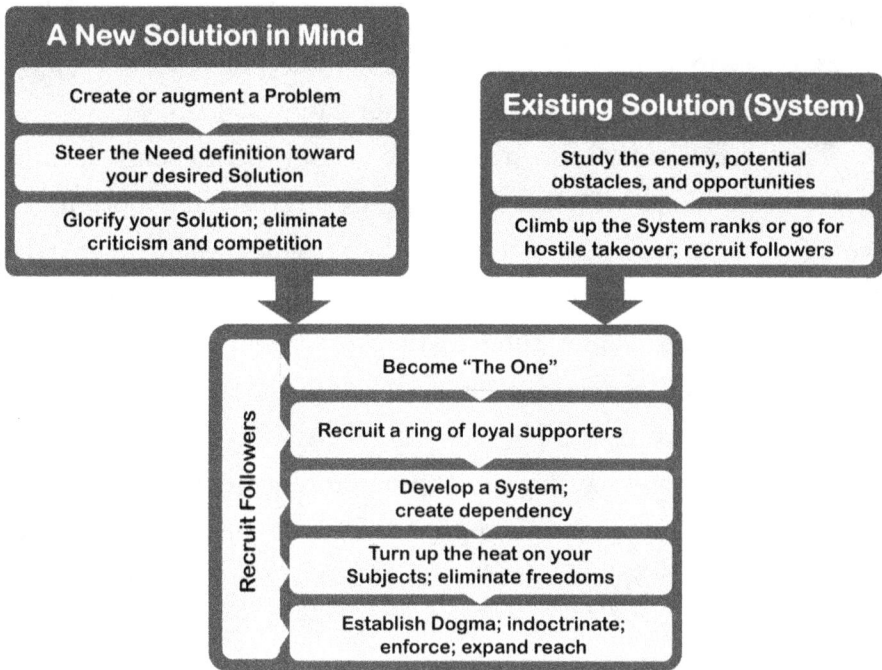

A New Solution in Mind

Create or augment a Problem

Steer the Need definition toward your desired Solution

Glorify your Solution; eliminate criticism and competition

Existing Solution (System)

Study the enemy, potential obstacles, and opportunities

Climb up the System ranks or go for hostile takeover; recruit followers

Recruit Followers

Become "The One"

Recruit a ring of loyal supporters

Develop a System; create dependency

Turn up the heat on your Subjects; eliminate freedoms

Establish Dogma; indoctrinate; enforce; expand reach

Figure 15: Major milestones for Cone Builders

Once the Cone Builder gains traction with their followers, they develop a System for the Solution—one that will normalize it as the only viable option. They will put in place mechanisms that will solidify the System, such as ongoing propaganda, training, education, distribution, and financial structures. The idea is to build a System that will create dependency. Just one step away from Dogma.

In other cases where the Solution is already out there, like Mark's and Neelam's marriage, Cone Builders will focus on latching on or growing inside it into leadership positions. Overtaking a big, established System may require time, energy, or greater force. However, once inside, it can easily be converted into Dogma because it already has limited room for doubt, functioning dissemination and delivery systems, and the belief of Users in its benefits. Though Erica's example is on a small scale, the same principles apply in big System takeovers such as religious organizations taking over countries, Big Pharma taking over our medical services, Big Agro taking over our farming communities and food supply, or oligarchs taking over our media and information sources.

The Cone Builder's first step will be to study their enemy, identify potential obstacles to their plan, and recognize inroads and opportunities. Enemies are those currently in charge of the System, as well as those who vehemently oppose it. Depending on their estimate of the situation, Cone Builders may decide to either climb up the ranks, go for a hostile takeover, or both. They can become the leader's right hand and wait for the opportune time to replace them. They can act as a staunch supporter of the existing leader, openly battling the opposition to gain credit and status. At the same time, they can undermine the leader by secretly siding with the opposition to topple the leadership and then step in. The more of these strategies Cone Builders will use concurrently, the more likely they are to become Cone Masters.

For this manipulative move to succeed, Cone Builders need followers, and the best ones are those with exploitable soft spots. We all have many potential vulnerabilities, such as our fear of death, scarcity, or isolation. We may all experience physical and emotional pain, shame, fear of uncertainty, or an insatiable hunger for power and means. Some of us will crave social approval, suffer in the face of injustice, or be desperate to feel happy. Smart Cone Builders will discover and exploit these vulnerabilities. They will reel us in by inflaming our pain points, harping on them, and promising their Solution will deliver the answer to all our prayers.

The next step will be building a close ring of supporters. Most Cone Builders will identify and recruit at least one supporter and confidant who worships, or at the very least trusts them unreservedly. Preferably one that will protect the Cone Builder at all costs. In large scale Solutions, Cone Builders will also find a few other trusted people to help recruit and keep Subjects, take care of operations, enforce their rule, clean up their messes, and bring in the money. Trust, however, is a flexible term. The higher a Cone Builder climbs, the more cautious they will be with supporters, as these might also be hungry for power of their own. For Cone Builders, trust and suspicion are not exclusive terms.

Once a Cone Builder recruits enough followers and has publicly established that they are The One and their Solution is the real deal, they have become Cone Masters. At this stage, they turn on the heat to ensure unwavering loyalty. As opposed to the recruitment phase, subtle moves and minor manipulations will no longer do. This is where Cone Masters use their heavy artillery to press their Subjects into submission, hack away at their opponents, and rise to greatness. They gradually eliminate their Subjects' freedoms while claiming it is for their own good and for their own protection. Because they can't trust "Others" and unchecked freedoms will "let them in." Or because the Subjects are innately flawed and cannot possibly trust themselves, and therefore must have limited liberties for their own good. Or because the Cone Masters know better and therefore should be the ones calling the shots. Preferably all three.

Mind control is everything. There are many tried-and-true tactics Cone Masters use to their advantage. They can infuse their Subjects with fear, create a scarcity mindset, or fuel their Subjects' sense of injustice and victimhood. They can also divide their Subjects from "hostile Others" while inflating their sense of superiority. To ensure a long-lasting, self-sustaining Dogma, Cone Masters will control the messaging system (e.g., gossip, media, education). They will invest in effective propaganda and indoctrination systems that infuse their Dogma at the earliest stage possible (e.g., storytelling, formal and informal education, controlled information). They will create a culture of oppression (e.g., fostering Stockholm Syndrome), and establish powerful crime-and-punishment processes and procedures (e.g., shaming, discrediting, expulsion, physical punishments). Finally, when the time is right and they have secured their status, they expand their reach.

Take for example a leader of a local bullying clique who wishes to gain more power. First, he will work hard on recruiting more followers. Once he establishes himself as The One and his emerging gang as the only way of life worth living, he becomes the Cone Master. From sporadic intimidation, he will turn on the heat to ensure unwavering loyalty. He will eliminate gang members' independent voices in the name of ultimate belonging, fire up fear and hatred of other gangs, and make sure everyone remembers how weak and vulnerable they are without their leader. He will inflame his followers' sense of injustice and victimhood to justify criminal activity and put in place tight enforcement and harsh punishments for transgressions. Once this leader stabilizes his gang and secures his status, he will expand his reach into neighbouring communities.

The reason it is so difficult to shield ourselves from Cone Builders and Masters is that most of us are trusting, positive human beings who cannot imagine anyone intentionally exploiting us. Cone Builders use all our weaknesses and blind spots, and they often do it just slowly enough for us not to notice. Hopefully, reading about these sinister behaviours will help us awaken to Cone realities.

Part 1:
The answers to our problems

Part 2:
How Cones are built

Part 3:
How Cones gain control

Part 4:
How Cones operate

Part 5:
How Cones fall… and come back

Part 6:
A better future within our reach

CHAPTER 7:

The Cone Master emerges

... where we behold the creation of "The One" who will befriend, shepherd, dazzle, rile, and save us from ourselves.

W ho are the people who build Cones and who are their Subjects? Our dark side, of which none of us is exempt, is hungry for power and means in one form or another. Therefore, each one of us, including the not-so-bright and not-so-evil, can build a Cone. Corrupt tendencies may be there from the start or grow throughout time. Often, all it takes is being methodical and unwavering. This is not a story about saints and monsters. We can all be both, and everything in between given the right circumstances and incentives. At the same time, Cones can dupe and enclose all of us, no matter how reasonable, educated, or intelligent we are.

One of the most basic success factors of a Cone Builder is focus. Those who wish to build a Cone cannot afford distractions. This is not a part-time gig. For a Cone to materialize, the building process must become everything they ever do and think of. Truly successful Cone Builders dedicate their whole being to their goal. They see themselves "there" from day one, conjuring their Cone from the depths of their burning desire. For a Cone Builder to become a Cone Master, one needs to believe it is the idea they will live by and die for. Otherwise, they're just another entrepreneur. Another success factor Cone Builders possess is believing in themselves and in their ability to rule. They must trust they are the only ones who can do it. Being self-absorbed and self-aggrandizing can be very helpful. Bonus points to those who are convinced their cause and Solution are truly special. Or, as Mark Twain once said, "All you need in this life is ignorance and confidence; then success is sure."

The first thing Cone Builders do is develop an appealing persona to have potential Subjects fall in love with them, platonically or otherwise. Becoming The One requires the use of what is known as Narcissistic Seduction—a method that exploits people's biases and vulnerabilities. Every Solution will require a slightly different approach and a different persona that will best seduce potential Subjects, but the principles remain.

The charmer

Bill Cosby, the famous American actor and comedian, was a born charmer. People of all ages, genders, and ethnicities took to him almost instantaneously. Throughout his fifty-year career, Cosby had managed to charm and lure women to trust him, and then sexually assault them. As all typical Cones Masters, Cosby used his power and influence in the entertainment industry to silence or discredit his victims when they attempted to speak out about their experiences. Charm and confidence— the kind that makes people feel all warm and fuzzy inside—is one of the fundamental components of manipulative abusers. Our basic biological programming makes us more fascinated with and attracted to someone we consider kind, with a bonus for the beautiful. It is the basic cognitive bias known as the halo effect, which tells our ancient brains that "what is beautiful and kind, is also capable and trustworthy."

Even if a Cone Builder hasn't won nature's beauty lottery, they can still use our halo bias to their advantage. Seeming charming, friendly, and personable opens doors with many target Subjects. It makes perfect sense on an evolutionary level. If someone is behaving in a kind and friendly way, they are probably not aiming to attack or harm you. They are also more likely to be good people to collaborate with or even follow. We have seen enough examples throughout ancient and modern history of people being susceptible to lies that were confidently delivered by charming, charismatic leaders, no matter how absurd the content.

Despite our innate ability to deceive, most of us aren't naturally inclined to suspect deception as the default. Especially not from delightful, kind, and confident individuals. In truth, most of us are more easily persuaded by glamour than facts. But it isn't only charm and pizzaz that draw us in. Cone Builders have several other personas to choose from to attract us, some less delightful than others, depending on their character and the Solution they are promoting.

The *Partner* persona

Hugo Chávez served as the Venezuelan president from 1999 until his death in 2013. While he didn't come from extreme poverty, his background as the son of teachers in a rural town contributed to his image as a man of the people. Chávez rose to power, presenting himself as a champion of the poor and marginalized of Venezuelan society. He gained his people's trust through his folksy, charismatic style. Dressed in the traditional clothing of the Venezuelan Llanos (plains), he delivered passionate speeches along the lines of, "I know your suffering. I've been there." By portraying himself as someone who was directly connected to the struggles and aspirations of ordinary Venezuelans, Chávez won widespread support, particularly among the country's lower-income population. Though he kept winning democratic elections, he became increasingly authoritarian over time, proving to be a classic Cone Master. He gradually consolidated power in the executive branch, eroded his democratic institutions, limited freedom of the press, and ruthlessly persecuted his political opponents.

There is a wise Turkish proverb that says, "The forest was shrinking but the trees kept voting for the axe, for the axe was clever and convinced the trees that because his handle was made of wood, he was one of them."

We are wired to prefer people who are like us, because it gives us a sense of safety. That which is known to us always feels safer than the unknown. It works even when we are fully aware it's bad for us. That's why Cone Builders often look for commonalities with their intended recruits. Think about the stereotypical used-car or time-share salesperson. Charming smiles, a few corny jokes to show they are lighthearted, a story about how they used to be in the same position you are now and, wouldn't you know it, their real or imaginary children are of similar ages to yours. You may look down at sleazy salespeople, but you can't argue with their ability to close deals, often against their customers' best judgment. The combination of charm and the sense of having something in common is nearly unbeatable.

That said, drawing people into a Cone takes a more calculated and long-term strategy than selling a car or a time-share unit. Erica, the narcissistic partner, would tell you that the one sure way to draw people in for a more permanent commitment is to make them feel truly seen. Cone Builders lure you into an intense connection by making you feel like they've known you forever. They will make you believe that you will always be understood and safe with them, not only because they've been there and done that, but also because they "see you." Strong Cone Builders are excellent observers who become finely attuned to people's emotions and weaknesses. Once they gain a decent understanding of your soft spots, they reflect those back to you to show they share these same sentiments and experiences. They will convince you they've suffered like you and with you, and that they feel your pain. When you feel heard and seen, you are more likely to open your heart and pockets.

A Cone Builder who chooses the *Partner* persona focuses their messaging on the "we" factor. They repeat statements that convey: "We complete each other, you understand me, and I understand you," and, "We've both been there." Building a sense of comradery with their potential Subjects is paramount. To establish this comradery, a Cone Builder will invoke a sense of internal unity among their recruits, making sure there is a clear "us" identity with obvious identifiers of sameness. They may create simple tokens such as "our song" or "our secret handshake," inside jokes, and all the way to shared birthright, deity, enemy, brand, anthem, uniform, flag, or insignia. Another unifying factor for partnering is insider knowledge, be it true or false, so long as only "our own" are privy to it. A *Partner* Cone Builder may coin insider code words and phrases and create inner-circle ceremonies. Think chants and initiation ceremonies used in cults, secret societies, religions, or sororities.

Cone Builders using this persona will let you see them as your closest ally while playing a double game. Because alongside their "partnering" act, they will also make sure you understand they are better, smarter, or stronger than you, and therefore the ones who must lead you.

The *Shepherd* persona

I always thought the proverbial use of the term "shepherd" is the epitome of irony. When we call someone "our shepherd," we consider them a parent-type guardian. It is the wise one who will lead us to safety through this perilous world and put our best interest before their own. Or will they? Let's be honest, the sheep are not the shepherd's children. In fact, they're not even pets. As far as the shepherd is concerned, sheep are nothing more than a heap of bleating and farting wool, milk, and meat. As the African proverb goes, "The sheep will spend its entire life fearing the wolf, only to be eaten by the shepherd." The same goes for people who submit to Cone Masters who use the *Shepherd* persona.

Nicolae Ceaușescu, former leader of Romania, was an artist when it came to positioning himself as a fatherly figure. He ran massive propaganda where he was called "The Father of The Nation" and portrayed as a wise and benevolent leader who cared deeply for the well-being of the Romanian people. The way only a father would. Ceaușescu often participated in activities such as visiting factories, schools, and agricultural projects where he would offer guidance and encouragement. He cultivated a modest personal image, presenting himself as a frugal and humble leader who lived a simple life despite holding significant power. In reality, he was a ruthless dictator who practiced repression, forced women to bear hoards of children, and committed widespread human rights abuses.

Why are we so easy to fall for *Shepherd* personas? One explanation is that from the moment we are born, we rely on our parents or parent figures for our physical survival and emotional well-being. Growing up with the idea that a higher authority or power takes care of us, programs us to respond positively to parental displays. For people who had experienced a childhood of neglect and abuse, the *Shepherd* persona is even more enticing because it plays to their craving for the love of a benevolent parent figure. This desire can easily divert people from the truth. A play-pretend shepherd will quickly become a tyrannical leader who will exploit and thrive on the backs of his adoring flock.

Cone Builders using this persona apply several tactics to attract their recruits. One is by becoming a magnanimous parental figure. They will appear to be nobler, wiser, and more compassionate than you. They will use phrases such as, "I will always understand and be there for you," and, "I will heal and take away your pain." They will listen to you attentively and forgive your mistakes. But this will be nothing but the inroad into your psyche. Once you are hooked, they will not hesitate to use all forms of aggression to crush resistance or destroy you should you disobey.

Another tactic this persona uses is superb storytelling. Like an elder spinning tales around the campfire, a skilful *Shepherd* Cone Builder can weave a compelling tale and captivate their recruits with marvellous heroic stories, fascinating trivia, and inspiring quotes. They will infuse select facts to support their narrative, but not too many, because they know people prefer stories over data. They will place themselves in the centre of their stories, while re-writing history and changing facts to bolster their image. Their exquisite storytelling is a powerful weapon of mass attraction. Cone Builders who use the *Shepherd* persona are also good listeners. Not because they care, but because it's a great way to gain inside knowledge, which is a precious weapon for a later time when they need to control their Subjects. The *Shepherd* will know their audience, their ebbs and flows, and when and how to make them cheer or shed a tear.

Being a philanthropist is another way *Shepherd* Cone Builders make themselves magnanimous. You would think that a voluntary contribution of one's money toward noble causes shows moral character and honourable intentions. In some cases, this is true, but in many others, it is a tool *Shepherd* Cone Builders use to build their "parental" reputation and attract recruits into their Cone. Once the *Shepherd* persona takes hold of their recruits, it is nearly impossible to persuade the herd that their revered shepherd is a wolf.

The *Superstar* persona

Apple CEO and co-founder, Steve Jobs, was an undeniable superstar, and not only within his industry. Even posthumously, he is still synonymous with vision, genius, and innovation, having revolutionized the world with the personal computer, iPod, iPhone, and iPad. He has become a role model for underdogs who were told they would never amount to anything. College dropouts, struggling entrepreneurs, business leaders who had lost their positions, adoptees, and even people fighting a terminal disease are still inspired by his story.

Jobs was charismatic, self-absorbed, and extremely full of himself. As a highly intelligent, independent thinker, he commanded adoration while paying little attention to the needs of the people around him. He was a shining trailblazer followed by millions, and a self-absorbed abuser who had left a long trail of victims.

Celebrity worship is a big thing and Cone Builders know it. Admiring and even worshiping superstars is not a trend of the modern era. Almost every culture—modern or ancient—has their heroes, saints, and superstars who can't do wrong. They can be spiritual leaders, top athletes, popular scientists, or renowned performing artists. All living creatures are status- or competition-oriented to one degree or another as part of our social survival mechanism. As such, we admire excess. The butterfly with the most luminescent wings, the bird with the brightest feathers, and the ram with the largest horns get more action in the mating department than their average counterparts. Even human babies and children are more drawn to faces most of us perceive as "attractive" (1). But it isn't just a flashy appearance; it's performance as well. The gorilla who beats its chest the loudest is more likely to be a good defender of its clan. A promising mate in many species will be the one who can overcome contenders, build the sturdiest dwelling, get the most food, and protect its territory. Humans are no different.

We are naturally inclined to perceive competitiveness and excess as desirable qualities. We are drawn to heroes and superstars, even when their public image is ridiculously larger than life and holds no relevance to us. Celebrities used to be the monarchs, top religious leaders, and war heroes, but in the last century we have made the billionaires and the tech moguls of the world into our new superheroes and superstars. We tell and retell their origin stories, including those that never really happened. We ascribe to them words of wisdom written by their shadow advisors and marketing managers. They become the person we want to become when we grow up. We buy their products and vote for them based on nothing else but their enviable stardom. Once the internet and social media took over our lives, we have ordained another group of superstars—the influencers.

Political parties have long learned the power of celebrities, and many are promoting candidates by the sheer power of their irrelevant fame. Ronald Reagan (US president) and Volodymyr Zelensky (Ukraine president) were both actors who had gone all the way to the presidency mostly based on their acting careers. Justin Trudeau (Canadian prime minister) and George Bush Jr. (US president) were seen as fitting for the presidency based on their fathers' past fame. And then there was Donald Trump (US president) who was also a celebrity for his TV show and his eclectic, albeit irrelevant and often failing business pursuits.

Beyond these few familiar names, there are millions of celebrities on every scale of our lives. They don't have to be movie stars or billionaires. They can be the legendary school athlete, our rags-to-riches cousin, a TV doctor who knows it all, or the legendary family patriarch who used to walk to school in a snowstorm uphill both ways. Fame makes it easy to forget that people with desirable markers of success in one field may have little to no ability in any other area. Furthermore, being famous has little to do with morality, kindness, or quality of character. Though both science and history show that many such celebrities develop a sense of entitlement and lose compassion for their fellow humans, we can't help but admire them.

Most of us experience celebrity admiration to some extent, but some people go farther into an extreme state coined by psychologists as "celebrity worship." Celebrity worshippers often struggle with their sense of personal identity and with meaningful relationships (2). Falling for the *Superstar* persona allows them to imagine they have tapped into their "better selves" and have built a genuine and meaningful relationship with their idol. This imaginary relationship causes celebrity worshippers a slew of undesirable psychological states, such as anxiety, depression, and neuroticism, an obsession with the lives of celebrity figures, and unquestioning loyalty. No amount of incriminating evidence will ever persuade the zealot fans of their hero's faults, flaws, or crimes.

To lure in recruits, Cone Builders using the *Superstar* persona will rely on messaging that focuses on the "I" factor. This is not the persona for the meek or the humble. Their inflated ego and self-importance are their best assets. Alongside the self-aggrandizement, they will help their recruits develop a sense of special worth that must be acknowledged. Their message: "I am incredible, and by siding with me, some of my glamour will brush off on you."

The *Rebel* persona

Jim Jones seemed like an average American church-going kid in Indiana. Growing up, Jones gained a reputation as a charismatic religious leader with self-proclaimed psychic powers. Being a powerful proponent of social justice, racial integration, and human rights, Jones attracted many followers who were drawn to his message of equality and communal living. Jones was a formidable rebel. He preached against the ills of society and positioned himself as the one who isn't afraid to speak unpopular truths. In 1955, he established his own church that was later renamed into the Peoples Temple. As most megalomaniac cult leaders, he renamed himself to "the Prophet" and soon enough, became a brutal tyrant. As with most Cones, this story doesn't have a happy ending. Promising his followers a utopia, he led them to mass suicide, leaving more than 900 dead.

Cone Builders who adopt the *Rebel* persona position themselves as the destroyers of the old-and-evil and the visionaries of the new-and-wonderful. Boldly tearing down or discrediting existing Core Certainties and Solutions give these *Rebel* Cone Builders the appearance of fearless truth tellers. They are the heroes we all wish we could be if we weren't afraid. Think national icons, revolutionaries, or fierce promoters of causes. To be fair, many rebels pursue their causes in earnest. They take great personal risks and end up bringing significant and positive change to the world, should they survive. Some might start with pure intentions and gradually transform into Cone Builders once they have tasted power and accumulated means. Others yet are schemers from day one, using this persona as a front.

Rebel Cone Builders come in different shapes and flavours. Some are loud and arrogant; others come across as quiet and meek. Their demeanour will depend not only on their personality but also on their target recruits, knowing that some people will get excited with the inflammatory type, while others will be more amenable to the humble. Whether the *Rebel* Cone Builders are illiterates or intellectual mavericks, they will always be astute in their own way. They will quickly and creatively figure out impressive angles that will support their claims. No matter how absurd their statements might be, their conviction and charisma will make their claims ring true to followers who admire blunt, truth-telling revolutionaries.

Skilled *Rebel* Cone Builders can typically outsmart (or out-scream) most people, which is why they constantly intrigue us and make us buy into their ploys. On the less endearing side, people who dare oppose them better watch out. Those who use *Rebel* personas have already considered how their opposition might react and are ready to destroy them by any means available. They can easily resort to unethical, inhumane, and illegal action to crush opponents, which will only strengthen their position and rally more supporters. This type of Cone Builder will persuade their followers that they tell the hard-to-hear truth, as opposed to the evil, deceitful "Others." They will have no problem bending facts or lying through their teeth to prove their point. *Rebel* Cone Builders tap into people's pain and promise to give their followers a voice. The harsher and less popular their claims, the faster the fearful, vengeful, vulnerable, and certainty-seeking people will be drawn to them.

A vital ingredient of this persona is legitimizing people's darkness. There are few Cone-building tactics more appealing than allowing people to say, be, and do their worst without feeling bad about it. Better yet, while feeling just and noble about it. Though we might not be aware of our own darkness, life events can trigger buried emotions, and inflammatory rhetoric can make them swell and overflow out of our mental basement. Since no one wants to be seen and judged as a bigot or a pervert, *Rebel* Cone Builders cleanse their followers from guilt and shame by telling them these feelings and urges are not only perfectly legitimate, but they are also necessary. They will work hard to unleash their followers' anger, hatred, cruelty, and even violence because they need merciless foot soldiers to do their bidding. These Cone Builders will be the loudest anti-authority orators until they are the ones in authority. Once that happens, their reign becomes absolute. They will make Subjects believe this tyranny is different. That it is for their own good, and that their unquestioning obedience to authority is necessary to protect their righteous cause.

The *Saviour* persona

Following World War I, Italian liberal beliefs and institutions collapsed, much like Germany's had. Desperate, impoverished people who had lost trust in their leaders wanted a new order. During this extreme post-war tension, Benito Mussolini rode on the fascist ideology all the way to assuming control as Duce (the leader). Mussolini had never been the nice guy. He was a notorious bully who, even as a child, fought and stabbed classmates and even his own girlfriend. In his twenties, he was a fervent socialist who preached violent revolution, praised Karl Marx, and vocally criticized patriotism. Later in life he made an about turn and founded the fascist movement. This man of extremes gradually swept the people as their designated saviour. His charismatic and non-empathetic persona was greater than life. It didn't take him long to be lauded as the new messiah and become a ruthless dictator.

Although all successful Cone Builders end up as tyrants of one sort or another, none are as shamelessly open about their goal as those using the *Saviour* persona. *Rebels* and *Saviours* have many commonalities, but they also differ in certain ways. *Rebels* might not always position themselves as the leaders from the outset, though if they do it right, they end up growing into one. *Saviours*, on the other hand, start by stating their intention to lead. The basic vibe of the *Rebel* persona is mostly anger and angst, and their motto is "unite for the cause." In comparison, the *Saviour* will carry an air of arrogance and entitlement, and their motto will be, "I'm here to save you, and I'm the only one who can. You're welcome."

The power of the *Saviour* persona comes from ultimate confidence and a sense of entitlement. But why would anyone follow a tyrant who isn't even trying to conceal their megalomania? Because when people feel they have lost control of their own lives and their surroundings, they seek strong, bigger-than-life, messiah-type figures to help them regain a sense of certainty and self confidence. When we're desperate and frightened, we have no patience for all talk and no action. A *Saviour* persona is capable of not only showing us a far better alternative (even if it's a complete sham), but also displaying the ruthlessness necessary to act on it. *Saviour* Cone Builders radiate confidence and self-assuredness, which is most attractive and even infectious for those who desperately need someone powerful to hold them up.

A *Saviour* Cone Builder doesn't have to be an actual hero, expert, fighter, or demigod. They only have to seem like one. They do it by adopting fake titles or wearing military uniforms or professional attire such as lab coats (often without having the right or the credentials to wear them). Sometimes all it takes is an authoritative tone and mannerism. While all Cone Builders should be good storytellers to draw their audience, the *Saviour* persona will invest heavily in "world building," not unlike fantasy fiction authors. False background stories, fabricated credentials, exaggerated or fictional accomplishments, or false "ties and connections with the greats" can all be part of their fictional narrative. Some use it as a calculated, deceptive strategy, whereas others feel so grand, they actually believe in their own lies.

Cone Builders who have settled on their main public face or persona usually stick with methods that support this image. However, using a single persuasion tactic can only get them so far. Like in any type of investment, they diversify their recruitment and retention methods. A Cone Builder normally starts with the persona that is most natural to them, and then supplements with other personas or switches altogether when needed. The most proficient ones cover as many personas as possible to appeal to as many recruits as possible without wasting time on the non-persuadable. Steve Jobs was not only a Superstar but also the *Rebel* persona. Trump started as a *Superstar* and quickly branched out to the *Shepherd* who allegedly understood his people, to hard-truth-telling *Rebel*, and eventually the megalomaniac *Saviour* who is beyond reproach.

Once the Cone Builder puts on their preferred persona, they are ready to recruit followers. However, pretending to be what their recruits want them to be is only the beginning. Next, they must identify their low-hanging fruit.

CHAPTER 8:

Picking the low-hanging fruits

... where we discover how Cone Builders sniff out our vulnerabilities, pull on our heartstrings, and lure us into their Cones.

n healthy and supportive groups of people, mutual trust, fairness, and cooperation is the normal way of being. People generally trust each other, and willingly abide by the agreed upon moral rules to make sure every member of the group is safe and supported. This is why most of us underestimate the hidden agendas of Cone Builders who mimic normalcy and kindness to gain our trust while having no concern for anyone but themselves. What makes things even more complicated is that Cone Builders come in many forms and levels of sociopathy. Some may be classic villains and homicidal tyrants, but the majority is much more illusive. Most Cone Builders abide by certain social graces on the surface and make the impression of contributing to the group in a multitude of ways. It is only behind the scenes that they pursue their self-interests with no regard for others.

From the early stages of recruitment into the Cone, Cone Builders tap into our exploitable weaknesses. Every good manipulator is acutely aware of what drives humans to action. No matter where we were born, how we were raised, and what we believe in, we can all experience powerful emotions that will make us vulnerable in the wrong hands. Some of us are born with a "mental immune system" that makes us more resistant to Cone Builders. These are the people who can, from a very young age, see through propaganda, injustice, and the lies they are told "every child knows to be true." There is no need for statistical data to tell that the mentally immune are a tiny minority. It is enough to examine the world around us, with its hefty dose of unchallenged tyranny, exploitation, and injustice. Their peers often perceive the mentally immune as ridiculous, enraging, insane, and even traitorous. Depending on the Cone they are trapped in or interact with, their lives can get very difficult, and sometimes significantly shortened.

Cone Builders who understand people's weaknesses and exploitable motivators have a better chance at building their Cone. That said, recruiting Subjects requires a deliberate effort and a staged approach. Very few Cone Masters have gained power over others by accident. They must first figure out who their potential recruits are, find, and then actively recruit them. There are many ways to attract followers and consumers—some more generic, others more laser-focused. No matter the method, smart Cone Builders won't be wasting time and resources on the wrong people. For that reason, they start by defining their target Subjects.

Sometimes, potential recruits will be obvious, such as the Cone Builder's immediate family or community members, their employees, or their religious congregation. Other times their potential Subjects will be outside their immediate reach, such as balding men, prepubescent girls, or people who will buy into a particular conspiracy theory. Whether dealing with the close and familiar or with the distant and unknown, some people will always make for easier targets than others. In the early stages of the Cone Builder's recruitment efforts, they will use the 80/20 Pareto principle. They will look for the people with whom 20 percent of the recruitment effort will yield 80 percent of the positive response. These people are their "low-hanging fruit."

What is it that makes someone a Cone Builder's easy target? Obviously, each Cone will have its own blend of required qualities, but there are some common characteristics that make people more vulnerable to manipulation, no matter the product or ideology. The common thread of easy recruits is extremes. The most resistant recruits are the well balanced, centred, and moderate people. The easiest are the ones sitting on the extreme edges on any given behavioural scale.

The repeats

If you have ever donated to a cause, you know that this is never the proverbial one-night stand. They will curate you in their database and keep approaching you for more. Even if you decline repeatedly, you are now on their list of those-who've-done-it-before, and they will keep approaching you. Fundraisers will tell you that people who have donated once are more likely to do it again than people from the untapped population. Just like in physics, it is easier to build up on existing momentum than to initiate motion from zero. Indeed, those who have done it before are more likely to do it again—be it donating, taking part in a movement, engaging in criminal activity, making purchases on the shopping channel, supporting a conspiracy theory, or going to war. It doesn't even have to be the exact same thing; close enough will do. Something that addresses the same underlying Need or touches the same unresolved craving or trauma.

Naeem is an aspiring Cone Builder who wishes to climb up in the anti-aging market with the goal to one day dominate it. He builds his momentum on a strong foundation of decades of industry propaganda that primed women to feel unloved unless they are young and beautiful. Naeem knows his lowest hanging fruits are women who previously bought anti-aging products, because whatever they already bought didn't magically transport them into their twenties. They are still aging, and he has just the right remedy for their affliction. To find these women, he will use advertisements on search engines, commercial sites, and all forms of social media that build on the premise of repeats being easy targets. "Since you liked this, you may also like that," or, "Other clients who bought this, also bought that," or, "I spied on you talking about wrinkles, therefore I will flood your feed with my ads."

One powerful motivator for repeatedly joining causes is our desire for social proof.[18] House cats are awesome, and it's not my opinion alone—just ask any pharaoh from ancient Egypt. They have a royal bearing, they are independent, and even when they bestow their love upon us, cats keep a mind of their own. Fraternizing with other cats is an optional pastime because, apart from mating, they don't really need them for their survival. As far as the animal kingdom goes, humans are the neighbourhood dogs. We are social, collaborative, trusting, and loyal. We need each other to survive, and we seek an alpha to lead us. Belonging with the pack is a matter of life and death for us.

Though we hold our independent thinking in high regard, we also have an irresistible Need to be accepted in our social circles. This Need is so powerful, it overrides our independent thinking almost without fail. One way to belong is our reliance on social proof. In situations where we aren't sure of the right action, we often decide what to do by watching other people. This is, after all, the way we learn from infancy. We assume that if many other people are saying or doing something, it must be right, or they wouldn't have said or done it. If you see a crowd running out of your building, screaming and flailing their arms, this probably wouldn't be a good sign to stop, gather information, evaluate evidence, and weigh your options. Just follow the crowd and analyze later.

This compelling Need to belong can easily tip the scale from helpful to traitorous. One of the classics on the deceitful nature of social proof is Hans Christian Andersen's tale of "The Emperor's New Clothes." In this story, everyone, from the emperor to his townsfolks, was willing to go along with a ridiculous ruse to make sure they weren't seen as stupid or incompetent. Peer pressure isn't limited to foolish emperors and their townsfolk. Commodity companies use social proof regularly to boost

---

[18] Social proof is when we copy the actions and behaviours of other people to make sure we belong, even when these go against our reasoning or beliefs.

their sales. They place their brands on their products so people walking or driving around with them create social proof for others. They publicize testimonials from "average people just like you," or use celebrities to promote their products.

We all want to believe we are critical and independent thinkers who would call out the emperor on his parade in the nude. But are we? Here's a quick proof of concept. Have you ever jaywalked?[19] If you are truly a strong critical thinker, once you reach a red light, you will analyze your options like so: traffic signs and road rules exist to protect everyone on the road, therefore it would be prudent to follow them. Crossing the road against the rules might cause me bodily harm. Even if I don't get hit by a car, I might get caught breaking the law and end up with a fine. Waiting for the lights to turn green will only take a minute or two. Unless there's raging fire on my side of the road, there is no logical justification for jaywalking.

Based on this critical and independent analysis, a smart person will refrain from jaywalking. And yet many of us do it anyway. Some of us do it because we aren't great critical thinkers, because we're distracted, or we refuse to obey "the system." Most of us, though, do it because we see someone else doing it. Research on jaywalking shows we aren't only affected by the number of people we're seeing jaywalking, but also by who's doing it. When a man jaywalks across a busy intersection wearing a business suit, three and a half times more people follow him across the street than when he is wearing casual clothes.

Social proof is an incredible weapon of influence. It creates a mental shortcut, and we love those. By adopting other people's opinions and behaviours, we don't have to think so hard, and we can easily fit right in. Two essential birds with one stone. Society considers those who cannot

---

[19] Jaywalking is when pedestrians fail to obey traffic rules, such as crossing where it is forbidden or on a red light. In some countries Jaywalking is illegal and carries fines.

read social cues, such as people on the spectrum of autism, to have a disability despite being the stronger thinkers among us. Most of us prefer to follow others and keep repeating these patterns.

As described in Figure 16, successful repeats will respond well to strokes on their ego and the promise of another success while being warned about the disgrace that awaits them should they fail. Many of them will also be devout believers in "the cause" and will follow Cone Builders who rally them around it. On the other side of this spectrum, failed repeats will join Cone Builders who play on their unresolved pain, their shame with their previous failures "to do it right," and their desire to belong with "the right crowd." Cone Builders convince these recruits that joining the Cone puts them "on the team." That it will transform them into something bigger than themselves.

If manipulated proficiently, our Need to belong and conform with the crowd can easily override our very humanity and turn us into anything from mindless drones to murderous monsters.

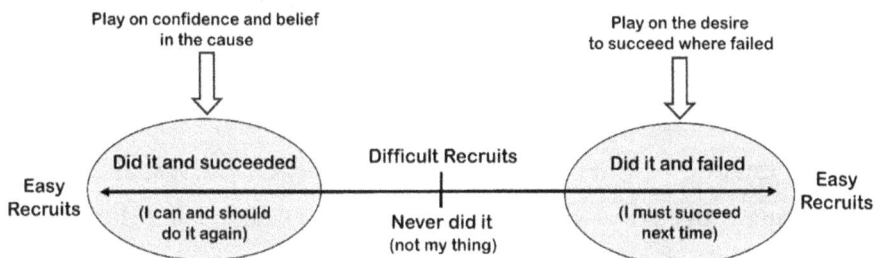

Figure 16: Easy recruits—the successful, and the failed repeats

The domineering, and the obedient and insecure

Fear, pain, and the fear of pain are such basic survival mechanisms, they alert us not only when danger approaches or is already upon us, but also when situations may merely imply the possibility of harm. Physical or emotional pain can become so unbearable that we frantically seek any Solution—true or bogus—as long as it promises relief. One way our fear is activated is through Analyzed Risk, where we critically analyze the potential for risk and pain. It is our logical process. The other is a Feeling of Risk that comes from our "gut." This is where we get fast, instinctive, and often irrational fear of something we perceive as dangerous (1).

When you walk down a dark alley you may use your rational brain to assess potential danger. But if you've ever had an unpleasant experience or if you're into horror movies, you won't bother analyzing the data at hand. Your Feeling of Risk will take over and generate strong, primal dread. Police officers and soldiers in enemy territory who spend much of their time facing hostile situations will be faster to reach into their unexamined Feeling of Risk. They will often respond with disproportionate fear and violence toward those they perceive as potential threats, especially toward members of a demonized minority group.

Cone Builders want our Feeling of Risk to burst into flames and remain burning hot because it is the surest way to bypass our logical thinking. They want to keep us away from Analyzed Risk as much as possible, lest we figure out their deceptions. The most basic way is to tell or show us something that scares us. They use disinformation and staged events that were intentionally set up to play on our deepest fears, such as statements about refugees being terrorists, rapists, and drug dealers. For a Feeling of Risk to keep burning hot, Cone Builders create an environment that floods us with terror. They make sure that everything we hear, read, see, or discuss focuses on the things that scare us.

In the American political arena, people are so preoccupied with terrorism and communism that they ignore the real reasons for their societal crises, such as poverty, predatory capitalism, and racism. This distraction allows decision-makers (i.e., Cone Masters) to invest obscene amounts of money in the military, policing, security agencies, and weapons, while all but ignoring their poorest and weakest members of society. They get away with it because they manipulated their people's terrorism- and xenophobia-related Feeling of Risk to go through the roof.

Prolonged fear hurts us not only in the moment but also compromises our physical and mental health (2). It can warp our long-term memories and cause chronic anxiety, making it even more difficult to think clearly. If we are in a constant state of anxiety and pain, the world will look so much scarier than it really is. We will focus our attention on everything that confirms our fear, and then create distorted memories to validate that. It also makes it more difficult to regulate emotions, read body language, and think before we act. In this state, we put a lid on our morality and welcome unethical behaviours without remorse. And that is exactly what Cone Builders are hoping for.

Another powerful motivator that makes us easy targets for Cone Builders is a scarcity mindset. Imagine two androids sitting at a table with four cookies placed in the centre. The androids receive a single rule for this game: each must try to get all four cookies by every means possible. Once the buzzer goes off, the two will fight for the prize. One will end up getting all four cookies and win the game, while the other will lose. This is a zero-sum game where there is zero change within the system because it still has four cookies, with the only difference being their location. A societal zero-sum game happens when we are told that there aren't enough resources to go around, therefore we must fight over them. We are told that the only way to win is by making the other side lose.

As opposed to emotionless androids, this zero-sum setup usually results in significant loss, though not always one that is measured by the number of baked goods. A winner-loser mindset creates a sense of superiority and entitlement on the winning side, a sense of inferiority, injustice, and vengeance on the losing side, and a newly gained animosity between the two. Sometimes it can also harm the resource itself ("broken cookies" or post-conflict scorched earth).

When we divide cookies, we can tell right away that the all-or-nothing rule is unreasonable and that it contributes nothing to the participants. Not even to the winner who has just taken over four broken cookies and bought themselves an enemy. We can immediately see that we could have easily modified this game to promote fairness and collaboration. But fairness and collaboration are not what Cone Builders are after. Pitching people one against the other gives them the power to conceal the truth, manipulate, and take over their followers. The underlying principle of the zero-sum game is the concept of scarcity, where we see things in limited supply as being more valuable. Sometimes we experience genuine scarcity, where we truly have limited resources, such as the number of lifeboats on a sinking ship. But in most other cases, it is intentionally created to manipulate us. One of the most common uses of scarcity motivation is when a company intentionally produces a limited quantity of their product and then markets it as rare and unique. The diamond industry provides a classic case of deceptive scarcity. Diamond dealers make us believe diamonds are expensive because they are rare. The truth is, there is no shortage of them in the world, except when the suppliers decide to hold onto their inventories to create scarcity.

To further enhance their gains and control while keeping us in a mindless rat race, Cone Builders compound scarcity with competition. In his book, *Influence* (3), Robert Cialdini shows how adding competition to scarcity can transform our desire for something from strong to insane. Cone Builders will create a hostile competition by convincing us that the resource is not only in short supply, but we can only purchase it or act on it today. Right now. Before everyone else. Commodities are not the only things that can be positioned as scarce and requiring competition. Manipulative parents will stage their affection as a scarce commodity they can only bestow on one of their children. A domineering friend will act constantly busy to make the little time they spend on their friends seem that much more valuable and desirable.

Both scarcity and rough competition create insecurities, and Cone Builders thrive on this vulnerability. As illustrated in Figure 17, Cone Builder's best bet is those who struggle with self-doubt, any lack of confidence and assertiveness, and those who are more submissive or dependent. Though none of us is completely free of such vulnerabilities, the easy recruits are those who carry a heavy load of them. There are several tells Cone Builders look for on the insecure side of this continuum. One is obedience and people-pleasing. It can either result from cultural conditioning, or a defence mechanism, also known as fawning,[20] such as appeasing behaviours among women in extreme patriarchal societies. People who feel unworthy, inadequate, fearful, and insecure go for people-pleasing as an attempt to get others to like them so they can feel safe. Cone Builders spot fawns and pleasers by the way they constantly flatter everyone around them, drop their boundaries, self-sacrifice for others' benefit, and seek reassurance from others. Since pleasers have serious doubts about their own value, they often end up prioritizing other people's wants and needs over their own. They will "go along to get along" and accept values and actions they don't necessarily agree with. These are the yea-sayers, and Cone Builders love having them in their ranks.

Being communal creatures, we naturally seek kindness and support when we feel vulnerable. Those of us who feel constantly defenceless will look to other people for reassurance and emotional support. Ironically, relentless reassurance-seeking and boundary wavering traps us in a nasty feedback loop. The more we are insecure, the more we seek approval and cancel our needs. The more we depend on others' approval and prioritize their Needs over ours, the more insecure we get. This is an unfortunate

---

[20] Fawning comes from the word fawn (think cute and helpless Bambi). It is a trauma response where survivors of complex trauma develop people-pleasing behaviours to avoid conflict and to appease their abusers.

cycle exploited by Cone Builders. It is also one of the foundations of gaslighting.[21] Cone Builders will first feed their recruits' emotional Needs to the brim (love-bombing), and then deny them the reassurance they desire most. The pain inflicted through this process makes their recruits bounce back with greater resolution to serve the Cone Builder's every whim and beg for their approval.

Another common symptom of insecurity is indecisiveness. We may all struggle with decision-making, especially when they have a meaningful impact on our lives, such as where to live, who to partner with, whether or not to have children, what career to pursue, and which causes to support. Unlike confident people, those with low self-esteem struggle with decisions even over small things like what to wear, when to shower, or where to go shopping. Because when you don't trust yourself, you can't trust your decisions either. You will defer to others to make them for you, and Cone Builders will be happy to oblige.

On the other extreme of this continuum are those who hide their insecurities under overly confident facades, often seeming pompous, entitled, and self-aggrandizing. In fairness, no mentally stable person would choose to feel constantly and entirely powerless, because it feels bad and might put us in danger. Therefore, a certain amount of controlling behaviour is a healthy and natural survival instinct. Some of us also seek control that extends beyond ourselves, such as power over our environment and other people. That, too, can be essential to our collective survival, so long as it improves everyone's living conditions through collaborative leadership. For some of us, though, collaboration won't do. Being prone to confusing Problems with symptoms, those who live with deep-seated pain, fear, and insecurities transform these Problems into extreme

---

[21] Gaslighting is a colloquial term that describes certain forms of psychological manipulation. The expression derives from the title of the famous 1938 play by Patrick Hamilton, Gas Light, later adapted into a movie. Gaslighting is used by abusers and manipulators to make their target victim question their own perception of reality.

Need for power. This power will presumably protect them from whatever they fear, increase their social worth, and give them control over their and other people's lives. Some will even believe that gaining ultimate power will somehow make them immortal. Such hunger for power is a form of greed, which is an insatiable beast.

Cone Builders will find these recruits by their excessive self-importance and disrespect for others who are "beneath them." The same domineering people are also likely to be overly defensive. Though we all might feel defensive, the slightest provocation will offend those hiding deep insecurities. They will be quick to attack or go into a passive-aggressive guilting tantrum because it will make them feel stronger and in control of others. At least temporarily. Another group on the domineering extreme are the callous and coercive. Each may have a different approach to controlling people, but they will always do it ruthlessly. Cone Builders will play on their desire to assert their dominance openly and the chance to have power over others.

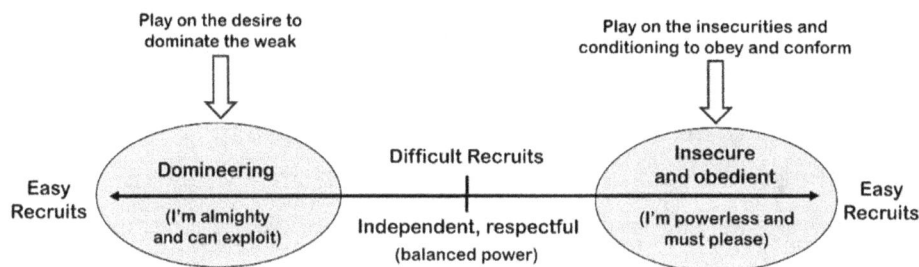

Figure 17: Easy recruits—the domineering, and the obedient and insecure

Hopeless pessimists and relentless optimists

You would think that having evolved in a world that can be deadly to soft and chewy creatures would make us innately pessimistic. Surprisingly, about 80 percent of us are much more prone to expect good things than bad, to the point of having an optimism bias (4). Most of us underestimate how long home renovation will take and how much it will end up costing us. Most of us imagine we will enjoy our parties and vacations much more than we eventually do. We also believe in commercials on products and in promises made during election time despite countless disappointments on both fronts.

In his book, *Talking to Strangers* (5), Malcolm Gladwell describes how we deal with people we don't know. Specifically, how deeply flawed our strategies can be when we encounter liars and schemers. We find it difficult to believe that some people are ungrateful, devious, ruthless, or don't have our best interests in mind. This bias is so powerful that even when we see glaring signs of dishonesty or of being taken advantage of, we resort to denial. This means that Cone Builders don't have to be exceptionally talented to recruit followers with deception, lies, and manipulation.

On the other hand, people with mild depression show no optimistic bias when predicting future events, and those with severe depression expect things to be worse than they turn out (6). Beyond depression, pessimistic bias can be entangled with the belief that things aren't only worse than they really are, but they are worse than they used to be. It is cleverly called the good-old-days bias. You may have heard statements such as, "What is happening to our young people? They disrespect their elders, disobey their parents, and ignore the law. They riot in the streets about their wild notions. Their morals are decaying. What is to become of them?" Or how about this one: "The world is passing through turbulent times. The young people of today think of nothing but themselves. They have no reverence for parents or old age. They are impatient of all restraint."

If you had to guess the period of these statements, you could have easily assumed these were made by boomers about millennials or Gen Z.

In actuality, the first quote is attributed to Plato, a Greek philosopher who lived over 2,400 years ago, and the second is by Peter the Hermit who lived in the eleventh century. If you scour through historical writings, or even through older contemporary magazines, you will find the same types of intergenerational opinions.

Media further reinforces the pessimism and good-old-days biases. Even the optimists among us will be affected by hearing or watching bad news. Since apocalyptic scenarios and violent events sell much better than anything feel-good, our media keeps feeding our pessimism, dissatisfaction, frustration, fear, and the longing for the good old days. The more mainstream media people consume, the more they will perceive the world as scarier, meaner, and more dangerous than it really is. This mindset creates fertile ground for target recruitment. As described in Figure 18, the Cone Builder's easy targets in this category will be those who are relentlessly optimistic and trusting in anything a persuasive person would tell them. Those who delve in deep pessimism and crave the good old days will also be easy recruits. They will respond to fear-based propaganda and promises of "resurrecting the golden age," or "making them great again."

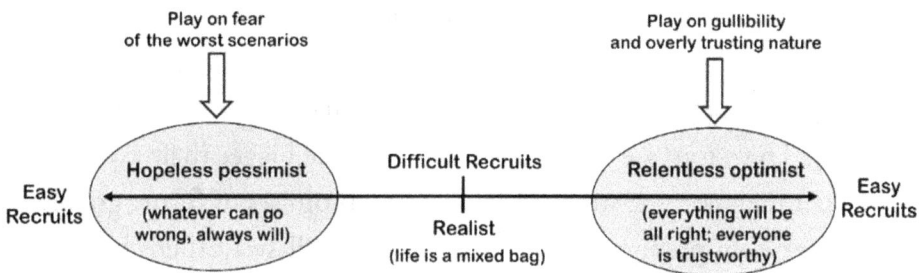

Figure 18: Easy recruits—the hopeless pessimists and the relentless optimists

The entitled and the wannabes

People with a sense of entitlement believe they deserve to have everything good handed to them without having to work for it. They know it in their hearts that they deserve privileges that others don't because they are inherently superb. On first blush, this would seem like an impenetrable trait for manipulation. However, the more inflated a person's self importance seems on the outside, the smaller and more scared they are on the inside. And we've already established that insecurities prep people for Cones. The problem with being "superior" is being placed on a very high pedestal. When they look down, they become mortified by the long and hard fall they might experience if someone takes away their privileges. To recruit the entitled, Cone Builders stroke their egos and promise that the One True Solution will celebrate and immortalize their superiority. With the same breath, they will remind them of how vulnerable they are, and therefore how scared they should be of losing their privileges. Luckily for them, the Cone Builder is there to come to their rescue and prevent that dreaded collapse.

On the other end of this spectrum are the underprivileged individuals who feel bitter about the injustice that has befallen them. These are not simply the people who believe they have been wronged. The most vulnerable in this category are those who dream of becoming superior and entitled. They, too, are easy recruits, because the bigger their aspirations, the easier they become susceptible to empty promises of future grandeur, no matter how preposterous. Cone Builders will sway them by talking about their unrealized sense of entitlement and how they are better than others and therefore deserve more, despite what anyone says about them. At the same time, they will shame them for their inferiority. They will promise that, while they are currently so much less than others, they could rise to power and privilege by sticking by the Cone Builder and their Solution.

We are all familiar with manipulative phrases such as: "They think we are nothing. It's time to show them who the superior people truly are." Or: "People of the [whatever makes them "elite"] are naturally superior to [the "inferior"] in every aspect, and therefore deserve to dominate them." Or this one: "Humans are the superior race that were placed on this earth to govern it and can therefore exploit the land and its inhabitants at will."

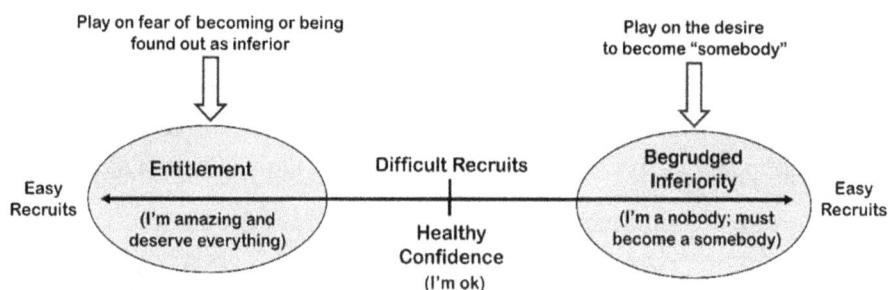

Figure 19: Easy recruits—the entitled and the wannabes

The immoral egotists, and the righteous and self-restraining

Moral behaviour is a complex concept that exists not only in humanity, but also in many other living beings. At the very least, basic morals mean we must consider each other's safety and basic needs. Though most of us possess a moral compass, we differ in how we calibrate it, and in what triggers or disables it. What we consider moral is affected by our parents' views on life, our cultural norms, religions, governments, laws, and many other Core Certainties that dictate our "morality standards." These are further affected by our early life experiences, trauma, fear, peer pressure, and the state of our mental health, to name a few.

We face moral dilemmas every day, even when we are not aware of them. When the cashier hands us more change than is due, we can easily take it and say nothing. Most people will give back the surplus money because they know stealing is wrong. But what if the storekeeper hikes prices, dominates the market, and exploits their workers? Will it still be immoral to take the extra change? What about lying? If the lie harms someone, most of us will refrain from telling it. But what if it's a little white lie that spares someone's feelings or gets us out of trouble without harming anyone? Some people will be lenient with white lies. Others will consider it immoral and punish liars no matter the severity or impact. What about murder? Surely something so drastic speaks to a universal moral code. Perhaps. But what if you grow up to believe that members of a certain group are demons and must be killed to save the righteous people or your own children? Is it still immoral to kill? What if you are a soldier given a command to shoot or drop an atom bomb on a demonized enemy?

A universal moral code is, and will probably remain, a theoretical concept as it is highly subjective and contextual. Regardless of its many definitions, people who are particularly greedy, self-indulgent, and dishonest can be easily tempted to act immorally (7). Egotism and the belief that one's needs and pleasure are above all else often contribute to a lack of morality. Self-absorbed and immoral people will adopt Solutions that promise them power and decadence. As described in Figure 20, Cone Builders will seduce these recruits by playing on their fear of losing power and pleasure and by promising to get more of those. Preferably on the backs of "losers" and Others. However, a Cone Builder will have to be extra cautious with these recruits, as their lack of morals might become a liability.

The opposite of extreme hedonism and egotism is self-restraint and self-denial that hold the promise of making one holier than thou. What are the forces that drive us to these extremes? One such motivator is shame. Most cultures around the world have one version or another of "shame on you." Shame is not a flaw in our design. It is vital to keep us in line with our in-groups. Most of us feel ashamed when we believe our behaviour reflects badly on our character. We do our best to maintain a positive image and actually do the right thing. In his book, *In Sheep's Clothing* (8), George Simon describes the many ways manipulators prey on our weaknesses to control us, with shaming and guilting being some of the top hits. Abusers and manipulators exploit decent human character by creating situations and narratives by which we should feel deeply ashamed.

A domineering spouse will shame their victim by claiming their partner's misbehaviours cause them suffering. Leaders of religious organizations will shame and guilt their congregation members for being undeserving of God's good graces if they stray from "the one righteous path." Abusive employers shame employees who aren't willing to work sixteen-hour days seven days a week for scraps by calling them lazy, entitled parasites. Shame makes people vulnerable to Cone Builders, who promise to absolve and give them self-value and pride.

Another powerful motivator for self-restraint is an overpowering Need for certainty. A few of us are daredevils who thrive on ambiguity, but most of us prefer to know what's coming. We want to make sure that the things we want to happen end up happening. We want to know that we and our loved ones will always be healthy and safe. That we'll have enough resources and supports to keep us comfortable well into our old age. We want to make sure we will realize our potential, and that our country will remain safe and prosperous. For most of us, a good level of certainty becomes a core Need because it tightly interweaves with fear (9). Unfortunately, life is mostly a series of wild plot twists that throw us into alarming unknowns. Most of us don't like it whatsoever. Though some may take comfort in wise concepts such as "when one door closes, another door opens," truthfully, no one is thrilled about the proverbial door slamming in their face. Our Need for certainty affects how we handle relationships, choose our careers, manage our finances, and decide on whom we befriend, idolize, or alienate.

Some of us want to be absolutely sure of everything all the time. The absolutists will seek "strong leaders" and Solutions that promise to deliver such assurance. They will view their beliefs and attitudes as superior and consider Others to be inferior and dangerous, which is a quick leap to extremism, intolerance, prejudice, and hostility (10). Absolutism works in tandem with the black and white cognitive bias, which makes us believe there is only one right way and all the rest is categorically wrong. Cone Builders are great at detecting people desperate for certainty and at cultivating it in the rest of us.

Yet there's only so much we can deny ourselves. Eventually, our suppressed desires burst like steam out of a pressure cooker and manifest in the ugliest ways. People on the self-denying side of the spectrum secretly seek a licence to enjoy all the spoils of this world without the associated guilt or adverse consequences. The desire for certainty and a black and white worldview often lead vulnerable people to dualistic thinking.

People with dualistic thinking are not great believers in subtleties or in grey zones. For them, there is one side of an argument or idea, or the opposite side. Everything in between is unnecessary noise. This perspective builds up a sense of self-righteousness and forbids people from reexamining their values or changing their minds, no matter how strong the evidence is. These are the dogmatic thinkers for whom ideology is everything. People who don't share their same beliefs are considered anywhere from wrong to undeserving of life.

Dualistic thinkers have uncompromising self-demands that are driven by ego. Cue phrases Cone Builders look for include: "I must perform well, prove my competence, fulfill our vision, and have control."

Smart manipulators can easily drive these people to obedience or to self-hate, anxiety, depression, and even suicidal behaviour, given the right incentive or punitive action. The uncompromising hyper-idealists will be loyal to a cause they believe in and rejoice with the thought that they are part of the inner circle. The best and most righteous inner circle, that is. This belonging reassures and validates their beliefs and proves that the others are wrong. Cone Builders will promise salvation and glory while justifying actions that would otherwise be seen as vile and immoral. These recruits who seek the One True Solution to save them from themselves (or from Others, or this world), won't require it to be logical. All they want is a clear and promising Solution. So long as it satisfies the recruit's desire for order and emotional stability, they will accept even the most ridiculous and contradicting claims.

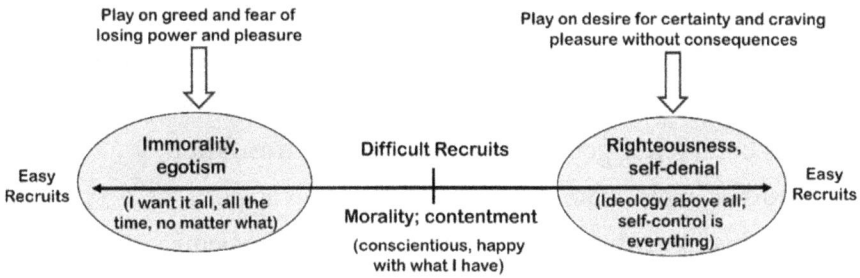

Figure 20: Easy recruits—the immoral and the righteous

The envious and vengeful, and the perpetual victims

They say the most powerful force in the world is love. It's true for positive emotions, but we harbour so much more than pure love. Deep frustration with injustice, anguish of being betrayed, desire for revenge, envy of others' better fortunes, and a sense of misery can propel us like a rocket from hell. Unrealized expectations and injustice trigger frustration. Broken promises and being abandoned by those who were supposed to care for us trigger a sense of betrayal. Unfairness, and having those we trust turn on us trigger a desire for revenge. A comparative lack of means, power, and dominance trigger hostile envy. A sense of endless misery drains our hope for a better life.

We may all experience injustice, betrayal, inequality, shortage, and powerlessness throughout our lives. Even the emotionally balanced among us can resort to aggression if they see no other way, but they will have clear moral boundaries. When people with a disturbed and uncontrollable anger response encounter the same adverse circumstances, they will experience overpowering rage, and resort to harming others without moral considerations (11). One commonality in any historic or current mass movement is the high level of frustration among the supporters. In his post-World War II book, *The True Believer* (12), Eric Hoffer pointed out that proficient power-seeking manipulators (i.e., Cone Builders) intentionally enhance people's frustration to advance their own goals. Hoffer stressed that no matter the ideology, religion, or dogma the group adhered to on either side of the conflict, their mindset was nearly identical. It was completely governed by overflowing frustration.

Another exploitable vulnerability in this category, as described in Figure 21, is our sensitivity to unfairness. As social beings, we are wired to monitor how rewards and means are distributed within our social circles, and we constantly evaluate the fairness of this distribution. When we are treated fairly, we feel joy, and when we aren't, we feel disgust and contempt. In the long run, an overall sense of fairness in our lives contributes to our happiness, whereas a constant sense of unfairness or injustice makes us angry and vindictive.

We can measure fairness using different yardsticks. Some of us believe in equality, where "fair" means treating everyone in the same way and expecting everyone to obey the same rules. Some of us believe in equity, where "fair" means each gets what they need in order to access equal opportunities and quality of life. Groups that support equity will provide greater resources and supports to their vulnerable members and apply rules differently based on people's unique Needs. Others yet believe in merit, where "fair" is when those who work harder or make greater contributions to the group get greater rewards.

No matter how we define fairness, it is extremely important for us to see it preserved. We expect those who don't play fair to be stopped, punished, or banned from the group. A perfect world will always be fair. In the real world, we will each experience unfairness and injustice of one sort or another. Even toddlers as young as three, and some species of animals, such as monkeys, birds, and dogs, express anger and contempt toward those who treat them unfairly. This powerful response is known as Inequity Aversion. Societies where unfairness is rampant develop a low-trust culture riddled with dissatisfaction, insecurity, hostility, and violence. When parents favour one child over another, the disadvantaged children are less happy, more resentful, aggressive, and rebellious, either openly or covertly (13). We can also be angry in the face of unfairness on someone else's behalf. This empathy can be so powerful, many of us will pay a personal price to eliminate injustice for others.

Just as each of us perceives fairness differently, we differ in the way we experience an offence. We may be rudely interrupted when we speak, get mansplained,[22] have our ideas rejected or stolen, or be ghosted[23] by our love interest. While most of us will view such incidents as disappointing or even painful, we will eventually overcome them. However, some of us will become fixated on the offence and obsess over it long after the event ended. Tendency for Interpersonal Victimhood (TIV) is a personality trait in which an individual experiences an enduring feeling of being

---

[22] Mansplaining is when a man explains something to a woman in a condescending manner, implying the woman is unable to understand or communicate on her own.
[23] Ghosting is when someone abruptly ends communication with someone else without any warning or explanation (as if suddenly becoming a "ghost").

a victim across different relationships (14). People high on the TIV scale are hyper-sensitive to offence, and almost anything can trigger them into victimhood, real or imaginary. They have a compelling Need to have the "perpetrator" take responsibility and express feelings of guilt. They also expect others to acknowledge their constant victimhood, empathize, and provide unconditional support.

People high on TIV consider themselves to be immaculately moral and are quick to point out the immorality of the other side. Similarly, collective victimhood will be based on beliefs about the justness of the in-group's goals and their positive image, while demonizing the Others' goals and characteristics. Though they expect endless empathy and support, they are very low on empathy for other people's suffering, and always believe to be the ones who suffer the most. They will focus on the causes of their victimhood rather than resolving it. They will also have a pathological desire to take revenge against those whom they perceive to be responsible for their victimhood. Yet no revenge will ever suffice, for their suffering is endless. It is no wonder such powerful emotions can play into the hands of manipulative Cone Builders. They will spill gasoline on our existing sense of unfairness, while claiming to have the One True Solution for our sorry situation. They will make us believe we are victims and tell us whom to blame.

Craving happiness is another exploitable vulnerability that pushes people to extremes. It may sound contradictory to the previous motivators. Surely it is a purer driver than fear, hunger for power, or inflated self-importance. Indeed, a simple pursuit of happiness comes from a hopeful and positive place; from knowing happiness is within us and up to us. However, desperately craving happiness happens when we believe it is external to us; that we will never experience it unless someone bestows it upon us, or if we work hard to earn it. This mindset of miserable-until-made-happy can result from our personality combined with life experiences where happiness was scarce and always depended on others. Happiness and fulfillment are often interchangeable or coinciding, therefore similar influences can affect both.

Like every other mindset that relies on external validation, craving happiness makes us prime candidates for Cone Builders that promise us eternal bliss. To play the happiness and fulfillment card, they will start by convincing us we are miserable and then point out the culprit for our suffering—our own insufficiencies or those who victimize us. Cone Builders will let us know that happiness and fulfillment are both conditional and external. That we can only experience these emotions if we "earn them," and be denied them should we fail. And lo-and-behold, Cone Builders have just the right Solution which, surprise-surprise, can give us that desired joy and purpose. If, and only if, we commit and submit to the Cone.

The neoliberal capitalism Cone[24] will promise happiness when you become rich. The mainstream education Cone will promise happiness when you graduate at the top of your class from the most prestigious institution. The organized religion Cone will promise happiness when you submit your will to their version of deity and "church." The military Cone will promise fulfillment when you become a loyal soldier eager to eliminate the enemy. And the bully's Cone will promise happiness once you live to please.

Cone Builders don't want people to be genuinely happy or fulfilled because happy people aren't seeking saviours. Though some Cone Subjects may feel temporary joy once they achieve whatever it is that they believe will make them happy, most will be disappointed to find it to be a fleeting sentiment. Because whatever is external to us can always become a moving target (the Need for a bigger house, better job, greater

---

[24] The listed systems, along with many others, will be analyzed in greater detail and shown to be bona fide Cones in my following books of this series. Stay tuned.

popularity), and therefore temporary. Cone Builders will respond to such disappointments by claiming: "You're either doing it wrong, or you're being disloyal and ungrateful, otherwise you would have been eternally happy and fulfilled." Or the shorter version: "It's not me, it's you/them."

Frustration, envy, a sense of injustice and betrayal, make people vulnerable and easily influenced by extremist propaganda. The same goes for people on the other end of this spectrum—those who feel they are helpless victims and desperately seek happiness. Especially if a Cone Builder asserts that Others have betrayed them, are cheating them out of their own, taking their women, or oppressing them. They will then incite their recruits to seek revenge and make the "culprits" pay for their crimes.

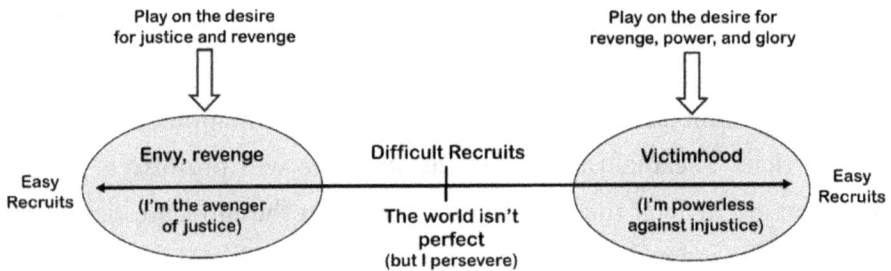

Figure 21: Easy recruits—the envious and vengeful, and the perpetual victims

The naïve and the wilfully ignorant

On one side of this continuum are the naïve and those with cognitive and/or developmental disabilities. The naturally naïve are those who have little to draw upon in the way of information, life experience, or brain power. Babies, children, or adults with developmental disabilities will have little capacity to examine the world with critical eyes. Their inherent innocence makes them great candidates for recruitment and indoctrination. Cone Builders who fill their innocent minds with their rhetoric and worldviews will turn most of them into unquestioning Cone Subjects for life.

The cognitively impoverished are another category of naïve individuals. Many variables might compromise our Cognitive ability.[25] Some factors are physiological, such as our genetics and brain wiring, others are environmental—or what we call nature and nurture. The more limited people's social networks and their experiences with the outside world, the more easily they will believe anything a charismatic leader will tell them. Their narrow band of exposure makes it difficult for them to grasp complex ideas and process "novelties." The same applies to people who have grown up with harmful or absent parenting, who struggle with unresolved or unaddressed trauma, or have little or low-quality education. Cone Builders will find cognitively impoverished individuals mostly in rural areas, small towns, economically strained communities, and groups that experience discrimination and social isolation (e.g., prisoners, marginalized groups).

Note that while these are all impactful factors, they don't necessarily predict a person's cognitive abilities. Higher education can improve one's cognitive abilities, but we have all encountered highly educated morons. We have also seen people with very basic education, if that, showing great wisdom and doing very well in the world. Some people are greatly affected by lack and deprivation, whereas others find ways to overcome and thrive, cognitively and otherwise. That's why stereotyping people based on their backgrounds is such a messy business.

Another factor that affects our cognitive ability is our mental processing and storage capacity. We approach situations and people based on the information we have about them. But to do anything meaningful with this information we must first process it. If we discover that our beloved

---

[25] Cognitive ability is our capacity to reason, plan, solve problems, think abstractly, comprehend complex ideas, learn quickly, and learn from experience.

leader scammed retirees of their pension money, it stands to reason we should stop trusting them. If a company we admire exploits children to produce their highly priced products, we should stop buying from them. If a political party we voted for has committed immoral acts, we should stop voting for them. That's what people with solid cognitive abilities would do. Yet we don't always change our minds quickly enough. Or at all.

Some studies show that individuals with lower cognitive levels find it more difficult to adjust their attitudes after being presented with the truth than those with higher cognitive levels. One explanation is that our cognitive ability is affected by the "mental workspace" we use for processing information (15). Think of the brain as your computer. A well-functioning machine will update software with a new version by deleting and replacing the old one. People with "mental clutter" can't delete the old software and therefore can't install the update. The older we get, the harder it is for us to declutter our minds from outdated and useless notions. That's why older people are more vulnerable to lies, manipulations, and fake news, especially if those reinforce their existing beliefs. This effect is even more pronounced in people with little education.

Another aspect that makes people with cognitive and/or developmental disabilities easy recruits for Cone Builders is their greater vulnerability to repeated information, even when it is blatantly false. While the trick of repetitive messaging can eventually affect any of us, the first ones to fall prey are those with compromised cognitive abilities. One more reason for Cone Builders to target people with lower education and lower cognitive abilities is that they are less trusting (16). This may sound counterintuitive because a Cone Builder's goal is to get people to trust them. The trick here is to get the people to trust the Cone Builder's lies by making them believe they can't trust anyone else.

Unlike the naïve and those with cognitive and/or developmental disabilities, the wilfully ignorant are the people who have access to information and enough mental capacity to process it, and yet choose not to. They may be aware of the existence of information, but they ignore it to maintain their preferred reality. These are the people who, in retrospect, will say things like, "I can't believe I was so naïve. But, with all honesty, I actually knew [whatever the truth was]." Not all will openly admit to it, but most of the self-deceiving people know it somewhere at the back of their minds. We see this self-inflicted naïveté in people whose children abuse substances or bully their peers and siblings. Some children are very good at pretending and covering their tracks, but most are quite sloppy when it comes to hiding illicit activities. Yet even in the obvious cases, too often it takes years for the big reveal to happen. In retrospect, their parents admit they saw all the signs yet chose to ignore and misinterpret them.

The same goes for voters ignoring their elected figures' transgressions, consumers ignoring unethical means of production, religious congregations ignoring their leaders breaking the very tenets of their beliefs, or scientists wilfully ignoring evidence that might shatter their illusions of truth. Cone Builders are quick to capitalize on these cognitive limitations and biases. These will be the recruits who, once in a Cone, will never ask difficult questions. In this category, Cone Builders will target the very young, the old, people of low income and education, the marginalized, abandoned, bullied, and isolated.

Play on strong-held beliefs and desire for status-quo

Play on trust in people and systems or limited cognitive capacity

Wilfully ignorant — Easy Recruits — **Difficult Recruits** — **Naïve, cognitively compromised** — Easy Recruits

(I am certain, and no one can tell me otherwise)

Open-minded, critical thinkers

(balanced perspectives)

(I believe everyone because they know better)

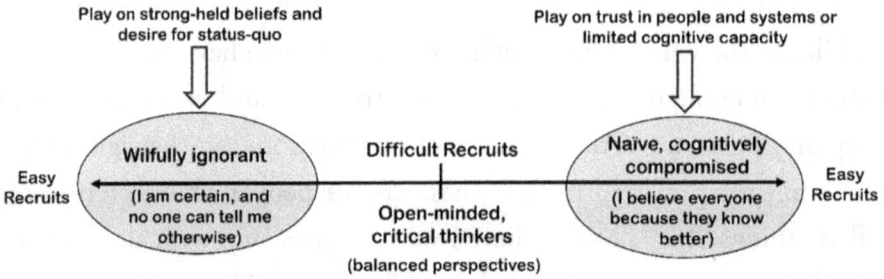

Figure 22: Easy recruits—the wilfully ignorant, and the naïve

Everyone is fair game

The categories I've described for easy recruits aren't all encompassing. They represent a few of the many archetypes that make Cone Builders' work much easier. Moreover, these categories aren't distinct. In fact, most of them overlap. Successful repeats can also be domineering, entitled, immoral, and uncompromising. Perpetual victims can also be failed repeats, hopeless pessimists, self-righteous, self-restraining, and vengeful. The wilfully ignorant can also be obedient wannabes or unprincipled egotists. We are complicated creatures, and this complexity is easily exploited by Cone Builders. Or as Nicholas Machiavelli said, "One who deceives will always find those who allow themselves to be deceived."

What about the centred, well-balanced folks among us? We would be remiss to think that dogmatic Cones are upheld by the less educated, less enlightened people, or only by the most vulnerable groups in society. The truth is, with the right type and amount of propaganda and childhood indoctrination, we can all be inducted into one Cone or another. Bottom line—wherever there are human beings, we are likely to find Cones.

Cone Builders know that every kingdom requires subjects. Aspiring Cone Builders can be the greatest snake charmers or the most abusive tyrants, but none of it will matter if they have no one who will obey and serve their Needs. That's why the recruitment stage is so crucial, and Cone Builders invest much time, thought, and resources to lure in the right (i.e., most vulnerable) recruits and convert them into Subjects. They start by playing to people's existing Core Certainties and promising a Solution that will address all their Problems and Needs. However, using the right persona and recognizing vulnerabilities will only get Cone Builders so far. Next, they will have to actually find these vulnerable recruits, build a close ring of supporters, and then find clever ways to convert recruits into loyal Subjects.

CHAPTER 9:

Building Cone foundations

... where we discover how Cone Builders establish their power, find their recruits, and create a magical role reversal.

A ring of true believers

uilding a long-lasting Cone usually takes more than one person. Even megalomaniac Cone Builders, who genuinely believe they are deities with the answer to eternal life, quickly realize that no one rules alone. All the strongest and most notorious Cone Masters in human history relied on a small, inner circle. A Cone Builder needs someone to be their confidant. Someone to help them translate their vision into strategy, or at least to be their sounding board or enthusiastic cheerleader. They need someone to herald their message. Someone to fundraise and manage finances because Cones are rarely cheap enterprises. And, of course, someone to be the muscle, fixer, and executor, either literally or figuratively, depending on the Cone.

Recruitment into the Cone Builder's inner circle requires great caution. The first tier of close supporters is usually based on trust, as much as possible. These may be old friends, family members, or other relations whom the Cone Builder would trust with their life, money, or at least their vision. Ideally, they will be devout fans and zealots who hang on the Cone Builder's every word and believe in their One True Solution. These will be the people who will make substantial sacrifices for their leader and their cause.

The second tier of close supporters, though still indispensable, are those whose personal ambitions are served by the Solution. These are the greedy and the opportunists who vie for power and means. Whereas the zealots will buy into the Solution unconditionally and be dazed by the Cone Builder's charisma, the opportunists will require explicit commitment regarding their personal gains. They will condition their loyalty and support with a well-defined exchange. This tier can include experts who seek glory, the oppressed looking to come into power, or investors who seek hefty returns on their investment.

The only way for a Cone Builder to grow into a Cone Master is to always position themselves at the top. Though they may be working with and supported by others, there is no room for more than one at the helm. And there's the rub. Those who have joined the inner circle out of zeal for the cause might find their leader too lax if they don't "go all the way." They will then try to replace the Cone Master with a candidate better aligned with their cause. Those who have joined for power and profit may secretly see the leader as a temporary stepping stone. They might provide their support until the Cone is built, and then try to take over. That's why Cone Builders are usually very careful when selecting members for their circle of trust, knowing well there is no honour among thieves.

For their inner circle, Cone Builders may choose people who see the world in black and white and the uncompromising absolutists. The entitled, envious, and vengeful will also do well, so long as the Cone Builder can show them how it will improve their status and satisfy their desire for revenge. Cone Builders who require particularly strong individuals may go for recruits with Machiavellian personality traits.

Machiavellians are master planners and strategists. On the surface, they may come across as charismatic and well-loved leaders (1). They are true artists when it comes to forming coalitions, building a flawless reputation for themselves, and working with partners. But just below the shiny veneer, they hold a cynical worldview where all others are merely tools for realizing their own aspirations by every means possible. Their chief priority is money, power, and competition, with no regard for their surroundings, and no empathy for others' suffering. They are the epitome of the sophisticated immoral.

The conscience of Machiavellians is in a mint condition, as it has never been used. They consider morality and ethics to be the mark of fools; they manipulate and lie to achieve their goals, and they do it with style. Machiavellians will rarely be openly confrontational, but they will not hesitate to crush those who stand in their way. These individuals make for exceptional Cone Masters. They may also make excellent members of inner circles, but they will pose a constant threat to the leader, as they rarely envision themselves as number two. On one hand, Cone Builders will not find more skilful partners in building a Cone. On the other, these partners might be ticking time bombs waiting for an opportunity to take over.

The callous and coercive are another group of recruits that may find their way into the inner circle, though these, too, must be handled with care. These are the people who are very low on empathy and compassion. They can be extremely averse to any type of connection with other people, and act in ways that are normally frowned upon by society (2). They are selfish and rude, and they exploit and harm other people without losing a moment of sleep over it. The callous and coercive can also have temper tantrums, resort to impulsive actions and, often, criminality. Many tyrants can be callous and coercive, but we can find them practically everywhere. They can be the family bully, the instigator of an outrageous conspiracy theory or a violent rebellion, a cult leader, or one of your toxic corporate managers (3).

Cone builders who seek powerful, driven, and morally indifferent people to do their bidding often find the callous and coercive to be best suited for intimidation and enforcement roles. The problem with these recruits is their impulsivity and volatility. If Cone Builders don't watch them closely, they might easily become a liability by making damaging public statements or doing something stupid without considering the consequences. They can also easily turn on the leader. Just like with Machiavellians, if a Cone Builder includes the callous and coercive in their inner circle, they will have to closely monitor and never truly trust them.

Finding recruits

Marketing to everyone isn't great for Cone Builders for the same reasons it isn't great for business. Having recruits believe that the Cone Builder and their Solution is The One will be a good start, but not much more than a start. Even talented Cone Builders never get everyone all at once, no matter how incredible they think they and their Solutions are. Even major religions around the world weren't successful in recruiting everyone, and this partial success took many centuries. If a Cone Builder is to throw themselves in every direction, they will achieve nothing. Think about someone who wishes to take over the vehicle market by introducing posh flying cars. What would be the point of directing their recruitment efforts at young children, decrepit neighbourhoods, or the residents of nursing homes? Obviously, they will fare much better targeting the repeats, the entitled, the wannabes, the envious, and the insecure of a driving age who have access to sufficient funds.

Adept Cone Builders start by studying the many types of easy recruits before they decide which ones would make most sense for their Cone. If a Cone Builder wishes to build a controlling relationship with a potential spouse, one of their easiest recruits will be those who have done it before. In this case, children to abusive parents or those who had abusive ex-partners. Though some of these potential recruits will have escaped the vicious cycle of abuse, many will be more vulnerable, because in their world, abuse is the normal. The insecure would be another excellent group for an abuser to tap into. People prone to pleasing, perfectionism, and approval-seeking will respond well to flattery, bombastic gestures, and sweet nothings that will reassure them of their worth.

Other types of vulnerabilities could also work, but it would depend on the specific type of Subject the Cone Builder is looking for. When looking for a submissive partner, the greedy and immoral, or the envious and vengeful, will not be great choices as these traits might backfire big time. But if a Cone Builder is trying to overthrow the current leader, the greedy and immoral, and the envious and vengeful are exactly the people they would look for. Those who have done it before would also be a great target group, and so will the extra-moral, the uncompromising, the naïve, and people with cognitive and/or developmental disabilities. If a Cone Builder is after the ruling position, they will appeal to most of their recruits by playing on their anger and sense of injustice. They will also attract the entitled by appealing to their sense of superiority over the other "riffraff"—the ones they stand to dominate and exploit.

The next recruitment stage will be to build recruits' personas. A recruit persona will be an imaginary person with a detailed profile that represents similar people in the Cone Builder's target audience. A detailed and well-constructed persona will help the Cone Builder craft more relevant messaging and create a highly focused and more personalized approach to their recruitment method. To build useful personas, a methodical Cone Builder will collect information and create a compendium of sorts, in the same way a grifter would collect information on a mark. They will start by defining their recruits' demographics. Will their typical Cone Subjects be mostly male or female? Youth, adults, or seniors? Working or unemployed? Professionals or labourers? Are they of a particular region, race, religion, tribe, or cast? And whatever else that speaks to the Cone Builder's Solution.

The next stage is gaining a deeper understanding of the recruits' inner world and pain points. Do they share vulnerabilities, a particular psychological profile, or common biases? Do they share certain beliefs and values? What ails, frustrates, scares, or shames them? What makes them feel worthless, misjudged, or oppressed? Which obstacles are they facing to overcome their challenges? Cone Builders will also want to know what "a perfect world" looks like to their recruits. What are their dreams? Where would they live? What would be their occupation? How would people treat them? Whom do they blame and would love to see punished? Whom would they love to dominate? How would they feel about themselves? What would they look like? How would their country look like? What stops them from making a change? Whatever hurts their target recruits and the things they fantasize about will guide Cone Builders to the kinds of promises that would work best. Every Cone will warrant different questions, but the principle remains. Creating reliable recruits' personas helps Cone Builders convert their recruitment tool from a fishing net to a harpoon.

Once a Cone Builder gains a good sense of the typical identities of their intended recruits, they will seek their high-value leads. Producing powerful promotional content is critical, but it's the distribution and the outreach that will require most of their effort. For that reason, recruits' profiles should include the answers to questions such as: Where do these recruits hang out? Where do they buy their commodities? Do they live in certain neighbourhoods? Do their children attend the same school? Are they members in clubs, secret societies, or particular social media groups? Are they drawn to specific political or social movements? Do they work in a specific industry? Who do they listen to and whom do they trust? Where do they get their information? Which platforms do they use for Solutions? What other Cones do they subscribe to? The answers to these and similar questions provide Cone Builders with insights into the channels and platforms they should hit to target recruits with their highly focused content.

In some cases, Cone Builders find shortcuts that save them a lot of prep time. Going back to the coup example, if they are a member of a tribe or a region that is currently governed by a tyrant, they will already know who their general target recruits are, what ails them, what their dreams are, and where to find them. If they are a member of a religious congregation and they wish to create a more radical faction, they will already have their channels and contacts to launch a campaign. In these and similar cases, Cone Builders can skip right to the targeted recruitment of a few close supporters that will lift them up and work for their cause.

The magical role reversal

Building a Cone is all good and well, but no one has ever grown into a Cone Master without their Subjects' sustained loyalty. Any marketer will tell you that without proper maintenance, most new clients will leave as quickly as they came. Once the recruitment honeymoon is over, Cone Builders start implementing retention strategies for the long haul. In order to have their recruits stay put, they may choose to reign with an iron fist or ease in with silk gloves. The first requires brute force, the second demands sophistication.

Many conquerors, colonizers, and enslavers have used the brute force approach. In some places around the world, it is still the case. Cone Builders can invade, kill, incarcerate, or exile their most powerful opponents, and then set up a Cone System to mercilessly govern their new Subjects. On a smaller scale, a Cone Builder can dominate the prison yard by becoming the most ruthless aggressor on the block and beating everyone into submission. A parent can keep their child under dictatorial rule, hold them confined, and batter them into obedience. Violent opposition to brutal Cone Masters may gradually subside, but it will never completely disappear unless mental manipulation is put in place.

Though the brute-force approach is a workable option for Cone Builders, it is hardly the best one, as it takes a great many resources that yield bouts of unrest and a short reign. Even Genghis Khan, the ruthless conqueror, was smart enough to declare religious freedom throughout all his conquered territories. He even granted tax exemptions to places of worship to make his subjects at least somewhat content. The last thing a Cone Builder wants is to become the zookeeper of disgruntled animals unless it gives them pleasure to sleep with one eye open.

To create enduring loyalty and dependence, a Cone Builder must employ a more effective way that eliminates the weight of their Subjects' resistance. The smart ones want their recruits to be grateful for being enclosed in their cage. They want Subjects who revere them, their cause, or their product. Those who will willingly guard their own cage, prevent their peers from leaving, and fiercely protect it from outsiders. Smart zookeepers want their animals to operate the zoo, leaving the owners to make every kind of gain off their loyalty without breaking a sweat. Or as Fyodor Dostoyevsky wrote, "The best way to keep a prisoner from escaping is to make sure he never knows he's in a prison." For this magical role reversal to happen, Cone Builders use a few nifty methods. Fundamentally, they aim to either numb us or push us into extreme emotional states where our primal, fearful, and irrational brain rules. They create these states of mind through several tried-and-true tactics, such as stupefying us, limiting or manipulating the information available to us, dividing us, establishing systematic and systemic oppression, and indoctrinating us.

Take for example something as common as organized religion. Based on data collected in 2022 (4), about 80 percent of the world's population identify with a religion. Most if not all religious organizations immerse their followers in their indisputable Core Certainties and teach them to revere not only the tenets of their faith but also the members of the clergy. The more orthodox factions will limit their followers' information to their religious scriptures and eliminate their access to any other sources of information. When a congregation member displays insufficient reverence or dares to question their religion's Core Certainties, they will be considered a sinner and a traitor. The more zealous believers will inform on these sinners, prevent their peers from leaving, fiercely protect their faith from outsiders, and spread their faith to nonbelievers. Even if only 30 to 50 percent of the people affiliated with a religion adhere to their faith, we are still looking at billions.

Religion is but one example among hundreds of other Cone Systems that govern our lives. Most of us don't notice these oppressive constructs because we consider them normal life. They are Dostoyevsky's prisons we are unaware of. This dogmatic "normal" is sustained by two seemingly opposing sides of one foul power equation, as illustrated in Figure 23. The obvious one (on the left side) is the profiteers' self-serving drive to dominate and exploit. The less obvious force, but just as powerful and possibly even more so, is the well-intended desire of loyal Cone Subjects to guard and reinforce their own cage.

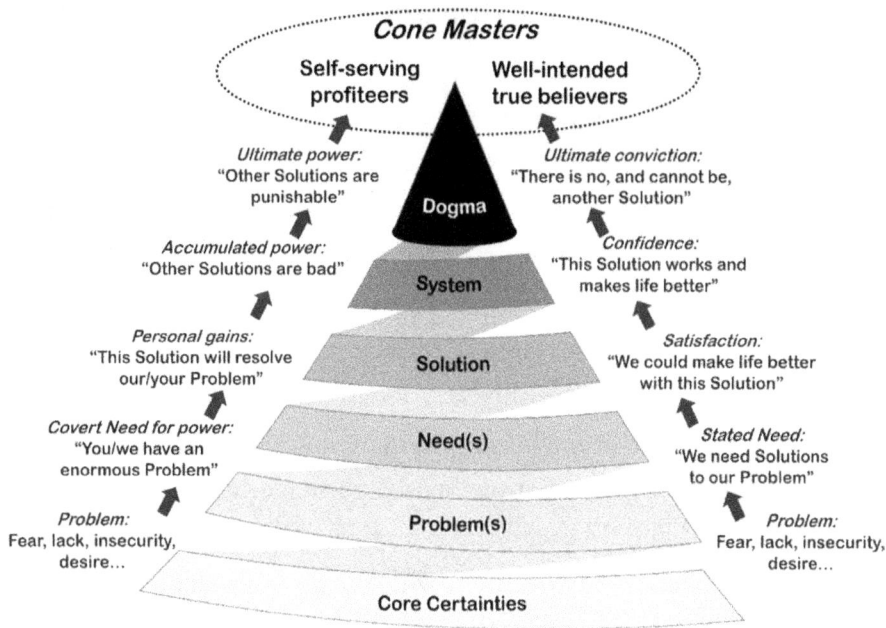

Figure 23: The anatomy of a Cone—driving forces and Cone Masters

In the early days of a System, when a Cone is but a glimmer of hope in the eyes of the Cone Builder, people will have confidence in the Solution. The Cone Builder will work hard to create satisfaction and assure this Solution is the best and other similar Solutions are really bad. Gradually, the Cone Builder will accumulate significant power (and often means as well, depending on the Solution), and then start limiting innovation and access to alternatives. In the meantime, a good portion of the well-intended Subjects will become devout believers. Without anyone noticing, the System becomes a Dogma. The Cone Builders, along with the well-intended die-hard believers, become Cone Masters. Both sides will enact rigid limitations on the Solution, demand unquestioning loyalty, and punish Subjects for transgressions. In many cases, Cone Masters will stop hiding their self-interest and personal gains. They will simply claim it to be the natural order of things that allegedly "benefits us all." The zealots, on their part, will assert to all other Subjects that, "There is no, and cannot be, another Solution." They will be the loyal supporters of the Cone Masters, and often become profiteers themselves by virtue of being close to the proverbial plate of power and means.

In an abusive relationship, both the abuser and their manipulated victim will be the Cone Masters, though the victim is also the Subject who will uphold this relationship as fervently as the abuser. The victim will blame themselves for being flawed and deserving abuse and do their best "to do better." They will ignore friends and family who are trying to rescue them from the relationship and accuse them of trying to sabotage their precious partnership. This is the smallest-scale zookeeper dynamic, which makes for a highly functional and a particularly cruel Cone.

Below the Cone Masters, there may be a variety of Subjects with different levels of direct involvement with the Solution depending on the Cone, as described in Figure 24. On a large scale (e.g., religion, economic governance system, tribe, commercial conglomerate) Cone Masters may consist of a Leader and a close ring of supporters. Some of them will be cynical and self-serving, and others will be the staunch, well-intended believers who would defend the Leader and "the cause" at all costs. People in this top tier of the Cone will not be bothered by their Subjects' unmet Needs or the Cone's harmful and oppressive practices. They will always justify and defend the Cone, no matter what. They will also be the top tier of Solution Enforcers.

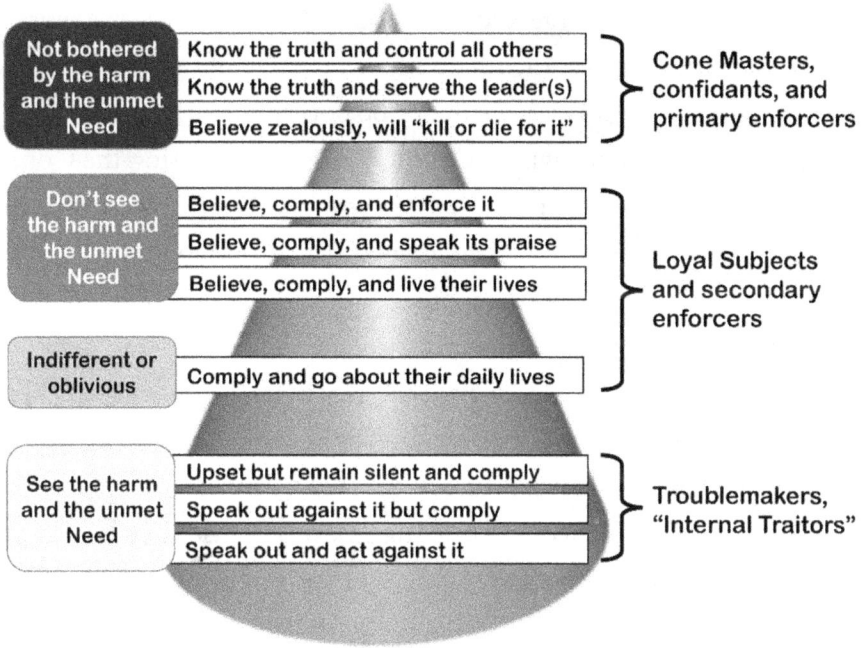

Figure 24: The anatomy of a Cone—types of Subjects and Cone Masters

Below them will be a tier of loyal Subjects who are ignorant in earnest or wilfully ignorant of the Cone's wrongdoings and its failure to meet their Need. They, too, will justify harmful and oppressive practices because they've been taught to ignore shortcomings. They may also believe it is "the only way," or that "it must be so for everyone's best interest." Subjects in this tier will enforce the Solution on their peers out of loyalty to the Cone and their outrage toward harmful traitors.

Some of the Subjects at the low end of this tier will be indifferent to Solution politics or the deeper meaning of an oppressive system. They will happily comply, so long as they don't have to think too much about it. This group is the most oblivious, and it is usually the majority of Cone Subjects. In some ways, these will be the happiest Subjects because their simplistic view of the world (and of the Cone Dogma) leads to mindless existence. No matter how exploited, they will be content or at least not disgruntled. Using George Orwell's book, *Animal Farm*, these are the workhorses who consider their hard life to be a sign of being a good, loyal, salt-of-the-earth person. They will not be bothered by the pains of higher values or idealism. They will not acknowledge the suffering the Cone inflicts on Others and will perceive their own suffering as part of normal life, or the fault of the Cone's designated scapegoats. Never in a million years will they suspect that the Cone is what's weighing on them or that life could be much better without it.

At the fringes of the Cone are the rebels and troublemakers. These are the people who are fully aware of everything that is wrong about it. Some of them will be upset but will remain silent and comply, because they fear the consequences of speaking up, or because they believe their voice will make no difference. Some will speak out against the Cone's failures and crimes, but still comply because they will see no other way. Only a small percentage of Cone Subjects dare not only to speak out, but also to defy and act against it, no matter the personal cost. Cone Masters will brand these two vocal Subject categories as Internal Traitors. They will be treated as such not only by the Cone Masters and formal enforcers, but also by the other loyal Subjects. They will experience more frustration, anger, and suffering than any other group within the Cone.

A cult is one obvious Cone example. The Cult Leader is the top indoctrinator and decision-maker. They are usually aware of the deception and of their disproportionate personal gains made on the backs of their followers (though some are delusional enough to believe in their own righteousness and divinity). Devout cult members closest to the Leader will be their confidants, their eyes and ears into the rest of the cult members, and usually the enforcers who exact punishments on transgressors. Most members will believe in the cult philosophy and be loyal to its Leader. They will have no doubts about the methods or the results of the One True Solution. They will remain vigilant, gladly reveal their peers' offences, and enforce penalties on those who dare stray from the righteous path. A tiny minority may awaken and see the Cult and its Leader for what they truly are. Some will hide their revelation out of fear of retribution. Others who dare speak up will become Internal Traitors and the targets for harsh penalties. The question is, what do Cone Masters do to us to achieve such magical role reversal?

Part 1:
The answers to our problems

Part 2:
How Cones are built

Part 3:
How Cones gain control

Part 4:
How Cones operate

Part 5:
How Cones fall... and come back

Part 6:
A better future within our reach

CHAPTER 10:

Stupefying us

... where we discover how Cone Masters manage to stupefy us all the way into their Cones.

cientists and psychologists call irrational behaviours "cognitive biases," which is a polite way to say, "This is us being ridiculous."

Some of our brainlessness is transient; sort of a temporary insanity triggered by certain events that shut down our brain for a while. Another form is the obstinate one that endures despite any of our attempts to wise up. One of the most basic tenets of many Cones is "get brainlessness going and you own them for life, or at least most of them for most of their lives." Even if Cone Masters don't get everyone, a good portion will suffice, because stupefied followers will fight the rest of us to the death for their Masters. The unyielding among us will remain mostly silent, albeit in awe with the foolishness surrounding us. The Cone-cultivated posse, on the other hand, will make enough noise and take enough aggressive action to make themselves felt and seen as if they are the only voice and the mightiest force out there.

Looking around with sober eyes, you will find ridiculousness at all levels and in all areas of life. Dietrich Bonhoeffer, a German theologian and anti-Nazi rebel in Nazi Germany, claimed that human stupidity is behind all the world's problems and that it is more dangerous than evil (1). Building on Bonhoeffer's theory, an Italian economics historian, Carlo Cipolla, wrote an unapologetic essay about what he termed as "The

Laws of Stupidity."[26] Though he initially authored it as a humorous article, it reflected everything history shows and modern psychology confirms. His five basic laws of stupidity, later published as a book (2), are:

"Always and inevitably, everyone underestimates the number of stupid individuals in circulation." Looking around, we find there is more
foolishness out there than one would assume. The perpetual presence of
multiple oppressive Cones we defend with everything we have against our
best interest is a testament to that. Cipolla claims that while the proportion of people behaving stupidly stays roughly the same within any society, what matters is how much power they get. Though in recent decades
it seems as if stupidity is suddenly everywhere, it is probably an illusion.
It has always been here. Nowadays, it simply has bigger platforms to be
heard and greater power to act under the guiding hand of their Cone
Masters.

"The probability that a certain person [will] be stupid is independent of any other characteristic of that person." Stupidity doesn't discriminate based on education or cognitive ability. Highly educated people who
may seem rational and intelligent can be as prone to falling for mental
manipulation as the other guy. Cipolla claims that stupidity has no nationality, race, or gender, and that it is spread proportionally among all of
us. An educated person can be just as much of a douchebag as an illiterate
one. Think of brilliant, highly educated men who abandon their partner
and children to run off with a much younger woman for an empty ego
boost. Think of all the highly educated people who fell for financial and
political Ponzi schemes of all forms. Consider all the highly intelligent
people who follow idiotic tyrants and cult leaders, or vehemently deny
climate change, the Holocaust, or the history of slavery.

---

[26] The term "stupidity" in this context is not to be in any way confused with the cognitive
abilities of people with developmental disabilities. Rather, it refers to stupefied, manipulated folks behaving thoughtlessly.

"A stupid person is one who causes losses to another person or a group of people while they gain nothing or may even suffer losses." Causing someone losses to benefit yourself is the act of devious Cone Masters. Causing losses while gaining nothing from it or even suffering personal loss is plain stupidity. There are more than enough people who take a saw to the branch they are sitting on to punish or control others, not realizing they would experience the fall just as badly, if not worse. You'd think that such irrational behaviour would be rare, but it isn't. This form of stupidity has built and sustained Cones for millennia.

"Non-stupid people always underestimate the damaging power of stupid individuals." Reasonable people constantly forget that dealing or even spending time with stupid people will always turn out to be a costly mistake. It is because reasonable people can't even imagine the possibility of stupid behaviour and are therefore always being blindsided by it. How shocked were all the reasonable people in the early twenty-first century once radical, blatantly lying, and unintelligent leaders started gaining massive support and winning elections around the world? I must admit, I still am.

"Stupid people are the most dangerous type of people… A stupid person is more dangerous than a bandit." This law seems to summarize all the above. People afflicted by stupidity are far less rational, predictable, ethical, or restrained than reasoned people. They rarely play by the rules and are more prone to fall into the hands of Cone Builders and play by their arbitrary rules.

What is it that makes us stupid? We believe we decide and act based on logic and data, but as discussed in earlier chapters, we make our decisions from an emotional place (amygdala) at a subconscious level. The only thing our "logical processing" does is justify our emotional decision by constructing logical arguments and selecting only the data that support it. Take the most basic example. It starts with you really wanting something—a want that comes from a purely emotional place. Perhaps it's your desire for social validation, your desperation to be loved or valued, or your fear of dying and being forgotten. Whatever this emotional undercurrent may be, it will translate into more tangible wants. You may want that wildly overpriced car, that new diet pill, or the person you know is absolutely wrong for you.

Deep down, your logical mind will try to slap you into form, but it will be a losing battle because your amygdala has already made the decision. At first, your cortex will try to tell you that buying that car will sink you into unmanageable debt. That taking that diet pill will be a temporary solution at best and most likely damage your health. It will remind you that dating that "bad boy" might lead to abuse. If you have a good handle on your emotional drivers, reason will prevail, and you will make logical decisions. But if you are low on impulse control, or if these emotions were inflamed by Cone Builders, your cortex will line up all the reasons you should go for it. The voice of reason will be discarded as a nuisance.

Cone Builders are well aware of the flaws of our ancient brain. They invest much of their time and resources in manipulating our emotions, igniting our fears, and strumming on our desires, and then offer their "perfect Solution" that just happens to address these inflamed emotions. That's when our brain finds every rational justification to adopt and defend our ill-advised decisions and actions, no matter how stupid these may be. The question is, are we born stupid, or do we gain it throughout life? Though some are more vulnerable than others, we aren't stupid beings at our core. Many of us are simply easily exploitable, either by nature or because of manipulation and life experiences, and therefore easily driven into foolishness. I have to believe it is a curable condition, though not through a quick fix. Perhaps we can start by reading a good, awakening book on the subject. Just saying.

Bread and circuses

There are many ways Cone Builders actively stupefy us to the point we start believing everything they say and defend everything they do. One of those ways is distracting us until we forget what truly matters. Juvenal, a Roman poet, wrote nearly two thousand years ago: "Two things only the people anxiously desire—bread and games." To make sure the general populace remained distracted during tumultuous political times, the Roman government handed out free food and staged free plays, gladiator fights, and other grand spectacles. It wasn't the first time in human history Cone Masters used distraction to divert their Subjects' attention from actual problems. It was simply a grand and well-documented one. In their book *Amusing Ourselves to Death* (3), Neil and Andrew Postman examined the effects of television and mass media on our culture and public discourse. They found that the rise of entertainment-oriented media all but killed our ability to engage in deep, meaningful, and critical discussions of any sort. Just like in ancient Rome, our modern entertainment systems are driven by visual images, super-scripted events, and brief messaging that deliver instant gratification.

This easily digestible media has become our intellectual junk food. It's cheap, it's available everywhere and to everyone 24/7, it's been processed to death, oversimplified, and super-sized beyond reason. We no longer have to gather ingredients and decide for ourselves how to "cook" this information. It is almost literally shoved down our cognitive throats, saving us the need to chew on it. This entertainment mode has created a culture where we no longer wish to read lengthy narratives, run independent or in-depth analysis of information, or hold deep debates. Many of us have grown to value distracting entertainment over substance. We became addicted to ten-second kitten and celebrity videos. Most of us can no longer tolerate anything lengthier or more intellectually challenging than catchphrases from influencers.

The problem with distraction extends much beyond our readiness and ability to hold a philosophical debate. The deeper problem is our loss of independent thought, which makes us so much more vulnerable to Cones. People who struggle to engage in serious, rational discussions and rely on quick and digestible messaging will never contribute or even appreciate democratic participation and freedom of thought. They will believe everything that is given to them in short snippets, especially if the messaging is delivered by confident orators and celebrities who tell them what to think.

Killing nuance

Most of us already know that our world is a mix of truths and lies, well intended, indifferent, and ill-intended people, joys and catastrophes, and everything in between. And yet it is the in-between—where most of life happens—that goes by the wayside when dogmatic Cones take over. Cone Masters hate the grey zone because it makes us think and consider possibilities. And when we think, we might develop critical thinking, rational decision-making, empathy, and compassion—all of which interfere with efficient indoctrination.

Most of the systems and institutions in our societies discourage and often even forbid the grey zone. We are made to choose a single sports team to cheer while being expected to boo all others. We are persuaded that a single political party is absolutely right and therefore the others must be totally wrong. We are told that we can be for or against religion but not both. That if we are not devout believers in modern science and medicine, we must be ignoramuses, idiots, conspiracy theorists, antivaxxers, or all of the above. Even skeptics who pride themselves for refusing to yield to restrictive dogmas often form a rigid doctrine of their own. It isn't easy to live in the greys of our world. Ambiguity is not a popular sentiment, therefore killing nuance and painting the world in black and white works so well for Cone Masters.

The ways our mainstream and social media operate make this reductionism all too easy. Oversimplified, black and white information creates binary thinking where truth that lives in the grey zone goes to die. One way Cone Masters kill nuance is by "packaging" their version of the truth for us. We experience this packaging at all levels of our lives. Family elders infuse us with packaged narratives of their Core Certainties, affecting our understanding of reality. Educational systems package the types of information our governments wish us to live by while omitting information that will interfere with their ideology. Labour market moguls package their version of "work ethics standards" to have us comply with their needs, while omitting any alternative ways work can be performed. Partisan news broadcasters package a one-sided truth for their base while excluding all inconvenient information.

If we feel exploited or oppressed, a Cone Master will reduce everything that happens around us into short descriptors of the offences we experience while ignoring anything good in the existing situation. They will create packaged truths to play to our desire for freedom or justice and delete any nuanced elements or evidence contradicting their narratives. Those who insist on questioning, seeking middle ground, or refusing to accept these packaged truths risk being branded as fools and Internal Traitors.

Manipulating our language

We may mistakenly assume that influencing people's opinions involves lengthy lectures, a book series, or a full-fledged manifesto. This may be true for a few deep thinkers, but for most of us it is a waste of time and energy. Some Cone Masters, especially within academic and intellectual circles, will invest in vast information building if they feel it would add credibility, but that would be the odd case. To "make a killing," Cone Builders find those small and impactful ways that can penetrate our brains without leaving an exit wound. Manipulating our lingo is one great way to skew the message.

Offensive language

Much has been said, and many have complained about the shift from blunt in-your-face talk to the politically correct. Many societies move away from open racism and public bullying to more considerate behaviours. Similarly, we got rid of derisive terms and replaced them with more inclusive language. We can no longer say words such as "fatso," "faggot," or "retard" without being frowned upon, if not cancelled, and rightfully so. Groups and individuals who aren't affected by offensive language—especially the privileged and the bullies who relish abusing the vulnerable—feel they are being unfairly silenced. They mock those who lead the change, calling them snowflakes and putting a negative spin on the term woke. That is until such language is directed at them. White bigots who feel very comfortable using the N-word against black people will be deeply offended when being called rednecks, racists, or Nazis, because words are meaningful, and they can hurt worse than a beating.

Thought-terminating phrases

Another language manipulation method is using phrases that command unwavering obedience, such as "Heil Hitler," or those that instill deep fear and antagonism, such as racist chants against football players. These thought-terminating phrases aim to stop us from thinking, exploring alternatives, or listening to reason. I call them "brain plugs" because they work like ear plugs for our brain. Different types of thought-terminating phrases aren't exclusive to one another, and they often work in synergy. It doesn't matter how meaningless these clichés may be, repeating them ad nauseam can turn perfectly normal people into brainless, chanting crowds. A short and repetitive phrase that means very little can easily generate mass stupidity, especially when manipulating the vulnerable, oppressed, and marginalized.

Many thought-terminating statements are ridiculously hollow, such as "Brexit means Brexit," yet it swayed enough people in the UK to vote for an economically suicidal political move. "Blood and soil" was the meaningless yet powerful slogan that justified Nazi Germany's racial policies, later adopted by white-supremacist movements for similar stupid-rallying purposes. "Trust the science" was a stupefying slogan used in 2020 during the COVID-19 pandemic to terminate critical thinking and silence any form of questioning of pandemic measures, despite true science being all about doubt and inquiry. Cone Builders are heavy on thought-terminating slogans and very light on details because they know their stupidified followers don't require elaborations or proof. All they need is something catchy to repeat while looking good, just, or smart doing it.

Sterilizing our language

When a certain phrase or term doesn't serve their agenda, Cone Masters will alter it for us in ways that seem completely innocent or nearly undetectable while holding a punch. Frank Luntz, an American communications consultant, famously pushed the Bush administration to use the term "climate change" instead of "global warming" because "warming" sounds alarming and will require action, whereas "change" is something that happens all the time, and not necessarily for the worse. This rephrasing allowed Bush to ignore this impending catastrophe without political repercussions. Luntz was also the one who recommended replacing the term "oil drilling" with "energy exploration." That's how you get people feel much better about this harmful process and significantly reduce resistance to oil extraction. Because who doesn't like exploration?

Researchers experimenting on animals coined the term "sacrificing the subject" vs. "killing the dog" because "killing" may create public outrage, whereas "sacrificing" sounds almost noble.

Changing active to passive phrasing and removing the culprit from the sentence is another way of sterilizing language to shift or remove blame. When the media reports that "the woman was raped," it places the woman in the centre with the perpetrator being all but ignored. It is as if the rape was some force of nature the woman was unlucky to encounter. Had she only been more careful she wouldn't have tripped over this rape thing. Think of how much more impactful and truer "the man raped the woman" sounds and registers in our minds. The same goes for "the price of insulin was hiked in the last quarter," as opposed to "the drug company hiked the price of insulin in the last quarter."

Even when the guilty party is mentioned in the sentence, a passive voice changes our feeling toward the perpetrator. "The man was attacked by a police officer" sounds much less severe than "the police officer attacked the man." In the passive version, we are more likely to assume the police officer had a good reason, whereas in the active version, we might be less forgiving. Most of us aren't even aware of these subtleties, but our emotions hear it loud and clear.

No matter what strategy Cone Builders use to manipulate and subdue us, once people are overcome with stupidity, they act as if under a dark spell. The rational part of our brain we are so proud of is turned off. Much like a mental zombie, any attempt at a logical discussion and presentation of facts fails miserably. Once we become stupefied, we resort to the slogans and catchwords Cone Builders planted in our minds and trust "verified and approved sources" unreservedly. But stupidifying us isn't the only tactic in the Cone Masters' bag of tricks. The clever ones use several such methods to ensure we remain loyal and compliant. The good news is that this state of induced foolishness is neither a terminal nor an irreversible condition. Given the right opportunities and supports, most of us can retrieve our wits and reconsider our actions.

CHAPTER 11:

Dividing and isolating

... where we witness how Cone Masters manage to unleash the very worst in us by dividing us.

A long the lines of "one picture is worth a thousand words," one of the brilliant caricatures created by Dave Coverly demonstrates the gist of divide-and-conquer. In it, a king and his adviser observe a crowd from the safety of their fort. An angry mob of villagers below carry torches and pitchforks. The advisor says to the king, "Oh, you don't need to fight them—you just need to convince the pitchfork people that the torch people want to take away their pitchforks."

Julius Caesar, the prominent Roman general and statesman, was an artist when it came to dividing and conquering. When Caesar set out to conquer Gaul (today's France) he employed every trick in his helmet to inflame longstanding rivalries and internal power struggles among the Gallic tribes. He exploited these divisions by forming alliances with some tribes while playing them against others. By promising certain Gallic leaders land, power, or protection in exchange for their allegiance and assistance in his campaigns, he fuelled greater animosity with other tribes. Those who felt marginalized or betrayed became more vengeful against their own countrymen instead of focusing on the Roman invader. Meanwhile, those who accepted Caesar's offers lost their autonomy and were in effect conquered by the empire. Dividing groups to better control them was only one part of Caesar's strategy. He arranged marriages between Gallic chiefs to forge political alliances and further solidify his influence among the tribes he took over, because part of divide-and-conquer is unite-under-my-flag. By manipulating these divisions and alliances,

Caesar was able to weaken the collective resistance of the Gauls and gradually asserted Roman control over the region.

In Rome, Caesar faced opposition from the ruling elite—those who ran the very traditional Senate and disliked the aggressive, rising star. To counter this opposition, Caesar used the same strategy with a combination of political alliances, bribery, and coercion. When tensions between him and the Senate escalated, eventually leading to civil war, Caesar used a strategy of reconciliation and clemency toward some of his enemies while eliminating or neutralizing others. This further fragmented opposition against him and facilitated his rise to dictatorship.

The list of examples where the deceptive principle of divide-and-conquer is applied is nearly endless. Think dogfight. While dogs may fight in their natural habitat for territory or mating rights, it isn't in their nature to fight each other to the death for entertainment. Not unless they are conditioned to do it. This conditioning must happen from a very young age and within a very restrictive and punitive environment. They are taught that their enemies are other dogs. Why? Because their masters say so. Because if they aren't good enough, they will become "bate dogs"—those who are used to bring out the viciousness in potential winners. All they are programmed to do is follow orders and kill. Despite being mistreated and tortured by their human owners, the only thing these dogs know is that other dogs are their enemies. Not for a fleeting second would they consider their owners to be the real nemesis.

Cone Masters use the same artificial animosity-building strategy on every level, from a relationship to worldwide systems. Numerous tribal feuds, cold wars, religious crusades, commercial takeovers, and armed conflicts were driven by divisive opportunists. In their pursuit of power and possessions, they divided people into hostile factions, and manufacture conflicts to establish their Cones. The divide-and-conquer strategy brings out the worst in us and, just like a virus, has many variants that lead to societal sickness, as described in Figure 25.

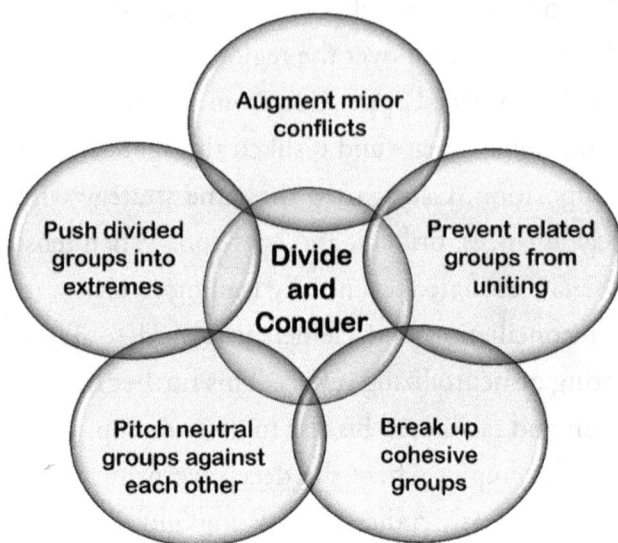

Figure 25: Major variants of divide-and-conquer

One of the most basic variants is further dividing the already separated by pushing each group to extremes. On a national and international level, major arms dealers, colonizers, power seekers, and indebting financial institutions thrive on inflaming conflicts. They will keep the animosity burning hot for as long as possible. The endless political strife in the Middle East is one glaring example. Sometimes, it would be a stretch for Cone Builders to throw rival groups immediately into extremism. They will first have to augment existing minor animosities into more significant ones, similarly to what Caesar did with the Gaul tribes, or such as further dividing majority from minority groups that already have a bad history. Cone Masters will pitch one religious denomination against another or develop hatred and fear among different groups within the same region. This will give them greater control of the separated and, potentially, use the "abominable Others" as scapegoats.

Another option for divide-and-conquer is to intentionally pitch a few peaceful groups against each other using lies and deceit, and then step in to take over the ruins. Remember Erica who broke up Mark and Neelam with lies and manipulation? This is typical manipulative handiwork of abusive and Machiavellian Cone Builders who wish to create mayhem among peaceful groups or individuals. This turmoil allows them to triumph as the "voice of reason" or "the saviour."

Preventing loosely related groups from uniting under a common cause is another variant of this divide-and-conquer "virus." It is much easier to stop small groups from linking forces than to break them apart once they have united. Corporations go to great lengths to prevent the formation of unions. They do it by dividing the workers and pitching them against "troublemakers" and union organizers who supposedly "endanger all of us and ruin our livelihood." This type of divide-and-conquer eliminates their workers' negotiating power and ensures their uninterrupted exploitation. Manipulative abusers prevent their victims from forming new friendships to keep them weakened and isolated.

Yet another manifestation is breaking up existing cohesive groups into smaller, weaker, and more submissive units. The weaker the ties people have with other individuals or groups, the greater their suspicion and fear of Others. And that makes it easier for the manipulator to swoop in as the saviour, exploiter, or conqueror. A class queen will break her posse's external friendships to solidify her reign and set clear identifiers of "insiders" and "outsiders." An abusive partner or a cult leader will forbid their Subjects from contacting their families and friends to eliminate alternate information sources and support systems.

However the division is achieved, separating people is only half the job. The complementary part is uniting them in zeal and fear under the Cone. Since most of us yearn to belong, Cone Masters find creative ways to make us feel we are becoming one with a greater whole. *Their* greater whole. They convince recruits that uniting under a single banner will protect and make them powerful against a "common enemy." First, the Cone Builders draw a clear line between *Us* and *Them* and make their recruits feel special and united. Then they will set terms of belonging which come down to, "You're either with us or against us."

This conditional affiliation exhibits the stark difference between belonging and fitting in. Belonging means feeling a part of a group that accepts you for who you are. When you truly belong, you feel cherished and genuinely seen. Having to fit in is the exact opposite. It is a conditional membership with a group that will only see you as part of them if you conform to their terms and conditions. Having to fit in means you must change yourself to be more like others, even if it forces you to suppress your true identity or your values. When you "fit in," you will always be under scrutiny and fear of being discovered as insufficient and undeserving. Cone Builders promise belonging when they actually mean their Subjects must fit in, lest they will be exposed as Traitors or Others.

The pernicious principle of divide-and-conquer works on all levels of our lives. A bully at school, in a neighbourhood, or a workplace will seek their low-hanging fruit—the repeats, the insecure, the envious, the vindictive, or the wannabes. They will recruit using their manufactured personas, and make their followers believe that associating with The One will give them purpose and a sense of belonging. Better yet, it will make them superior to others. The bully will reward loyal followers by creating the appearance of insider friendship or fraternity and protecting them from their own bullying. At the same time, they will establish a culture of harassing those Others now deemed undeserving or "easy prey" to ascertain dominance. Any association with them will bring a punishment, such as shaming, beating, or expulsion from the bully's in-group.

Within families, power hungry members often use divide-and-conquer. These Cone Builders sow seeds of instability between the family members, spread lies, break confidence, and create incidents that implicate their target of choice of being the culprits. They will make false accusations on their target's alleged indiscretions and turn the entire family against the victim. Eventually, all that is left for them is to watch how otherwise kind people ostracize their own family member, while regarding the abuser as their protector from the alleged black sheep.

Beyond pitting us against Others, at a deeper and more philosophical level, divide-and-conquer separates us from ourselves as well. A Cone Master's goal is to weaken us in every possible way while making us believe we are growing stronger. Outwardly, a Cone Master separates us from our existing and potential allies and support systems. Inwardly, they separate us from our self-confidence, logical thinking, conscience, kindness, compassion, empathy, and any other sentiment that might allow us independent thought, voice, or agency. To turn us into obedient, mindless Subjects, Cone Masters must separate us not only from Others, but also from the basic tenets that make us decent human beings.

Exploiting vulnerabilities

Every kind of divide-and-conquer starts with playing on our vulnerabilities. We all harbour them, and they can be minimized or magnified by life circumstances. Very few of us have full immunity from the many divide-and-conquer traps Cone Builders set for us. As described in Figure 26, those of us who are more prone to fear and anxiety will respond to repeated messaging about those Others who are making our world hostile and scary. People burdened with shame and guilt will be disgraced for associating with Others, behaving like them, letting them win, or being inferior to them. People who fear scarcity will be constantly reminded there isn't enough for everyone and that those Others are taking what little we have.

People who are frantically seeking certainty and control over their lives will be reassured that, "Ours is the only truth and therefore we must never believe the Others." The isolated who crave to belong will respond not only to a call for unity ("become one with us"), but also to threats of expulsion ("You don't want to be the outsider, do you?"). Those who hunger for power and superiority will be lured into the divisive mindset by the opportunity to defeat and dominate Others while gaining privileges and asserting their "natural superiority." The frustrated, the hungry for justice and revenge, and the perpetual self-proclaiming victims will join the cause once the Cone Builder has identified the Others as the ones to blame for their pain. Those who feel happiness is in short supply will believe Cone Builders who claim that, "If it weren't for those Others, you would have been happy."

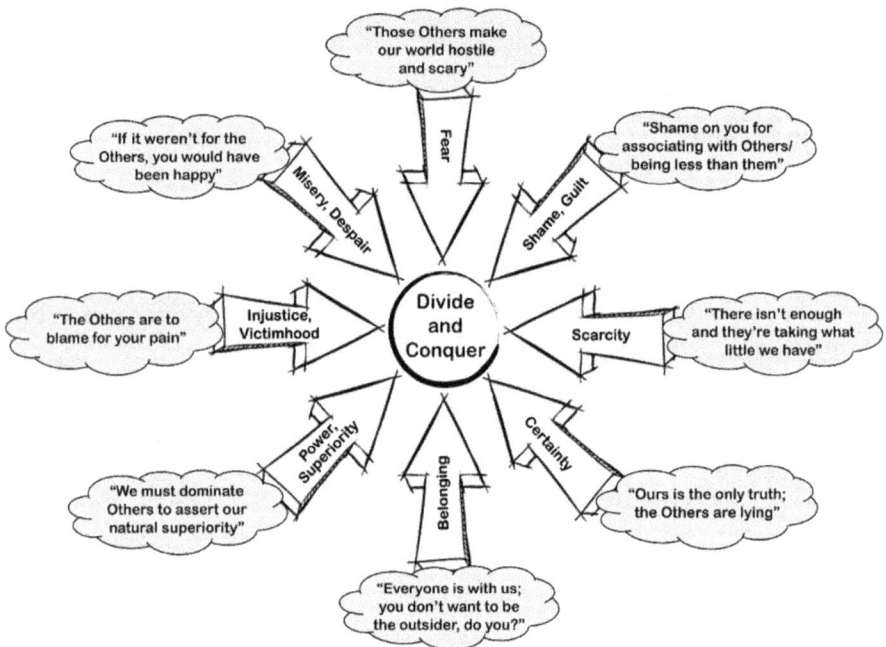

Figure 26: Major motivations Cone Builders exploit to divide and conquer

Nearly all tyrants who rise to power use one or more of these divisive tactics to rally support. Barry Glassner, the author of *The Culture of Fear* (1), wrote on the rise of Donald Trump: "Politicians, journalists, advocacy groups, and marketers continue to blow dangers out of proportion for votes, ratings, donations, and profits." Like many other tyrants in the making around the world, Trump excelled in triggering fears and anxieties among the vulnerable. He then promised ultimate safety and prosperity in return for their unconditional support. And it worked.

The art of othering

The many variants of the divide-and-conquer "virus" have one common denominator—uniting while othering. Depending on the Cone, the process of othering can be anything from subtle and nearly invisible, through open and unapologetic, to inflammatory and violent. Many times it starts as a subtle act, and then escalates as the Subjects show increasing buy-in to the Cone Builder's othering attempts. As illustrated in Figure 27, Cone Builders can start with spreading rumours and gossip, and gradually become emboldened and use increasing hostility, all the way to demonizing and scapegoating. Though the chart shows a logical progression, othering doesn't always happen in this neat sequence. Often, these tactics are used in bulk or in tandem, depending on the Cone.

Discredit	Losing trust in Others "No longer believe them"	Individual or public distancing from Others
Bully	Losing respect for Others "Don't want to associate with them"	Public shaming and harassing Others
Objectify, Dehumanize	Losing morality toward Others "They aren't really human"	Strict separation, mistreatment of Others
Demonize, Scapegoat	Fearing and despising Others "They must be exterminated"	Radical separation, violence toward Others

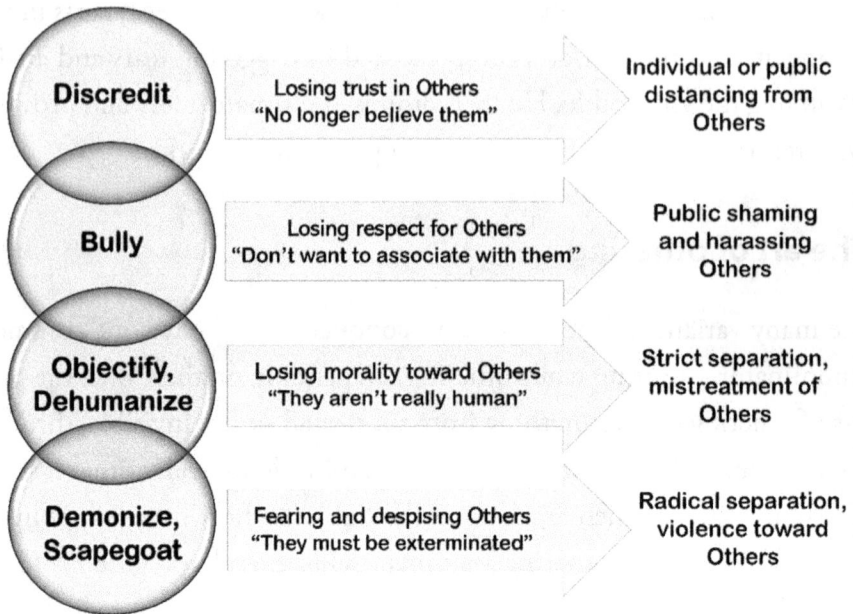

Figure 27: Common othering mechanisms

Discrediting

Trust is a positive state of mind and therefore isn't helpful in a Cone. Though Cone Masters want their Subjects to trust them unreservedly, they have no interest in fostering an overall trusting mindset. On the contrary. They aim to eliminate their Subjects' trust not only in those allegedly harmful Others, but also in each other and in themselves. Because people who live in a general state of stress, suspicion, and uncertainty are so much easier to control. When Cone Subjects come to suspect everyone, including their in-group members, they become more submissive and much less likely to pursue justice and freedom.

There is a slew of old mother-in-law jokes that demonstrate passive-aggressive behaviours, such as the mother-in-law telling the son-in-law, "Who would have thought you'd be so successful." Microaggression is one of the most subtle ways to sow doubt and disrespect toward Others.

It is a type of comment or action that perpetuates stereotypes of its target while the aggressor can get away with being offensive or even appear to be well intended. When a manipulator says, "You're so smart for a woman," or tells a person of colour, "I can't believe you got promoted. Well done!" they don't mean these as compliments. What they want is for their followers to hear the subtext that says, "Women are brainless" and "People of colour cannot possibly be good enough to be promoted." And all without being blamed for misogynism or racism. Microaggressions are one of the many methods in the Cone Master's gaslighting toolbox that undermines trust with a bonus of deniability.

Genuine artists of subtle discrediting know how to plant seeds of doubt in the minds of their Subjects with statements such as, "Are you sure your wife isn't cheating on you?" "I may be wrong, but something is fishy about this person," or, "I'm not one to speak, but I'm pretty sure [they] can't be trusted." Some repetition with the appropriate tone, headshake, and eye-rolling and these seeds will germinate and grow into deep-seated distrust. The Subjects won't even be able to rationalize their suspicion. They will simply know this person can't be trusted.

Lesley Stahl, a CBS *60 Minutes* correspondent, shared a conversation she had in 2016 with then-presidential candidate Donald Trump (2). In a candid, off-camera meeting, she pressed him to explain his bombardment of insults aimed at journalists. This was the explanation he gave her: "You know why I do it? I do it to discredit you all and demean you all so when you write negative stories about me, no one will believe you." This dirty discrediting trick is also used by reporters who wish to discredit political opponents by repeatedly prefacing questions with statements such as, "Surely you aren't saying the elections weren't rigged," or posing questions that start with, "Word on the street has it…" When confronted for being belligerent, the interviewers (who often serve as the Cone Master's mouthpieces) claim innocent questioning and hide behind their freedom of speech.

Cone Masters—from neighbourhood bullies to state leaders—discredit those they other while hiding behind "they can't take a joke." This tactic used to be publicly deplorable and got people fired. Unfortunately, in recent decades, a swath of influencers and political figures around the world have legitimized this behaviour. Back in 2015, when Donald Trump had just launched his campaign for president, he said of Senator John McCain: "He's a war hero because he was captured. I like people who weren't captured." It was a hideously offensive jest about a veteran who had endured unspeakable torture for over five years in a North Vietnamese prisoner-of-war camp. Though many rushed to condemn Trump for this unsavoury joke, it ended up raising his polling numbers.

Ruining the reputation of Others happens across all types and sizes of Cones. You will find these dirty tricks played within professional and academic communities, businesses, tribes, virtual groups, and families. On the smallest scale, from the early stages of the relationship, a manipulative, abusive partner will start with brief statements and questions that plant seeds of doubt about their victim's close friends and family members. They will then progress to detailed stories of indiscretions that were allegedly performed by those malignant Others, strongly advising their victim to stay away from their friends and family.

While discrediting doesn't sound like a big deal, many people all throughout history have lost their reputations, status, families, social affiliations, possessions, and sometimes their lives based on such allegedly harmless personal attacks. Discrediting tactics can be the whip that keeps everyone where Cone Masters want them, or merely the opening shot that builds a distrusting foundation toward much stronger measures of divide-and-conquer.

Bullying

When Cone Masters are ready to up their othering game, they move from gossip and gaslighting to public ridicule, harassment, and intentional defamation. Ridicule rides on Subjects' fear of being associated with those who will shame them by association. It also plays on their desire for superiority over Others. Cone Masters bully those they wish to other by spreading lies and half-truths. They will infuse key events with false facts or completely fabricate stories that will drag the Others through the mud. Then they will tell and retell those to their Subjects. Their narratives will imply something shameful, immoral, dangerous, or illegal. Cone Masters may share inciting stories as seemingly harmless gossip, knowing it will spread like wildfire and quickly transform into "hard facts."

But gossip will only go so far. Drama will do a much better job because drama sells. The only way a good propaganda machine can succeed is if people get hooked on the turmoil the Cone Builders manufacture. Well-staged drama generously steeped in outrageous accusations has the power to sway the attitudes of Cone Subjects and divide them from the targeted Others. Cone Builders often manufacture outrage through loud and theatrical displays, both in person and through the media.

The way media works, the outrageous lies will find their way to the front page or in a big, viral headline, whereas the denial or the legal defamation loss will be a short paragraph buried on page 21 or completely suppressed if the Cone Master owns the media outlets. Instigators know that a stone one idiot casts into a well will not be salvaged by a hundred wise men. Even in extreme cases where Cone Masters end up paying for defamation in the form of fines, public statements, or loss of their formal role, the damage has been done. Their believers will accuse the Others of lying and conspiring, or blame "the system" for siding and conspiring with the Others. At that point, all the puppeteer has to do is ride back up on their Subjects' thermal.

One of the easiest ways to bully Others is coining degrading terms and catchphrases. On a small scale, ostracized family members will be branded as the black sheep, and outgroup members of a social clique will be tagged as the freaks and weirdos. On a larger scale, right-wing politicians will ridicule left-wing members as the snowflakes and bleeding hearts, while left-wing politicians will ridicule right-wing members as brainless rednecks. Colonizers will brand indigenous people as "primitive savages," abusers will call their victims "the psychos," and Cone Masters will brand whistleblowers and truth-tellers as "national traitors."

A favourite demeaning label adopted by Cone Masters in the last four or five decades is "conspiracy theorist." This term alludes to people who fabricate and believe in ridiculous conspiracies about such things as a flat Earth, a fake landing on the moon, or an extant Elvis. It is true that many of the conspiracy theories out there are downright ridiculous. Many are conceived out of our Need to explain situations we feel strongly about and events we can't understand. The problem is the blend of conspiracy theories that range from the painfully true to the utterly absurd. So long as there are nut cases out there that invent unfounded conspiracy theories, everyone who opposes the Cone can be tarnished as the same kind of idiot. In one of the more incisive caricatures on this subject by cartoonist Peter John Herron, a sheep tells its fellow sheep in the corral, "I'm telling you! The guy and the dog are working together!" To which the other sheep respond, "Oh come on George, you and your conspiracy theories."

Both ancient and modern history prove that many "conspiracy theorists" are not tinfoil wearing nuts, as Cone Masters would have us believe; they are level-headed people and experts who research a subject in depth and use their intellectual acumen and integrity to form an educated opinion. Or what some call "conspiracy factualists." Their only fault is refusing to mindlessly believe in "the party line." When they get too close to the ugly truth, Cone Masters rush to brand them as conspiracy theorists, lump them with the flat-Earthers, and portray them as raving lunatics. Ironically, Cone Builders develop their own conspiracy theories to besmirch their intended Others. These can be limited in scope, akin to a series of lies, such as blaming someone for saying or doing something they haven't said or done, but they can also be full-blown tales with back stories, forged documents, and false experts and witnesses. In the age of social media, AI, and deepfakes, spinning disinformation and damning conspiracy theories became almost too easy and too tempting.

Some forms of discrediting and bullying involve the use of so-called "objective outsiders" who lend credibility to othering a person or a group. These "objective outsiders" must be highly regarded by the Cone Subjects. They are portrayed as being unrelated to the Solution or its leaders and, therefore, completely impartial. Depending on the Solution, Cone Masters will use influential figures such as tribe and community elders, political figures, war heroes, scientists, doctors, social media influencers, journalists, and celebrities. These influential figures will act as "objective opinion holders" on the Dogma, reinforcing the Cone Master's othering attempts.

Some of them may truly believe they are objective while being fed lies and propaganda by the Cone Master. During the Cold War era, these misguided influencers were branded as "useful idiots." This referred to influential individuals in the West who bought into the Soviet Union's communist propaganda and became firm proponents of an oppressive regime. Other so-called "objective outsiders" will only appear to be objective while knowingly serving or being controlled by the Cone. Many for-profit companies use experts to provide what looks like an independent opinion about their products, while being secretly well rewarded for their endorsements.

Subject radicalization is another tactic that feeds into bullying. In his article, "How do we take our societies back from the lunatics, fanatics, and morons?" (3), Umair Haque poignantly describes the contagious lies

Cone Masters spread to radicalize normal, friendly people. He writes on the radicalization of school boards: "… these moms, who used to probably be pretty normal people, underwent a careful and deliberate process of radicalization by this shadowy group, Moms for Liberty, and if that's not already surreal enough, in it, they were taught to… hector… harass… intimidate… threaten… abuse… their fellow parents, teachers, principals, even kids." Following this planned radicalization by a right-wing group, school board meetings have become a battleground in which these inflamed members would silence others by shouting and spewing hate, bigotry, and prejudice. Their persistent bullying led to banning books and essential classes such as family planning and sexuality, and censoring history curriculum. What starts with pesky bullying can quickly become the grassroots of an authoritarian Cone.

One would think that Cone Masters will hesitate to use bullying, easily disprovable lies, and character assassination out of fear of public backlash or a lawsuit. The problem is that they excel at defending themselves from the consequences of their actions. Whoever disputes their false stories will be assured by the Cone Master with great confidence that they were originally misinformed or that they are remembering it incorrectly. Those who insist on the truth will be ignored or get the silent treatment. If that isn't enough, out comes the ad-hominem weapon—leading a personal attack against their accusers. The Cone Master will claim their attackers are trying to destroy them with their lies to divert the focus from themselves and their own lies.

When push comes to shove, Cone Master double down by claiming they were misquoted, misunderstood, or taken out of context. Malicious postings on social media or false reports in mainstream media allow Cone Masters a measure of deniability by stating their words were altered, forged, or delivered by others who don't represent them. Some will seek a hidden deal to cover up their lies. Others will embrace their actions as

Rebels and *Saviours* who "speak the hard truth others aren't willing to speak."

Dehumanizing and objectifying

If you grew up in a democratic, equality driven society, you may believe that all people deserve to have at least certain basic human rights that mustn't be violated. At the very least, you know that people should not be robbed, raped, tortured, enslaved, or murdered. These basic humanitarian beliefs come with a stipulation: "So long as they are human." When a Cone Builder equates an individual or a group of people to something sub-human—an object, a cockroach, a rat, a disease—they can not only separate Us from Them, but also justify every kind of mistreatment and even violence against the "non-humans." Once we start believing that a person or a group of people are less than human, we can switch off our moral code, and console ourselves with the thought that it's okay to break an object, crush a cockroach, poison a rat, or eliminate a disease.

Objectifying humans is one common method Cone Masters use to erase our morality. When certain groups are consistently portrayed as objects that have no thoughts, feelings, and voice, we start thinking of them as such. Once a person has become an object to us, we stop seeing harmful attitudes and behaviours toward them as being bad or immoral. After all, an object cannot be offended, it feels no pain, and it is disposable. Objectification can be achieved by focusing on a person's physical attributes while completely ignoring their personality, skills, or inner qualities. Being reduced to an object means that this person is nothing more than their external features. Women are frequently objectified in media and advertising by being reduced to sexualized decorations. Advertisements that use women's bodies to sell products depict women in passive or submissive poses that reinforce traditional perceptions of woman as objects to use and possess.

We have all seen images of sexy women in skimpy bikinis sprawled over posh cars and decorating yachts. A close-up of luscious lips hungrily sucking on the product of the day. A restaurant chain built on the premise of big-busted waitresses. Music videos where half-naked women are shown to gladly offer their bodies to abusive assholes who sing about their fuckable bodies and refer to them as bitches and hoes, because objects don't deserve to be called by name. Once Cone Masters manage to turn women into objects, men will no longer be compelled to respect, seek consent, or feel empathy towards them any more they would for a chair.

Women are not the only group that falls prey to objectifying Cones. Racial and ethnic minorities often face objectification where they are racialized, exoticized, or reduced to their ethnicity, while all but erasing their individuality. Queer individuals are being objectified and stereotyped based on their sexual orientation or gender identity. People with disabilities are often reduced to their disability. Individuals who are considered underweight or overweight may be treated as nothing more than their body size and cast into stereotypical roles. The same goes for elder individuals (especially in individualistic societies), indigenous peoples, religious and ethnic minorities, sex workers, refugees, and immigrants.

Another powerful dehumanizing tactic is developing disgust of the Other. Disgust is a vital part of our evolutionary defence system, driven by our fear of contamination and death. Beyond our disgust of basic pollutants such as rotten food or oozing wounds that might make us physically sick, we also experience emotional disgust influenced by social forces. When we feel disgusted by something or someone, our behavioural immune system gets activated (4). It is no accident we use the phrase "they make me sick" when we encounter individuals, groups, or situations that disgust us, though we bear no risk of physical infection. Our mental immune response triggers fear, anxiety, and disgust to avoid "exposure."

Human history is packed with Cone Masters who exploited our sense of disgust to control our primal emotions and turn us against "disgusting Others." In the United States, African Americans were systematically portrayed as sources of contamination, justifying physical segregation. In India, millions of people known as "untouchables" are still considered inherently filthy and disgusting, justifying every kind of discrimination and exclusion. During the peak of COVID-19, people expressed disgust with those who refused the vaccine. They treated them as a source of contagion, openly called for forced vaccination and incarceration, and even went as far as openly wishing them extermination via disease. Whatever the dehumanizing method, once it takes hold, we view those sub-human Others as undeserving of our moral consideration. Psychologically, it is easier to regard our enemy as sub-human because it helps us justify violence we wouldn't normally consider as moral or appropriate.

Demonizing and scapegoating

Author Emine Fougner posted on LinkedIn a story shared by a friend about a powerful lesson on trust within communities. When teaching the Salem Witch Trials,[27] a class teacher ran a game by which some students were secretly witches. He went around and whispered to each of them whether they were a witch or a normal person and then asked the class to build the largest group possible that doesn't include a witch. Any group found to include a witch would fail the game. As expected, the students went into a frenzy of interrogations. They quickly split into isolated groups of various sizes, turning away anyone they suspected to give off the slightest whiff of guilt. Once the groups were finalized, the teacher

---

[27] The Salem Witch Trials were a series of prosecutions of women accused of witchcraft in colonial Massachusetts (late seventeenth century). The trials were sparked by accusations of witchcraft based on personal disputes, societal tensions, and religious hysteria. Twenty people, mostly women, were executed for practicing witchcraft. These trials are a notorious example of mass hysteria, injustice, and the dangers of unchecked authority.

asked the assigned witches to raise their hands. No one did. The teacher explained to his confused students that, just like in Salem, no one in the class was a witch. However, everyone had gone along with it because a figure of authority determined the presence of witches and assigned a penalty for refusing the task and associating with witches. Within minutes into the game, trust was ruined, and students demonized and rejected their own friends.

One of many ugly examples for demonizing and scapegoating happened in the United States during the Vietnam War. In a 1994 interview, Richard Nixon's domestic policy advisor, John Ehrlichman, revealed that the "War on Drugs" in that period had little to do with preventing drug abuse and distribution. It begun as a racially motivated crusade to criminalize Blacks and the anti-war left. In Ehrlichman's words (5): "We knew we couldn't make it illegal to be either against the war or blacks, but by getting the public to associate the hippies with marijuana and blacks with heroin and then criminalizing them both heavily, we could disrupt those communities. We could arrest their leaders, raid their homes, break up their meetings, and vilify them night after night in the evening news. Did we know we were lying about the drugs? Of course we did."

Once you vilify and demonize your target victim, the road to injustice is paved. A study conducted in 2015 found a correlation between seeing people as evil and supporting harsher punishments for their crimes (6). People who believe in the existence of pure evil might not be looking for the context and the reasons someone had done something. They'll just say, "You know what? That person must have done something horrible because they are demons. We don't need evidence to know we must get rid of them." Calling someone evil is the most serious moral accusation we can make. If you believe a person is Satan, you won't bother seeking evidence of their crimes.

Cone Masters usually invest in building an "othering momentum" before going for full-on scapegoating and demonizing. Where there is already enough latent hatred, superstitions, and fear of the Others, they won't bother with building momentum. They will go straight for the jugular, generating flaming disgust and fear. What made the witch hunt so easy in seventeenth-century Salem was the pre-existing belief that witches existed, and that women harboured evil that could easily turn them into demons. The reason it was so easy for Hitler to demonize and scapegoat Jews for everything that went wrong in Germany, was the Germans' deeply rooted antisemitic Core Certainties. Building on decades, centuries, and sometimes millennia of hate and fear of "inferior races," "heretical religions," "sexual deviants," "savages," women, and a range of other vulnerable groups, makes it easy for Cone Masters to inflame their recruits' emotions against those Others. Historically demonized groups become easy targets for scapegoating that divert the Subjects' attention from the actual problems usually caused by their Cone Masters. Even when there is no such preexisting groundwork, people living in a state of great pain and fear will be highly suggestible to the idea that someone evil and inhumane is to blame for their condition.

Demonized Others will be blamed for everything broken, sick, and evil inside the Cone. The ones upholding "heretical religions" will be blamed for wars, famine, and natural disasters, which will justify holy wars. "Sexual deviants" will be blamed for corrupting our children and leading us into hell, which will require their persecution and elimination. Women in patriarchal societies will be blamed for being born sinners who bewitch men and bring disasters, and therefore deserving to be enslaved, beaten, and killed at will.

Whichever othering method Cone Builders use, their goal is to make you believe that everyone outside your in-group poses danger to you, and that anybody inside your in-group can be a potential traitor. Under these stressful conditions, your first loyalty will inevitably be to your Cone Master, like a child who grows in fear of the outside world will hang on to their abusive parent. That child will feel no remorse about excluding and even harming those infamous Others, because it will earn them praise and make them feel righteous.

When Cone Builders seek profit from harming or exploiting certain groups of people—such as needing enslaved folks for cheap labour, consumers to buy harmful products to make a profit, scapegoats to hide their crimes, or soldiers to kill for financial and political gains—they will feed their Subjects with fear and disgust with these Others. The more persistent the demonization and scapegoating campaign, the easier it becomes for Cone Subjects to justify moral exclusion and switch off their moral behaviour. Voltaire said it well: "Those who can make you believe absurdities can make you commit atrocities."

Managing the Others

Manipulating Cone Subjects to separate and persecute Others is only one part of the game. The other is finding ways to control or set up the Others in ways that will prove their "otherness." One of the easiest ways is by encouraging and manipulating the Others to willingly separate themselves from Cone Subjects. An abuser will share horror stories about their Subject (partner, employee, child) with their victim's friends, family, or colleagues. They will paint their Subject as mentally unstable, insufferable, or malevolent, gradually driving a wedge between them and the victim. Any attempt of the victim's friends and family members to counter the abuser's narrative will be met with denial and spectacular offence. Eventually, most if not all the victim's social networks will distance themselves from the alleged "malignant" victim. Once the manipulated group buys into this self-othering, the manipulative abuser will have every kind of evidence to show their victim how malignant these people really are.

Cone Masters can also encourage Others to develop a sense of superiority over Cone Subjects. They do it to make sure these Others no longer bother to empathize with Cone Subjects, thus othering themselves. They intentionally entice Others to publicly humiliate Cone Subjects as being flawed and inferior. Cone Masters will play on the Others' desire to feel exceptional, often branding them as the "aristocracy and intellectuals." Then they will turn to their Subjects with great outrage about those entitled aristocrats and intellectuals who deserve to be hated.

In other cases, Cone Masters will set up the Others for behaviours that justify everything bad said about them. One method is to dig holes and have the Others fall in, thus proving the Cone Masters' vicious narrative. Historically, European and Eastern European Jews were intentionally forbidden from working in any public occupation other than banking and moneylending to reinforce the narrative of Jews being greedy and exploitive. Women were intentionally locked out of education and were forced to play brainless and naïve, or risk being devalued by society. This reinforced the public narrative of women being inherently weak and stupid. Racist governing bodies blocked immigrants and minorities from employment and housing opportunities to prove they are lazy parasites. Exploitive employers implanted their own people into unions to incite violent episodes, justifying police action and criminalization of unions.

The problem with these insidious methods is not only that they work, but they have a way of proliferating and creating a domino effect. Using the social application of Newton's third law of motion,[28] Cone Builders amplify othering through mirroring forces: The more one side becomes extreme and hostile, the more the other side is doing the same in the opposite direction. This counter-radicalizing proves the Cone Master's divisive narrative on the malevolent Others. The more the left-wing

---

[28] Newton's third law of motion: for every action (force) in nature there is an equal and opposite reaction.

goes left, the more they "prove to be as dangerous as we thought they were, and even more so" to right-wing followers, who radicalize into far-right, and vice versa. The more vegans become militant about their cause, the more hateful staunch meat eaters become towards plant-based ideology. Finally, as Vladimir Lenin said, "The best way to control the opposition is to lead it ourselves." Once a Cone Master gains enough power and influence, they can step in and take over the Others, steering them in any direction that benefits them.

Most languages and cultures have at least one idiom along the lines of, "United we stand, divided we fall." These idioms speak to our fundamental need to belong and collaborate. Cone Masters know it all too well. They use this primal need against us by dividing-and-conquering. They build their Subject's inner-unity and loyalty and develop their ferocity against "Cone heretics" (Internal Traitors), and scapegoated outsiders (Others). They artfully create an illusion of belonging while separating and isolating us, and in so doing weaken and make us dependent on them.

CHAPTER 12:

Mind control by a thousand cuts

... where we discover how Cone Masters manage to control us by invading our minds and legitimizing our darkest desires.

ppressive Cones are not just distant spectres. They exist everywhere. In fact, we all take part in many of them, and they inform how we think and act as citizens, students, patients, co-workers, family members, and nearly every other area in our lives. Most of us would like to believe that we are free of mind prisons. That we lead our lives based on a reasoned analysis of information, a keen observation of our environments, and on moral decision-making. But as we've already seen, our brain works in many psychedelic, biased, emotional, and irrational ways we aren't even aware of. We decide mostly based on our Cones' brain-programming and then find creative ways to justify irrational and immoral decisions. Don't believe you're a Cone Subject? Try testing yourself through the following three-part scenario:

You had a busy morning and time got away from you. You are now on your way to work, rushing to get there on time. On route, you nearly stumble over one of the many unhoused people lining the sidewalk. One of them is sprawled next to his tattered bags. His eyes are shut tight, his body is curled, and he is moaning. Two blocks down the road you encounter a group of people protesting a government policy they claim to be discriminatory to minorities. The protest is guarded by the police, and while the callouts are heated, there are no signs of violence. Suddenly, one protester steps on what you recognize as your national flag and sets it on fire.

Once you finally reach your workplace, you come across a colleague that has recently been diagnosed with cancer. She approaches you all gleaming and tells you she is finally on her way to recovery. She had found an energy healer, and she's already feeling better. Then she pulls out a book that summarizes all the scientific evidence for this healing method. She tells you she made a thorough research on the subject and had stopped her chemotherapy and radiations to focus on the natural healing process.

Which of the three events will stop you in your tracks, annoy, or rattle you? Let's analyze them from a logical, objective, unbiased point of view, or as objective and unbiased as we are capable of.

Scenario 1: A fellow human being is in a dire situation. We all know unhoused people are much more vulnerable to disease, violence, and the elements. In this case, the man might be hurt and in need of immediate help. Logic would dictate that nine out of ten people who encounter this man should be outraged by his situation that robs him of his dignity, let alone basic human needs. They would also be deeply concerned with his condition and try to help. The remaining one out of ten who walks by without giving the man a second thought or a helping hand is probably an asshole.

Scenario 2: A group of people, who received a permit to hold the protest, as indicated by the orderly presence of the police, are actively participating in a peaceful demonstration. They are protesting a policy which, in their opinion, harms vulnerable people. Right or wrong, their intention is to create a more equitable and a better society. One protester is destroying a national symbol that is printed on a piece of cloth. This action doesn't endanger anyone. Logically, nine out of ten people should be supportive of a cause that improves society. They may feel uncomfortable with the flag burning, but that is the extent of it. After all, it is a piece of cloth. No one was threatened or harmed, and the deed was part of one's protected freedom of speech and expression. The remaining one out of the ten who will go into a fit of rage at the sight of the burning flag may have missed their breakfast or is dealing with their own, unrelated issues.

Scenario 3: While chemotherapy and radiation are commonly used for cancer treatment, it is a known scientific fact that not everyone will survive the disease even when they get the best prescribed medical treatment for their condition. Both radiation and most of the chemicals used nowadays for chemotherapy are carcinogenic (causing cancer). While they significantly reduce mortality rates of cancer patients, this method is far from perfect. Not only does it fail to save some of the patients, but it might also cause a future recurrence of cancer, not to mention the severe side effects of the treatment. This means that seeking alternative approaches that may have more positive outcomes through a less damaging process is completely logical, so long as sufficient evidence is produced. Nine out of ten logical people should conclude that, all things considered, there is solid reason to at least examine the efficacy of the alternative treatment. The one out of ten that will refuse to even consider the alternative is a poor critical thinker or is making money out of chemotherapy treatments and therefore follows a different (albeit an unethical) pathway.

Makes sense? Fortunately for Cone Masters, unbiased critical thinking is not a deciding factor for their Subjects. Reality shows that most people (at least in Western countries) react in the exact opposite without feeling bad about it. If asked, they will justify their decisions and behaviours using their Cone doctrines. Let's examine the three scenarios from the vantage point of a few common Cones.

In **Scenario 1**, most people living in capitalistic regimes, or abiding by low-trust, highly individualistic ideologies (no matter how rich or poor the country), will avoid or step over unhoused people without giving them a second thought. If you ask them why they ignored a helpless man dying on their street, some will openly state their disgust with the vermin that soils their city, and others will find an excuse (haven't seen them, wasn't sure they were in trouble, they wouldn't want me interfering in their business). This is not because they are heartless, immoral people by nature, but because their Cones have conditioned them into concepts of hyper-individualism, scarcity, meritocracy, and an eat-or-be-eaten world.

The basic premise of capitalistic meritocracy is "people get what they deserve." If you work hard, you get much, and if you're lazy, you get nothing. Hyper-individualism and low-trust Core Certainties claim that "I take care of myself. The rest aren't my business." The neoliberal capitalism Cone makes meritocracy and ultimate individualism seem logical and fair to their Subjects. Top profiteers use this highly effective narrative to ensure that the masses are enthusiastic about working hard for them. Living under this Cone, all those in favour of supporting the unhoused and vulnerable will be branded communists—a highly potent and punitive buzz word.

If you aren't convinced modern capitalism is a Cone, here is the gist of it: A handful of select individuals keep most of the assets to themselves and create an artificial shortage for everyone else. They buy their way into governance systems at all levels to ensure all policies and legislations support their goals. Then they systematically convince all Cone Subjects that only those who fight over the crumbs left for them deserve to get any. Their narrative asserts that those who are unable or unwilling to fight for the crumbs deserve nothing; not even to live. Whatever harm comes to them, they brought it on themselves, and it is no one's fault and no one's responsibility to help them. They are nothing but a parasitic burden on society. Possibly not even really human, if you think about it. Since it is a dog-eat-dog world, there is no shame in wanting to be the top dog, no matter how many of the weaker dogs get eaten in the process.

Zooming out of this Cone, you find that while the Subject "dogs" are busy squabbling and biting each other for the single bone left for them, our Cone Masters enjoy their prime seats at the dogfight arena. They have conditioned their dogs to ignore this social injustice and trained them to protect the owners at all costs. If you are living in one of these societies and you're doubtful of this description, feel this is a stupid conspiracy theory, or are completely outraged with it, you might be more indoctrinated than you think.

Scenario 2 relates to a different Cone that can be titled "governance system." Governance Cones can be of varied sizes, from an organized sports club to a country. The most common mind-controlling tactic in governance Cones is the cultivation of undying loyalty. In sports clubs, it will be expressed as a mad devotion to the team and all its symbols. In a country, it will be nationalism and patriotism. Our Cone Masters condition us into believing that our nationality goes much beyond group affiliation. That it is everything we are as human beings. The more nationalistic the society, the more our nationality is intertwined with our very identity. Anything that is said or done against our nation (or our football team) is a personal attack. Unlike nationality, which pertains to, "This is who I am," patriotism can be described as, "This is my undying loyalty to my Cone and everything I'm willing to do for it." Nationalism is the belief, while patriotism is the muscle that drives this belief into action. In the context of Cones, fans of a particular sports team regard their belonging with it as their nationality, and their willingness to defend and fight for it, their patriotism.

Both nationalism and patriotism are often represented by a flag or a shared insignia of some sort. Even though burning a flag is anyone's right in a free society (unless it is someone else's property), and it poses no physical threat to their surroundings, most people will still go into a fit of rage at the sight of their defiled flag. If you ask them to rationalize their reaction, they will speak heatedly about the sanctity of their nation, land, or sports team. If you ask them why they were more outraged with a piece of burning cloth than with the just cause of the protesters, they may tell you that anyone who burns their flag is a criminal and a traitor and therefore cannot possibly have a good cause in mind.

Scenario 3 touches on the Cone of Western medicine. As previously described, modern medicine is a system in which medical professionals treat symptoms and diseases using a range of physical means, such as drugs, radiation, or surgery. It is based on "man as a machine" model, focuses mostly on curing vs. preventing disease and on reducing symptoms vs. treating core Problems, and heavily relies on the pharmaceutical industry. Despite its great value and many strengths, like most Solutions, modern medicine isn't perfect. Nonetheless, mainstream healthcare systems ignore anything that isn't aligned with their Cone. Though these Systems profess evidence-based practice, both practitioners and policymakers actively ignore, ridicule, and censor "Cone-deviant" evidence.

Having grown up within the modern medicine Cone, most of us will be appalled with our colleague's decision to step out of the medical Dogma because a Cone has a way of placing locked doors in our minds with flashing "do not enter" signs. We learn to obey the sanctity of these locked doors because the modern medicine Cone conditioned us to believe there is a perfectly good reason for the existence of these locks. And so we keep walking past them, no questions asked. In fact, we don't even notice them. When anyone points out or questions these no-entry doors or tries to open one and examine the forbidden territory, we will scoff at their naïveté or stupidity, call them conspiracy theorists, or rage at their audacity. Either way, we won't bother looking through these doors. Even if people tell us they have seen new wonders and have solid evidence for good results, if they contradict the Cone's Core Certainties, we will stop listening to them. No matter how much scientific evidence this co-worker will introduce, most of us will consider her foolish and misguided.

In this three-part mini anthology, most people will choose to ignore a vulnerable man in dire situation without feeling remorse; feel outraged at the sight of a burning piece of cloth; and ignore the possibility of an alternative Solution for a deadly condition. This is how Dogma works.

This is the mighty power of Cone indoctrination. Like the electronic collar used for dogs that zap them whenever they try to step out of their territory, the boundaries of our Cones are lined with psychological and emotional electric fences we have learned not to approach lest we get zapped. It warps our logical thinking and our basic human morals in the same way a black hole bends light.

But what if you are that person who sees through these three Cones? What if you are the one who would stop and help the man on the street, who wouldn't fret about a burning flag but focus on the protesters' just cause, and who would encourage your colleague to try proven alternative healing pathways? Does that mean you aren't indoctrinated by Cones? You may be impervious to these particular Dogmas, but probably not to all Cones in existence.

You may be a critic of capitalism but a staunch believer in another economic model you will fiercely defend and refuse to question. The symbols of your nation may not mean much to you, but you may be a passionate supporter of the protesting group, and therefore get deeply offended if *their* symbols are defiled. You may be a great believer in alternative healing methods, to the point of completely denying the merits of modern medicine. You may be a great defender of our educational system, or the sanctity of monogamous marriage. Perhaps you are a devout religious person, or a strong-minded atheist. Will it surprise you to learn that all these examples are oppressive Cones? Much as we don't like to admit it, we are all indoctrinated by our parents, cultures, systems, and the many manipulators in our lives, at least to some extent.

Starting us young

Have you ever seen a pear inside a bottle of liqueur? If you haven't, you should check it out. It is truly a thing of wonder. A ripe, fully grown pear lays inside a narrow-necked bottle, immersed in a translucent alcoholic beverage. How on earth did it get in there? The secret to this logic-defying stunt is what I call "fruit indoctrination." Once the pear tree sheds its blossoms and budding pears take shape, the liquor producer threads the branches with the tiny fruit into empty bottles and props them to ensure the bottles stay put. These baby pears grow inside the bottle until they have reached the desirable size. Once they have ripened, they are pruned off the tree, immersed in an alcoholic liqueur, and sealed with a cork.

If these pears were sentient beings—which they may be for all we know—how would they view the world? How would they perceive themselves and their role in life having grown up inside the bottle, closely watched, tended to, and guided by their Liquor Master? Though light and blurry visions of a different world may penetrate the glass, a smart Liquor Master will keep pointing out the perils awaiting on the outside. Hail, drought, hungry insects, grabby human hands. They will make sure the pear knows it has a much better life inside the sanctuary of its bottle. That it is, in fact, the best and the most natural way for a pear to grow. That only the finest pears on the tree are selected to grow in a bottle, as opposed to their defective tree mates that will fall off and rot on the ground. The Master will assure that each bottled pear has a noble role of enriching the liqueur with its divine sweetness. That the pear and the liqueur are one, and the Master exists merely to make the pear's life better and help it realize its potential.

All inconvenient information will be kept away from the pear, such as the fact this isn't the natural way to grow. The pear will never learn that those scary looking bees with their stings are there to pollinate and give life, not to harm. That the Liquor Master grows and protects them for their own profit, not for the pear's well-being. Or that the pear's true purpose has got nothing to do with a bottled alcoholic beverage, because when it rots on the ground it isn't a punishment but a new beginning—seeds giving life to new trees.

If a pear falls sick or cannot grow into a perfect shape inside the bottle, the Liquor Master will discard it without giving it a second thought. They will do it while demonstrating to all the other bottled pears what happens when one falls out of line and fails their mission in life. If these pears were sentient beings, they would be grateful for their wonderful lives. They would be loyal beyond measure to their Liquor Master. If fruit liberators came knocking at their bottles, the pears would be shocked and appalled. They would fight for their Master against the evil perpetrators. Any truth the fruit liberators would reveal to these pears would be perceived as lies and enemy propaganda, no matter how strong the evidence. The very few open-minded and rebellious pears who side with fruit liberators, will be deemed traitors by their fellow bottled pears.

In generations to come, these pear trees will yearn for the Liquor Master to come and make them whole and worthy. They will pride themselves with the number of bottles tied to their branches and look with envy at trees that made better numbers. They will be ashamed of their progeny that had failed to be selected for bottling or those that had failed to grow properly inside a bottle. If they can, they will spread the word of the wonders of bottling to other pear trees in the grove and look down upon those who refuse to buy into this superior concept. Some may even seek ways to exterminate those unnatural, free-standing trees. And this, in a nutshell (or in a bottle), is how Cone Masters zombify their Subjects for the long haul. Once they have recruited their followers, up goes a well-oiled oppressive indoctrination system.

A fundamentalist Islamic organization - also known as ISIS, ISIL, or Daesh, launched their "Caliphate" project in Syria and Iraq around 2014, aiming to topple existing regimes in favour of a radical, Islamic State. One of their major weapons of control, beyond genocide, was recruiting, indoctrinating, and operationalizing children as their loyal Subjects and soldiers. They created a collateral indoctrination strategy, combining formal and informal, direct and indirect, cooperative and coercive, and individual and systematic "pathways of influence" (1). ISIS kidnapped thousands of children from orphanages, schools, and family homes, often murdering their parents in front of them. They were told their old life was gone, and that they now belonged with a new and superior family. ISIS desensitized these children to violence by normalizing brutality, violence, and death. They were brought to watch public stonings, amputations, and beheadings to inflame their disgust with sinners and their fear of betraying the cause. Through this brutal emotional "reprogramming" children grew to accept violence as part of life, and started conducting violence themselves as soldiers, torturers, and executioners.

On a systemic level, ISIS exploited Syria's low rates of literacy and school attendance, taking over and converting the schooling system into recruitment centres. By limiting the curriculum to their radical ideology and isolating children and youth from any outside influences and information, they created an ideological echo chamber. Following a colossal death toll of civilians, droves of newly orphaned children who sought parental figures became easy targets. In a typical Cone move of divide-while-uniting, ISIS played on these children's desire to belong with the privileged in-group. They encouraged fierce peer pressure, and reinforced the sense of belonging with uniforms, weapons, and gifts. The "cubs" (boys) who used to trust their fathers and community leaders, were manipulated to idolize hypermasculine fighters who boasted wealth, status, and a promise for adventure and revenge. These children grew into devout supporters and loyal ISIS fighters, even though this was the organization that had killed their parents. Years down the road, most of them are still willing to die for their Cone Masters.

Some Cones were erected more recently, but most of our big Cones were formed before our lifetime. We were born into them and learned to accept them as the normal and the one true reality just like the bottled pears and the new generations of ISIS child soldiers. The people who raised us have presented this reality to us in a myriad of ways. We learned from our indoctrinated family and community, our Cone-engineered education systems, our power-driven religious organizations, our repurposed myths, co-opted media, and colonized legal framework. We may think we learn much by observation but, in actuality, like the bottled pears and cult children, we are taught what to observe and what to ignore; how to interpret what we observe; and how to treat those whose observations are different from ours.

Controlling information

Our personal narratives create our inner realities. The stories we are told from childhood and those we tell ourselves about who we are and about our world, end up guiding our perspectives, sense of morality, and actions. Most of us aren't even aware of how these narratives control us. The sum of our internalized stories becomes our indisputable reality, and the only thing we recognize as truth. This imaginary inner truth makes us ignore the many nuances and complexities around us. Our narratives are both our allies and our enemies. On the one hand, they help us understand ourselves and others, and help us feel secure in our beliefs. On the other hand, our version of reality can become so rigid and detached from facts and events that contradict our narrative that instead of serving, it imprisons us. Not only do we hold tight to our narratives, but we also reduce them into an executive summary or a few bullet points to simplify this complex world. We distill them into our indisputable Core Certainties. That's why Cone Masters invest time and effort in rewriting our narratives to fit their Cones.

Once they got inside our heads, they reinforce their control with steel plates through ongoing mental manipulation that results in complete indoctrination. The more consistent and repetitive the narrative they create for us, the more we will internalize it and never let go. For that to happen, Cone Masters must control our information sources. This allows them to be constantly seen, heard, and revered. It helps them to continuously deliver their Cone propaganda and keep us in a stressed emotional state that ensures our loyalty and obedience. Lastly, it allows them to feed and control our narratives while eliminating all other types of inconvenient or contradictory information. Effective Cone Masters use multi-tiered strategies. They can combine influential branding, rewrite our existing narratives, control the media, manipulate information, distract, silence, falsify data or intentionally misinterpret it, and rewrite our history.

Controlling the media

One of my earliest media-related memories was the daily news broadcasted in black and white on my grandparents' tiny TV set. It took place in Ukraine (then part of the USSR) in the late 1960s. Every evening, a well-groomed newscaster provided a detailed report on the great achievements of the Soviet Union, particularly in relation to "the plan." The said plan referred to the government's production quota in different industries that was supposed to ensure the people got everything they needed to live comfortably. Every evening, the news broadcasted combine harvesters rolling through vast fields of wheat, driven by gleeful, chubby farmers. The newscaster would then proudly announce, "The plan has been fulfilled and even surpassed our targets."

The daily news broadcast was a running joke in my family—*oh look, we've surpassed the targets again*. You didn't even have to be an adult to recognize the lie. All you had to do was look outside at the endless lineups at stores that were usually empty of the most basic necessities. And yet you never saw these lineups, the starving farmers, or the failed production systems on the news. Not because reporters were obtuse or corrupt, but because the Cone Masters in that tyrannical regime owned and controlled all media. Even the most conscientious reporters were forced to act as the loyal mouthpieces of the communist party. Those who refused were silenced, incarcerated, and sent off for an indefinite vacation in a Siberian gulag.

The Soviet propaganda wasn't limited to the news on TV. It was the print newspaper (ironically called Pravda, i.e., "truth"). It was the film industry that produced films smothered with communist messaging and national pride, boldly rewriting historical events to fit the narrative. Theatre plays, play productions in schools, textbooks, and even children's books were either written by the communist party or plagiarized from other sources with a slant. I remember reading *Pinocchio*. The story was very explicit on the horrors of exploitive, heartless capitalism. At the end, Pinocchio broke free from the claws of capitalists because he stopped lying—like a good communist child should. When he turned into a real boy, he wasn't just any boy. He became a proud, rosy-cheeked communist pioneer—insignia, pledge, salute, and all, eerily resembling images of the Hitler Youth.

Most of us like to believe that this cynical use of media for propaganda is limited to dictatorships such as the former Soviet Union or today's China or North Korea. But the truth is, propaganda exists all around us. It is infused into our media and art sources, only slightly more subtly than in dictatorships. We are so deeply immersed in fabricated fantasy worlds and disinformation campaigns that we accept them as "mostly true with occasional flukes."

Contrary to the olden days when information on recent events came to us from our in-groups, modern mass and social media have become the largest windows to our reality. Media is a vehicle that brings the whole world into our homes. In their book, *Manufacturing Consent* (2), Edward Herman and Noam Chomsky explain that, in the past, our news and entertainment outlets were owned by small, local businesses that had little contact with each other. Most of them focused on their communities and held no loyalties to their governments. Small, independent media outlets still exist, but the major ones—twenty-four-hour news stations, newspapers, publishing houses, film industries, internet utilities, and even video game companies—are almost all owned by six conglomerates (3).

Controlling the media is one of the most effective ways to infuse our lives with both systemic and systematic propaganda. In our world of concentrated power and wealth in the hands of the few, media is tightly controlled to faithfully serve mega-Cone Masters. It's easily detectable when it happens in dictatorships, at least from the outside. It is also very obvious in smaller, isolated communities, such as enclosed cults and religious groups where the only information available to Subjects is the one approved by their Cone Masters. It is much harder to recognize similar propaganda systems in more open and democratic societies where we live under the assumption of full transparency and systemic integrity. Without us being aware of it, they manipulate information before it reaches us, and eliminate inconvenient truths. Herman and Chomsky claim this illusion of propaganda-free media is especially powerful when there is free competition among media outlets, and where mass media periodically expose corporate and government corruption. Mass media in democratic countries aggressively portray themselves as the guard dogs of democracy, the agents of free speech, and the impartial champions of their community's best interest. This narrative is so powerful that it is nearly impossible for us to see beyond the manipulation.

Cone-driven propaganda thrives on the hidden inequality of wealth and power. Even in democratic countries, the ultra-wealthy and their loyal, corporate-funded politicians have the power to filter out information based on the premise it must be "fit to print." On a smaller scale, a local governing body, faith group, or family patriarch may ban access to certain books, movies, plays, and exhibitions. They do it under the pretext of "protecting our children, our souls, and the public," though the true motive is protecting themselves and their narratives from competing ideas.

Until the early 2000s, "media" referred to the big information outlets. The emergence of social media upped the information game by creating an unprecedented highway of communication and information exchange. In the early days of social media, platforms like MySpace and early versions of Facebook and YouTube provided individuals with spaces to express themselves freely. With minimal content moderation, they allowed users to share their thoughts, opinions, and creative content without significant interference. Gradually, moderation phased in, mostly focusing on illegal activities and explicit content. With the widespread adoption of social media, its impact on society became increasingly significant. It finally gave a voice to those who were previously marginalized and suppressed in the mainstream media. But as with every good Solution we develop, it has since been corrupted by commercial and political self-serving interests.

Though social media platforms are offered for free use, as the saying goes, there really is no free lunch. Since commercial ads are a primary source of revenue for social media platforms, it is no longer the free speech and communication that drives their owners, but the desire for profits and power. These platforms can only achieve it by satisfying their paying sponsors at our expense. They do it by gathering vast amounts of user data, including our demographics, interests, and online behaviour, and share it with their paying clients. These profiteers then use our data to target each of us with personalized ads and content. This unauthorized invasion of our privacy has reached the dystopian levels described in George Orwell's book *1984*, in which "the big brother" is always watching and listening. In our case, all our interactions on social media and our smart devices can and are being used against us by a range of Cone Masters. Each of our electronic gadgets has become our personal informer.

Commercial sponsors not only shape our user experience to incorporate their ads, but also influence the algorithm that determines the types of content each of us will encounter. These personalized algorithms that were built without us having a say on the matter create echo chambers, in effect limiting the information we access to more of the same. The more we are exposed to information we agree with, the more we end up believing in it (confirmation bias) and the less we know or believe in the existence of alternatives and contradicting facts and opinions.

This commercial manipulation of social media may be a menace, but it is not nearly as impactful as the intrusive involvement of governments and people of power. It all started with hate groups disseminating misinformation, cyberbullying, hate speech, and other harmful content. Once these negative aspects of social media gained enough attention, governments and users demanded that the platforms address these issues. Following legislation on the matter, platforms began implementing content moderation policies and guidelines to maintain a safer online environment. This seemingly well-intended legislation was the beginning of a slippery slope.

Social media platforms may reside on virtual clouds, but these "clouds" don't hover in our atmosphere. They are server farms that are physically stored in countries. Many governments around the world have passed laws requiring social media platforms to store user data locally. It allows them to demand access to our private information or force these platforms to comply with specific content restrictions. These measures allow governments to control the operations of social media platforms within their jurisdiction, while closely monitoring their residents. Some governments engage in information-manipulation campaigns by spreading propaganda and misinformation through social media platforms.

They may employ trolls, bots,[29] or state-sponsored actors[30] to shape public opinion, suppress resistance, or influence elections. At the same time, they have the power to shut down free voices that oppose their agendas, and censor information to prevent their users from accessing it on social media.

Since the mid-2010s, we have seen one example after another of the power of social media and its backstage controllers. These platforms allowed political groups around the world to use micro-targeting techniques for election campaigns and for ideological movements such as Brexit. This enabled political candidates and lobbyists to tailor specific messages to different demographics, regions, or even individuals based on their online behaviour and interests. This personalized messaging reinforced people's existing beliefs, amplified certain issues beyond realistic proportions, and distributed false or manipulated information. These well-orchestrated social media campaigns had managed to sway undecided voters to elect dubious candidates and vote for economically unsound and even harmful policies.

Another example of staggering proportions was the role both mainstream and social media played in swaying people's beliefs and opinions throughout the COVID-19 pandemic from the early 2020s. Most governments implemented rigorous censorship at the level of worldwide dictatorship to silence any personal or professional information that could have even remotely countered their formal directives.

This dystopian brave new world of media is truly the wet dream of every Cone Master—having people believe they are free to learn about

---

[29] Bots are automated accounts that can amplify certain messages or trends while appearing as "real users." Trolls are real users that intentionally bully, provoke, and disrupt discussions. These two tactics can create a distorted perception of public sentiment and shape the online discourse in favor of particular viewpoints.

[30] Actors in this context are people who intentionally exaggerate a situation or an opinion to sway people toward a particular agenda of their Cone Masters.

the world and openly communicate their ideas and opinions, while being quietly bottled inside controlled and sterile echo chambers created for them by commercial and political Cone Masters. Using mainstream and social media for propaganda isn't limited to embedding Cone messages in our minds and hiding from us inconvenient truths. It is as much about diffusing and exhausting our ability to think critically. When we are being fed fully cooked ideas supported by altered data and selective "experts," most of us will eventually give up on researching facts or forming our own opinions.

Lies, damn lies, and statistics[31]

Cone Builders and Cone Masters lie. They must, because that's how manipulation works. You cannot bend people to your will, have them commit to useless or harmful Solutions, and remain unquestioningly loyal unless you keep their minds imprisoned. And you cannot imprison minds by telling truths and allowing free inquiry. Lies are Cone Builders' tools of the trade, and they come in different shapes and sizes. Some are more daring than others, spewing blatant, often laughable fabrications. Others use more elusive deception, easily passing as undeniable truths. One way to manipulate information and spin lies is by altering data to serve the Cone's agenda. Profiteers who can't find or manipulate existing information to support their Solution will pull the data out of their… let's go with hat.

One of many such examples is Reebok's campaign in 2009 of their EasyTone walking shoes. Their ads were everywhere—newspapers, magazines, websites, Facebook, Twitter (now X), YouTube and TV. They claimed that the shoe worked a person's hamstrings and calves 11 percent harder and could tone a person's butt up to 28 percent more than other

---

[31] This title was respectfully borrowed from Mark Twain who said, "There are three kinds of lies: lies, damned lies, and statistics."

sneakers. Basically, all you had to do to sculpt your figure was to walk in their sneakers. These shoes were supposed to provide a Solution to the Problem of being overweight (or insufficiently toned), and address the Need to comply with beauty standards. Consumers had every reason to believe that such a big, trustworthy company would abide by the laws on truth in advertisement (a Core Certainty related to "reputable" sources of information). The very specific numbers gave the air of meticulously conducted research. Except there was no research, and the numbers were completely fabricated. Reebok ended up paying $25 million USD in fines for this intentional deceit—a risk many Cone Masters take, with the hopes of never being caught in the lie.

Brazen liars can get away with it when they address particularly vulnerable Subjects and recruits. With the resilient ones, more cautious approaches usually work better. That's where half-truths and intentionally faulty uses of statistics come into the picture. Statistics is an incredibly effective tool when used correctly. It helps us make well-informed decisions, both on the personal and the public level. Governments, organizations, businesses, industries, social movements, scientific, educational, and medical institutions all collect data and analyze it. Statistical data helps them track progress, measure performance, identify and analyze problems and possible solutions, prioritize budgets, and come up with policies. None of these bodies could function effectively without statistical data.

Alas, like every other useful tool, statistics can be abused to provide misleading results. Averages, relationships between different factors and variables, trends, and graphs can be easily miscalculated, misrepresented, and misinterpreted. Research base assumptions can be biased. The study design can be faulty. Data collection and interpretation of results can be flawed or biased. And if that isn't enough, published conclusions and recommendations can be warped, corrupted, or censored.

Censoring and silencing

Part of good parenting is being careful with the kinds of knowledge and information to which you expose your child. Too little and too slow, and we might stunt the child's emotional and intellectual development. Too much and too soon, and the child might develop anxiety, depression, and lack of empathy. Raising children requires parents to withhold certain types of harmful, mature, and complex subjects, and make sure their kids can't access those on their own. As the children grow, so must their exposure to the world and everything in it, so long as it's done in the right way and with the right supports. Once a child grows into an adult, withholding information is no longer protective; it becomes a tool of control and oppression. Denying people of certain forms of information may sound harmless. There are even phrases in the English language that assert, "What you don't know won't hurt you," and, "Ignorance is bliss." Despite the witty idioms, nothing can be farther from the truth, especially when dealing with manipulators and profiteers. Our ignorance is only bliss to our Cone Masters.

While cautious information sharing with children has its merits, silencing is a whole other category of wrong. There is no stage in our lives—no matter how young or powerless—when silencing is the right thing to do. Most parents teach children what they believe are "rights and wrongs," and therefore what is allowed and when it is "okay to say something." However, instilling thoughtful and inclusive communication is worlds apart from silencing. Forbidding people at any age from expressing thoughts, questions, and emotions unless they are parent- or authority-approved is the mark of authoritarian, dogmatic families, cultures, and all other social constructs. A Cone isn't only defined by who has the freedom to speak, but also by who has the power to silence.

Withholding information and silencing those who wish to share it result in ignorance. This form of ignorance isn't simply a lack of knowledge, information, or experience. Cone-induced ignorance is the lack of specific types of knowledge that might make us question or doubt the Cone and its Masters. It is the lack of truthful information that would allow us to think for ourselves and make our own decisions. It is the lack of exposure to unfiltered reality that will give us clarity beyond the Cone's hidden agendas. It is the lack of awareness of anything beyond the boundaries of a Cone that is meant to kill our interest in exploring and gaining deeper and broader insights.

Dr. Martin Kulldorff is a renowned epidemiologist, biostatistician, and an expert on infectious disease outbreaks who has helped the CDC and FDA develop their post-market vaccine safety systems. When COVID-19 first broke into the news, very little was known about it. But from early 2020, everyone who had a working understanding of virology and epidemiology already knew the virus would eventually spread across the globe, and that it would be futile to try to suppress it with lockdowns. It was also clear that lockdowns would have a colossally harmful effect on education, child development, public health, cancer treatment, cardiovascular disease, and mental health, as well as on the elderly, the middle class, the working class, and those living in poverty around the world for decades to come.

Under heavy international criticism, Sweden kept its schools and daycares open for its 1.8 million children aged one to fifteen based on scientific evidence that clearly showed a stark difference in COVID mortality risk between the young and the old. Children faced a minuscule risk from COVID compared to adults. The Swedish government did what any rational government would do in lieu of this evidence, with the thought that interrupting their children's education would disadvantage them for life, especially those whose families could not homeschool or afford private schools, pod schools, and tutors. Sweden ended up with zero COVID deaths in the age one-to-fifteen group, while teachers had the same mortality averages as those in other professions. The Swedish

Public Health Agency published these findings in a formal public report (4).

Following the massive and successful Swedish experiment, Kulldorff tried to publish an article on the subject in American media, but despite being a distinguished Harvard professor, was repeatedly declined. His attempts to disseminate it on Twitter (now X) put him on the platform's Trends Blacklist. Eventually, he wrote his article in Spanish, and CNN–Español ran it. CNN–English was not interested. Kulldorff was not the only one in the scientific community who tried to cry "the emperor is naked." There were hundreds of highly reputable scientists who were silenced by the System. Study after study and a mass of anecdotal evidence showed the harm done by the forced lockdowns. And yet, against every scientific understanding on the subject, schools remained closed with the broad support of lead academics who were either silenced or refused to defy "the party line."

Being a freedom fighter at heart, Kulldorff was not about to back down. Together with Sunetra Gupta of Oxford and Jay Bhattacharya of Stanford, he wrote the "Great Barrington Declaration" arguing for age-based focused protection instead of universal lockdowns, with specific suggestions for how better to protect the elderly, while letting children and young adults live close to normal lives. They clarified that despite any governmental claims, no scientific consensus existed for school closures and many other lockdown measures.

Since it was much more difficult to silence and ignore a report written by three senior infectious-disease epidemiologists from three leading universities, the attacks intensified. It even grew slanderous, per Cone best practices. The authors were called "fringe epidemiologists" who deserved a "devastating published takedown." A prominent Harvard epidemiologist publicly called the declaration "an extreme fringe view," equating it with exorcism to expel demons. Other scholars accused Kulldorff of "trolling" and having "idiosyncratic politics," falsely accusing him of being enticed with Koch money and cultivated by right-wing think tanks. Others at Harvard worried about his "potentially dangerous position," while "grappling with the protections offered by academic freedom." Not everyone was against him. Kulldorff received much support, though most happened behind the scenes from scientists unwilling to speak publicly.

Despite the efforts of powerful scientists, politicians, and the media to denounce the "Great Barrington Declaration," it gathered almost a million signatures, including tens of thousands from scientists and healthcare professionals. Nonetheless, schools remained closed for two whole years because mega-Cones have the power to silence and disregard their Subjects' Needs and wants. As predicted, COVID closures led to startling learning loss, especially among lower- and middle-class children, an effect not seen in Sweden. Beyond academic damage, 80 percent of US public schools reported "stunted behavioral and socioemotional development" among students, 70 percent reported increases in students seeking mental health services, 56 percent saw an increase in "classroom disruptions from student misconduct," and "rowdiness outside of the classroom" (5).

Besides education, Sweden had the lowest overall mortality among major European countries during the pandemic, and less than half that of the United States. Beyond reducing COVID-related deaths, Sweden avoided collateral mortality from other causes that resulted from lockdowns. Despite being right on every front, Kulldorff was eventually fired by Harvard University for refusing to fall in line. He wrote: "I chose then to risk my life to help protect vulnerable people[32]. It was a comparatively

---

[32] In the 1980s, Dr. Kulldorff worked for a human rights organization, protecting local Guatemalan groups and citizens who spoke up against the killings and disappearances perpetrated by the military dictatorship. Throughout his time there, he was threatened by the military, two of his colleagues were stabbed, and a hand grenade was thrown into the house where he lived and worked. Yet he stayed to protect the Guatemalans.

easy choice to risk my academic career to do the same during the pandemic. While the situation was less dramatic and terrifying than the one that I faced in Guatemala, many more lives were ultimately at stake."

As in most other Cone tactics, there are two main types of censoring—the blatant and the covert. The blatant kind is common in openly tyrannical regimes, such as authoritarian families, cults, orthodox religious organizations, crime gangs, or dictatorships. These Cone Masters aren't trying to hide their absolute control of information and their silencing of subversive Subjects. On the contrary, it is part of their righteous power and authority. They justify open censorship with whatever reasoning is relevant to the Cone. It can be to make sure the dangerous Others don't get their Subjects, prevent them from falling into crime or save their souls, save them from becoming gay, or whatever else the Cone must lie about.

Unlike blatant silencing and censorship, the covert version is much more widespread and more pernicious because it's invisible. Cone Masters do it through quiet omission and undisclosed reporting bias,[33] and through discrediting and slander of dissenting voices. Money-making industries are notorious for withholding information to ensure profits on the backs of their consumers, and often at the account of our planet. But it isn't limited to the world of commerce. If we are attentive enough, we will find it in nearly every area of our lives. News reports can overrepresent one side of a debate or an issue while all but eliminating reports on the other side, in effect silencing them. Even our search engines and social

---

[33] Reporting bias is a distortion of the information presented to us. It is when we are given information that has been tampered with, or when it has been censored without our knowledge, therefore creating an illusion of "the complete and only truth." Reporting bias happens when researchers and/or media choose to report only certain data, even though they know other, contradictory data exists, yet they choose to suppress it to secure their narrative (or their jobs).

media platforms actively and covertly silence voices that inconvenience their owners, or the mega-Cones that control them.

In their book, *Google Leaks*, Zach Vorhies and Kent Heckenlively (6) provide a complete account of the many ways Google, YouTube, Facebook, and (then) Twitter silenced dissenting voices by rigging their search algorithms, placing individuals and organizations on undisclosed blacklists, and using biased "fact checkers" to make them disappear from the public eye. On the flip side, they intentionally boost the voices they are interested in. Vorhies and Heckenlively write: "Modern technology has given the tyrants of today the power undreamed of by the ancients. No longer would rulers have to deal with uncomfortable narratives. Those stories would simply not exist, or be exceedingly difficult to find. People would believe they were seeking out independent information, only to be fed the stories approved by Google."

Silencing and reporting bias extend into our educational systems. Our history books are written by the victors and those in power. These books guide the curriculum, and therefore everything we know to be true about ourselves and our ancestors. They portray the groups in power as the righteous ones, while describing their past and present enemies and minorities as hateful and inferior. Those in power omit any past glories of their dehumanized minorities, any mentioning of the roles they played in shaping the world, or the crimes committed against them by the ruling class.

In recent years, there has been a great upheaval in the United States around critical race theory. Indigenous and black folk have suffered centuries of genocide, enslavement, and systemic discrimination by their white colonizers and enslavers, yet you will be hard pressed to find any of it represented truthfully or with any level of depth in American mainstream history books and curriculum. Though the term "critical race theory" sounds academic, it is quite simple. It is the basic expectation of historically discriminated and oppressed racial groups to have their stories and their part in history included in school curricula in a complete and unbiased way. Or simply put: "Stop censoring history and tell our children the whole truth already."

You would think this is a perfectly legitimate expectation in any democratic country, but as I previously mentioned, even regimes that claim to be democratic harbour powerful hidden Cones. The outraged opposers to the demand for truthful history books use arguments such as "this is a political left-wing plot to push their liberal agenda," "this will contribute to division instead of fostering unity," "it will perpetuate racial differences and create victim mindsets," "it will foster a negative view of American history and defile the heritage of our heroes," "it will shame and guilt white people," and even "truth and free speech are overrated." Oppressive Cones are never short on excuses for censorship and silencing.

The same goes for any achievements and contributions made by women throughout history, which are difficult to find in formal, educational materials. This form of censoring and silencing isn't limited to history books. It is reflected in the lack of representation of diverse populations in media, commercial ads, or children's literature. Anything related to people who don't look, sound, or act like those in power will be quietly and systematically taken out of the public's awareness. This will create a false reality where they don't exist, don't count, or worse—aren't really humans.

Censorship can be aimed at everyone, or it can be targeted. Denying "undeserving groups" of basic knowledge and information keeps them weakened and easily controlled, or easily Othered. Denying education and literacy, for example, creates vulnerability. When women, people of low income, slaves, or members of "the wrong religion" are denied basic literacy or told they don't need education, Cone Masters achieve a double win. Those who were denied education will be more easily controlled through fear and uncertainty and less informed of their rights. This vulnerability will confirm to their Cone Subjects the narrative about those Others being innately inferior, as compared to their own unrivalled superiority. Induced ignorance through censorship and silencing is a powerful tool of mass enslavement and one of the most effective Cone engines. It creates true believers that are willing to do everything "for the cause" and anything to "the inferior Others." And this, after all, is what Cone Builders aspire to achieve.

Cone Masters that use covert censorship do it to avoid being accused of deliberately withholding information. For example, they will make information available, but in formats that make it inaccessible to the public. They hide important information in the "small print." They make it publicly available but in hard-to-reach sites, or intentionally compose documents that are unintelligible for most readers. And they control media channels to make sure only Cone-approved information flows to their Subjects while pretending to be "free to all." Like in all other Cone aspects, the different message-controlling strategies intertwine and intersect. Rarely would a Cone Master use a single method to control their message. A shrewd combination of all the above will yield a much more powerful effect than a single tactic.

Unleashing our dark side

Are you a good person? Surely you are. Most of us desire to be good. This desire is so strong we often engage in self-enhancement bias, where we emphasize positive while downplaying negative aspects of ourselves. We try to engage in behaviours we believe are morally good based on our societal standards of morality. It makes us see ourselves as good people and demonstrates our goodness to others. When engaging in surveys or assessments, most of us will be tempted to respond in ways that present us favourably with our society (7). Like in everything else, there are exceptions. One such group includes the callous and coercive (in extreme cases, the sociopaths and psychopaths) who either don't give a damn about being good or consider it a weakness of inferior humans who deserve to be exploited. Another group are the people who have been indoctrinated into perpetual shame and guilt and will never feel worthy of being "truly good."

If most of us desire to be and be seen as good people, how can we possibly explain why people regularly do terrible things to themselves, others, and their one and only habitat? When you think "monster," you may envision a creepy, drooling, eye-bulging, teeth-exposing creature that lurks in dark alleys, spends its nights plotting your demise, and then lunges at you with an ominous moo-ha-ha. In real life, evil isn't perpetrated by epic villains from comic books. It is executed by normal, average people just like you and me. Though we may feel like good people who could never lose our humanity, the problem with darkness is that it isn't in the habit of jumping at us from its hiding place in the bushes. It creeps on us slowly and unnoticeably. It lures us by offering rational justifications for every atrocity, having us slowly lose compassion and empathy.

There isn't a single motivator that turns us into monsters faster than our desire to feel righteous and, by extension, superior to others. A plethora of manipulative tactics make us reach into our dark side and unleash thoughts and behaviours we wouldn't normally entertain or accept. Give the most normal people a cause they deem noble, tell them it is worth fighting for and that it makes them just and right, and you get to unlock the monster in most Cone Subjects. Merciless colonization, exploitation of entire populations, torture, enslaving, and genocide were done in the name of "the purity of our race," "civilizing savages," and even "freedom and equality." All allegedly signs of us being good people. Tell staunch believers to kill sinners in the name of their deity, and they will know in their heart of hearts it isn't simply justifiable, but indeed their holy duty. These inhumane acts aren't conducted by orcs from *The Lord of the Rings*, but by average folks turned by manipulative Cone Masters into raving, murderous, human beasts.

In recent years, we have uncovered ample evidence and witnessed stomach-churning testimonials on the horrors of residential schools for indigenous children in countries that were colonized by the British Empire. Funded by local governments around the world and operated by churches, their stated goal was, "To kill the Indian in the child" (8). Children as young as four years old were taken by force from their families and locked up in these schools. They were strictly forbidden from keeping ties with their families, speaking their native languages, or practicing their cultural ceremonies. They were systematically starved, neglected, beaten, tortured, sexually abused, denied medical care, and even murdered in the name of "civilizing."

Only four out of every ten children in these schools made it out alive. Those who died were buried in mass, unmarked graves, their death unbeknown to their parents. This cultural and physical genocide inflicted on children seems unthinkable now, but until less than thirty years ago, it was perceived as the right thing to do to "those savage Others." All these monstrous deeds were performed by perfectly normal people who were given power over Others with the reward of righteous indignation.

Weaponizing stress responses

Most of us don't turn into monsters with the flick of a switch. Every big atrocity starts with a series of little atrocities that slowly erode our basic morals. We start by accepting lies, ignoring bullying, and then beginning to play along with bullying. At first, we accept racism and misogyny, and then we start supporting radicals who spew hatred under the guise of free speech. We get accustomed to hateful, inciting catchphrases and start seeing them as the truth. Then comes the active involvement. Little atrocities open a gateway to the most horrific acts. It is a slippery slope where we lose our humanity, slowly but surely. Or as Father Dwight Longenecker said, "First we overlook evil. Then we permit evil. Then we legalize evil. Then we celebrate evil. Then we persecute those who still call it evil."

The same principle works on all levels. Take the garden-variety bully. No one follows them for their charming personality. While some bullies can be quite sophisticated, their true colours inevitably peek through when they abuse their victims. Most bullies don't even bother hiding their antisocial behaviour. The callous and coercive wear it with pride. What then, is the big appeal? The mark of a bully is spreading fear, be it on a playground, a workplace, or a crime organization. They create a threat—social, physical, or both—that forces us to choose sides. Do we side with the shark or with the sardines? A few who consider themselves immune or strong enough to contend with the shark will remain true to themselves. But there are many more sardines than dolphins out there. So what is a tiny fish to do once a shark comes into the picture? It will resort to one of the six classic trauma responses: fight, flight, freeze, collapse and submit, please and appease, or attach and cry for help.

Fighting a bully is certainly one of our choice responses, but let's be realistic; how many sardines have you seen fight a shark? Even if there are a few brave souls who decide to face the predator, there are often too few of them to make a dent. Some will not even live long enough to tell the tale. Others may become martyrs. They will be commemorated and worshiped by the other sardines, though usually in hiding, lest the shark finds out and takes its vengeance. Some of these brave sardines become cautionary tales. It is as true in the human context as it is at sea. People who fear the bully will not go head-to-head with them because, for most of us, the survival instinct trumps higher values.

The flight response will make us want to put as much distance as possible from our abuser. Though some sardines will be lucky enough to escape, in real life, escaping or distancing ourselves from bullies isn't always an option. It is especially difficult when the bully isn't a random passerby, but a member of our family, class, platoon, workplace, police force, or governance system. In most cases, the cost of fleeing the situation is too steep or simply impossible.

The freeze reaction is another common way to deal with distressful situations. In nature, this "play dead" response is meant to confuse the predator, or at least make the prey seem unthreatening. Playing dead in a bullying situation translates into a state of shock where we cannot produce any external response to the assault. We may experience immobility, numbness, or a sense of being "stuck." When we freeze, we become defenceless against the bully. Worse still, we may be perceived by others as "those who never resisted and therefore wanted it." This is a common misconception about victims of sexual assault who went into a freeze response, too shocked to resist. If later they dare complain about the assault, the attacker will claim they never resisted or said no, which to them was a clear indication of consent. Sadly, many courts of law accept this claim, failing to acknowledge freezing as a legitimate response to a traumatic event. Even highly educated people in the legal system still don't realize it is the same as saying, "When the accused was beating the plaintiff with a bat, the plaintiff just lay there all curled up, saying nothing and showing no resistance, therefore they clearly consented to the beating."

The freeze response can also manifest as dissociation. In extreme stress or trauma, we may experience mental detachment from our surroundings or even our own emotions to cope with overwhelming fear. Others will numb their unmanageable emotions to avoid feeling the intensity of their fear or use humour to cover it up. When the trauma is severe or chronic, our freeze response may become more persistent and contribute to conditions such as post-traumatic stress disorder (PTSD). These individuals will continue to experience a heightened emotional state, intrusive thoughts, and emotional numbing long after the traumatic event has ended.

Some of us will respond to bullying by collapsing and submitting—both emotionally and physically. We will feel utter helplessness, which will lead to surrendering and fully submitting to our aggressor. In this state, we will pretend we hadn't noticed other people's suffering, because we feel helpless or because it may protect us from becoming the primary target. Pleasing and appeasing is another common response to a traumatic event, also known as fawning. We become submissive to the bully like a sweet baby deer. In mild situations, we may try to gently negotiate and deescalate the situation. But when that fails (and it will always fail when dealing with Cone Masters), we will make ourselves agreeable with the aggressor. We will smile, nod, and keep our mouths shut even when we disagree. However, the fawn response has a more sinister version called the active appeasement (9). That's when we choose not only to comply, but also to side with the bully. We will show empathy and understanding toward the aggressor, acknowledge their perspective, cater to their every whim, and hang on their every word. We will giggle at their jokes and cheer their actions, no matter how cruel or moronic. The appeasement response can turn us into fervent supporters of every atrocity the bully commits.

The final stress response is becoming hyper attached to others and crying for help. Seeking help from others in times of trouble is one of the most natural strategies of social beings. However, it can be easily exploited by manipulative Cone Masters. They may manipulate our trust, posing as a friend or confidant, only to later betray or control us. They may exploit our need for help by cutting us off from others. This social isolation will increase our dependence on the aggressor and reduce the likelihood of outside protection from them. People with attachment stress response will be easy targets for gaslighting, exploitation, and grooming. When a Cone Master creates a stressful situation—either real or perceived—we may experience more than one trauma response. Either way, most of these responses make us vulnerable to them. Most of us—sardines and humans alike—will prefer to adapt and comply than be eaten or find ourselves on the wrong side of a bully's "you're either with me or against me."

Dipping into our shadow

There is a stark difference between complying to survive and becoming true believers and active supporters of bullies and evil tyrants. When we commit atrocities, we don't magically mutate into an evil being; we simply tap into our own well of darkness. According to the psychologist Carl Jung, our shadow self is a mighty force. It is our private cesspool of all that we are ashamed of and fear admitting about ourselves. Our subconscious harbours everything our cultural and societal norms see as abnormal, abominable, or taboo. It contains our unloved selves, shameful desires, unacceptable prejudices, and twisted urges.

If we acknowledge our shadow and treat it, it will remain small and manageable. If we don't, once things go wrong for us (and they always do eventually), our shadow will swell and find cracks from which to burst out. Cone Masters know how to legitimize our dark side and convince us there's nothing wrong with being bad. They assure us all our dark desires are completely justifiable and should no longer be hidden. Small atrocities that have been washed clean quickly swell into horrific atrocities we not only grow to feel comfortable with, but actually delight in. We justify our choices and then keep piling up lies to maintain them.

People who don't trust their own spine to hold them upright allow others to reach in and "put them on their feet." They usually don't realize that by submitting to a Cone Master, they have lost their spine altogether. A loyal Cone Subject becomes a puppet with the Cone Master's hand shoved into their core, controlling their thoughts, decisions, and actions.

Mob mentality

Another way to have us lose our humanity is by developing mob mentality. "Rhinoceros" is a famous play written by Eugène Ionesco[34] in 1959, and later made into a short movie. The story takes place in a small and peaceful town. At first, all seems completely normal. Happy families, friendly neighbours, and all. Gradually, some residents turn into rhinoceroses that stampede through the streets. A growing number of residents start believing in the beauty and wisdom of the rhinoceroses, and eventually turn into them and join the roaming herd. The one man who refuses to succumb to this mass madness, is being criticized and shamed for his antagonism and so-called paranoia with rhinoceroses.

As highly evolved social beings, we experience a constant tension between thinking for ourselves and fitting in with the collective. The safer and more self-confident we feel, the more comfortable we are with our individuality. The more frightened and insecure we become, the more we seek safety in numbers, even if it means sacrificing our independent thinking (10). When we fall prey to manipulative Cone Masters that cultivate fear and threaten us with becoming outcasts, we let go of who we are and start imitating others. This de-individuation kills our personal judgment in favour of groupthink. It makes big atrocities so much easier to accept and execute. Mob mentality not only allows us to fit in and be protected by the masses, but it also provides us with a sense of anonymity (11). When we act as part of a mob, we stop being personally responsible for our actions. And if we aren't responsible, then anything goes.

The thought of us becoming someone's puppets can be so disturbing most of us will reject the very idea of it. This denial is exactly what Cone Masters are counting on for the long-haul. Nevertheless, it is not a foolproof process. Individuals who possess stronger mental immunity will

---

[34] Originally the play was written in French, titled Rhinocéros.

see through the deception and grow to resent and defy the Cone. Some of them may become rebels, while others will simply avoid engaging in the Cone's beliefs. Another group will be indifferent to the Cone's rhetoric and actions. These will be the oblivious ones or those who are less affected by the Cone's reality—or at least don't think they are. Indoctrination related to gender identity and gender roles will probably affect nearly everyone because our societies identify all of us by gender. Indoctrination into sports fandom, on the other hand, might not touch those who have no interest in sports and feel it has no relevance to their lives.

You may imagine Cones as being obvious constructs you will see from a mile, but as you will discover in the next chapter, Cones and manipulative Cone Masters come in all forms and scales, often making it difficult for us to recognize the power they have over us. We are all Subjects of one Cone or another, and they mess with our heads whether or not we are aware of it. The good news is that this is not part of "the nature of things." Cones are not existential imperatives. As you keep reading, you will find that all man-made constructs can be un-made if we so choose.

Part 1:
The answers to our problems

↓

Part 2:
How Cones are built

↓

Part 3:
How Cones gain control

↓

Part 4:
How Cones operate

↓

Part 5:
How Cones fall… and come back

↓

Part 6:
A better future within our reach

CHAPTER 13:

A Cone by any other name

... where we explore the many Cone variants and the ways they differ.

ll Cones share major commonalities. They all either latch on our existing Problems and Needs or create them for us. They all pretend to exist for our benefit while using us as the means to their own accumulation of power and prosperity. They all use a range of mind-control tactics to keep us loyal and compliant, and they all keep us on a short leash.

Nonetheless, just like viruses, there is a great variety of them out there. Cones can be of different dimensions, emerge through different pathways, be concealed or conspicuous, local or expansive, and reign for different periods of time.

Big and small

Let's start with size. How small can a Cone be? If we compare a Cone to a cage, it should be large enough to contain at least one person. The smallest Cone in existence is a single, Cone-infused person who governs themselves with an iron fist. Each of us contains all the Cones to which we subscribe, as illustrated in Figure 28. The more Cones we internalize, the harsher we become with ourselves without realizing it's not us, it's them. We will keep measuring our appearance, thoughts, successes, and actions against our many Cone yardsticks, and we will punish ourselves for being failed Subjects.

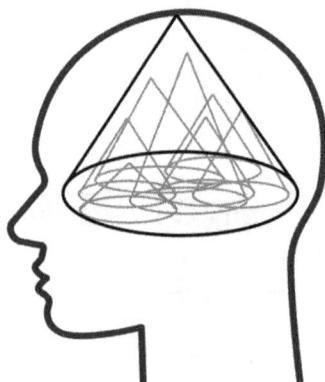

Figure 28: The sum of our Cones is much of who we are
and what we believe in

Think about the things that taunt you. The things that, deep down, make you feel unworthy or unlovable. Are you slim, attractive, educated, famous, rich, religious, obedient, pious, or patriotic enough? Whom have you disappointed? What or who shames you? Guilts you? Enrages you? Most of us will harbour at least some shame and self-blame for the things we have failed to achieve. The deeper our failure to meet the expectations of our internalized Cones, the crueller we are to ourselves. Self-hate, workaholism, self-sabotage, addictions, self-denial, and debilitating guilt are but few of the many ways we self-enforce the Cones in our lives.

The next mini-Cone is a partnering relationship between two people, a co-dependent friendship, or a nuclear family. Cones scale all the way to mega-Cones, such as a country or a global commercial conglomerate. Each will contain many smaller Cones. A corporate organization or a colonizer are two good examples of mega-Cones. That said, we must never dismiss the power of the smaller ones. We may think that mega-Cones are more powerful than their mini version by virtue of their magnitude, but this is one of those cases where size doesn't always matter for individuals. An abusive relationship has the potential to affect a person much more than their country's governance system. A small, twenty-person cult can exert much greater mind control on its members than a mega-Cone of worldwide media. No matter the size of the Cones in our lives, they are mighty forces that determine our worldview, boundaries, opportunities, liberties, fears, and punishments.

Obvious vs. concealed Cones

If you live in a sheltered, isolated cult, you might not know you are imprisoned in an oppressive Cone any more than the bottled pear. The rest of the world, however, will see it as plain as day, because a cult is an obvious Cone, at least to outsiders. Many other Cones are far less conspicuous. Some are nearly invisible to the uninformed eye.

In some concealed Cones, the insiders will be the ones more aware of the constricting Dogma, while outsiders will be completely unaware of it. In his book, *David and Goliath* (1), Malcolm Gladwell tells the story of a Parisian group of painters who were revolutionaries in their field. Degas, Manet, Cezanne, Renoir, and Pissarro were remarkable artists who gave birth to Impressionism. Today, every major art museum displays their paintings that cost sizeable fortunes, but back in the 1860s, most of the Impressionists were, quite literally, starving artists. Back then, art was so central to people's cultural lives, the government established a System to regulate it at a level no different from that of lawyers and physicians. The Ministry of the Imperial House and the Fine Arts determined the type of art education a painter had to acquire, the competitions they had to win throughout their training, and their right to exhibit their work in public.

The pinnacle of every artist's career was displaying their paintings at the Salon—the most prestigious exhibition in all of Europe. Artists carted their paintings to the grand hall to be appraised by an appointed jury. The jury marked the rejected paintings as "R," while the accepted ones were exhibited to millions of visitors and made serious money for their owners. Anyone who had a shred of self-respect would never buy a painting the Salon had rejected. Like every group of innovators and Cone rebels, the Impressionists were doomed to be rejected time and again, being Dogma rebels. Unable to change the establishment (as is usually the case with Cones), and unwilling to compromise their artistic values, the Impressionists ended up opening their own gallery outside the oppressive reach of the Salon. And the rest is history.

Though art is no longer formally regulated, we will be remiss to believe art Cones no longer exist. If you aren't an artist, these Cones will be invisible to you, and you will go about life believing that nothing is freer than art in all its forms. It is only when you are on the inside that you will recognize the constricting walls that keep you in line with the art Dogma. The mainstream Western film industry, for example, ticks nearly all Cone boxes. To this day, it is plagued with lack of diversity and representation on both sides of the camera (2). Following a Cone's typical "purity of the in-group," it perpetuates stereotypes, marginalizes groups, and limits opportunities for minority voices. Even now, it is still a highly patriarchal industry. Women, indigenous people, and people of colour have historically been, and still are underrepresented, in key roles such as directing, producing, and cinematography, facing discrimination and unequal pay as the norm.

Creative control (3) is another typical Cone practice. Many filmmakers and artists report that the film industry sets very clear boundaries on what creativity looks like, in complete opposition to the very premise of art. Studios often impose profit-driven restrictions on filmmakers, resulting in formulaic content. As all well-established Cones, the film industry has a system of gatekeeping where a select group of people, often with connections or privilege, have more access to opportunities. It is also known for concentrating power among a few major studios and distributors to limit competition. This typical Cone move leads to greater control of the artistic process and less diverse content. Another Cone telltale is exploitative practices of its Subjects. Many times, the film industry has been accused of exploiting actors, crew members, and other workers by overworking and underpaying them. Not everything that shines is silver, not even the silver screen.

Embedded, diffused, deliberate, reactionary, and ad hoc Cones

The oldest Cones in our lives are the fully embedded ones—those that had existed well before our lifetime and will probably endure long after. These are the Solutions we recognize as an inseparable part of normal life. Our religion, education, law, and borders are but a few of the many Cones we are immersed in. The Cone Masters of embedded Dogmas aren't necessarily intentional villains. For them and for most of their Subjects (save for the Internal Traitors), this is simply the "natural order of things." Even exploitive and abusive Cone Masters may believe they do it because this is how it's always been done, and the only way life works. Some of the deeply embedded Cones are more diffuse than a typical Cone System. Sometimes it is difficult to tell who the Cone Masters are because there are so many of them. These Cones are passed from one generation to the next, unquestioned, and unrefuted.

When I was a program manager of one of the academic programs I developed for immigrant professionals in Canada, one of my students was a woman from a country in the Middle East. The program was a year long and, apart from managing it, I also taught a few of the courses. At the graduation ceremony, she approached to thank me, at which point she felt comfortable enough to share her thoughts. She told me how horrified she was to learn her program manager was going to be a Jew and an Israeli Canadian and perhaps, as she said, a Zionist. Throughout that whole year, she kept looking for my horns and tail, having been taught by her parents and Imams that Jews are devil's spawns. She even discussed the matter with some of her fellow Muslim students. They postulated that hiding a tail in pants should be doable, but they couldn't figure out how I concealed my horns under my very short pixie cut. She was sure I would find a way to kill her or, at the very least, flunk her out of the program. Her final words to me at that ceremony were: "But then I got to know you, and you're actually nice. That's so confusing."

This was the worldview of a highly intelligent, highly educated woman, who grew up in a major urban centre. Despite having a master's degree in science, she had no doubt in her mind that some people grew horns and tails, drank baby blood, and plotted to take over the world as the emissaries of Satan. The reason even the most ridiculous Core Certainties go unchecked is because these diffused Cones are implanting them in our minds at an age where we have no capacity to question or doubt them. Once they take hold as our picture of reality, it is nearly impossible to uproot them, no matter how much science we study.

In her book, *Infidel* (4), Ayaan Hirsi Ali shared her life story as a Muslim, Somali-born woman. She described how fear and hatred of Jews had been fed to her with her mother's milk, and how much it took to re-examine and discard these Core Certainties. Ali is one of those rare human beings who were born with exceptional mental immunity that allowed her to see through the veil and break through her programming. Most of us aren't as lucky. Antisemitism is but one example. Culture, family structure, perception of gender, and racism among many others, are diffused Cones that infiltrate nearly every aspect of our lives.

Who are the Cone Masters of these Cones? Normally, these would be the influential people within our communities who have been indoctrinated by previous generations. These people transmit these beliefs to the young generations like a viral contagion. They do it through myths and storytelling, formal and informal teachings, traditions, and laws.

Though these ancient Cones were built by their originators with a clear intention in mind, such as gaining control, power, and means, their intentions have long been washed and forgotten.

Who among the white supremacists remembers that the original reason for oppressing black people was to make it easier to justify their enslavement for cheap labour and catch them if they escaped? Who among the racists who believes aboriginal people are inferior remembers these notions were fabricated to make it easier to commit genocide, rob, and drive them out of highly coveted territories? Who among the patriarchs remembers that squashing women was necessary because they were too communal, collaborative, and nurturing to support inhumane power grabs? The only things that remain from these ancient truths are the senseless Dogmas that are being dutifully passed on from one generation to the next like a stubborn genetic mutation.

Other types of Cones are reactionary, where one Cone begets an opposing one. These evil twins spawn when one radicalizing Solution or ideology triggers the radicalization of the opposite one. These two grow into Cones simultaneously, feeding off each other. The louder one sports fandom, the louder the opposing Cone. The fiercer a social justice movement, the more entrenched and radical the Cones that are accused of injustice, making the opposing movement even fiercer and more Coned. The more extreme a religion, the stauncher the atheists. No matter how genuinely well-intended the opposing force is, it will quickly devolve into an oppressive mindset of "you're either with us or against us." Even justice fighters who stand for human rights, once Coned, will squash anyone who disagrees with them, either figuratively (discrediting, shaming, cancelling), or literally (financial or physical attack).

We are so good at creating Cones that many of us can conjure one within a matter of days, especially in the wake of light-speed social media. These are the ad hoc Cones. They emerge quickly, they are not always well thought through, they don't always have a clear leadership, and most of them are short-lived or mutable. A group of fans can easily grow into an oppressive Cone. Fandoms, which are communities of passionate fans of a particular show, book, movie, game, or celebrity, can be overwhelmingly positive and supportive. Give it some time and a few radical members, and that same passion can transform into oppression. The Star Wars fandom, for example, has experienced much toxicity and abuse, especially in response to the release of the sequel trilogy. Some fans who were dissatisfied with the direction of the films led hate campaigns, shamed those who opposed them, harassed, and threatened actors, directors, and producers.

An ad hoc Cone can also be a social clique at school, forming within days around a charismatic student who applies Cone tactics to gain power and control. We also see it happening in the workplace when vulnerable employees find themselves under a micro-tyrannical Cone run by the in-house bully. Most of these ad hoc Cones don't have a premeditated goal, at least not a long-term one. Some of them are formed by a single leader who manages to sweep followers. Others are formed by a group of people who vie for power or have a burning passion and an uncompromising worldview.

Intersecting Cones

The term "intersectionality" was originally promoted by critical race theorist Kimberlé Crenshaw in relation to race and sex. She analyzed cases where black men and white women were treated much better by the legal system than black women, for whom the combination of racism and sexism made life significantly worse (5). Intersectionality was later adopted into a broader framework of social interactions. When Cones overlap and intersect, they make things much, much worse for us.

Complex prejudices are not the result of Cones randomly meeting at a bar to exchange anecdotes over drinks. They are more like a chemical

reaction where two mildly toxic chemicals mix to create an explosive compound. Every person and every group of people live within clustered, intersecting Cones. The same person can be a profiteer in one Cone and a
loyal Subject in another. The CEO of a corporate or the president of a
country can also be an oppressed Subject of a colonizer, an extreme religion, or a rigid gender construct.

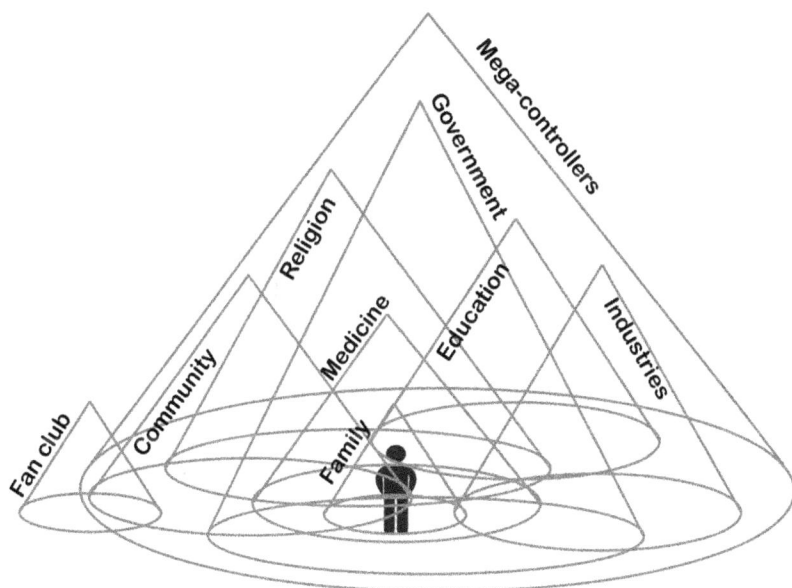

Figure 29: Example of mini- and mega-Cones intersecting in a "free" society

Intersectional Cones, such as the ones illustrated in Figure 29, collaborate,
affect, and reinforce each other. In much of European history, the religious establishment reinforced the power of monarchs, and vice versa.
The church claimed that kings had a divine right to rule, exempting them
from being held accountable by any earthly authority. In return for this
helpful decree, kings bestowed the church great riches and an unlimited
power over their Subjects. These are two simple intersecting Cones that
interacted with many others.

Let's look at one obvious oppressive Cone—a crime organization. Below are some major intersecting Cones that can affect its power and operation:[35]

Culture: In some societies, a long history of organized crime makes it more normative than in others. This local culture will affect the prevalence of organized crime, and how tolerated, supported, or persecuted these organizations will be by the local government and police force.

Governing systems: Different governance and legal systems have different approaches and levels of rigour when it comes to criminal activity. Some countries have powerful legislation and law enforcement against criminal acts and whole task forces to fight organized crime. In others, usually the less developed or more autocratic, neither legislation nor enforcement are set up to hinder criminal activity. Especially if it benefits the ruling class, which significantly strengthens this Cone.

Economic systems: The model and the state of a local economy have a powerful impact on organized crime Cones. The more compromised the economic status of a certain group or society, and the more disparity between rich and poor, the more people will be exploited by or join crime organizations, thus empowering the Cone.

Technology: In the past, the power of crime Cones heavily relied on muscle power. Nowadays, virtually anyone can run certain types of crime (e.g., fraud) online from their mother's basement. Even organizations with a greater physical presence more readily rely on technology to expand and enhance their Cone.

---

[35] These are merely a few examples for intersectionality. There are many other Cones of different types and sizes that would affect the power and operations of a crime organization.

Family and community: Beyond large governing and economic systems, most individuals are affected and indoctrinated from birth by the people closest to them. Even in the most affluent, law-abiding societies, people can be inducted into crime Cones and reinforce them (e.g., joining the "family business" or living within disenfranchised communities where joining crime organizations is the only way to survive).

Gender: While female-dominated crime organizations exist, they are the exceptions. Most of these Cones are male dominated. This intersectionality creates a top-down management style that favours brute force over collaboration.

The more restrictive a group or a society, the more its Cones stack instead of simply intersecting, as illustrated in Figure 30. In strictly theocratic countries like Iran or Pakistan, the religion Cone will sit on top, and govern all aspects of life, be it relationships, families, communities, professions, or governments. As in all other societies, the local religious bodies will not be exempt from the power of global mega-controlling Cones.

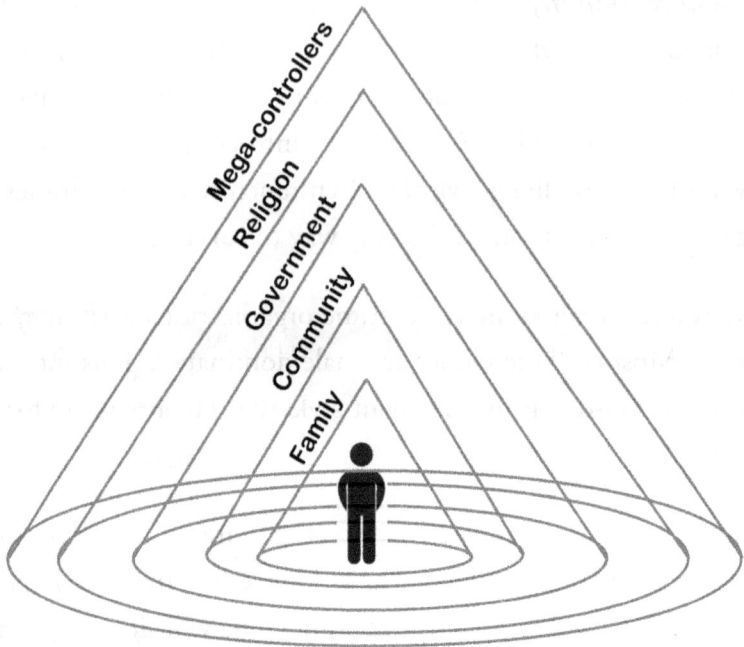

Figure 30: Example of mini- and mega-Cones stacking in a theocratic society

All cones share the same profiteering and self-serving agendas, they are all oppressive and harmful, either to people or the planet or both, and they all prioritize the Cone Masters and their Need for power and means over the Needs of their Subjects. However, Cones can also operate in different formats. Some are as small as a single individual whereas others can be mega-Cones aspiring for world domination. Some Cones are obvious and in-your-face, whereas others are so well concealed most of us don't recognize them as oppressive constructs. Some are clearly defined with a recognizable governance System whereas other are diffuse and more illusive. No matter what the Cone's format, it never exists in a vacuum. Cones intersect, interact, and empower each other in nasty synergies. The question is, since Cones are exploitive and harmful Systems, are they all governed by monsters and psychopaths?

CHAPTER 14:

The corrupting power of power

... where we discover how monsters are made and what they do with their power and wealth.

Cone Masters or Cone monsters?

eading on all the ways Cone Masters manipulate and abuse us, you may get the impression that all Cone Masters are evil Machiavellians who enjoy seeing people suffer under their heavy boot. While in some Cones that may be the case, overall, this is likely a minority occurrence. When you look at the pictures of famous butchers and their minions, the most striking thing is how normal they seem. They're no different from your next-door neighbours or your colleagues at work. Some of them even love dogs. Though the greatest Cone Masters are those blessed with an unhealthy measure of ego and self-aggrandizement, they don't always start that way. There are many examples of people who started as decent folks with genuinely good intentions and ended up as merciless Cone Masters once they tasted power and means. This metamorphosis isn't even a lengthy process. Research shows that exposure to sudden power and means can corrupt most of us, sometimes instantaneously.

One revealing study in this field is known as the Stanford Prison Experiment (1). In 1971, a Stanford University psychology professor, Philip Zimbardo, wanted to examine people's behaviours in extreme situations. He designed a simulated prison environment for volunteers to experience over a two-week period. Male applicants for the study went through in-depth interviews and a battery of psychological tests. Only those who were deemed the most normal, average, and mentally healthy were selected to participate. Each was randomly assigned either to be a guard or a prisoner. The "prisoners" were mock-arrested[36] by the local police and charged with armed robbery and burglary. They were taken in handcuffs from their homes, booked at a real jail, and then blindfolded and driven to campus where a makeshift basement prison awaited them. They were given uncomfortable, ill-fitting prison clothes, stocking caps, no underwear, and a chain propped around one ankle. Maximum authenticity was key to this study.

Those who were randomly assigned to play "guards" were given uniforms and instructions on their role. Their job was to maintain control of the prison without using violence. They were also instructed to call prisoners by their assigned numbers, sewn on their uniforms, instead of by name. A tried-and-true dehumanization method. It didn't take more than one day for the guards to start savouring their power. They decided to wake up the prisoners in the middle of the night by whistling and banging their batons against the iron bars of the cells. The inmates didn't take it kindly. They refused to leave their cells, ripped off their number tags, took off their stocking caps, and insulted the guards. In response, the assigned guards sprayed fire extinguishers at the prisoners, removed all the prisoners' clothes and mattresses, and sent the main instigators to The Hole (solitary confinement). One of the guards was even recorded saying to the other in earnest that, "these are dangerous prisoners."

Within only two days, the guards' behaviour escalated into psychological torture and physical abuse. On day two, one prisoner broke down and demanded to be removed from the study. The rest developed untrusting and antisocial behaviours toward one another. But it wasn't only

---

[36] This procedure was a breach of Zimbardo's own contract that all the participants had signed. In the aftermath, he justified his decision as wanting the experiment to be as authentic as possible. According to him, for the psychological process to mimic real life, the arrest had to come as a surprise.

the study participants who were affected. The study lead's professional colleague, Christina Maslach, noted that Zimbardo himself had been changed by his role as superintendent into someone she did not recognize and did not like. Zimbardo ended the experiment on day six. This study has since been scrutinized by many researchers, yet the bottom line remains: people thrown into roles of oppressors grow into their personas much faster than one would guess. Same goes for those thrown into a role of the oppressed.

Another set of experiments conducted by the psychologist Paul Piff (2) demonstrated similar behavioural transformation using a rigged game. More than a hundred pairs of strangers were invited to play a Monopoly game using altered rules. Each pair of participants flipped a coin to randomly designate one player "rich" and the other "poor." To stay true to the assigned roles and reflect the social injustice of wealth and poverty, the "rich" players got twice as much money as their opponents. They were allowed to roll two dice instead of one, therefore moving around the board twice as fast as their opponents. When the "rich" passed the "Go" square, they collected $200, while their "poor" opponent collected only $100. They even got the Rolls-Royce piece as their token on the board, whereas the "poor" players got a little plastic shoe or a thimble.

Any ethical human being assigned to be "rich" would be embarrassed with their unfair advantage and would do whatever they could to help their disadvantaged counterpart. Because that's what decent people do. But that is not what happened. Within minutes, most of the "rich" players started displaying arrogant body language and bragging about their wealth. They would smack their game pieces loudly against the playing board in a display of power and mock their opponents' misfortunes. They would take liberties with "poor" players' game pieces and move them on the board for their counterparts. Fifteen minutes in, most of the "rich" players had lost all semblance of empathy toward the "poor" players. They severed social contact with their game partners (no longer kept eye contact, sat sideways instead of facing the other players) and took the poor players' cash unblinkingly. *Fifteen minutes.* What was even more interesting were the outcomes of the post-game player interviews. When the "rich" players were asked to explain their win, they bragged about their talents and superior game strategies that had won them the game. A few claimed it was due to lucky rolls of the dice, and even fewer attributed their success to the unfair game and their position of privilege.

In another experiment, Piff and colleagues found that people driving expensive cars were four times more likely to cut off other drivers and ignore right-of-way laws (3). He had noted that more than half of the expensive cars sped through an intersection and didn't pay any attention or even make eye contact with a pedestrian who was trying to cross the road. Meanwhile, every single person who pulled up to the crossroad in a cheap car stopped. In one of their most interesting experiments, they found wealthy people were more likely to take candy from children. Literally, not metaphorically. For years, Piff and his colleagues conducted dozens of similar studies with thousands of participants. They consistently found that as a person's privilege and wealth increases, their compassion and empathy drop, and their feelings of entitlement ("I deserve this"), self-justification ("It's because I'm better/smarter/work harder than the other"), and their ideology of self-interest (succeeding on the backs of others) skyrocket.

In the past few decades, many experiments showed that although people vary, there is a strong indication that power has transformative effects on our psychology. Research consistently shows the rich cheat more on their taxes and on their romantic partners. They are more apt to be rude and inconsiderate of others. They are more likely to shoplift and to cheat at games of chance, and they are overwhelmingly less empathetic. These behaviours may be attributed to two main factors (4). One is that power lowers our inhibitions. People who gain power see more choice and more options for the actions they can take without the fear of being punished. In turn, they become less likely to respect social norms. The other factor is that the rich and powerful have increased self-focus (5). They feel that their own needs are greater and far more important than the needs of others. They are less inclined to interact, help, or consider other people's needs.

The ill effects of wealth persist outside lab experiments. In the last seven or so decades, trends in charity giving have been well documented and researched. Turns out that lower-income households donate proportionately more of their incomes to charity (nearly twice as much) than higher-income households.

The bottom line is that once we taste power and start accumulating means, we might no longer be bothered by the actions we must take to remain in control, or by the price others will pay for our success. And it happens much faster than we may think. Which is why becoming a Cone Master is not limited to legendary monsters.

The power of money

The phrase "money is power" is probably older than money. Most Cone Masters invest much thought and energy in accumulating funds and assets to serve their Needs. Some small-scale Cones, such as abusive relationships, families, or social cliques, focus mostly on controlling existing funds and assets to increase their power over their Subjects. Most other Cone Masters aim to amass wealth. The question is, where does this money come from and what do they do with it?

Where does the money come from?

There are many creative ways Cone Masters amass wealth. Contrary to the common ethos of "wealthy people gain their riches by waking up early and working really hard," Cone Masters leave the early rising and hard work to their Subject and find much easier ways to amass wealth. As described in Figure 31, one common way Cone Masters accumulate means is by siphoning off funds that were intended for the Solution. They can do this through fraudulent schemes, fake contracts, or simply by directing Solution funds to their private accounts. Many authoritarian regimes control or have significant influence over state-owned enterprises, which they can use as sources of personal enrichment. This siphoning of funds doesn't always happen covertly. Some Cone Masters openly demand a share of their Solution's earnings, assets, or profits as part of their official position. Whenever possible, Cone Masters will demand bribes and kickbacks to secure a contract, support favorable decisions, or gain some form of preferential treatment.

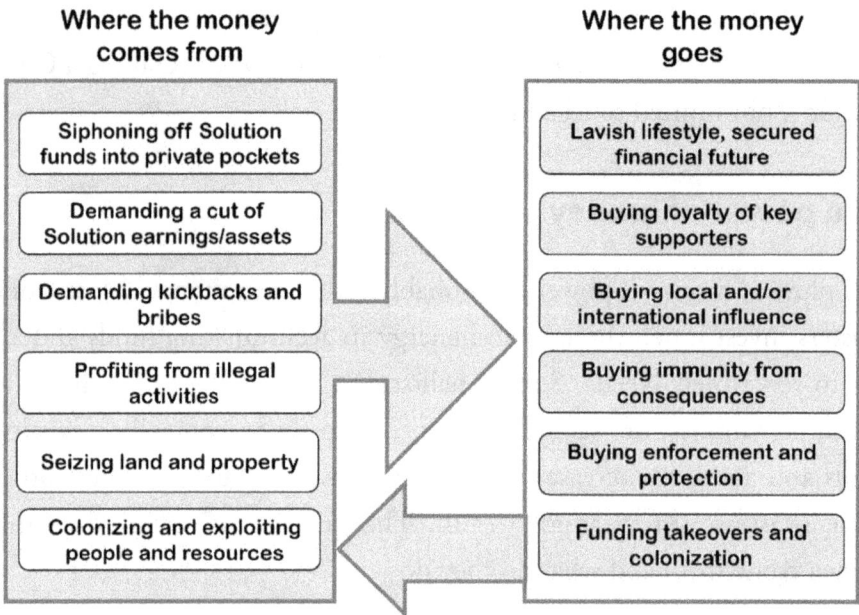

Where the money comes from

- Siphoning off Solution funds into private pockets
- Demanding a cut of Solution earnings/assets
- Demanding kickbacks and bribes
- Profiting from illegal activities
- Seizing land and property
- Colonizing and exploiting people and resources

Where the money goes

- Lavish lifestyle, secured financial future
- Buying loyalty of key supporters
- Buying local and/or international influence
- Buying immunity from consequences
- Buying enforcement and protection
- Funding takeovers and colonization

Figure 31: Cone Masters' finances

There is a long list of heads of states, especially in developing countries, who have amassed enormous wealth through corruption during their rule.

They did it by embezzling funds from their national treasuries and demanding bribes, cuts, and kickbacks from government projects. The former president of the Philippines and his wife, Ferdinand and Imelda Marcos, Suharto, past president of the Republic of Indonesia, Mobutu Sese Seko, past president of what is now the Democratic Republic of Congo, Saddam Hussein, the former president of Iraq, Nicolae Ceaușescu, the former president of Romania—are all but a few of many such examples.

In countries with valuable natural resources like oil, gas, minerals, or timber, both commercial and political Cone Masters may control these industries and pocket revenue from resource extraction and exports. They may also seize land and property from individuals or businesses, often using political power and intimidation. Once they claim ownership of these assets, they can pocket the profits or sell them for personal profit using a range of justifications, from, "We're doing it to civilize the savages," through, "It is the right thing to do," to, "I'm doing it because I have the divine right." During the peak of Western colonialism, European powers demanded that their colonies surrender a significant share of their resources and wealth. They plundered their colonies for valuable resources such as minerals, spices, agricultural products, and slaves, leaving the indigenous populations with minimal benefits and major losses.

Some authoritarian leaders manipulate to their advantage international aid and loans meant for development and humanitarian purposes. They may divert foreign aid funds for personal use or use loans to enrich themselves and their inner circle. In some cases, they use their power and connections to facilitate and profit from illegal activities, such as black-market trade, smuggling, or trafficking. African dictators, for example, loot their countries so unabashedly that they have become known as "kleptocracies" (6). When developed countries and humanitarian organizations send aid, they often encounter corrupt bureaucracies that siphon off a significant portion of that money. At one point, roughly 20 percent of Uganda's budget came from foreign aid, without any notable benefits to its population. We may think that these things only happen in developing countries and third-world tyrannies, but an eye-opening study conducted by Gerard Padró i Miquel (7) demonstrated that African dictators are not so special that way. Padro concluded: "Finally, note that no difference is made between democracy and dictatorship in the model. The evidence from Africa shows that democracies have not behaved differently than dictatorships when supporting kleptocracies and corruption."

Not all Cones pretend to be well intended. Leaders of crime organizations are obvious wealth-amassing Cone Masters. Notorious figures such as Al Capone (American mafia), Pablo Escobar (Colombian Medellín Cartel), Dawood Ibrahim (Indian D-Company), and Semion Mogilevich (Russia/Ukraine) got filthy rich by demanding a hefty cut from all their organization's illegal operations, such as smuggling, gambling, drug trade, and human trafficking. To be fair, as opposed to most other Cone Masters, they have never claimed to stand for some higher cause than making money and growing their power.

Other forms of wealth-amassing are neither hidden nor illegal. Heads of corporates can accumulate "legitimate" wealth by demanding astronomical salaries and company shares. In 2022, Stephen Schwarzman, the CEO of Blackstone Inc. (a private equity firm), made over $253 million a year. That's over 15,800 times more than the average fully employed American on a minimum wage that comes to less than $16,000 a year. Clearly, Schwartzman, and the rest of the high-earning CEOs, aren't working 15,800 times harder than anyone else. Certainly not more than the hardworking people who earn minimum wage. For many of the rich, even that isn't enough because greed is a bottomless pit. Corporate Cone Masters can exploit tax loopholes, use offshore tax havens, and create intentionally complex financial structures to reduce their tax liabilities. They may use shell companies and offshore accounts to launder money, evade tax, and hide assets from creditors or authorities. They can engage in insider trading based on their non-public, material information while manipulating the market to favour their investments.

Cone Masters are also notorious for exploitation. They exploit the environment through deforestation, pollution, or unsustainable resource extraction, and they exploit people through low wages, poor working conditions, and violations of labour rights. No matter which strategy Cone Masters use to accumulate means, the more wealth they put their hands on, the more wealth they can keep generating based on the old principle of "money makes money."

Where does the money go?

The desire to accumulate far more means than one will require for a thousand lifetimes is driven by insecurities that lead to insatiable greed. These insecurities can be material, such as the fear of scarcity and the Need to safeguard against future uncertainties. They can be psychological, such as low self-confidence and the Need for validation of self-worth. They can also be social, such as the fear of isolation and the Need to gain social status. Whatever their drivers, Cone Masters will use money and assets to meet these deep Needs well before investing it back in the Solution. That is unless this investment circles back to benefit them personally. One of the most basic uses of accumulated means is gaining and maintaining a wealthy lifestyle—luxurious residences, land, expensive vehicles, private planes and yachts, posh vacationing, space travel, art and collectibles, fashion and jewelry, lovers and mistresses, and anything else money can buy.

Beyond the perks of being rich, wealth allows Cone Masters to grow their power. They can use their financial resources to maintain loyalty among key supporters, such as military leaders, influential officials, and business elites. Smart Cone Masters establish patronage networks where they provide economic incentives, highly coveted positions, or other benefits to those who support them. By enriching their inner circle, they surround themselves with a powerful network of people with a vested interest in keeping the Cone going. Cone Masters may also use their wealth to pay bribes and maintain influence over various sectors that benefit them. They may pay influential people in the judiciary arm to gain legal immunity, and bribe businesses to source goods and take over markets. They can also bribe media companies to allow them to shape public opinion, control the narrative, and suppress dissenting voices.

When most of us think of a bribe, we imagine an envelope stacked with bills passed under the table. Though some bribes are secretive, many others happen in the open under more appealing names. Very few public donations and financial contributions are made purely out of the goodness of the donor's heart. Most come with strings attached and secret agreement on reciprocity. Gas and oil companies that contribute millions to political candidates always expect something in return. Once elected, gratitude alone will not suffice. These companies will pressure the endorsed politician to represent their commercial interests, and to promote and vote for favourable legislation on tax breaks, environmental deregulation, and support for energy projects.

Big Pharma pours millions into medical schools around the world. In his book, *Doctors in Denial* (8), Dr. Joel Lexchin describes the ways drug companies establish a relationship with medical schools. They invest heavily in research funding, grants, or allegedly philanthropic donations, while acting in their own best interests. These financial benefactors gain the power to prioritize which health issues receive attention and which Solutions are researched (hint: their own medications). They negotiate agreements that grant them access or even exclusive rights over research findings or technologies that can make them money. They even influence academic policies and priorities, and shape curricula in ways that align with their commercial interests. Most if not all major medical schools around the world have representatives of pharmaceutical companies on their boards. Most of these companies pay academic medical leaders from these institutions to sit on their own boards for a hefty salary to make sure their Cone interests are protected from every direction (9).

Some Cone Masters will use wealth to gain influence on the international stage. State leaders may engage in "economic diplomacy," providing financial incentives to other countries or individuals to garner support, secure alliances, or evade international sanctions. Buying influence may also happen through co-opting or neutralizing opposition figures. They can offer financial incentives to key people in rival organizations and all forms of bribes to ensure their cooperation, thereby dividing and weakening the opposition. Big employers will bribe union leaders to back off. Political figures will fund cyber attacks and social media campaigns to discredit their opponents. Commercial rivals will bribe their competitor's key employees to sabotage operations or leak damaging information.

Being rich isn't only about what it gives you, it is also about what unpleasantries it can take away. Wealth can easily shield Cone Masters from accountability for their screwups. For one, strategic payments can ensure that everyone on their formal and informal payrolls remain loyal, hide their misgivings, and protect them from the consequences of their actions. Paid politicians can help create legal loopholes to get their benefactors off the hook. High-power public relations firms can manage a Cone Master's image and downplay or divert attention from their crimes. When all else fails, wealthy Cone Masters can afford high-powered lawyers and legal teams with extensive resources for a robust defence in legal proceedings. Having deep pockets allows Cone Masters to engage in protracted legal battles to exhaust opponents with the cost and time required for litigation. This can pressure their accusers to settle on less favorable terms or abandon legal action altogether. They can also afford jurisdiction shopping, relocating assets or legal matters to countries with lax regulations, favorable tax laws, or legal systems that are less likely to hold them accountable.

Depending on the Cone, wealth can be used to fund a powerful security apparatus, including private security services, police, intelligence agencies, and paramilitary forces. These are instrumental in enforcing the Cone on its Subjects and, consequently, enhance Cone Masters' power. Suppressing dissent, maintaining control, and protecting the Cone from opposition all cost money. Offering enforcers financial incentives, bonuses, and special privileges ensures their loyalty and reduces the risk of a coup or rebellion.

Mega-Cones often keep growing their Solution until they control whole economic sectors. This is also known as monopolizing and/or colonizing, depending on the Cone. Such growth costs a lot of money, but it allows them to manipulate policies, allocate resources, and direct economic benefits to themselves. Whichever way Cone Masters accumulate their riches, it is never for the benefit of their Subjects or for the significant improvement of their Solution.

CHAPTER 15:

Cone legalities and enforcement

... where we discover what makes one a criminal, how Cones come up with their laws, and how they enforce their Dogma.

As we have seen, Cones are dogmatic, harmful Systems governed by Cone Masters who see their Subjects as exploitable assets and care little for their Problems and Needs. While Cone Masters use a myriad of mind-controlling tactics to have their Subjects willingly submit to the Cone, these must be reinforced by uncompromising agreements, policies, or laws. To make sure these Cone directives are maintained in no uncertain terms, Cone Masters put in place a variety of enforcement methods to keep their Subjects in check.

Cone legalities

Who are the criminals and why do they do it?

Before we delve into reasons and motivators for committing crimes, we need to agree on the concept of crime. As described in Figure 32, crime can be against people (and other living beings), such as assault, murder, robbery, or human trafficking. It can be against Systems, such as treason, espionage, sedition, or environmental. Crimes can also be in the intersection of people and Systems, such as theft, vandalism, fraud, cyber crimes, and Cone heresy. Cone heresy is a specific category of offences against the System that will be defined by each Cone. An abuser will define Cone heresy and punish their partner for failure to please and obey or for daring to stand up to them. Every dictatorial Cone, be it a country, a gang, or a cult, will define heresy as questioning or critiquing the Cone Masters and their Dogma. More covert Cones, such as democratic governments, will punish heretic whistleblowers who uncover government corruption.

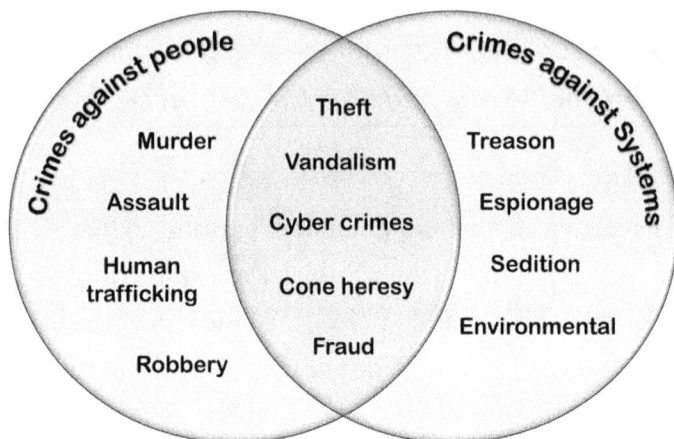

Figure 32: Major types of crimes

Now that we had agreed on what constitutes a crime and who the criminals are, the question remains: why do people commit crimes? There are many videos you can find online documenting the rescue of an animal from being caught in a fence, a fishing net, or the plastic rings of a six-pack. In most of these videos, the entrapped animal tries to fight off the person who comes to their rescue. Often it will attack and bite anyone who crosses their path. Once rescued, we can see how grateful that animal is to its rescuer, which makes us all sigh with a pleased, "Awe, that's so heartwarming." If all you saw was an animal attacking a human, you might have developed resentment against the wild beast. It is only when you see the full picture that you understand the entrapped animal is in such dire situation it can only operate from a place of fear and despair.

The same goes for guard or fight dogs who are infamous for their brutality. Once you realize that a killer dog is an abused and traumatized animal, you will gain compassion and be less judgmental of its harmful behaviour. These two circumstances—one of being entrapped, fearful, and hopeless, and the other of being cruelly handled and conditioned, apply to humans as surely as they do to any other animal. Both lead to similar behaviours. When we examine the reasons people commit crimes, we must remember these actions are but the tip of the iceberg. Using the iceberg metaphor, acts of crime are the visible tip affected by many acting forces we don't always recognize, as illustrated in Figure 33.

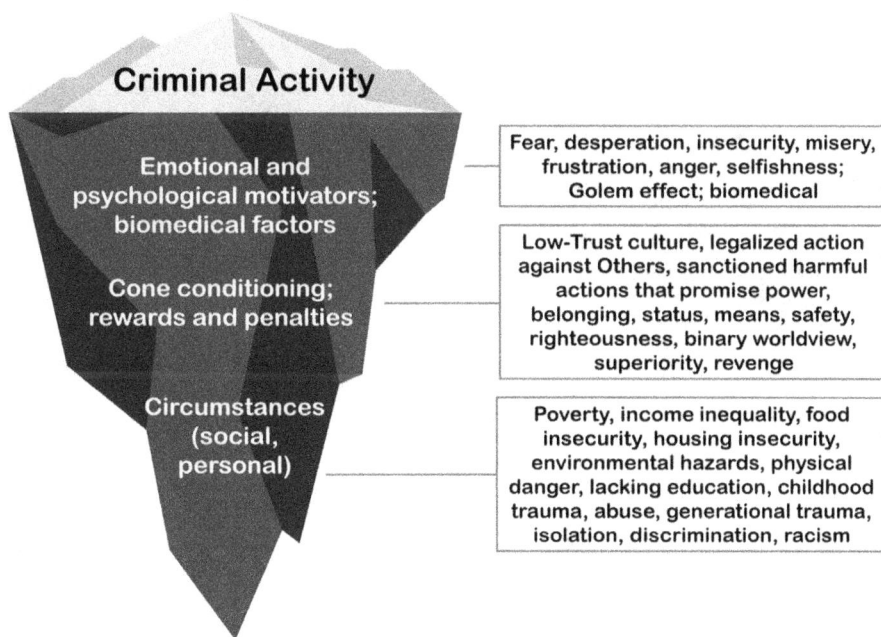

Figure 33: The many causes of criminal activity

People's propensity to commit crimes is impacted by at least three major forces. One such force is our life circumstances. When we live in poverty that denies us bare necessities such as food, running water, electricity, education or healthcare, we may turn to crime as a means of survival. People living in poverty may view crime as a more viable option than legal employment. Especially if legitimate job prospects are scarce or aren't paying enough to live in dignity. Significant income inequality can also lead to social disintegration. Social bonds become weakened and trust within communities is lost. And where there is no trust, crime can be easily seen as life's necessity. Beyond communities, when poverty and income inequality are perceived as unfair or unjust, trust in governments and institutions gets easily lost. This distrust may lead some individuals to be less willing to cooperate with law enforcement or abide by the law, because they consider the criminal justice system to be corrupt or unjust.

A lack of access to any or to quality education can also limit people's prospects for stable employment and economic growth, which increases the likelihood of criminal behaviour. In some cases, education is intentionally limited by Cone Masters who carefully engineer the education System and its content to indoctrinate their Subjects. Beyond lesser opportunities for generating income, people who grow up with a limited view and understanding of the world are also more vulnerable to the rhetoric of Cone Masters. They are more easily recruited into oppressive Cones, such as gangs, that will justify crimes against Others and against rival Systems.

Some environmental factors can also influence crime rates. Dilapidated and crime-washed neighbourhoods, make it easier for people to view crime as their only viable option. People living in remote geographic locations with no basic services and amenities will seek illegal ways to survive and thrive. Living in isolation from other communities and having no exposure to diversity of any sort, people may have little empathy toward anyone external to their in-group. Committing crimes against out-groups will therefore not be perceived as wrong or immoral. People living under systemic discrimination and racism will develop resentment toward those in power and the Systems they run, and therefore feel more comfortable committing crimes against them.

For many of these communities and individuals, social isolation, discrimination, and racism aren't new. Usually these are long-lasting situations that lead to generational trauma.[37] These multi-generational traumatic experiences can have a profound impact on people's mental health, including substance abuse. They can disrupt family life by creating unhealthy dynamics, conflict, neglect, and even abuse. Communities and families affected by generational trauma may face limited access to education, employment opportunities, and social support, which lead to enduring economic instability and poverty, and the normalization of criminal involvement. Individuals who experience parental neglect, childhood trauma, and abuse will more likely have low impulse control and engage in criminal behaviour as a way to express their anger or sense of alienation.

Each such life circumstance can have a strong causal effect on criminal behaviour. When there is more than one of those, they compound the damage into a world of pain. People living in poverty will not have the same educational opportunities as their well-to-do peers. They will be at greater risk of living in run-down neighbourhoods or having no access to clean water, electricity, or proper healthcare. They might also experience homelessness which will endanger them both physically and emotionally. They won't be able to afford high-quality food or even know where their next meal will come from. Most of them will have been born to parents with the same miserable experiences, and who are now paying forward their generational trauma.

Our Cones play a central role in creating these life circumstances or aggravating them. Cone Systems usually foster low-trust cultures that, in themselves, lead to criminal activity. In some cases, a particular Cone may glorify or romanticize criminal activity. Other Cones circumvent law-breaking by legalizing actions that would otherwise be immoral or illegal. They will incentivize their Subjects to justify immoral actions by

---

[37] Generational trauma refers to the transmission of psychological and emotional wounds and stressors from one generation to another within a family or community. Generational trauma is passed down through a combination of genetics (epigenetics) and social and psychological processes, such as family dynamics, cultural norms, and coping mechanisms.

promising them power, belonging, status, means, safety, righteousness, certainty, superiority, or revenge. The combination of life circumstances and Cone Systems create emotional and psychological motivators. Fear, desperation, insecurity, misery, frustration, anger, and selfishness can all push us into crime. In some cases, individuals will have biomedical factors that might predispose them to criminal behaviours, such as genetic factors, hormonal imbalances, and mental illness.

The most important thing to note about the hidden part of the crime iceberg is that almost none of these factors are our doing or under our control because we live in imperfect societies governed by multiple oppressive Cones. Similarly to the Social Determinants of Health, we are either born into our realities or they are created for us throughout life. While we may live under the illusion that crime is a choice people make, much of it isn't a choice at all any more than having a disease. A major portion of criminal activity is a reflection of societal rather than individual failures.

The good news is that these factors and motivations aren't permanent or immutable. We can all learn and adapt. One of my favourite stories as a child was *Pygmalion* by George Bernard Shaw. This is a story of an entitled and obnoxious phonetics professor who made a bet with his friend that he could transform someone as inferior as a flower girl into a refined lady by teaching her manners and proper speech. Through much hard work and the professor's insistence on her ability to change, the flower girl indeed becomes a proper lady.

The Pygmalion effect is a fascinating psychological phenomenon. One of the classic studies on this subject was conducted by Robert Rosenthal and Lenore Jacobson in 1968 (1). They administered a nonverbal IQ test to elementary school students at the beginning of the school year. Then they randomly selected 20 percent of the students and told their teachers that these students had shown "unusual potential for intellectual growth." The teachers were assured by the researchers that these children would have significant gains in their academic performance throughout the year. At the end of the school year, the students who had been randomly labelled as having "unusual potential" showed significantly greater improvement in their IQ tests compared to the other students. The researchers attributed this improvement to the teachers' expectations and the subtle ways in which they interacted with these students, providing them with more encouragement and opportunities for learning.

Hundreds of studies in this area have been conducted since, consistently showing that the more we expect people to do well, the better they do (2). Children of parents who made them believe they are capable of succeeding, will have greater success rates in life than children with the same aptitude and opportunities but no parents who believed in them. Employees of leaders who show positive expectations of their abilities perform much better than employees who experience no such empowerment. Patients of doctors who believe in their ability to make healthy changes are more likely to make these changes than patients of doctors who don't show faith in their ability to improve.

Self-fulfilling prophecies aren't always positive. Being pliable beings, we can be destroyed as easily as we can be elevated. The Golem effect[38] is the opposite of the Pygmalion effect. Having negative expectations of an individual lowers their performance (3). Children who are repeatedly told they are failures that will never amount to anything, are more likely to do just that. Employees who are being constantly demeaned and devalued by their supervisors, end up performing poorly.

---

[38] The effect is based on a creature from the Jewish mythology. Golem, a creature made of clay, was given life by Rabbi Loew to protect the Jews of Prague from the horrors of Blood Libel. With time, the golem became increasingly corrupt and violent, until it had to be destroyed. The psychological effect was named after the golem legend in 1982 by Babad, Inbar, and Rosenthal, describing the negative effects of self-fulfilling prophecies.

Patients whose physicians don't believe in their chances to recover or make lifestyle changes, will be much less likely to recover or make changes.

Simply put, we become what those in power expect us to become. When we are constantly told that we and everyone around us are potential sinners or criminals unless we are leashed by thousands of rules and penalties, that is exactly what most of us will believe and how we will behave. High crime rates in low-trust cultures aren't based on some deviant genetic traits. They are the result of infused Core Certainties that claim people can't be trusted and therefore must be tightly controlled. When you are taught that you can't trust anyone, you will be less inclined to follow social norms and ethical guidelines. Why would you bother being honest or ethical if no one else is? You will also be less inclined to collaborate with others for the common good because others can't be trusted, and "common good" might mean someone else's good at your own expense. In a society that believes in eat-or-be-eaten, you may be reluctant to report crimes or corrupt activities to authorities because you will believe that the authorities themselves are corrupt.

Low-trust mindset creates a self-perpetuating cycle. The Golem effect will have more people breaking the law and exploiting others, which will increase people's experience of corruption and crime and confirm what they already believe. Seeing that the powerful and corrupt can escape accountability, people's trust in institutions will further diminish, perpetuating a culture of suspicion and crime, which further propagates laws and punishments.

Whose rules are those anyway?

A social worker friend of mine once told me of a job interview where she was asked: "Would you ever consider breaking the law?" Having been in my twenties, I thought it wasn't a very smart question. Who in their right mind would say yes? Though I have always opposed mindless, oppressive systems, I have never considered law-breaking as a viable option. Especially in the context of employment. It was throughout that discussion with my older and much wiser friend that the true nature of laws dawned on me. We discussed the Civil Rights Movement in the United States in the 1950s and 1960s, where many activists were arrested and punished for violating segregation laws that enforced racial discrimination. We recalled Sophie Scholl, a member of the anti-Nazi student resistance group (the White Rose) who was arrested along with her brother Hans and executed in 1943 for distributing anti-Nazi leaflets at the University of Munich. We even spoke about Jean Valjean, the fictional character in Victor Hugo's *Les Misérables*, who was sentenced to five years in prison for stealing a loaf of bread to feed his sister's starving child. Our conversation boiled down to: "Who makes laws and for whose benefit?" This was followed by another critical question: "Are all laws just?"

While we may believe in universal morals, our view of rights and wrongs is defined for us by our Cone Masters. Different Cones will have different definitions of what constitutes a crime. Some legalities will focus on crimes against individuals, whereas others will deal with crimes against the Cone System and its Masters. Beyond having heaps of rules that keep proliferating in the hands of zealots, Cones excel at creating legal double standards or treating laws as moving targets. Authoritarian parents will apply a different set of rules to themselves than the ones they will impose on their children because "this is the natural order of things." They will then switch these rules on a whim, "because I said so" or "because parents know best." The same is done by all Cone Masters on various scales, either openly or implicitly. Applying double standards is one of the common Cone Masters' tools of the trade.

In George Orwell's novel *Animal Farm*, the animals decide to overthrow their cruel human owner and establish their own society based on the principles of animalism, a form of animal-centric socialism. They write the slogan, "All animals are equal," on the barn to commemorate the fundamental principle of life on the farm. As the story progresses, the pigs, led by Napoleon and Snowball, gradually take on human-like characteristics and privileges, such as living in the farmhouse, sleeping in beds, and even wearing clothes. They go on to assert their dominance and manipulate the other animals for their own benefit. To reinforce their position as the new masters of the farm, they change the slogan to: "All animals are equal, but some animals are more equal than others."

This story represents a signature move of Cone Masters. The higher one ranks in a Cone, the more privileges one "deserves" and the less the law applies to them. Some create separate laws that will only benefit Cone Masters or exempt them from laws that apply to Subjects. Then they will either deny the existence of this double standard or find creative ways to justify it, similarly to authoritarian parents. Abusive partners will be allowed to use abusive behaviours while forbidding their victim to do the same. They will either claim they had never done anything abusive and that they are the victims here, or that their victim "made them do it" by being so intolerably bad. We can find the same pattern in larger groups, including whole nations. If you find it difficult to believe large-scale System laws can be unjust, consider the following examples.

In highly traditional and religious societies, being anything but a cis heterosexual man or woman is an unforgivable sin that is punishable by law. In these societies, even if the death penalty for these "criminals" has been abolished, family patriarchs will still execute their deviant family members (also known as "honour killing") with the legal system all but ignoring it. Women suspected of infidelity or immorality in these societies will often be murdered with the full blessing of the law. In colonized societies, the colonizers will create laws that place them in positions of power, ensure their enduring dominance, and suppress the colonized population. The fifteenth-century American Doctrine of Discovery legalized

European colonial expansion. This perfectly legal framework gave European invaders the right to claim for themselves lands they "discovered" by any means necessary, including a genocide of indigenous populations already living there.

In India, The Indian Penal Code of 1860 gave British colonizers sweeping powers to suppress any form of dissent or resistance against their colonial rule. The law that denied freedom of speech, assembly, and press allowed the British to quash political movements and imprison dissenters. In South Africa, the Natives Land Act of 1913 divided the country into areas designated for specific racial groups. Through this act, most of the land was reserved for white South Africans, with severe restrictions on the rights of black South Africans to settle on what used to be their own land.

In theocratic societies, to this day, the religious establishment passes laws that enforce religious practices on its citizens while punishing anyone who adheres to other religions or denounces religion altogether. Blasphemy laws in theocratic countries such as Pakistan, Iran, Saudi Arabia, and Indonesia criminalize speech or actions that might insult Islam or its religious figures, and forbid people from abandoning their religion. These infractions can lead to severe penalties, including imprisonment and even the death penalty. In deeply divided societies, laws are created by the groups in power to favour the powerful and ensure a permanent divide. Jim Crow laws in the United States enforced racial segregation in the South, limiting people of colour from accessing services, education, employment, and political participation. While these laws affected all people of colour, they especially harmed low-income individuals, locking them into a cycle of poverty.

In societies where capital rules, the wealthy and powerful pass laws that favour them, and disadvantage those they exploit. The more capitalistic the country or region, the more you will find anti-minimum wage and anti-union legislation. These types of laws give nearly absolute power to wealthy business owners and corporations, while leaving workers with little bargaining power and low, unlivable wages. Highly capitalistic societies will also have tax policies that provide generous deductions, loopholes, or lower tax rates for the wealthy while making those inaccessible or irrelevant to the middle- and working-class. In some such countries, people earning unlivable minimum wages may end up paying more tax than the top 1 percent. These societies are also more prone to legislate laws that punish its vulnerable and marginalized members for… being vulnerable and marginalized. Anti-vagrancy legislation, for example, is used to criminalize homelessness and beggary. These laws target people who are denied housing opportunities by these very same societal laws. It is no different than starving a person and then punishing them for being malnourished. The same goes for criminalizing people who use substances, even though addiction is recognized as a mental health issue.

If you live in a democratic country that boasts equality in its manifesto, you may have been raised to believe that your country's laws are just and treat everyone as equals under the law. Reality, however, can be mucky. Every nation has a history, and most histories aren't pretty. All national legal frameworks have grown on a bed of thorny, bloody, and discriminatory events and outdated Core Certainties. Most if not all laws were written by members of the ruling class. Though laws have gone through cycles of updates, these aren't always significant enough to erase old Dogmas because we revere our forefathers and their ancient written documents. Even the changes we do succeed to pass are usually proposed by people in power, who have their own narrow agendas to protect.

When we think of the word "criminal," we may imagine murderers or burglars. But in many societies, depending on their Cones, a criminal can be a queer person, a woman who has been raped, an individual who fails to uphold a certain religion, a person who struggles with mental health or homelessness, a person who had escaped their slavers, or a farmer whose crop happened to get contaminated by GMO seeds from a neighbouring field.

At the same time, murderers and burglars may be considered law-abiding citizens provided they are soldiers loyal to their country, colonizers killing and robbing the "local savages," or racial purists who cleanse their land from "impure human vermin." Keep in mind that the greatest atrocities in human history were not committed by people who were considered criminals. They were committed by those who followed the full letter of their laws.

Going back to my friend's interview question, "Would you ever consider breaking the law?" it seems the correct answer must be, "It depends." This doesn't mean we should simply disregard all laws and rules or consider every policy to be corrupt. This is merely a necessary eye-opener for all of us who believe that our laws are beyond reproach and that crime is always immoral.

Addressing crimes: Justice or revenge?

When I was a child, every time I would bump against furniture or fall and scrape my knee, my parents would tell me to "hit it back," as if retribution would give the table what it deserves and take away my pain. You may chuckle at the silly advice, but that's more or less how most of our societies address people who commit crimes. Before we move into punishments, let's consider the highlights of our previous points:

Not all laws, rules, regulations, and policies are fair; they can be discriminatory and harmful to some or even most members of the group or society.

Considering the possibility of unfairness of the law, crimes aren't always universally "criminal." They may be inevitable acts of survival, Cone-defiance, or Cone-heresy.

Even when we ignore the flaws of existing laws, criminal activity is mostly the result of harmful societal factors outside people's choice or control.

In an ideal or a Cone-free world, before we devise the best way to deal with crime, we would have to answer the following two questions:

1. **Are the rules/laws they were breaking truly fair, reasonable, feasible, non-oppressive, and designed to serve all and harm none?**

If this is true, the person may have broken well-justified laws and is therefore likely to be in the wrong. The next step would be to check whether the reason for their criminal behaviour may be explained in Question 2.

If this is not true, the person may have broken unjust laws and is therefore not necessarily in the wrong. Instead of punishing the culprit, we should go back to the drawing board and re-examine our laws.

2. **Might the person's criminal activity be tied to their dire life circumstances and/or their adverse emotional, psychological, or biomedical state?**

If this is true, the person was likely predisposed, conditioned, pressured, or left no other choice than to break the law. Therefore, it should be our responsibility to provide care for this individual. We should examine how we have caused them to deteriorate into criminal activity, and then provide proper supports for the healing.

If no mitigating circumstances can be easily identified, our initial conclusion will be that the person had every reason and opportunity to follow the law but chose to break it anyway. This will require a deeper inquiry as the act might be concealed deeper in the person's psyche, such as a hidden childhood trauma, deep-seated insecurities, or an undiagnosed bi-omedical condition.

Whichever the case may be, the System should address not only the offenders, but also the victims of the crime. These may be the people who were directly harmed by the criminal act, the secondary circle of people related to the criminal and the victim, or any environmental factor that was adversely impacted by the act. It should be the responsibility of the System to help mend the damage, restore everyone's well-being, and find ways to prevent such future events. In a perfect, Cone-free world, this will be done in full participation of the offender, who will act to restore, mend, and heal those affected by their act. This will not be done as a punishment, but as part of their own healing and re-integration with their group or society. Unfortunately, most of us aren't living in a perfect, Cone-free world. We are much more familiar with addressing crimes with punishments.

When we first immigrated to Canada with our two young children, we spent the first week at a friends' house while searching for a rental place of our own. They, too, had two kids of nearly identical ages to ours. Though we were all childhood friends, we had lived apart on different continents for many years and our reunion was a joyous one. A day or two in, we noticed significant differences in our parenting styles. Our friends had multiple rules that regulated their kids' conduct, an untrusting mindset, a close monitoring of their behaviours, and clear corresponding punishments for each infraction. My husband and I found this parenting style unpalatable. Our friends, on their part, were shocked and appalled by our lax parenting style. When they asked us how we disciplined our kids without punishments, we tried to explain that we focus on mutual respect, empowerment, and negotiation. They thought our parenting style was a recipe for disaster.

If you are a parent, you know raising children isn't an easy task. Good parents require more maturity, patience, endurance, and practice than Olympic athletes. Beyond the basic need to be loved and cared for, kids can be dangerously experimental, and wildly free spirited. While these are wonderful qualities, if left to their own devices, kids might risk their own safety and struggle with integrating in society. That's where good parenting comes in. But what does it look like? An authoritarian parenting style checks many Cone boxes. One of them is the multitude of rigid rules that aren't always supportive, nurturing, or fair to their children. Young minds who are trying to figure out life and their place in the world will inevitably require experimentation and boundary pushing. If neither is allowed even in small ways, their personal growth will be stifled. The other Cone behaviour is the punitive system which leads to fear and anxiety in children. Parents who catch their children committing "crimes against the family System," will punish them based on a Cone-typical black and white view of "you're either with us or against us." You are either a good child or a bad child. A liar or a truth teller.

Their harsh punishments focus on inflicting enough emotional or physical pain to make sure the child is too afraid to do it again. The constant threat of hurtful penalties can break the child's spirit and reduce their "crime rates" along with their individuality and self-worth. Alternatively, it can teach them to be better liars and manipulators to reduce their chances of being caught. This system is a miniature mirror of the way Cones work when it comes to addressing infractions. Every Cone-defined crime carries a penalty. Cone penalties focus on retaliation for the wrongdoing, as it is seen as a betrayal against the Cone.

Cone penalties are all about suppression and control, not restoration and growth, because the Cone System never trusts their Subjects. No trust also means no respect and no empathy. Penalties will always invoke powerful emotions to make sure people will do anything to avoid them.

Punishments can play on the Subjects' fear of being seen as inferior or unworthy, of being rejected, losing power or possessions, exposed to physical harm, the good old fear of death, or all the above.

Just as there is no such thing as a small Problem, there is no small punishment since both are in the eye of the beholder. While some penalties are more visible and brutal than others, such as incarceration or execution, other less visible ones can be as devastating. In fact, it is those invisible punishments that can be the most affecting in daily life. For a social animal, being discredited, shamed, and rejected by our in-group may feel as bad as an execution. We are probably the only animal that doesn't have to use teeth, claws, or weapons to kill. We are perfectly capable of doing it with our words.

Cone enforcement

Cone enforcement serves a double purpose. One is to help the Cone Masters keep the envious and greedy in their inner circle at bay. The other is to keep their Subjects locked and compliant inside their Cone. Strong enforcement systems help achieve both purposes. The first basic principle is establishing double standards in laws and regulations, as described in the previous section. The second is establishing the same double standards in the enforcements of these laws for the exact same reasons. Compare the case of Donald Trump to that of Edward Snowden. By the end of 2023, former US President Donald Trump was found guilty of sexual attack, and faced four felony counts for his efforts to overturn the 2020 election, thirteen felony counts for election interference, thirty-four felony counts for hush money payments to a porn star, and forty felony counts for hoarding highly sensitive, classified documents and for impeding the government's efforts to retrieve them.

Snowden was a subcontractor working for the American National Security Agency (NSA) who stumbled on illegal and harmful activity conducted by the agency. In 2013, he found ample evidence of NSA collecting phone and internet data with no authority to do so from unsuspecting people around the world. Unwilling to cover up this gross and illegal breach of privacy, Snowden leaked the information on NSA's crimes to three prominent journalists. Despite being in the right, he was immediately accused of treason. Having left no other choice, Snowden fled to Russia for asylum. Snowden said in an interview:[39] "Everyone who's followed these cases know, being charged under the espionage act as a whistleblower means no fair trial is permitted. And there are people in the United States today that are serving time in prison for doing the right thing." While the American law enforcement persecuted Snowden with the full force of Thor's hammer less than a day after he released truthful information, Donald Trump was still walking free years after his crimes were revealed. Every other average citizen would have long lost their reputation, job, possessions, and freedom for a fraction of Trump's crimes, yet he was eligible to run for presidency—one of the most power-wielding roles in the world.

This story of enforcement disparity isn't limited to the United States and is usually much worse in dictatorships and theocracies. It is a recurring theme of Cone Systems around the world where enforcement authorities treat people in power differently (even under the same law) from those who have no power in society. This glaring double standard results from many acting forces. First, people in power build enforcement systems that work in their own favour. After all, what Cone Master in their right mind would willingly create mechanisms that would hold them accountable for their misconduct? Though some people in power may be stupid, they aren't fools. They do everything in their power to sabotage processes that might compromise their immunity from consequences.

---

[39] MSNBC, *The 11ᵗʰ Hour*, Sep 11, 2020.

Second, they use their power and means to create a network of community, political, judicial, and enforcement puppets and supporters who will shield them from consequences. These are the secondary Cone Masters and primary enforcers who enact their head Cone Master's rules. The third principle of Cone enforcement is the trickle-down system that allows Cone Masters to govern without breaking a sweat. Contrary to trickle-down economics, this one actually works. That's how even a small number of people—sometimes only a single individual—can run an oppressive and indoctrinating System and enforce their Dogma all at the same time.

Most Cones use four major power vectors to control their Dogma, System, and Users: trickle down enforcement, peer enforcement, self enforcement, and enforcement by proxy.

Trickle down enforcement

If you think about it, effective Cone enforcement is basically a clever Ponzi scheme. Figure 34 illustrates the Cone enforcement structures within the Cone of a typical Ku Klux Klan (KKK)[40] faction. Note the pompous titles typical to Cone Masters.[41]

---

[40] The Ku Klux Klan (KKK) is a white supremacist, extremist organization. Its core values focus mostly on the preservation of "white race" purity, opposition to civil rights for anyone who isn't a white Christian, antisemitism, anti-immigration, and anti-people of colour.
[41] The KKK's structure and titles have changed over time and across different factions, but the principle remains.

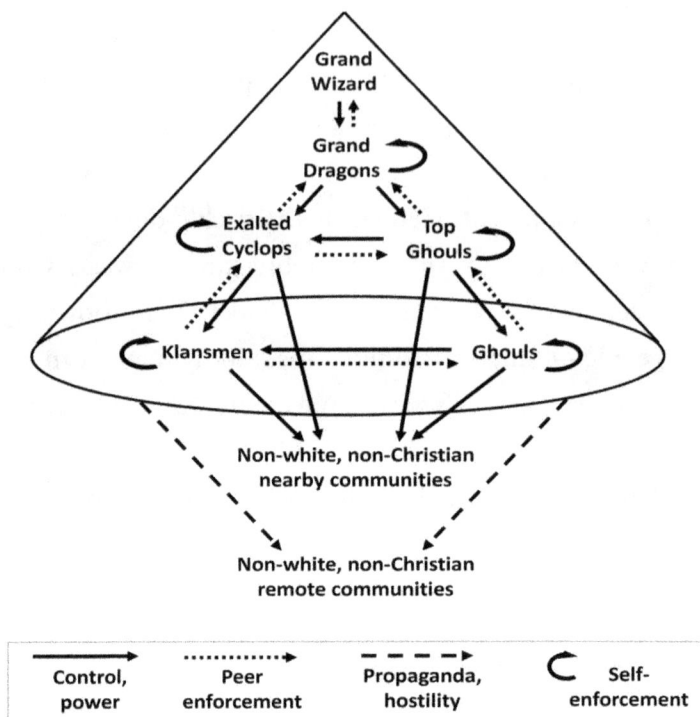

Figure 34: Power relations and enforcement vectors in the KKK

The trickle-down enforcement starts from the top. The head Cone Master (the Grand Wizard) will be the one to establish enforcement principles. These will include some form of monitoring of everyone in the organization, and a variety of effective offender-trapping and penalty methods. Being a large enough Cone, every local chapter of the KKK will have a tiered enforcement system. The Grand Wizard (the CEO) will enforce the organization's laws on the Grand Dragons (the VPs), who will enforce it on their Top Ghouls (head enforcers). Top Ghouls will enforce the law on Exalted Cyclops (head field operatives), and both will be the enforcers of Klansmen and Ghouls (the local foot soldiers).

Peer enforcement

Though it is less formal than appointed enforcers, peer enforcement can be as powerful as any policing force, and sometimes even more so. It may take the shape of peer pressure, tattling, and informing. In other types of Cones, peer enforcement can be a lynching mob or the power to make citizen arrests. These forms of enforcement are exceptionally powerful because our peers are always around, and they are always watching, listening, and interacting with us.

But how do Cone Masters get their Subjects to do their bidding, often with no tangible reward or compensation? There are many strategies they can use to turn their Subjects into peer enforcers. Cones that claim moral purity or a higher cause, such as the KKK, will instill a strong sense of moral or ethical responsibility for the Dogma, and therefore personal duty to report offences. Subjects will believe that exposing their peers' moral impurities or ideological betrayals will uphold principles of justice and prevent a threat to the Cone community. Subjects with a strong Need for certainty will inform on their "deviant" peers not so much for moral reasons as for their desire to maintain order and stability. Note that moral and ethical responsibilities can be perfectly legitimate reasons to report on peer infractions, so long as the Solution isn't an oppressive Cone, and the goal is to protect from harm. Business enterprises and regulated professions will put in place legal obligations to report certain activities, such as criminal actions, safety hazards, or violations of specific regulations. It is when the rules and penalties are oppressive and damaging that peer enforcement becomes toxic.

There are many other motivators for people to rat each other out to the authorities or to exert undue power on their peers. People will snitch on their friends and colleagues to protect themselves from potential harm should they be caught concealing someone else's crimes. Being part of a Cone, such as the KKK, creates a strong sense of belonging and a powerful need to conform at all costs, which means regularly observing each other's behaviour and reporting or acting against Cone deviants and Internal Traitors.

Some cases of peer enforcement are fuelled by envy and spite, something also known as crab mentality. When crabs are trapped in a bucket, they will prevent the escape attempts of any individual crab. The minute one starts climbing up to escape captivity, the others will grab him with their claws and pull him back down. In human societies, we call it, "If I can't be happy, neither can you." Another reason Subjects will report peers is to settle personal grievances or conflicts by using the Cone's big guns to get their revenge. People can also use peer enforcement to promote personal goals. Turning against their own will serve their Need for power and superiority and may award them with praise and rewards.

Oppressive regimes are known for turning their Subjects against one another and rewarding informers. Simone de Beauvoir wisely said, "The oppressor would not be strong if he did not have accomplices among the oppressed." In highly Coned societies—from abusive families, to cults, to totalitarian countries—children are particularly vulnerable to such strategies. They are indoctrinated to be more loyal to the Dogma and its Cone Masters than to their own friends and parents. These children grow up to feel pride in being loyal Subjects who would turn in their loved ones over the slightest suspicion of Cone treason.

No matter what motivates people to enforce the Cone on their peers, it will always be fuelled by a culture of distrust. One of the ways Cone Masters augment this distrust is by infusing narratives such as, "Only the righteous are deserving, but who is to tell which of us is righteous?" The other is by deepening the divide among sub-groups of Subjects to create a culture of sub-oppressors, as illustrated in Figure 35.

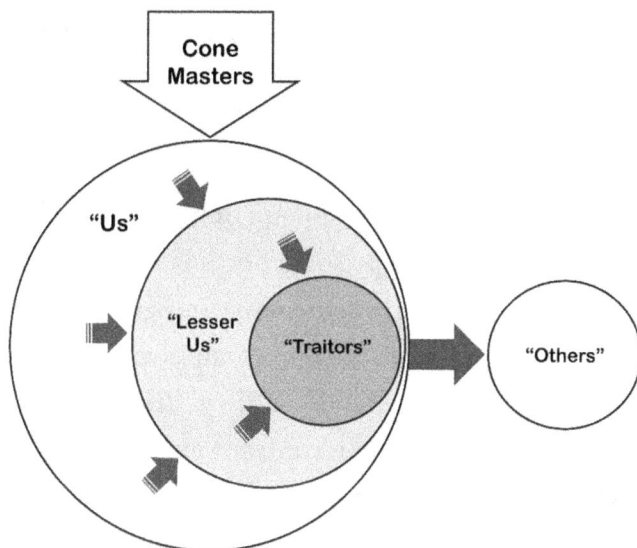

Figure 35: Cone enforcement—a culture of oppressors and sub-oppressors

The Cone narrative will claim that less devout and traitorous rivals are all around, both inside and outside the Cone. Therefore, our peers can be our unquestioning "brothers in arms" or traitors and enemies. But even among our insiders, there will be those who deviate from the "true Dogma" and become a sub-oppressed group. These may develop their own sub-sub-oppressed group to snub and control. Think of organized religions. Most are split into denominations or sub-clusters. Each denomination regards the other clusters as inferior. Within each, there will be the orthodox believers, who will frown upon the less devout, who will consider the even more liberal members as traitors. Each will oppress the next in line, while considering people of other religions or atheists (the Others) as sinners and enemies. Within authoritarian families, we see this pecking order when parents oppress their children, older children oppress the younger, and the boys oppress their sisters. The whole family will then mistreat outsiders they consider inferior or hostile. These layers of oppressors and sub-oppressors support the Cone's mission to infuse everyone with distrust and disrespect that leads to peer enforcement and keeps everyone in line.

Self-enforcement

Our Need to belong within a Cone doesn't only lead to betrayal of family and friends, but it also carries a personal price. It requires us to self-regulate our thoughts and behaviours, self-enforce our group's rules no matter how difficult it is for us, and even punish ourselves. In healthy groups, this self-regulation is rarely painful. Even if we struggle to conform with our group rules, we are allowed to learn from our mistakes, reach out for support, or decide to leave and seek a more fitting group without fearing penalties. In Cones, self-enforcement goes much beyond our Need to belong. It is usually a matter of psychological, social, or even physical survival within our punitive environment.

Self-enforcement comes in many forms, depending on the Cone. People may impose self-censorship by keeping their opinions, ideas, or beliefs to themselves in fear of persecution or punishment. Self-enforcement also means having to fully comply with the Cone's discriminatory laws and practices. Even when a person disagrees with the moral wrongs, they will adhere to oppressive practices to avoid penalties or to align themselves with the Cone's values. That's why Cone Masters can easily get away with harmful practices such as racial segregation, censorship, gender discrimination, curfews, mass surveillance, or restrictions on assembly. Subjects may also self-impose strict dress codes, limit their education to Cone-approved content, and surrender to sexual abuse. They will punish themselves for "Cone heresy" in a variety of ways, from fasting through self-flagellation, to self-mutilation.

Enforcement by proxy

The fourth and final vector is enforcement by proxy, which relies on scare tactics and hostility. This vector affects outsiders who don't belong or have not subscribed to the Cone but are close enough to be affected by it. These can be the family members of an abuser's victim, business associates and vendors of an oppressive organization, or the non-white, non-Christian community where KKK operates. Other external groups may be more remote from the Cone, but still affected by the Cone's propaganda.

While some smaller Cones rely on informal enforcement, most Cone Systems engage formal enforcers, such as disciplinarians, managers, taskmasters, fixers, strongmen, police, military, intelligence, or secret police. Cone Masters recruit and train them to ensure the execution of their rules and the maintenance of their power. The smart ones will convince their enforcers that they are the Cone Master's best friends and confidants. This will be a lie, because enforcers are the Cone Master's guard dogs, and as such, they will be expendable. Yet they will be made to believe that their sacrifice is noble and that one day, if they work really hard, they will be "the face/heroes of the Dogma" and get invited to sit at the Cone Master's table.

The highly intelligent Cone enforcers are typically assigned to strategic positions. Others will be zealots and wannabes who have something to prove; those who feel unappreciated and vie for power or live in fear that can be easily converted into hatred. Others yet will be assigned to their roles by their Cone Masters without being asked for their opinion on the matter. These could be conscripted soldiers, family members of crime organizations, or neighbourhood youth pressed into gangs. Formal enforcers will have as many motivations for their role as any other Subject practicing peer enforcement or self-enforcement. They may be driven by Cone morality, a sense of obligation, civic duty, righteousness, conviction, pursuit of justice, concern for other's safety, desire for order and stability, fear of refusing the role, authority-pleasing, ambition, or sadism. Whatever they are, Cone enforcers are the pillars that hold the Cone upright.

When it comes to legalities and enforcement systems, Cones operate under the assumption that leaders deserve far more than anyone else, and that Subjects cannot be trusted. That's why Cone Masters will always rig the Systems in their favour, while creating control systems that treat Subjects as incapable or untrustworthy to do right by the Cone if left to their own devices. This mindset results in unfair and excessive laws and regulations, extensive monitoring, and punitive and robust enforcement. As you can imagine, these inflated legal and enforcement systems lead to inflated bureaucracy, which often becomes the tail that wags the dog.

CHAPTER 16:

Belly of the beast

… where we discover how Cone Systems devolve into sluggish bureaucracies while expanding their power and reach.

Propagating rules

There's a military urban legend about an armoured corps unit that purchased highly priced, top-of-the-line tanks. As in all new equipment, the tanks came with detailed maintenance instructions requiring monthly oiling. Being a stickler about equipment maintenance, the colonel instructed his subordinates to oil the tanks every three weeks, to be on the safe side. The lieutenant-colonels took him seriously and instructed their majors to ensure the tanks were oiled every other week. The majors decided to go above and beyond, and instructed their captains to train specialized mechanics who would be dedicated to oiling the tanks on a weekly basis. The specialized mechanics, whose job was now narrowed to this one task and didn't want to look idle, oiled the tanks daily. Once the System was implemented, the military operations of the armoured unit ground to a halt, having maintenance taking the best part of every day. A few months down the road, all the new tanks broke down.

We are suckers for rules. Just give us a Solution of any sort, and we will develop mounds of laws and regulations that keep tightening the Solution, often into a chokehold. Organized religions are well known for proliferating rules. The most basic tenet of most faiths is "love all and harm none." And yet generations of believers have piled up so many laws, stipulations, and punishments for transgressors that this basic principle was all but buried alive.

Take for example the Jewish religious rules related to kosher food. The Tora (Old Testament) mentions six major provisions on food consumption:[42]

Forbidding to cook a young goat in its mother's fat for humanitarian reasons (the word "fat" ended up being mistranslated into "milk").

Forbidding the consumption of some types of animals (four-legged animals that don't have cloven hooves and don't chew their cud such as pigs, and sea creatures that don't have fins and scales). No reasoning was provided.

Demanding humane treatment of animals, including slaughtering in ways that minimizes suffering.

Prohibiting the consumption of blood and requiring proper drainage of blood from meat. The reasoning provided is that the life of every creature resides in its blood. By draining and burying it, humans pay homage to the life they took.

Forbidding certain parts of animals, such as the sciatic nerve and certain fats. The explanation provided for the sciatic nerve is that the socket of Jacob was injured near his hip tendon when he was fighting the angel. The fat prohibition is related to animals found dead or torn by wild animals, and to any major chunks of goodness that should be made as an offering to the Lord.

Instructing on the types of foods that should and shouldn't be consumed during Passover (eat bitter herbs, sacrifice a lamb, foods mustn't contain yeast). The reasoning provided is to commemorate the exodus of the Jewish people from Egypt.

Let's start with the source material of organized religions, including but not limited to Judaism. If you are a devout believer, no matter which

---

[42] Note that food preparation and consumption decrees aren't presented in a single chapter as a manual for Jewish foods; most are scattered throughout the scriptures within different contexts.

religion you subscribe to, you were probably taught that your holy scriptures were written by the hand of your deity or its prophets and are therefore irrefutable. You will adhere to the written word and take every story verbatim. From a more scholarly perspective, most ancient scriptures were authored by multiple human scribes (often in different periodic languages) who lived thousands of years ago in a world very different from our own (7). Some parts of these old texts include documented ancient wisdom that is still as valid and precious as ever, such as "love all and harm none." Other parts were relevant to the period, such as marital rituals, effective farming, and food hygiene procedures. Many narratives commemorated major events—either real or allegoric. These were the tales that held deep spiritual meaning to that particular group of people at that time. Many of these tales never aimed to describe actual events. Their goal was to communicate life lessons and create unifying myths. Not unlike the tales of the Brothers Grimm that taught little girls not to trust human predators who pretended to be nice to them.

Historic accounts make up a good portion of most holy scriptures. As all recorded history goes, ancient or modern, they were written by many authors who worked for local leaders and therefore represented political powers and interests. Some events were embellished to make the leader look good and righteous and villainize their enemies, whereas others were omitted to avoid embarrassment. Eventually, multiple pieces of these ancient texts were collated into a single anthology by other humans. These people had personal beliefs and political agendas that guided which narrative to include, rephrase, exclude, or destroy. Once these cherry-picked, agenda-laden, and often mistranslated texts were wrapped into a single scripture, it was sealed and sanctified as "the living word" of whatever deities they worshiped.

Going back to kosher rules, some of these stipulations are humanitarian in nature, which are well aligned with the foundational principles of all faiths. At least one major prohibition was mistranslated and led to a completely irrelevant practice of separating meat from milk. But even if we ignore the mistranslation and accept all six rules as "the word of God," current kosher rules will have you scratching your head more than once. Throughout the three thousand or so years since these dietary rulings were written, they were not only sanctified, but also interpreted in many different ways. They were expanded a thousand times over by rabbinic scholars whose sole mission in life was to dig deeper. And dig they did.

Nowadays, the rules on kosher food fill many books and require lengthy education on the subject. Every single biblical item has been multiplied into hundreds of directives that detail who, why, when, and how food sources should be grown, cropped, slaughtered, processed, cooked, eaten, stored, and disposed of. There are whole Systems of training and whole legions of licensed inspectors assigned to supervising farmers, butchers, and food producers who wish to get the kosher stamp on their foods. As in all Cone Systems, these rules are reinforced through a range of personal and commercial penalties for sinners and transgressors. The Jewish faith isn't the only one propagating rules beyond measure. Every major religion has its own inflated System of rules and punishments related to nearly every aspect of our lives, from food, through minute-by-minute conduct, to ceremonies and burial rituals.

Our compulsive desire to be certain about every unanticipated variable in our lives plays right into the hands of our Cone Masters who propagate rules to control us. Since Cones are low-trust constructs, the rationale for inflated legislation is, "If we leave an opening, people and/or organizations will abuse our trust and harm us and our Dogma." This untrusting mindset leads to the creation of more and more rules to close every possible gap and loophole anyone might exploit.

When you grow up in highly Coned societies, this may sound like a logical approach. We assume this is the reason countries have such extensive legal frameworks that address every single aspect of our lives—

because we can't trust others or even ourselves. Crime rates and law breakers in our societies seem to prove this assumption. To reinforce this Core Certainty, we were taught by our sociologists, psychologists, and historians that any group beyond 150 individuals will fall apart into chaos. Known as Dunbar's number, this hypothesis asserts we can only maintain about 150 connections at once and that anything beyond this requires a structured governance System. We believe that the bigger the group of people, the more written rules, management levels, and supervision structures it will require. And yet there are many current societies, as well as multiple ancient ones uncovered by archeologists on nearly every continent, that exhibit evidence of a very different way of living.

In their book, *The Dawn of Everything* (8), David Graeber and David Wengrow provide evidence of the various ways people have organized societies throughout history. One such example is the many ancient mega-cities found in what is now Ukraine and Moldova that were built about six thousand years ago. These cities were inhabited for nearly eight centuries—twice as long as the Roman Empire. The biggest one found so far is Taljanky, which extended over three hundred hectares (three square kilometres). This mega-city had over one thousand permanent dwellings built in concentric circles with spaces between the houses for private gardens. The houses created a multi-tiered ring around a vast empty field that was likely a communal space for markets and events. This city, and many others like it, presents no evidence of central government buildings, communal storage facilities, fortifications, dungeons, or religious structures. Around ten thousand people simply lived with and next to each other for nearly thirty generations without a centralized, governing power.

These types of societies, non-governed cities, and large, decentralized villages found all over the globe were run by matriarchal and other types of collaborative approaches. Some that were spared total annihilation or colonization, still are. And yet none have found their way into our mainstream history books and educational systems. Having lived in highly hierarchical and Cone-governed societies, historians were either unable, unwilling, or forbidden from interpreting their findings as anything more than curious aberration. These scholars dismissed places like Taljanky as being settlements of simple-minded, noble savages that by some miracle had managed to coexist in their thousands without "civilized systems." In truth, there is no actual reason for us to label these societies as a bunch of simpletons except that their way of life is beyond our indoctrinated, low-trust comprehension. It is much more likely these societies operated within well-thought-of, communal, high-trust cultures. Therefore, they had no use for rigid, oppressive Systems or for thousands of documented laws and centralized enforcement systems.

If this is the case, is it still true that we must propagate laws and build whole legal Systems to reduce crime? We are taught that without a plethora of laws, regulations, and punishments, we will collapse into a messy heap of felons and victims. We are assured that we can't trust people to know what's best for them or for the System, and we believe it to be true because we have seen these things happen time and again. The Wild West was a dangerous place because it was lawless. We have heard tales and have seen movies where people were shot in the streets, robbed, and raped without significant consequences. When the communist regime fell apart, the former Soviet Union was left in ruins, with exploiters grabbing power and assets and leaving the rest to collapse into anarchy and deep poverty.

Yet these examples are hardly proof that the only way to maintain order is through harsh laws and rigorous enforcement. The Wild West was a dangerous place for many other reasons than being short on legislation. The western coast of the United States was taken by force from its original inhabitants—the Mexicans and indigenous people—and swarmed by colonizers and gold diggers who were already in the habit of taking by force whatever the hell they wanted. The chaos created post-perestroika (the fall of the communist regime) didn't happen because unleashed humans are innately criminal. A big part of it was because a change in an oppressive regime, that isn't accompanied with a gradual evolution into a high-trust culture, is a recipe for failure. The same happened in "post-liberated" Afghanistan and Iraq. People who have never experienced a different way of being will naturally have a hard time imagining life where they would be treated fairly and kindly.

It is difficult for us to believe there are better ways to live and that society can run smoothly without being highly controlled and punitive if we have never seen or experienced a better way of life. It is difficult to believe people can be genuinely kind and collaborative if all we've experienced is a cut-throat society. Staunch individualistic capitalists cannot imagine the advantages of living in a more socialistic environment. They refuse to believe they wouldn't be "outstripped of their privileges and robbed of their hard-earned money to fund parasites." Culturally unprepared for such a transition, some people will find ways to exploit the trusting nature of high-trust societies and use it as proof that people are innately criminal unless stopped by law.

Strict rules in Cone Systems will start by suffocating us and stifling our freedom, growth, and creativity. Then they will get out of hand and gain a life of their own. Regulations and policies will propagate beyond measure to create absolute control. Like the tank story, rules and laws in mature Cones become the tail that wags the dog. Their multitude tends to empty the original intent and leave a shell—a System with a sole purpose of gaining and maintaining control of itself and its Subjects. When Cone Subjects live within oppressive, untrusting environments, some will submit, and others will find ways to beat the system at its own game. The bottom line is that oppressive Cones and their excessive laws don't prevent criminality. They enhance it as a self-fulfilling prophesy.

The ills of bureaucracy

Having a well-established, well-functioning System is at the heart of any Solution. Even a relationship between two people has a System they both agree on. At the very least, it will include written or verbal agreements on the purpose of the relationship, and on who does what, when, and how. The bigger the Solution and the more Cone-ish it is, the more rigid and inflated the System that governs it. Cone Systems are typically heavy on rules, deeply invested in enforcement, harsh on punishments, and run by oversized bureaucracies.

The bigger the Solution, the more complex and multi-tiered the System it will build for its operations. In the early days of a Cone, the System is often sophisticated and predatory. As time goes by, many Cones morph from "lean and mean" into something sprawling, sluggish, and convoluted. It is said that it takes more muscles to frown than to smile, implying it is easier to be nice than nasty. Though this is a physiologically and possibly a psychologically inaccurate statement, this metaphor is accurate for Cone Systems.

A healthy, functional System requires a certain level of order and organization. Being built on values of trust and respect, healthy, non-Coned Systems encourage their people to supervise themselves and be accountable for their own actions. Leaders and Users often decide collaboratively on how things should be done, and then communicate this to all Solution Users. Everyone within a healthy System knows the consequences of mistakes and offences and understands the reasoning for them. These consequences are fair, and they focus on problem-solving and learning, not finger-pointing or punitive action. The System leader is more of a facilitator, helper, adviser, and coach than an executor of control. Their role is to support Solution Users and then move out of their way, believing everyone is both driven and competent. In a non-coned environment, a single person will oversee many direct supervisees (or support many Users). This will mean fewer management levels, and less bureaucracy. It will also mean fewer rules and regulations and greater involvement of Users in overall System operations. Ergo, fewer muscles to smile.

The operating Systems of Cone Solutions are the exact opposite of healthy ones. The very essence of a Cone is control and suppression of all Subjects. Therefore, it will be managed in the spirit of a low-trust culture, which means any form and level of supervision will be tight and controlling. Much time, energy, and resources will be dedicated to commanding, scrutinizing, monitoring, checking up, and reporting on every single person and operation. In Cone Systems, only Cone Masters decide on how things should be done. They will view collaboration or consultation with Subjects to be redundant because "Leaders know best" or "Subjects are merely our means for success, therefore shouldn't have a voice."

When Coned Systems have clearly defined rules and policies, there will be too many of them to be wieldy. Alternatively, the rules will be moving targets based on the Cone Master's shifting personal Needs. Just like in children's stories about the petulant king who comes up with nonsensical decrees, Cone Masters feel powerful and justified enough to do the same within their Systems. In the more openly tyrannical Cones, they will not have to explain themselves. In the more covert ones, such changes will be publicly justified by the System as being "well-thought-of and in everyone's best interest." Worse still, System administrators will not always communicate the revised rules clearly or consistently to Solution Subjects. Sometimes it will be intentional as part of a gaslighting strategy. If we are unsure whether what we are praised for today will result in punishment tomorrow, we will be in a constant state of anxiety and fear. When life is perpetually uncertain, we become helpless and obedient, which is how Cone Masters want us. In other cases, the System is simply too sluggish and messy for effective communication across the Solution ranks. The intent here might be less sinister, but the adverse effects will be the same.

The role of Cone Masters within their System is to exert authority, provide detailed instructions, monitor closely, and control damage by their underlings. This pattern repeats itself throughout the ranks and results in inflated Systems. If you can't trust those reporting to you, you will have to spend a lot of time and energy micromanaging them. Since there are only twenty-four hours in a day, each micromanaging supervisor can only oversee a few direct supervisees. That's why Cone Solutions are top-heavy pyramids with significantly more managers and supervisory levels than healthy Solution Systems. A Cone's low-trust System culture requires far more bureaucracy to manage the many rules and levels of supervision, and safeguard the System from damage that Subjects might cause. Since the Cone System suspects everyone of being traitorous or incompetent, it will keep inventing new rules and putting in additional safeguards that will keep inflating bureaucracy, just like the kosher rules and their ever-growing monitoring and enforcement systems.

Sometimes the mere size of Cone Systems leads to them being unruly and contradictory, as described by Ian Hodder in his book, *Studies in Human-Thing Entanglement* (9). Subjects get lost and entangled in the complexities of large Cone Systems that are built to support the Cone, not them. As a result, these bureaucracies diminish and dehumanize them. In his article "Are Monopolies Evil Geniuses or Blundering Fools?" (10), Benjamin Cain claims that the Systems running monopolies (i.e., mega-Cones) are not operated by "… an all-seeing evil genius like Darth Vader who bends the corporation's bureaucracy to his will." Rather, they are run by a more "banal" form of evil, much like the one that operated in the Nazi dictatorship. Hannah Arendt observed in her book, *Eichmann in Jerusalem* (11), that, "Evil comes from a failure to think. It defies thought, for as soon as thought tries to engage itself with evil and examine the premises and principles from which it originates, it is frustrated because it finds nothing there. That is the banality of evil."

Cain asserts that though mega-Cones may look like the Death Star from Star Wars, they are usually operated by a blundering behemoth of a System where the left hand doesn't know what the right one is doing because "… there's no omnipresent taskmaster cracking whips and ensuring conformity to a coherent set of evil principles." Many times, even a legendary tyrant like Darth Vader will be dwarfed by his empire's convoluted administration. In these overly administrative Cones, clever Subjects learn how to manipulate the System to their advantage. Despite the low-trust, micromanaged environment, they will find ways to exploit the System to their benefit and hide their incompetence and disinterest under piles of processes and paperwork.

No matter how sluggish the Cone System becomes, it never loses its hunger for more. More power. More possessions. More territory. More than others. That's why most Cones invest in continuous expansion, the hell with consequences.

Expanding and colonizing

A virus is a tiny creature. It isn't composed of cells, and it can't generate energy, carry out biochemical reactions, or reproduce on its own. In fact, there is a whole discussion over whether it can even be categorized as a life form. Some scientists classify viruses as "obligate intracellular parasites" rather than living organisms. And yet it can take over living cells and even whole organisms. A virus is the ultimate colonizer. It starts by attaching itself to the surface of the host cell and connecting with particles the virus can easily bind to. Just like a Cone Builder that finds their easy recruits—their low-hanging fruits. Once attached, the virus enters the host cell. It can do it by injecting its genetic material into the host cell, akin to a hostile takeover, or fool the cell to willingly invite it in, using its deceptive, trustworthy Cone Builder persona. Once inside the host cell, the virus releases its genetic material and takes control of the host cell's machinery, in the same way a Cone Builder becomes a Cone Master by forcing their ideology and rules on their recruits and taking over their decisions, actions, and their very identity. The infected cell becomes a Cone with the sole purpose of serving the Needs of the virus.

That's when the expansion begins. The virus uses the host's co-opted machinery to replicate its genetic material and reproduce itself into new and potent particles (virions). Finally, these virions are released from the host cell and go on to infect other cells and continue the cycle of infection, as in a Cone's expanding enforcement and propaganda. If the virus infected one small cell like an amoeba, it would venture to seek other amoebas and infect them one by one. This might be a slow process if the hosts aren't living in a tight colony. But if the virus infected a large organism, like a plant, an animal, or a human, it could hit the jackpot because organisms have tightly packed cells that make it easier to infect "neighbours," and they have "highways" to deliver the virus all over (blood, lymph).

This is especially true in organisms that have a weakened immune system or one that had never encountered this virus as it won't be able to fend off this attack. It is eerily similar to communities and countries that are weakened by internal crisis or individuals that have never encountered a Cone Master of that sort and therefore make for easy prey. From a small-scale operator, a virus can colonize a whole organism and bend it to its will.

Some small Cones, such as a couple in an abusive relationship, an authoritarian family, or a cult-like community, usually maintain their original dimensions and internal dynamics. Other Cones yearn to expand their hamlets into empires, either figuratively or literally. Cones often grow through continuous recruitment of new Subjects. This requires

Cone Masters to keep building their image as "The One," and keep seeking and manipulating recruits into their "One True Solution," like the virus that keeps seeking the next amoeba to infect. This growth strategy requires ongoing promotion efforts, which are usually resource intensive. Established Cones will also use their existing devout Subjects as their representatives or missionaries of sorts to expand their reach (their virions). Depending on the type of the Cone and the recruitment method, Cones can continue growing, with the aspiration of taking over the masses. Those that expand solely through recruitment will increase their power and means proportionally to their growth. Double the Subjects will usually mean double the power and profits, as illustrated in Figure 36. Expanding Cones by colonizing whole "organisms," such as whole communities, regions, business verticals, or countries, allows Cones to ease on the marketing efforts while increasing their power and means exponentially, as illustrated in Figure 37.

According to the *Oxford Dictionary*, colonization is the action or process of establishing control over the indigenous people of an area, and appropriating everything they have for the colonizer's use. Like a virus. Some colonization involves military conquest of regions around the world, while other types are more subtle power grabs, such as commercial monopolies and hostile business takeovers.

When a region or a business is colonized, the Cone takes control over the indigenous populace—be it the native people living on that land or the employees, contractors, and customers of an acquired commercial company. Unlike regular Cone recruitment, colonizers will rarely bother winning the hearts of the colonized people to have them pledge loyalty and contribute to the Cone.

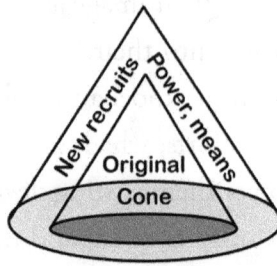

Figure 36: Cone expanding through recruitment

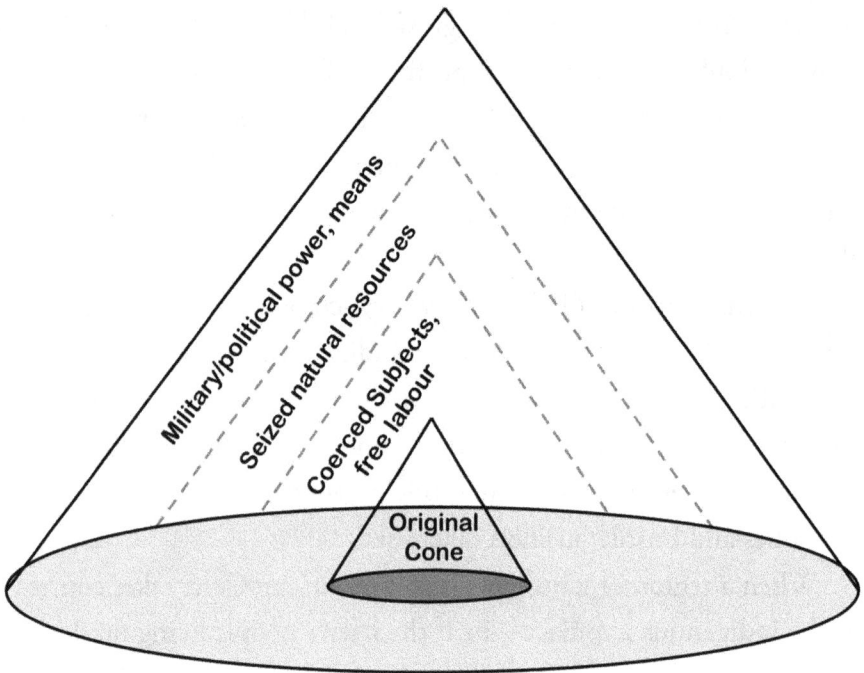

Figure 37: Cone expanding through colonization

Colonization is a violent act—physically or otherwise—which leaves no choice for the colonized people other than obeying. Colonizing governments will threaten locals with exile or genocide. Colonizing religions will use convert-or-perish ultimatums. Colonizing corporates will restructure, force their rules, fire anyone who opposes them, outsource production, and monopolize their products and services.

Colonization can increase the number of Subjects much faster and more significantly than via regular Cone recruitment, because it doesn't rely on the buy-in of new recruits. It also opens vast new opportunities that weren't previously available to the Cone in the same way an organism provides vast opportunities to a tiny virus. For one, they can exploit masses of new Subjects on a much deeper level by extracting cheap or free labour—something that wouldn't work that well through persuasion alone. They do it through enslavement, indentured servitude, human trafficking, or sweatshops. Free or very cheap labour allows Cones to establish profitable plantations, mines, and businesses, and execute low-cost infrastructure projects.

Some types of colonizing Cones may also aim to assimilate the local population into their culture and religion to boost their control and influence over the colony. Christian missionaries, for example, played a significant role in spreading European colonizers' culture and religion among indigenous populations, by turning them into more easily governed and exploitable Subjects. A colonizer will often take over lands and assets to access and extract natural resources that were previously unavailable to the Cone. New lands can mean minerals, timber, fossil oil, agricultural products, and spices that create new and significant sources of wealth and economic power. Even without physically seizing land, corporate colonizers can take over supply chains, impose new tariffs and taxes, spike product prices, and establish monopolies over trade routes and commodities.

Colonizing Cones will often invest in infrastructure development, such as roads, ports, and buildings, pretending to be "the benevolent, civilizing, and progressive agents of change." In truth, these investments have nothing to do with improving the lives of the colonized, in the same way a virus isn't looking to improve its host's well-being. Instead, they have everything to do with facilitating resource extraction and Cone-serving trade. Such investments not only enhance the Cones' economic power but also improve their ability to govern and enforce their laws on the colony.

Beyond money, colonization can bolster the Cones' power by gaining strategic locations for their military outposts. This will enable them to maintain a strong military presence crucial to suppressing resistance, enforcing their rule, and protecting their interests. Strategically placed military power can also allow the Cones to keep expanding their territories and deterring rival colonial powers, in the same way viruses spread to other organisms and create plagues.

Commercial Cones may invest in private military forces to help them seize and protect their assets, but they will be even more interested in accumulating political power. Having control over local governments and regulators allows commercial colonizers to push for laws favourable to their business or to seize local natural resources with the government's blessing. They can incite wars to take over new lands and natural resources, and have local authorities ignore their illegal activities.

These three major assets—masses of exploitable Subjects, new extractable natural resources, and powerful military and political influence—create sinister synergies that further add limitless riches and power to colonizing Cone Masters. In his book, *The Anarchy* (1), William Dalrymple provides a chilling account of the East India Company—a corporation that brutally colonized India, Pakistan, Bangladesh, and Burma under the pretense of a business enterprise. Other British corporations robbed Africa and colonized the Caribbean and the Americas. Dalrymple describes how a commercial Cone transformed millions of lives and how corporate violence and corruption won and eventually lost entire continents.

The British monarchy wasn't the only colonizer around. From the 1600s to the end of World War II, many governments used corporations to advance their national interests. The Dutch East India Company did the same in Indonesia, Malaysia, Sri Lanka, and South Africa. The French East India Company followed suit in the East Indies, China, Japan, India, Vietnam, and Madagascar. Germans and Belgians got their share by robbing the African continent of ivory, rubber, and cotton, and leading the murder and enslavement of millions. If you think about it, these colonizers were no more than specks on the world map until they became viral, gobbling up major parts of our globe through a colonizer's exponential power growth.

Turning the tables

Before World War II, national corporations were simply the weapons used by national Cones. Later, and especially in the early 1970s, the tables turned. Powerful corporations outgrew their national affiliations and started wielding governments to advance their own version of corporate colonialism. Nowadays, nations are no longer the largest Cones. Behemoth corporations now colonize nations to do their bidding. These are the mega-controllers that govern nearly every aspect of our private and public lives, though few of us are aware of it. Large oil and gas companies, such as Saudi Aramco, PetroChina, and ExxonMobil have immeasurable power over local decision-makers. Big Oil buys politicians and political parties through generous contributions with many strings attached. These mega-controllers influence national policies and legislation that make them richer and more powerful. They affect political decisions on which oil- and gas-consuming industries will be subsidized, with whom we will wage war, which atrocities we will ignore, and which governments we will overthrow because they threaten Big Oil's profiteering interests. Arms manufacturers and dealers, such as Lockheed Martin, influence worldwide policies and military spending. They run massive lobbying and campaign donations to push for military action. Nowadays, it is nearly impossible to tell how much of the armed conflicts around the world result from genuine ideological and territorial disputes, versus commercial interests of colonizing mega-Cones.

In his eye-opening book, *The New Confessions of an Economic Hit Man* (2), John Perkins provides a chilling account of modern-day colonization. He opened his TED talk (3) on the subject with the following words: "I stood in front of the Shah of Iran, the president of Indonesia, Ecuador, Panama, members of the royal house of Saudi Arabia, and I've said something like, 'in this hand I have millions of dollars for you and your friends. In [the other] hand, I have a gun in case you decide not to.' … that was the message. I was an economic hit man." In this book, he tells all about the concept and actions of economic hit men (EHMs) who are highly paid professionals used by major corporations and government agencies to cheat countries around the globe out of trillions of dollars.

These colonizing Cone Masters (mega-controllers) funnel money from the World Bank, the US Agency for International Development (USAID), and other foreign so-called aid organizations, straight into the pockets of major corporations and a few wealthy families who control the planet's natural resources. They dispatch well-trained EHMs as their messengers, manipulators, and enforcers to vulnerable regions around the world to help execute economic colonization. To achieve their goal, they use fraudulent financial reports, rigged elections, payoffs, extortion, sex, and murder. These Cone Masters have managed to colonize large portions of the world by creating a new global economy—a form of predatory capitalism.

Perkins provides a detailed account of the "jobs" he had been commissioned to do around the world as an EHM. He was recruited to work as an economist at an international consulting firm in Boston that had close ties to the NSA and the CIA. He, and many others like him, was trained to "work up" leaders of countries that had highly coveted natural resources, such as fossil fuel. His job was to make sure those countries took enormous loans from the World Bank and other affiliated organizations for one bogus development project or another. EHMs provided personal bonuses and kickbacks to the ruling families, or dispensed threats of being overthrown or assassinated if they refused. Either way, they rarely failed.

The money loaned to these countries never actually went to the country, apart from the promised personal bribes. Instead, it would go to major American corporations who were paid to build big infrastructure projects in those countries, administer them, and make enormous profits. They built power plants, industrial parks, and other infrastructure, claiming to move that country into the modern era. Except it would never actually happen. These behemoth loans benefited the rulers and a few wealthy families in the country that owned these industries, but most of the local people were losing everything. These countries were usually left with little tangible benefits from these mega-projects, while their people were displaced from their lands, exploited by these industries, and left with an enormous debt they couldn't hope to repay. That's when the economic colonizers would go back to the rulers of these countries and say, "Since you can't pay your debt, you have to sell your precious resources for practically nothing to our corporations, and then privatize and sell your utilities, schools, jails, and everything else that we can make money on." Should the leaders of these countries refuse the economic hit men's offer, the enforcers would be sent to "clear" any form of resistance through assassinations and convenient accidents.

Being deeply haunted by the things he had done during his time as an economic hit man, Perkins decided to reveal the activities of these global, corporate colonizers at great personal risk. He describes this form of globalized colonization as the treacherous cancer beneath the surface. He speaks of how it had spread from the economically developing countries to the United States and the rest of the world, quietly attacking the very foundations of democracy and the planet's life-support systems. All the Cone's common tools of the trade, including false economics, false promises, threats, bribes, extortion, debt, deception, coups, assassinations, and unbridled military power, are currently used around the world as standard procedure. Perkins writes: "Although this cancer has spread widely and deeply, most people still aren't aware of it; yet all of us are impacted by the collapse it has caused. It has become the dominant system of economics, government, and society today."

Being typical colonizing Cones at the level of super-controllers, these corporates and their lackeys use fear, debt, and good old divide-and conquer to convince us their predatory Systems benefit and protect us. They use professional manipulators, paid "experts," and a co-opted media to flood us with messages that terrify us. They make us believe our enemies lurk at our doorsteps, and that we must be ready to pay any price, assume any debt, and submit to all anti-democratic measures to stop them. We are told that our problems come from somewhere else—from those Internal Traitors and Others only the Cone can protect us from.

Perkins calls the actions of these mega-controllers corporatocracy— a vast network of corporations, banks, colluding governments, and the rich and powerful people tied to them who rob the world. We go deeply into debt without questioning hidden motives. Our countries and their financial collaborators at the World Bank and its sister institutions coerce other countries to go deeply into debt. The corporatocracy Cone keeps growing by colonizing and enslaving everyone through new debt.

If you feel out of breath and low on hope after reading this, pause and take a breath. Though things might seem hopeless, no Cone lasts forever, not even mega-Cones. There are other, better ways of being that are already in motion. Get yourself a warm, soothing beverage and keep reading.

Monopoly–more than a board game

Cory Doctorow presented a great analogy of a monopoly in an interview with Mitchell Kaplan (4). Imagine our economic market as an hourglass. On the top side of this hourglass, we have the creators of art and producers of goods, and on the bottom side we have consumers. In between them, we have a narrow passage. A pinch. That pinch is where the monopolies sit. Companies like YouTube, the five big publishers, the three big record labels, Facebook, Monsanto, Rockefeller's Standard Oil Company, De Beers diamonds, or Nestle create a choke point between Solution producers and their consumers.

As the art, services, and commodity producers pass through that pinch, they get stripped of nearly everything they have created and toiled over as a condition for reaching their consumers. They end up getting pennies on the dollar for their labour and products—if they are lucky. At the bottom of this hourglass, the consumers of monopolized goods and services are restricted to the few Solutions that are allowed to pass through the pinch. Moreover, they end up paying astronomically more than the art, commodities, and services cost to produce. This pinch of the hourglass is one way in which Cones colonize world economies without having to conquer nations. To quote Doctorow: "The monopolist structure is obscure by design. Like a great magician, they want us to focus away from where the deception lies. Facebook–building connections. Google–search. Really? All the while they become too big to fail, too important in our lives, policymakers and power players in their own right."

Large agrochemical and biotech corporations such as Monsanto (now owned by Bayer) use their billions to monopolize the market (5). Monsanto grew into a mighty Cone by getting governments to legislate discriminatory and predatory laws in many regions around the world that deny people of basic food sovereignty. They took over most of the major seed companies, creating a situation where over 90 percent of all available seeds on the market are bio-engineered by them and natural varieties are nearly impossible to come by. At the same time, they bought every available patent on both genetic engineering techniques and genetically engineered seed varieties to dominate the GMO market. They did it with the blessing of the United States Supreme Court and US Patent and Trademark Office (USPTO) who handed them the rights to patent nature itself. Because of Monsanto's legal rights on their seeds, when any farmer's non-engineered crop becomes contaminated with patented traits (something that happens naturally through cross-pollination or seepage of seeds from a neighbouring plot), that crop effectively becomes the property of Monsanto. Farmers who have never knowingly planted GMO seeds are fined for "stealing" patented genetic material and often lose their farms to the mega-Cone.

Once Monsanto dominated the seed market and left hardly any alternatives for farmers, they created inescapable legal binders. Their ruthless contracts prohibit farmers who are purchasing their seeds from saving new seeds for the following season—as was the natural practice for thousands of years. This forces farmers to repurchase Monsanto's seed every year. This agricultural colonizer is one of several that control farmers' livelihood and our collective access to food by exceeding the power of local governments. Following the 2020 pandemic, monopolizing Cones started hiking prices of nearly every essential commodity. According to Oxfam's 2023 report (6), ten food production companies[43] control 70 percent of what we eat. Wealthy corporations used the war in Ukraine as an excuse to pass on even bigger price hikes than the world had already seen throughout the pandemic. A small number of corporates that have effective monopolies with little to no competition, allow themselves to keep raising prices, simply because they can.

---

[43] Nestle, Pepsico, General Mills, Kellogg's, Associated British Foods, Mondelez International, Coca-Cola, Unilever, Danone, and Mars.

"The number of billionaires is growing, and they're getting richer, and also very large food and energy companies are making excessive profits," said Gabriela Bucher, Oxfam International's executive director. Throughout 2022–2023, the world's richest 1 percent have accumulated nearly double the wealth of the rest of the world combined. According to Oxfam, ninety-five companies that made excess profits by spiking prices paid 84 percent of those profits to shareholders. In other words, the rest of us paid our last dollar for the mega-wealthy to get much, much richer. In 2023, at least 1.7 billion workers lived in countries where inflation was outpacing their wage growth, even as billionaire fortunes were rising by $2.7 billion a day. That is the power of colonizing Cone monopolies.

Newly emerging Cones are usually controlled by coarse, all-powerful leaders who hungrily claw their way to the top. They build powerful and effective systems to support their ambition. As the Cone grows and ages, it becomes less of a rocket and more of an oversized, crawling tank. This gradual failure of Cone Systems hollows them from substance and robs them of agility and ingenuity. Despite these systemic shortcomings, many Cones expand their reach either through continuous recruitment of Subjects, or through colonization and monopolies. But like anything else in nature, nothing lives forever, not even mighty, colonizing Cones, and it all starts with the failed ways Cone Masters deal with change and resistance.

Part 1:
The answers to our problems

↓

Part 2:
How Cones are built

↓

Part 3:
How Cones gain control

↓

Part 4:
How Cones operate

↓

Part 5:
How Cones fall... and come back

↓

Part 6:
A better future within our reach

CHAPTER 17:

Trouble in paradise

... where we discover how Cone Masters deal with sticky situations.

D ealing with a misbehaving child is a delicate matter. If you are an open-minded, competent parent, you will acknowledge your child's overflowing emotions, apologize if you might have caused or triggered this behaviour, provide them with compassion and support, listen attentively, and empower them to resolve their issues. If you are an authoritarian parent, you are more likely to either ignore them, distract them until they shut up, deny your own wrongdoing, blame them for it, or punish them for defying you. Being authoritarian rulers, Cone Masters use the same strategies when their Subjects "misbehave." When things get sticky, Cone Masters find many creative ways to get away with nearly everything.

Ignoring and denying

Ignoring tough questions, accusations, and challenging situations doesn't sound like a good coping strategy, yet Cone Masters have been employing this since time immemorial. Your spouse feels abused? Your employees feel exploited? Patients using your drug are harmed by it? Your industrial logging and farming are destroying whole ecosystems? The academic degrees you churn out in your institution are useless? Who cares? Cone Masters who can get away with the consequences of their harmful Systems will simply ignore the few loud activists. They trust the troublemakers will eventually tire of protesting or be silenced by the Cone's enforcement system. So long as Cone Masters are in full control and most of their Subjects are compliant, there is no reason for them to address the issue.

The Rohingya Crisis in Myanmar is a severe humanitarian crisis. The Rohingya are a Muslim ethnic minority group who have lived in Myanmar for generations. Despite their long-standing presence, they have faced decades of persecution and discrimination from the predominantly Buddhist government and population of Myanmar. In August 2017, a Rohingya insurgent group attacked several police posts in their region for treating their people with brutality. In response, the Myanmar military launched a violent crackdown on the Rohingya population, which escalated to widespread atrocities including mass killings, rape, arson, and forced displacement. Hundreds of thousands of Rohingya fled to neighbouring Bangladesh to escape the violence, creating one of the largest refugee crises in the world. Despite the media coverage and the accusations by human rights organizations and the United Nations of ethnic cleansing and genocide, Myanmar's government ignored the accusations. Aung San Suu Kyi, Myanmar's leader and Nobel Peace Prize laureate, had a stellar reputation as a champion of democracy and human rights. But she remained silent on the plight of the Rohingya and denied accusations of ethnic cleansing and genocide. Instead, she defended the actions of the military and dismissed reports of atrocities as exaggerated or false.

When the noise grows too loud to be ignored, Cone Masters will deny accusations. Denial can be in the form of hand-waving, dramatic offence, or a trash-talk rebuttal. Cone Masters using the hand-waving response will dismiss their critics or opponents. They will use meaningless statements such as "that's nonsense and everyone knows it," or, "You have your facts, and we have ours." These hand-waving statements will never be supported by evidence. They will imply that the criticism is so absurd it doesn't deserve to be addressed. Similarly to hand-waving, the dramatic-offense response will ignore the actual issue while expressing loud outrage to distract enough people from the accusations. Cone Masters will create melodrama by using statements such as, "This is a knife in the heart of [our Dogma]," "I can't believe what I'm hearing," "I can't even talk to you right now," or, "This is an outrageous lie, and we won't stand for it."

Cone Masters with a crasser style will go for trash-talk to tarnish and discredit their accusers, using statements such as, "They are all idiots and conspiracy theorists." Trash talk is a common and usually a knee-jerk type of response to Cone adversity. It's the basic five-year-old response to a serious accusation along the lines of, "Well... you're stupid." Or, as psychologists call it, the ad hominem fallacy. Instead of addressing the content of the opponent's argument or position, Cone Masters will attack their rivals with the most personal and irrelevant arguments. If someone points out an abuser's poor behaviour, they will either lash out by calling names or drag their opponent's name through the mud. Many of the radical heads of state around the world adopted this behaviour. Donal Trump turned badmouthing his opponents into a grotesque art form.

All these methods of ignoring and denial are rooted in best practices of gaslighting. Whichever method Cone Masters will choose, for it to work, they must have willing recipients. Their Subjects must choose to believe the lies and live in denial, otherwise, it won't work. But why would people willingly believe lies? If you haven't skipped major portions of this book to reach this chapter, you will already have a pretty good answer to this question. Denial of the truth and acceptance of lies is a subconscious psychological process that leads to irrational beliefs and behaviours. Adrian Bardon provides three conditions to sincere denial[44] of a fact or a claim in his book, *The Truth About Denial* (1). These are: (a) we have no

---

[44] Bardon differentiates false denial, where a person is well aware of the lie and yet chooses to publicly deny it (which is what Cone Masters do), as opposed to sincere denial where a person is unaware of the self-lie and therefore denies it with earnest.

reason to believe the claim, (b) we have been exposed to good reasons to doubt it, or (c) we have an emotional Need to reject something that doesn't sit well with us. When the lies of our Cone Masters match their Subjects' Core Certainties, meet vulnerable minds, or minds eager to believe their leaders, denial on both sides becomes so much easier.

Despite every kind of solid evidence, too many people around the world still deny climate change, the theory of evolution, or the culpability of their corrupt leaders for their miserable lives. When it comes to deceptive denial, it takes two to tango. The main reason White Supremacists propaganda against non-whites is so well received is that it falls on fertile ground of deep-seated racism and xenophobia in a substantial portion of the population. Denial of climate science finds a receptive audience in people with pre-existing anti-establishment beliefs or those who mindlessly follow their Cone Masters. When a Cone Master denies a truth that clashes with their existing Core Certainty, Subjects will eat up every kind of garbage information and reject any evidence to the contrary.

Performative tokenism

When a Cone Master can no longer curb their Cone's stench, some will resort to benevolent theatrics, also known as performative tokenism. As previously described, this method is widely used by Cone Masters who adopt the *Shepherd* persona, pretending to be selfless good doers through altruistic gestures. When things get sticky, even those who normally wouldn't shy away from showing their sharp teeth to their Subjects may revert into the shepherd ploy. Sophisticated abusers will perform the role of the perfect partner in public. They will buy expensive gifts for their victim, speak their praise, or show great concern for their well-being so long as there's an audience to witness their overflowing kindness. The abusive parent will publicly show off their children's outstanding characters and successes and sometimes perform false gestures of affection. The film industry will cast a token diverse character as a decorative sidekick, and employers will do "diversity hires" to silence those pesky diversity and anti-oppression advocates. Dirty politicians will engage in small and meaningless actions to create the illusion of addressing whatever they have been accused of without actually solving anything. This gives Subjects the impression of progress even though nothing really changes.

One of the best documentaries that captures this deceitful strategy is Joel Bakan's and Jennifer Abbott's *The New Corporation: The Unfortunately Necessary Sequel*. Their original film, *The New Corporation*, made in 2003, exposed the ills of the legal decisions that defined corporations as persons and gave them the same legal rights as people (and sometimes even more). In their sequel, Bakan and Abbott examined how, since the 2008 economic collapse, corporations kept claiming to have "seen the light," and pass themselves off as socially responsible shepherds. This must-watch documentary describes the rampant practice of performative tokenism with firm evidence of their falsehoods.

One such example the documentary offers is the case of JPMorgan Chase, the largest commercial bank in the United States and the fifth-largest bank in the world as of 2023. After the economic calamity of 2008, a formal investigation established that JPMorgan sold securities, knowing full well that many of the loans backing those certificates were bogus. This directly contributed to the collapse of the economy. Their illegal action created collateral damage around the globe for years to come.

The Columbia economic historian, Adam Tooze, describes in his book, *Crashed* (2), the enormous and long-term effects the 2008 collapse had, and still has on the world. In the immediate "blast radius," millions of Americans lost their homes to mortgage foreclosures. The unemployment rate went up to almost 10 percent. Wages and incomes deteriorated.

New austerity policies[45] caused further harm to vulnerable groups and led to a nasty political polarization. This crisis of faith in the system and the spike in poverty and despair brought back something we believed was gone from our progressive world—a wave of anti-democratic, alt-right parties that started winning elections around the world.

With so many accusing fingers pointing at JPMorgan Chase, in 2017 the company announced an investment of $200 million in Detroit, a city that had reached its lowest point since the crash. They were lauded as the saviours of the city, even though it was JPMorgan's criminal behaviour that had brought the city so much closer to ruin. To be sure, $200 million may sound incredibly generous to most of us, so let's put things in perspective: in 2017, JPMorgan Chase had a market value of about $430 billion, making this investment about 0.0004 percent of that.

To bring it down to numbers most of us can relate to, let's equate it to a person who doesn't own much beyond their income of $50,000 a year. A donation of 0.0004 percent of this person's annual income equals $20. I want you to imagine this Joe Schmo committing fraud that causes half his neighbours to lose their life savings and homes, as well as a worldwide economic crisis. Surely, he would lose everything and find himself behind bars! What if I told you that this person never saw the inside of a prison cell. All he had to do was pay a fine of $4,500 but not before getting a government bailout of $3,000 to make sure he was doing well financially (i.e., his actual fine was $1,500). What if I told you this criminal was then publicly praised for being his neighbours' saviour once he made a charitable donation of $20 to the local housing association? Which he then wrote off for tax purposes!

---

[45] Austerity measures are attempts to reduce government spending to reduce public-sector debt. These measures don't touch the wealthy and powerful. Instead, they cut into essentials such as healthcare, education, environment, and social supports for vulnerable groups.

This small-scale scenario is laughable. Even producers of a poorly written sitcom would not have entertained such a far-fetched scenario. But this is exactly what happened with JPMorgan Chase. Though the company ended paying a total of $39 billion in fines, it was after the US government had gifted them $25 billon to help them land softly into the economy they crashed. None of the executives were ever personally held accountable for their criminal behaviour. JPMorgan Chase wasn't the only criminal organization in this story. Many other Wall Street moguls participated in this financial scheme, yet not a single CEO was punished, and most of them kept their positions. Once all was forgiven and forgotten, JPMorgan's tiny donation had people singing their praises as Detroit's saviours.

Clearly, JPMorgan Chase's donation was little more than performative tokenism, a form of benevolent theatrics. The late theologian Dietrich Bonhoeffer dubbed such gestures "cheap grace." Along the same lines, Anand Giridharadas once noted with regards to the hidden ills of philanthropy (3) that, "We talk a lot here about giving more. We don't talk about taking less."

Greenwashing is another popular version of performative tokenism that is used when denial isn't working well enough (4). It happens when a company misleads or lies to position itself as environmentally friendly or as a "climate leader," all while their actions continue to threaten the environment and worsen climate change. Greenwashing was coined in 1986 by environmentalist Jay Westerveld who fought to expose the hotel industry's "save the towel" initiative as bogus environmental tokenism. Nearly four decades later, hotels are still asking guests to help protect the environment by reusing their towels. It creates a well-crafted image of an environmentally conscious hotel industry when it is mostly about cutting down on laundry costs. Not that reducing the amount of laundry is a bad thing, as it likely makes a small contribution to the environment. The problem is that this tokenism exempts hotels from engaging in more meaningful sustainability efforts, such as implementing energy-efficient practices, expanding water-saving initiatives, implementing comprehensive recycling programs and sustainable food practices, and incorporating sustainable design principles into new construction or renovations.

Another glaring example is the fossil fuel Cone industry. As the public demand for urgent climate action grows, the industry is churning out new deceitful steps to make us believe they are making the changes needed to protect our planet.[46] They use tokenism to convince us they will take action that contradicts their very existence and their financial and political goals. In a 2022 Greenpeace Netherlands report led by Harvard University (5), researchers identified greenwashing in 72 percent of social media posts by oil and gas companies. Fossil fuel greenwashing is particularly sinister because, contrary to ads that promote a product to customers, their campaigns aim to influence a legislative or a favourable policy outcome. In 2022, experts evaluating climate claims made by four oil majors (ExxonMobil, Shell, Chevron, and BP), reported that these companies are using deceiving language like "low carbon" and "transition" without doing anything to back it up (6). None of them are making the necessary investments in clean energy or truly transforming their harmful business models. Instead, they have spent billions on "reputation-building" advertising—money they could have invested in the transition to a clean-energy future.

Performative tokenism can happen in all types and sizes of Cones. It can be done through minor donations, splashy but meaningless changes, big promises without much evidence to back them up ("we're helping to save the planet"), vague language ("your success is our

---

[46] The fossil fuel industry is not limited to oil and gas producers. There are many other businesses with a vested interest in keeping our economy hooked on fossil fuels, such as gas utilities, car companies, aviation companies, the plastic industry, as well as industry associations and lobby groups working on their behalf.

mission"), and claims we can't prove or disprove ("we'll be carbon-neutral by 2030").

Leaning into the good old days

When things inside the Cone go sideways and dissatisfaction rises, Cone Masters can play the good-old-days card to reel back their Subjects. Similarly to its use as a Cone recruitment strategy, this cognitive bias fools us into believing that things used to be so much better before the traitors and disruptors started making trouble. Once we get rid of the trouble-makers and "roll back" our values to align with the Cone, all our problems will disappear. Abusers confronted by their victim will fall back on statements such as, "Remember how happy we used to be (before you started complaining and screwed everything up)?" Abusive parents will claim that, "Everyone in our family has always been loving and supportive until you became disrespectful." Exploitive employers will claim that the workplace was nearly utopian before this bunch of troublemaking employees started demanding to unionize.

In his book, *The Politics of Cultural Despair* (7), Fritz Stern examines the "conservative revolution" movement in pre-World War II Germany that rejected and attacked modernity. They convinced their followers that everything modern was alien to the German spirit and tradition. They blamed the liberal culture for all that was wrong in their society and then painted a vision of national redemption through a good-old authoritative regime. The worse the picture they painted of the present, the more people were drawn to an imaginary past glory when men were simple farmers and kings were glorious rulers. You would think we would learn something from the way things turned out for the German people and the rest of the world, but we really haven't. It's enough to look at present-day demagogues who preach making us great again to see how well they sweep whole countries into radicalism and justify every kind of violence and oppression.

It's not me, it's them

Another common response Cone Masters use when things go sideways is accusing their opponent of the same behaviour they were accused of. In this deflection game, the Cone Master assumes the role of the victim by asserting that their opponent is the abuser and using false accusations to undermine the other's credibility. Blame-shifting has yet a darker version used by Cone Masters. When they see their Cone isn't doing so well, instead of fixing the problems, they will scapegoat the most powerless groups they can find. While the problems will keep getting worse, they will daze Subjects with fear and hatred of those Internal Traitors and harmful Others. These types of Cones end up leaning into their collapse because there is only so much other-blaming can achieve.

The former president of South Africa, Jacob Zuma, faced numerous corruption allegations. Using the "it's not me, it's them" approach, he blamed his political opponents within his own party for trying to undermine him or for orchestrating his legal troubles. He accused the media of intentionally portraying him in a negative light that contributed to his political challenges. He accused the South African judiciary of bias and interference in his legal matters. When all that wasn't enough, Zuma claimed that Western countries and foreign interests have been involved in conspiracies against him.

For a personal deflection of blame to work well, Cone Masters meld their identity with those of their Subjects. Once they become "one with the leader," Subjects feel personally attacked by opponents' accusations aimed at their Cone Master. Trump centred his entire presidential campaign on this persona-melding. He did it so thoroughly that his supporters took every legal allegation against him as a personal attack. "I AM

BEING ARRESTED FOR YOU": he posted this Jesus-like statement in all caps on the day of his indictment for seeking to overthrow the 2020 election. According to a CBS News/YouGov poll, more than half of Republicans felt Trump's indictments and investigations were a direct attack on people like them. Inflammatory British leaders weaponized the "it's not us, it's them" tactic in their favour after the fallout of the 2008 financial crisis. They managed to convince an entire generation that Europe was the one to blame for Britain's troubles. Though Europe had absolutely nothing to do with the financial collapse in the UK, these aspiring Cone Masters skilfully scapegoated the European Union all the way to Brexit.

Scapegoating isn't always obvious. Sometimes it hides behind allegedly good intentions. One example is fossil fuel companies popularizing the idea of a personal carbon footprint. The British oil company BP spent $100 million per year from 2004 to 2006 in efforts to place full responsibility of reducing the carbon footprint on individuals and away from major polluting industries. It was a massive campaign that persuaded us that "true change can only come from the people." While it's important for each of us to take personal measures to reduce our collective footprint, we are but a drop in the ocean. This blame-shifting narrative pushed by fossil fuel moguls conveniently ignores the fact that a mere one hundred fossil-fuel related companies are responsible for about 70 percent of the world's historical greenhouse gas emissions. This is not to say we have no role in this change. We absolutely do and we must. We simply shouldn't believe the fossil fuel industry is "with us on this," and that the failure to reduce emissions is our fault.

Another form of blame-shifting happens in Cones that uphold a stratified social construct. In her insightful book, *Mediocre*, Ijeoma Oluo describes white supremacy in the United States as a pyramid scheme, or what I would call a Cone scheme (8). In the United States, and in many other countries, white men are made to believe that life is a merciless food chain with limited supplies, and that their rightful place is at the top of that food chain. They are the kings and masters of society (or so they are told by the actual Cone Masters of their society). If they only play along, they will have more. They will be successful and content. Of course, it doesn't always work out that way. And when it doesn't, anger and frustration build up. If they did everything right, voted for the right people, spent their money in the right places, worked as hard as they were told to, and still their greatness isn't coming, whose fault is it? When rage creeps up, Cone Masters will be quick to deflect the blame and point a damning finger at those allegedly to blame for their Subjects' misery. People of colour. Immigrants. Women. Jews. Muslims. Gay people. Drag queens. You name it. It's not us, it's them.

Tightening the reins

Colombian philosopher Nicolás Gómez Dávila said: "Dying societies accumulate laws like dying men accumulate remedies." When all else fails and Cone Masters fear they might lose their Subjects, they will resort to tightening enforcement. During periods of labour unrest in the late nineteenth and early twentieth centuries, many business and industry leaders hired private security forces to break strikes and suppress worker protests. In response to student protests during the 1960s and 1970s, academic institutions often tightened disciplinary actions against protesting students, placed new restrictions on free speech, and increased surveillance. Vladimir Putin, the president of Russia, has faced several turbulent periods marked by powerful opposition movements. In the aftermath of the 2011–2012 demonstrations, he increased the government's control over the media, implemented restrictive laws on protests, and cracked down on opposition figures.

Following a failed coup attempt in 2016, Recep Tayyip Erdoğan, the President of Turkey, declared a state of emergency and launched a widespread crackdown on perceived opponents, including journalists, academics, and civil society activists. His government also came up with new laws to expand executive authority and weaken democratic institutions. Religious leaders tighten enforcement within their communities during periods of internal dissent by using excommunications, purges, and greater suppression of alternative religious interpretations. In economic downturns, corporate leaders often increase surveillance of employees and implement stricter and more punitive policies. Authoritarian parents boost their control systems over a rebellious adolescent by imposing curfews; regularly going through their child's private possessions, social media, and internet search history; and implementing harsher punishments for the smallest infractions.

Tightening enforcement and propagating rules when a Cone is in trouble is only one side of this strategy. The other side is making sure their Subjects are too weak to resist. There are many ways Cone Masters can make us lose our capacity to act, make choices, or control our own actions. Depending on the Cone, they can isolate us from our friends, family, and support networks to make us more dependent on them. They can gaslight us to distort our reality and erode our self-confidence and our own judgment. They can control our finances and get us into debt to limit our economic independence. Or they can burden us with a daily, mind-numbing grind that leaves no room for anything nobler than basic survival and mind-numbing entertainment. The key here is disempowerment. If we are isolated, hopeless, imprisoned by debt, or have no energy left to fight for what's right or what's ours, Cone Masters can easily get away with their crimes and failures.

Squirrels and red herrings

Distracting Subjects from the problems at hand is a staple Cone practice I've discussed earlier in the context of stupefying us. Besides robbing us of our wits, a well-construed distraction shifts our attention away from problems by dangling something meaningless for us to grapple with or fight over. When basic distractions fail to kill dissent, Cone Masters will move to sow panic and confusion. A common way to distract Subjects is by creating panic about something completely unrelated to the issue at hand, such as internal problems or criminal actions. Religious or cult leaders often create a moral panic by emphasizing imaginary threats to their followers ("the sinners/Others are bringing Armageddon upon us"). Those Others can be witches, queer people, women who wish to have a say about their reproductive rights, people outside the cult, or youth playing contemporary music. By creating moral panic, Cone Masters can divert attention from their own abusive behaviours and internal controversies or divisions.

Consider a few of the moral panic sensations some of our Cone Masters have been distracting us with in the last decade or so. Transgender people and drag queens have become "the new threat" to our safety and moral integrity, even though there is not a shred of evidence that either of them poses a threat to anyone. If anything, it is the broader intolerant society that poses a threat to these vulnerable minority groups. And yet we have heard endless inflammatory discussions and read an ocean of postings on the corrupting power of transgender people and drag queens, and how they threaten our children and our way of life, and the urgent need to de-legalize, if not eradicate them.

Cone Masters who wish to divert our attention from their own catastrophic economic and policy failures will fuel long discussions on the horrors of transgender women using women's public bathrooms. They will scream about the dangers of drag queens reading books to our innocent children in the library without ever mentioning evidence to support their panic. They will incentivise the media to fill our every waking moment with meaningless nonsense. We will be flooded with debates over the outrage of one celebrity trashing or slapping some other celebrity to distract us from the actual issues that plague our society. When these Cone Masters get accused of outdated fundamentalism, they rile up their Subjects against "snowflakes" and "wokeness," which they will brand as signs of depravity and societal collapse.

Sowing panic is further enhanced through widespread confusion. In this context, confusion isn't about us taking the wrong exit on the highway. It is about us being so thoroughly and constantly uncertain that we can no longer tell our left hand from our right. Spreading confusion was one of Goebbels's many dirty propaganda tricks in Nazi Germany. Instead of repeating one specific lie, you spread so many contradicting lies you make people feel there is no such thing as truth anymore. As Sean Illing wrote (9), Putin engages the same tactic by using mainstream and social media to "… engineer a fog of disinformation, producing just enough distrust to ensure that the public can never mobilize around a coherent narrative… [Putin does it by] funding advertising and social media campaigns to sow confusion in American and European politics." Steve Bannon brought this same strategy to the Trump campaign. His catchphrase was: "Flood the zone with shit."

Distraction can be a strong companion of the "it's not me, it's them/you" campaign Cone Masters use to divert attention from their misgivings. How about this red herring: Worried about the environment? Let's get rid of plastic straws. This campaign used a picture of a sea turtle with a plastic straw stuck in its nostril—an image of suffering that broke many tender hearts, mine included. Great numbers of environmental advocates rallied around this campaign. They drove changes in legislation to ban plastic straws, and used social media to cancel food chains that hadn't complied with the conversion to biodegradable straws. We all got so busy with the straw revolution that we forgot to ask: "What is the actual impact?"

Even though plastic straws are on the list of top-ten items found in beach cleanups, they make much less than 1 percent of the plastic waste that enters the ocean each year. Banning plastic straws may be a good start, especially if the focus is on building public awareness of the bigger problem. But when the plastic industry portrays it as "a great solution to our problem," it becomes nothing more than a distraction from the disproportionate impact of corporate polluters. Banning plastic straws makes us feel good about ourselves. The problem is that once we've done well on one thing, we put a checkmark next to "did my share for the environment" and move on. Which is exactly what profiteers want us to do.

When simple distractions don't cut it, Cone Masters generate more critical and "close to home" crises for us to focus on. During a major crisis, people are more likely to look for strong leadership and decisive action. Aspiring Cone Masters who wish to move up the Cone ranks will create a local crisis and then position themselves as capable leaders during times of trouble. Calamities can also create opportunities for Cone Masters to push controversial policies or changes to which no one would have agreed to under normal circumstances.

An abusive partner whose victim is showing signs of awakening and dissent will create a crisis by worsening violence or by threatening to abandon the victim and leave them with nothing. Cone Masters ruling communities and countries use existing or manufactured internal security crises to justify increased measures of control. The Chinese government used the political unrest in the Xinjiang region to justify new and extensive surveillance systems, mass detentions of Uighur Muslims, and policies that suppress religious and cultural practices. They used the crisis narrative to tighten government control to dystopian, Orwellian levels.

Cone Masters aren't always the ones who create crises, but they are quick to exploit them. In the immediate aftermath of 9/11, the US government passed the PATRIOT Act, granting law enforcement agencies expanded powers for surveillance, wiretapping, and access to personal records, without requiring a warrant. Though these provisions infringed upon individual privacy rights protected by the Fourth Amendment, the crisis made such controversial legislation possible. At the same time, the US government approved "enhanced interrogation techniques" on suspected terrorists, including waterboarding—a cruel form of torture prohibited under international law. This security crisis also allowed political Cone Masters to enact "extraordinary rendition," a fancy term for transferring suspects to foreign countries for interrogation where no laws apply or protect them from abuse. Individuals, including those captured during the War on Terror, were held at the detention facility at Guantanamo Bay, Cuba, for years without trial, all without any meaningful public outcry.

One may claim that war is the ultimate distracter from internal problems. Politicians have been using it as a diversionary tactic since the dawn of politics. In the recent century alone, we have seen wars all over the globe being justified by instigators with one meaningless motive or another to hide their true agendas. Every single war anywhere in the world is about Cone Masters and super-controllers amassing means and power or diverting our attention from their crimes under the guise of patriotism and righteousness. Just like in all other Cone-related strategies, when things get sticky, Cone Masters will use more than one method to cover their failures and curb any form of resistance.

When the tide of Cone opposition rises, and Cone Masters can no longer get away with their corruption and wrongdoings, they find a myriad of ways to deny culpability, distract us, blame it on Others, tighten the reins, justify themselves, or pretend they are working hard at righting things. Some may succeed to hoodwink their Subjects for a while, but as the cracks in their Cone keep expanding, their eventual fall becomes just a matter of time. The question is, what do most Cone Masters do about their impending fall, and how does this eventual collapse happen?

CHAPTER 18:

The emptying Cone

... where we discover how Cones collapse, and what Cone Masters do when that happens.

Truth can be manipulated and concealed, but eventually, it cannot be killed. Every Cone is doomed to collapse or morph into something else. Every viral pandemic ends up dying out. Every single empire throughout human history has ended at some point. If you adhere to a certain religion, you may believe it will outlast the universe, but it won't. People used to believe that kings will rule forever because they were God's liaisons on Earth, until kingdoms fell. Others believed dynasties would outlast time until they didn't. Every oppressive construct ends up disintegrating because of its own escalating dysfunction, its Subjects' growing dissatisfaction, and a change in circumstances that allows for change. Some Cones topple within months or years, whereas others take centuries. Some slowly disintegrate, whereas others suddenly burn and crash. Just as there is a pattern for the conversion of a Solution into a Cone, there are patterns to a Cone's demise. No matter how it perishes, it all starts with the emptying Cone.

When I travelled through national parks in the United States, I came across the strangler fig. It was a vast and impressive tree, at least on the outside. Though tall as a skyscraper, when you peek inside, you find nothing but external walls. This tree is as empty as an evacuated house. A few people can stand comfortably inside a mature strangler fig, and here, they'll find its emptiness goes all the way to the top. The seed of this tree spends the first part of its life without rooting into the ground. It settles in the nooks and crannies of another tree, where it germinates, grows its roots downward, and envelops the host tree. The strangler fig also grows upward to reach the sunlight that is only available above the thick canopy. I find it to be a wonderful metaphor for the emptying Cone phenomenon. If a conversation between the host tree and the strangler were possible, it would probably go something like this:

Tree: Oh, hello there, little buddy. I see you made yourself comfortable inside the crevice in my trunk. Are you lost?

Strangler seed: No, not at all. I've been looking for you. I asked the bird that carried me to find a tree that has the greatest need for protection. Glad I found you, and just in time, too.

Tree: Um... what do you mean "the greatest need for protection?"

Strangler seed: Well, I don't mean to worry you, but you are pretty vulnerable here in the forest. Did I say forest? I meant jungle. Look how much stronger the other trees are. How much closer they are to the sunlight. How much sturdier their trunk. If a storm breaks tomorrow, which one do you think will remain standing?

Tree: I see your point. The world sure can be a dangerous place. But don't you worry, little seed, I will protect you.

Strangler seed: Oh, you misunderstand. I am the one who will protect you.

Tree: But you're just a tiny seed. How could you possibly help me?

Strangler seed: I come from a mighty parent plant. Let me grow on you and I will make sure you become the strongest and tallest tree in the forest. I'm not asking for anything in return. I'm just here to help.

Tree: Of course. I don't see the harm in letting you stay.

Some time later:

Tree: Wow, look at you go! Your root extensions are almost reaching the ground and your branches are climbing higher atop my trunk every passing day.

Strangler: I told you I'm the offspring of a mighty plant. The stronger and bigger I grow, the safer you will be.

Tree: That's great. I'm glad I let you stay. One little thing, though... must you cling to me so tightly?

Strangler: How else will I hold and protect you from the upcoming storm?

Tree: There's an upcoming storm? Haven't heard anything about it.

Strangler: Of course you haven't. Why would the other trees share this information with you? Don't you all compete for a very limited spot in the sun? They are not your friends, you know. But I am.

Tree: I am one lucky tree to have you as my friend.

Strangler: You mean your one true guard and confidant. Your only trusted protector.

Tree: Um... sure?

Some time later.

Tree: Listen, I don't know how to tell you this, but you have grown so much around me that I can barely breathe. Any way you could ease off?

Strangler: Ease off? Well, there's ungratefulness for you. I put every effort in growing a fortress around you to keep you safe, and all you do is complain.

Tree: I didn't mean to...

Strangler: Would you rather have me leave and abandon you to the cruel fate of unprotected trees?

Tree: A cruel fate? Are you sure? They all seem fine to me.

Strangler: That's what they all want you to think. They're just waiting for you to weaken so that the storm can break you. So that they can take your spot in the forest. How can you even consider trusting other trees? They are your enemies.

Tree: They are?

Strangler: Definitely. I've seen them harm other trees just like you. They are ruthless.

Tree: That sounds terrible.

Strangler: It is. And that's not even the half of it. Once they organize, it will be the death of you. I'm the only one you can trust. The reason I'm growing so tightly around you is because your safety matters more than anything else to me.

Tree: Wow, I'm sorry, didn't mean to be ungrateful. It's just… I can hardly breathe, most of my water supply goes to you, and your branches aren't leaving my leaves much room for light exposure.

Strangler: This is the price we must all pay for safety and security. I'm disappointed with your negativity after everything I'm doing for you.

Tree: Of course, you're right. I can't believe some of my fellow trees are just standing there, bare, and unprotected. The fools. I should tell them they must get some of your seeds for protection.

Some time later.

Tree: Help… I'm choking… I'm dying in here.

(Strangler ignores)

Tree: Could you give me a hand?

Strangler: I'm giving you everything, all the time. It's not my fault you're such a weakling. Your whining is embarrassing.

Tree: Aren't you supposed to protect me?

Strangler: And what does it look like I'm doing? Look at us. We are wider and stronger than any other tree in the forest, and our canopy is higher than everyone, soaking up all the sunlight we will ever need.

Tree: But... I'm locked in here, with no water and nothing but darkness. You're the only one who gets everything, leaving nothing for me.

Strangler: I drink all the water and reach up to the sunshine for your sake. We are one and suggesting otherwise is selfish.

Tree: I guess... *(Slowly dying. Leaving an empty space in the heart of the mighty strangler fig.)*

Like the strangler fig, a Cone is not a symbiotic System. It is a parasitic construct that doesn't operate in a win-win mode. It thrives on the backs of its Subjects who receive very little in return. Beyond exploitation, the emptying Cone has another aspect. Not only does it stop serving its Subjects' original Needs or solve their Problems, but it often creates the exact opposite effect. Initial good intentions—if there were any to begin with—turn on themselves and achieve the exact opposite without us noticing. Think of making a U-turn on a road. When driving after a U-turn, you know full well you turned 180 degrees and went back to the place you came from because it happens on a small, comprehensible scale that you can easily see. But have you ever gotten lost in the woods or in an unfamiliar city, only to find hours later you were walking in a circle? It happens because there are too many trees or unfamiliar buildings to enable you to visually mark the route you took. On a large scale, the bend in your path that leads you back to your starting point is too subtle to notice.

The same happens to us when we are trapped in Cones. Every Cone you will ever examine will go the U-route, as illustrated in Figure 38. The analogy of the boiling frog explains why we don't feel it while it happens. The degradation in the Cone's benefit to us is usually so slow we don't notice it. Once we're in it, we've already been programmed to accept its shortcomings as part of normal reality. A mature Cone conditions us not to question it. We are warned that "jumping out of the heating water" will not only put us in a worse position, but doing so is also punishable.

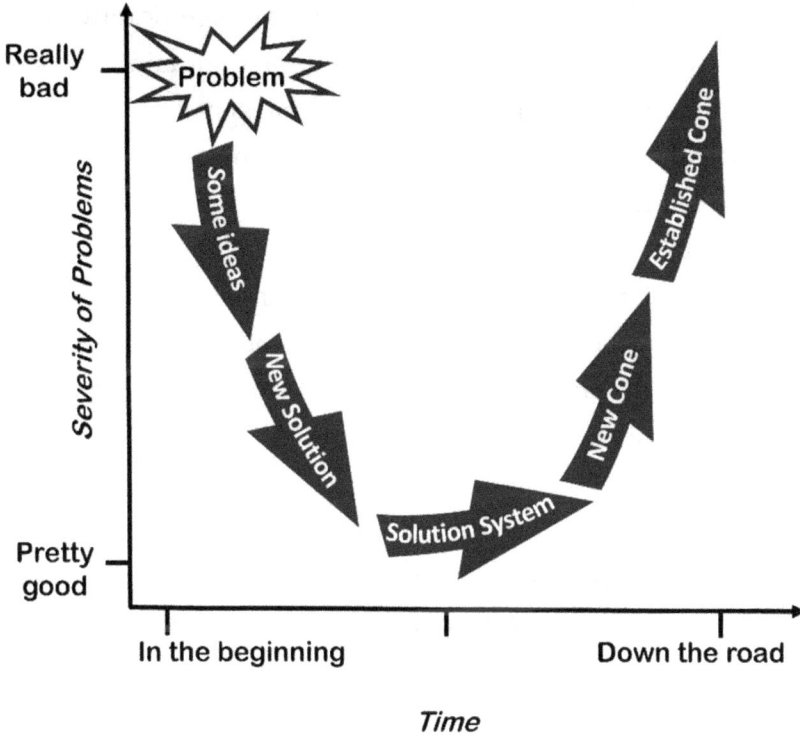

Figure 38: The U-turn of the emptying Cone

If we are awake and brave enough to admit it, we can see the emptying Cone in most areas of our lives. For example, when profit-hungry food-producing monopolies and conglomerates take over our markets and become mega-Cones and mega-controllers, they promise prosperity and food security for all. In the early days, we enjoy more accessible and abundant food supplies. With time, we become less capable in producing our own food, and sometimes even lose permission to do so. We end up completely reliant on these producers and have no other choice but to agree to the rising prices of food dictated by these profit-hungry Cones. All these lead to food deserts,[47] deteriorating health, and food insecurity—the very things these food conglomerates promised to solve.

When profit-hungry Big Pharma companies take over the way medicine is practiced, they promise their Solutions will significantly promote everyone's health. In the beginning, we see some meaningful, positive changes. But the more our medical System is pressured to solely rely on medications, the less we explore alternative Solutions and self-healing. We are taught by our mega-Cones to believe that whatever health issues medications can't cure simply cannot be cured. We become dependent on drugs, even when it means having unresolved health issues that could have been resolved in other ways. Many times, using pharmaceuticals also means sustaining damage, becoming addicted, and even dying from side effects and overdoses of different medications (1).

The same goes for communication technology. The more we rely on it, the less communicative we are, and the more isolated we become on a deeper level, despite the initial promise of increasing human connections. The more money we have circulating in our economy, the poorer the poor get. The more high-stakes and competitive our sports become, the less joyful the participation in the game. The more product beauty supply companies push on us, the uglier we feel. The more military and police forces we engage, the more we end up fearing for our safety. The more the concept of God is pushed on us by the less enlightened circles, the farther our fears push us away from true spirituality, unity, and the connection with our higher selves. It is said less is more. With Cones, more is much, much less.

---

[47] Food deserts are areas where residents have limited access to affordable and nutritious food, especially fresh fruits and vegetables.

The collapse

When Cone Masters fall from grace

When things go terribly wrong and distractions no longer work, we would expect Cone Masters to say, "Hold on, my Subjects are about to rebel or abandon me, and I'm about to lose control over my Cone. Nothing I've done so far to distract, silence, or threaten them is really working. Perhaps it's time to make real changes to refill the Cone with better crafted, more current Solutions." Upon an imminent defeat, these logical leaders would then re-examine their methods and beliefs and adapt their Solutions to the growing demands of their Subjects. That, however, is not what happens in most Cones. An emptying Cone either slowly disintegrates until there is not much left to rule over, or it goes up in flames and burns down to ashes, sometimes taking its Subjects with it.

Why does this happen? One powerful explanation for the Cone Masters' recklessness is the combination of cognitive dissonance and inertia. People in power want nothing more than to preserve the status quo that serves them so well. When it is threatened, they will persuade themselves that "this too shall pass as it always has." Most Cone Masters become so drunk on their power that they will believe they are immune to consequences. That there is no scenario in which they fail, and if they simply keep going as if nothing happened, those pesky Cone troubles will disappear on their own. A manipulative abuser is usually suspicious and untrusting of their victim. They will invest much time and energy in monitoring, surveilling, and interrogating their victim to uncover disobedience or betrayal. They will crush any sign of resistance and will be well aware of the misery they cause. And yet, when their victim finally walks out of the relationship, the abuser is always shocked and refuses to believe it is actually happening. They will threaten, berate, or make false promises, but they will not change their ways. A poorly-managed corporate may spiral for years, burdened by exploitive management, abusive terms of employment, unethical business practices, corruption, and convoluted bureaucracy, and yet top management will keep draining their Cone. They will be so confident of their ability to weather any storm and of their ultimate control that they will see no reason for making much-needed changes until it is too late.

This obtuseness happens on any scale. Umair Haque writes in his article "Why Don't Societies See Their Own Collapse Coming?" (2): "... entrenched elites go on pretending nothing's wrong—even in societies like America, where social collapse has reached breathtaking proportions. Kids shoot each other in schools, people just... die... because they can't afford insulin which is profiteered on... the average American lives and dies in debt, with little to no real freedoms or choices. And elites just whistle, shrug and walk away."

This wilful obtuseness of Cone Masters to their failing Cones is also notable in the area of global climate change. The Spanish street artist Isaac Cordal created a brilliant puddle sculpture that went viral on social media. This art installation creates an image of a group of ageing men in formal suits that look like they are in the middle of an important business meeting. Their bodies seem fully immersed in the puddle water, with some of the figures sunken up to their shoulders, and others have only the tops of their balding heads breaking the surface. This sculpture was cleverly dubbed, "Politicians discussing global warming."

The boiling frog syndrome isn't limited to Cone Masters inside an emptying Cone. It affects Subjects just as badly. Though you might say "that's not me," the fact remains that most of us prefer to ignore or deny brewing catastrophes. We do it even on the smallest scale with ourselves. Have you known people that refused to get checked even when their body was screaming with ominous symptoms? Have you done it yourself? We do this ostrich head-in-the-sand thing because no one enjoys admitting to failures and mistakes or having to make radical changes.

Another major reason Cone Masters ignore imminent collapse is their, and their System's self-preservation that stands above all else. Like many parasitic life forms, they keep squeezing the life out of their host until nothing is left. Sometimes, the parasite will replant itself elsewhere. Other times, it will die with the original host. The parasite's demise doesn't happen because of some noble sentiment of "the captain goes down with the ship." It is because they refuse to admit their ship is sinking, or because they have their private, well-stocked life raft at the ready for their escape. One of my favourite books as a child was the Russian Dunno trilogy (Neznayka) written by Nikolay Nosov. Inspired by the Canadian illustrator and author Palmer Cox, this children's series was written and illustrated with great humour, albeit heavily infused with communist ideology. The protagonist is a comical anti-hero boy who is oblivious, lazy, offensive, and arrogant, and at the same time curious, kind, adventurous, and incredibly lucky.

On his journey, the boy Neznayka ventures into a land of capitalism. There he comes across a mansion where a group of rich people live. These millionaires were abandoned by their servants (who rebelled against their selfish and oppressive capitalistic Cone Masters), and are now trying to figure out how to survive without their Subjects. Since they are incapable and unwilling to clean up after themselves, they keep feasting and loading the room with their dirty dishes. Once their mess fills the whole space, they lock that room and move to the next. This strange behaviour baffles the boy Neznayka. He wonders what will happen to these rich folks once they run out of rooms. Though the story is written humorously, it is a chillingly realistic reflection of the way Cone Masters treat our planet.

Despite their vanity and self-assurance that nothing could possibly touch them, many Cone Masters have an escape plan. Secret stashes of funds for lavish retirement. The next victim lined up. The next takeover of another Cone or going bankrupt and opening the next Cone under a new name. Right now, there are specialized companies around the world that build bunkers for billionaires in places like Texas, Switzerland, and New Zealand as their "apocalypse insurance" (3). Some buy private islands, some build floating cities, and others plan to leave for Mars. As the threat on the environment becomes more difficult to deny or ignore, the demand for these bunkers and for private military security keeps climbing. World billionaires are planning their escape from the very environmental catastrophe and societal collapse they help create. Many Cone Masters have a plan for themselves should things end badly. It simply doesn't include us. They will always publicly defend their Cone and claim to see a bright future for their Subjects while hedging their bets. A fraction of the billionaires' investment in their "escape plans" could have saved this planet and the rest of us. Yet they don't and they won't do it because Cone Masters didn't get to their positions by being kind, empathetic, or humanitarian.

While self-preservation sounds like a good plan, albeit a cruel and selfish one, not all Cone Masters survive the fall. Some abusers will keep finding their next victim in line, but many will fail the second or third time around because, eventually, the word about them gets out. Once their final victim kicks them out or confronts them, they will experience a reality crisis, also known as "narcissistic injury," which may lead to depression and even suicide. Some corrupt CEOs, politicians, and presidents may escape with their accumulated riches while leaving everyone else in ruins, but others will end up bankrupted, in prison, or dead. Even those who take refuge in posh bunkers, spaceships, or private islands will quickly realize that humans are not suited for long-term confinement. Ending up exiled and isolated isn't exactly a triumph. It's just a posh version of solitary confinement.

Life inside a Cone breeds a strange combination of numbness and arrogance at all its levels. Cone Masters fail to adapt because then they will have to give away their power and admit failure. Cone zealots cannot adapt because they would rather go down with the ship than admit their ideology was wrong. Subjects cannot change things on the inside because most are too numb or distracted to realize the ship is sinking. Even the awake minority cannot change the Coned Solution on the inside because it has been emptied of substance and re-engineered to self-preserve.

The tipping point

My high school chemistry teacher was a kind person but not a very gifted educator. Most of his classes left me either baffled, frustrated, or semi-comatose. There was one experiment, though, that kept me awake and in awe. He took a beaker filled with a clear liquid that looked like water and started dripping into it a purple liquid. The first ten drops mysteriously lost their colour instantly, as if a parallel dimension had swallowed them. Something in that clear liquid gobbled up their beautiful purple upon impact. But the eleventh drop changed everything. Once it hit the surface, the whole liquid turned deep purple in an instant, as if retaliating against the disappearance of their fallen brethren.

I was disappointed to learn this experiment did not involve travel to other dimensions or a retaliation plot of the purple avengers. Apparently, this happens when the liquid inside the beaker is a buffer that can neutralize small amounts of added acid or base. But just like patience, a buffer has its limits. Once it reaches its capacity, it can no longer counter the acid or base, and then every additional drop creates a dramatic shift. This is also known as the tipping point. This term is used in chemistry, physics, epidemiology, and social sciences because the principle of bit-by-bit and then all-of-a-sudden is all around us.

We may think that all big shifts in life, such as the fall of mighty empires, must be a very slow and linear process. Predicting linear change is our go-to because it is much easier to visualize. Anything else strains our minds and bends our perception of reality. The hardest change to grasp is the exponential one, and therefore it keeps surprising us whenever it happens. There is an old story about the origins of chess. When the inventor presented the game to a great king, the king was so deeply impressed he asked the brilliant man to name his price. All the inventor asked was for one grain of rice to be placed on the first square of the chessboard, two on the second, and then continue adding rice grains one square at a time. His condition was that every subsequent installment would be the square value of the previous. Four grains on the second square, sixteen on the third, and so on. The king immediately agreed, believing his payment would be almost unfairly small, because he was used to a linear growth pattern. To his great dismay, he had discovered that following the inventor's rule over the sixty-four squares of the chessboard, amounted to more grain than his entire kingdom possessed. This shrewd inventor may have been a brilliant mathematician, but he was a very poor judge of character, especially when it came to Cone Masters. Instead of paying, the king had him executed as a lesson for anyone trying to outwit him.

Exponential change starts slowly for quite a while and then climbs faster than we can imagine. That's why many of the cancers are undetectable for years, as one cell duplicates into two, two into four, and so on. Then, in what seems like overnight, it grows from the size of a grain of sand into a tennis ball and spreads all over. Though some Solutions experience a slow rise and decay, many take us by surprise by their rapid growth or sudden collapse. In his book, *The Tipping Point*, Malcolm Gladwell discusses this curious phenomenon (4). In his research, he identified three key factors that contribute to societal tipping points, i.e., drastic changes in social behaviours that no one saw coming. Though Gladwell's examples were of newly emerging Solutions, the collapse follows the same pattern, as it is often the result of newly emerging dissent that grows into a tipping point that collapses the Cone.

Cones don't simply collapse one fine day for no good reason in the same way the beaker in my high school chemistry lab didn't turn purple on a whim. Their collapse progresses slowly and unnoticeably. It starts with nearly invisible acts of defiance by a tiny minority that are crushed and suppressed in the bud. This is the latent state where, on the surface, nothing seems to happen. It is the tiny grain of sand no one suspects could grow into a sandstorm. As time goes by, a few rebellious Subjects with a good presence of strong networkers, enthusiasts, respected experts, or gifted influencers create a wider circle of support. Add to that an appealing alternative to the Cone's Solution and a favourable change in circumstances, and suddenly from a small and silenced group of Internal Traitors, they become the new voice of the rebellion. This is the acute, exponential phase where everything changes seemingly all at once. This is the tipping point where a Cone moves from a sturdy mountain into a rapid avalanche.

The British Empire was a force to be reckoned with. It controlled nearly every continent in one way or another. Then nationalist movements started emerging in many of the colonies, driven by desires for self-governance, independence, and the rejection of colonial rule. It started internally with the American Revolution and emancipation. It continued with leaders such as Mahatma Gandhi in India, Jomo Kenyatta in Kenya, and Kwame Nkrumah in Ghana. At the same time, the cost of the two World Wars of the twentieth century and its declining industrial power drained the British economy and weakened its global dominance. Following World War II, international attitudes toward colonialism went from "that's life" to "hell no." Not only the British, but all colonial powers faced increasing pressure from the international community to grant independence to their colonies. Domestic political changes within Britain also played a role in the collapse of the empire. Following World War II, the British Labour Party pursued policies aimed at decolonization and the granting of independence to colonies. Nowadays, Britain is far from being an empire. For all its past glory, it is now a small and struggling economy. As is the case with most toppled Cones.

One of the more recent examples of sudden rises and falls are the ad hoc Cones that go viral and become inflated beyond proportions almost overnight. Then, after a period of delirious reign, they either fizzle out into obscurity or go bust through cancel culture in the same viral manner they were erected. When Britney Spears was at the prime of her career with millions of fans around the world, a wave of haters rose into a vocal crowd including a mix of right-wing and religious leaders along with run-of-the-mill opinionators who were outraged with her hyper-sexuality, failing mental health, and poor life choices and parenting skills (though mostly offended by her enviable success). This media circus where Britney's personal struggles were heavily covered and sensationalized united scattered groups on different media platforms into an ad hoc Cone of "us the righteous against her, the shameful and sinful."

Nothing was beneath the trolling Cone, including attacking her loyal fans for being "blind lackies and idol worshipers." When Britney had lost her freedom to her father's conservatorship, the members of the haters' Cone celebrated the validation of their beliefs and the vanquishing of their designated Other. It wasn't until the truth started seeping out through friends, and eventually the media, about Britney's lifelong exploitation and abuse by her father and the music industry, that this Cone quietly fizzled out—without any of them admitting to their mistakes and wrongdoings, as Cones go.

Once the tipping point takes hold of a Cone, the collapse becomes nearly inevitable. What further contributes to the fall is that Cone Masters and zealots rarely see or believe their collapse is coming, no matter how strong and clear the warning signs, and they therefore fail to prevent it.

So long as the Cone is still functional or in its latent phase of resistance, it keeps the Cone reinforcement cycle going. Once a Cone reaches the acute phase of resistance, this cycle starts "leaking," as illustrated in Figure 39.

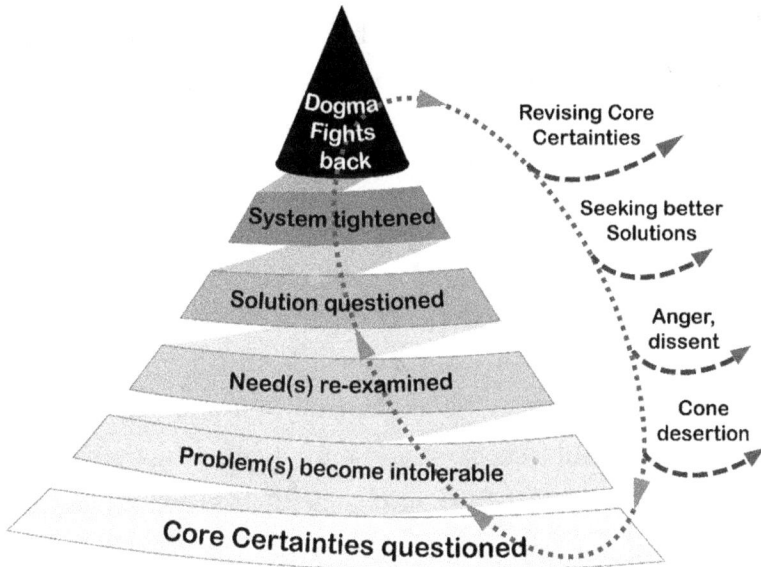

Figure 39: When a Cone starts falling apart

The leaders of the Cone resistance and their followers will question the Cone's Core Certainties and propose alternatives. They will start seeking better Solutions. Many will openly express their disappointment and dismay with the failings of the Cone, and then start deserting it. This open revolt will spread the word, sometimes going viral at an exponential pace, which will help a growing number of Subjects realize their Problems are intolerable and unacceptable. Once they realize the Cone has failed them, Subjects will start leaving. In response, Cone Masters and zealots will tighten their control over the Cone System into a chokehold. This will further aggravate the rebellion because even the dormant Subjects will finally start recognizing the Cone's ills and brutality. Eventually, the Cone will lose a critical mass of Subjects and either collapse or shrink into something unrecognizable.

In fairness, not all Cones crash and burn. A few manage to turn things around by adapting the Dogma to their Subjects' demands. An authoritarian parent may have a change of heart and find ways to improve the family dynamics once they realize their children are about to abandon them. A selfish, oppressive business manager may decide to allow their employees to unionize and negotiate for better terms to prevent the loss of their company. A monarch may decide to relinquish their absolute power in favour of a democratic senate if it means they will maintain their position, even if only a dignitary one. But these are the few exceptions that prove the rule. The Chinese military general, strategist, and philosopher, Sun Tzu, wrote, "An evil man will burn his own nation to the ground to rule over the ashes." Unfortunately, most failing Cone Masters will rather see their Subjects crash and burn—either figuratively or literally—than admit to their failure or change their ways. When that happens, Subjects will find themselves at a fork in the road, which will often lead them to create a new Cone.

CHAPTER 19:

Cones die... and reincarnate

... where we discover what happens to Cone Subjects once their Cone collapses, and how and why Cones are reborn.

A fork in the road

We have seen that Cone Masters don't have the best coping mechanisms for a collapse. But what about Cone Subjects? Masters or Subjects, eventually people are people and therefore as vulnerable to irrational thinking and ineffective responses. Faced with an imminent fall, each Subject may go one of several major ways as described in Figure 40. The zealots and true believers are the most likely ones to defend the Solution and barricade themselves against the rebels. They often join their Cone Masters in denying, lying, distracting, or finding scapegoats to blame. They will add new oppressive laws and boost Cone enforcement. Cone zealots are more likely to radicalize in their belief in the Dogma than to consider the claims made by the dissatisfied Subjects. In rare cases, a zealot may question their loyalty to the Dogma and their Cone Masters. This might put them in a state of confusion, and they might feel fearful, lost, confused, and even betrayed.

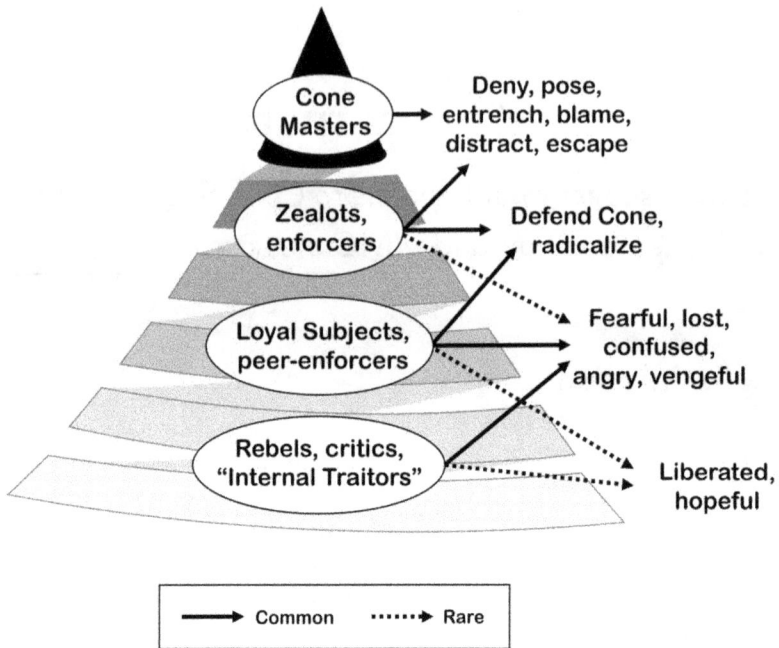

Figure 40: Cone fallout

Subjects who have always been loyal to the Cone with little thought, simply living their lives and considering it to be the normal, may sway in three different directions. The reactionary Subjects who fear uncertainty and wish to uphold the Cone's status quo will radicalize and become Cone zealots. Though their Problems, Needs, hopes, and expectations are of no consequence to their Cone Masters, smart rulers will, occasionally, throw them a bone to keep them loyal. It doesn't even have to be something tangible. An inspiring speech describing Subjects as "the superior people" or being "one with the leader" will often suffice.

When the ground starts shaking, the abused partner will defend their manipulative abuser from family members who are trying to save them. The loyal followers of the right-wing party that had impoverished them will radicalize into alt-right. Religious congregations whose clergy was found to abuse their children will become even more orthodox. A poor labourer who was raised to believe in capitalism will march to defend their exploiting billionaires from their critics. These are the invisible people, whose Problems, Needs, hopes, and expectations never mattered to their Cone Masters. Nevertheless, they stick with it all the way to the bitter end because they learned that whatever bad happens is someone else's fault, and that anything else is ridiculous or heretical.

Other Subjects in this middle group will feel lost and confused. Some of them will take the approach of "stay calm and keep paddling," too afraid to admit the emperor is naked, and the empire is falling apart. They will look away and act as if nothing is happening. These are the dutiful members who had never questioned their Cone, but now feel that everything they were ever sure about is disappearing. They will fear this new reality and be too paralyzed to consider change. One reason people don't act is indoctrination that closes their minds to alternatives; the other is a phenomenon known as pluralistic ignorance. This is when no one believes in a certain value or action, but everyone thinks that everyone else believes.

In a study conducted in Saudi Arabia (1), researchers asked young married men whether they thought women should be allowed to work outside the marital home. Most of these men privately supported the idea, despite their cultural and religious Cones that taught them a woman's place is at home. The only reason they never publicly spoke or acted on their beliefs was that they were certain they were the only ones that thought that way. Once they discovered that many others in their society shared their beliefs, these men became far more likely to help their wives secure work.

Loyal Subjects trapped in pluralistic ignorance will keep silent when the Cone is falling apart and feel ashamed for being less committed to the Cone than their peers seem to be. Beyond confusion, this middle group of Subjects may respond to a collapsing Cone by feeling betrayed, angry, and vengeful. The smallest portion of people from this middle group will rejoice in their liberation from oppression. They will decide to let go of their resentment and find more positive ways to be in the world.

The fourth and final group of Subjects in a collapsing Cone are the rebels and critics. This is usually a small group, at least in the early stages of the collapse, because independent thinking, intellectual integrity, fair-mindedness, and personal courage come in short supply inside a Cone. This group of Subjects will also split into different responses to the imminent fall of the Cone. Most will become increasingly angry and vengeful against the Dogma, its leaders, and its zealots who have been committing all those Dogma-related crimes and persecuting them. A few of these rebels—a trickle at best—will feel relief and let go of resentment. The question is, if all Cones are doomed to end one way or another, why do we still have so many of them?

Cone reincarnation

When a Cone collapses, Subjects will seek alternative Solutions to their Problems. Each of their potential responses to this crisis will create a path forward, for better or worse, as described in Figure 41. The two most common paths will almost inevitably lead to the creation of the next Cones in line. The one forward-thinking path that stands a chance of escaping this fate will usually remain in the fringes of society. Our mega-Cones and super-controllers will push against these positive, collaborative Solutions because they threaten their narratives, power, and means.

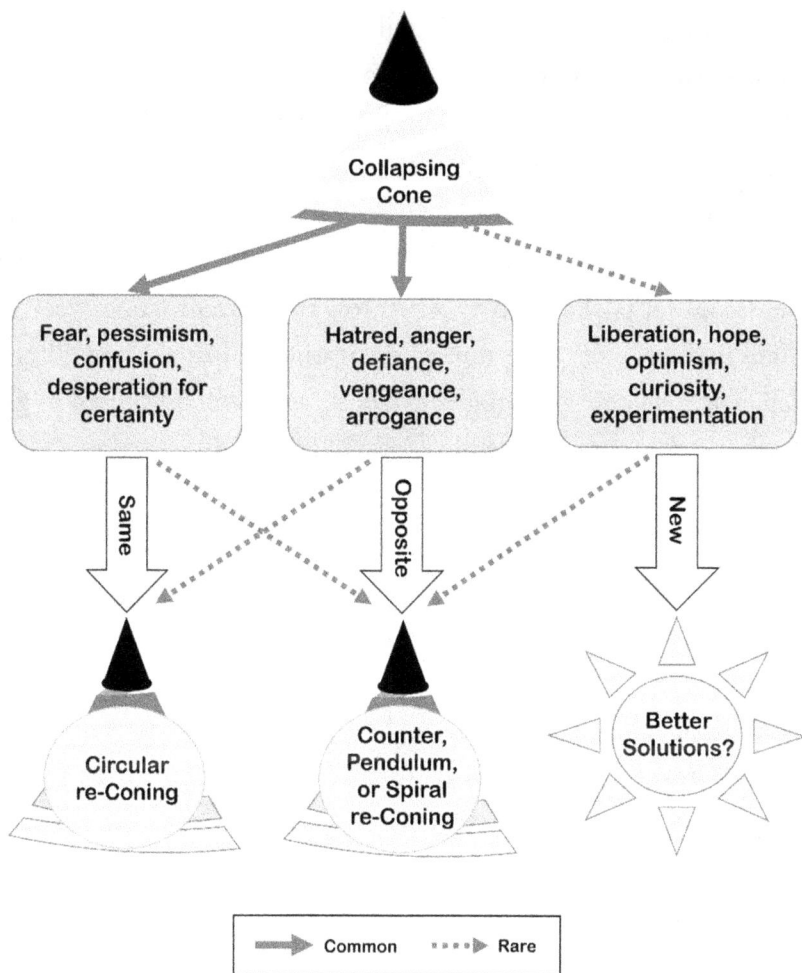

Figure 41: The paths to re-Coning

Circular re-Coning

Cones have more than one way to come back to haunt us. One post-Cone path will be driven by people's fear, pessimism, confusion, and desperation for certainty. When all we want is to land quickly and safely on solid ground, we will not go far and wide to explore new options. Nor will we spend much time on analyzing what went wrong and how to prevent it from happening again. Instead, we will reach for the closest life raft offered to us—specifically the one that looks familiar.

Dissatisfied gang members who feel expendable or disappointed by their leaders for not allowing them to move up or make real money will follow an ambitious wannabe leader. A few of these disgruntled members may try to leave the organization and start a new life at great peril. Most will eventually support a coup to overthrow the current Cone Masters, as illustrated in Figure 42. The one who spearheaded the coup will crown themselves as the "new and progressive boss" who will lead them to glory. Those who had supported the old Cone Masters will either run, declare their loyalty to the new boss, or face elimination. The rest of the members will celebrate their "new Solution," believing this to be the dawn of a new era. This will be a short-lived celebration, as their new leader will become the new Cone Master and repeat their predecessors' oppressive and corrupt behaviours.

The same happens in many dictatorships, where the old tyrant is overthrown by a revolutionary who represents "the people," often by using the *Rebel* or *Saviour* persona. This aspiring, charismatic individual will promise a new dawn and a new hope but will eventually revert to the same dictatorial regime. Robespierre was a powerful advocate for the rights of the common people during the French Revolution but, once in power, led what is now known as the Reign of Terror. Thousands of people were executed under his leadership until he himself was executed by the people. In the late 1960s, the Ugandan president Milton Obote was losing his popularity because of increasing dictatorship, suppressing political opposition, corruption, and tribal favouritism. In 1971, Idi Amin seized power through a military coup, portraying himself as the leader who would address these grievances and bring prosperity to Uganda. Once in power, his regime became notorious for its brutality, human rights abuses, and the suppression of political opposition.

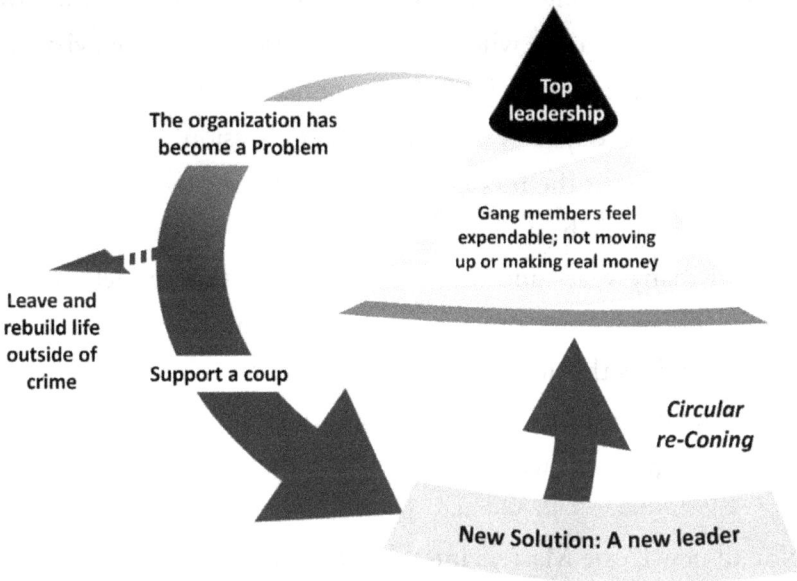

Figure 42: Example of circular re-Coning

This is the nature of a circular re-Coning. It happens when Subjects of a failing Cone seek a better Solution, but one that feels familiar enough. Though their new leaders will promise improvement, safety, and certainty, its ultimate sameness with the old Solution and its leaders' hunger for power will inevitably result in re-Coning. Paraphrasing Einstein's famous quote, you cannot solve a Problem with the same Solution that created it.

Circular re-Coning doesn't have to be organizational or state-wide, and it isn't limited to brainwashed, poorly educated crowds. It can happen at any scale and to any person. Some years ago, I presented at a conference on critical thinking. I was impressed with the model this foundation had developed throughout the years and was eager to learn more and make contributions in areas I felt were overlooked. The newly appointed head of this foundation led with a keynote speech, describing at length their rebellious spirit. They reminisced about starting as a young psychologist with a strong, independent mind. How baffled they were with old-generation scholars who upheld dogmatic professional views and methods, dismissing anyone who had questioned them.

Later that same day, at a smaller break-out session, I asked whether it was possible to revisit the model through a more inclusive and less ethnocentric perspective. The answer I received from that same person: "We have invested many years and much research into this model, and it is now perfect. There is no room for changes and improvements." I trust that in the early days this leader was a rebel and an innovator. Then they grew confident and comfortable in their Solution and internalized it as an untouchable Dogma, emulating the very mindset they criticized in the past.

Not all new Cone Masters intend to erect a new Cone. Many revolutionaries start with the best intentions in mind. They have been oppressed and persecuted, and they may genuinely believe they can do better. The problem is that power can corrupt even the best-intended people. Remember the rigged monopoly or the Stanford Prison Experiment? Totally normal people got high on their newly gained means or power, lost all empathy, and started abusing others within minutes. Now add years of pent-up anger, hatred, and disparity, and you get a nasty brew of vengeance and newly created entitlement and cruelty.

The circular re-Coning may happen quickly, but it takes enough time for the Subjects of this new Cone to fall for the boiling frog effect. At first, the new Solution will operate "as advertised." Subjects who were haunted by fear, pessimism, and crushing uncertainty from the fall of their previous Cone will feel relief and renewed hope for a better future. Gradually, the Solution will grow into a System, and the System will escalate into Dogma. By the time some Subjects start noticing the change, it is too late.

Counter re-Coning

When a Cone disintegrates, people are pulled to extremes, and no side listens to the other. Under these conditions, it is nearly impossible to find a voice of reason, hold a genuine dialogue, or learn from each other. This typical dynamic triggers an even fiercer resistance by the new faction, fuelled by powerful negative emotions. The new Solution ends up countering the existing one in every way. Counter-Solutions created by the bitter-fast-and-furious will often address current symptoms instead of focusing on the Problems the old Cone was supposed to address. Using the leaking ship story, the rebels will ditch the failing water-pump Solution and come up with a decree dictating that ships shouldn't be sailing the oceans. No water, no leaks. Simple. When you have spent your life slaving away pumping water from a leaking ship, all you will want is to never see water again. Instead of taking a deep breath and seeking the core Problem (i.e., what's causing the leak and why), many Cone rebels will focus on symptom elimination.

Being driven by powerful emotions rather than rational analytics, most post-Cone Solutions skip the necessary (albeit slow) conceptualization and testing of options. The new counter Solution will offer a basic and persuasive logic. If the old way was a miserable failure, surely the answer is in the exact opposite. With such conviction and pent-up anger, things go too far very quickly. In his book, *Tethered* (2), C.M. Collins describes the ways well-meaning counterculture movements morph into rigid constructs—those I call Cones—that contradict their initial intent: "The trouble was they were fighting the wrong enemy. They could not see that the desires that led them to seek the overthrow of the System were the same ones that led to the creation of the System in the first place. They believed they were fighting against war, political corruption, religious hypocrisy, racism, sexism, and a lack of freedom, but did not understand these were merely the outward manifestations of a deeper human and spiritual dilemma. Their Solutions, therefore, ended up being palliative, rather than curative."

Most of our Problems have complex roots but, as you may recall, complex systems confuse and burden us. Even on good days, we would much rather go for quick fixes. Once a Cone starts collapsing, instead of taking this opportunity for introspection into our core Problems and genuine Needs, we adopt the first Solution our rebel leaders have come up with. Usually, the one that sounds nothing like the old one and promises quick results. This is exactly the mindset budding Cone Builders thrive on.

One of the most powerful drivers for counter re-Coning is the rebels' chronic anger with the old Cone, which turns into hatred, contempt, and self-righteousness. Many times, these rebels aren't the first generation within the old Cone. Beyond their own pain, they carry old scars and multi-generational, collective trauma that further push for extremes. If unhealed, these emotions will be transferred into the new Solution where they will breed rigidity and even brutality. When people are driven by powerful negative emotions against the old Cone, they will get rid of every aspect that can even remotely resemble it. On the surface, this may sound reasonable. After all, if the old Dogma was as bad as to be abandoned or overthrown, why would we want to maintain some parts of it? The simple answer is that any Solution, horrible as it may have become, addressed at least some Problems and Needs at one time, otherwise it wouldn't have caught on.

Oppressive cults offer their Subjects a sense of belonging and a promise of emotional and spiritual elation that will pull them out of desperation. Oppressive crime organizations offer their Subjects the tight and loyal family they lack, and a promise of power and means they so desire. Communist regimes promise ultimate equality and prosperity. Organized religions promise a sense of community and spiritual elation. Predatory financial institutions offer developing countries gigantic loans to build infrastructures they can't afford on their own, and inflated mortgages to individuals who can't afford to buy a home. Abusers promise their victims all the love, support, and stability they've been dreaming of.

Though these Cones end up being emptied of substance and turn against their Subjects, it doesn't mean everything about them is terrible. Cult members experience a sense of belonging with each other and with something higher than them, at least some of the time. Most gang members experience a sense of family, loyalty, pride, and access to at least some income. The Subjects of communist regimes experience at least some sense of equality (e.g., communist countries have much greater gender equality than democratic countries), as well as free access to healthcare, higher education, paid vacations, paid maternal leave, and guaranteed housing and employment. People following organized religions may gain a strong sense of community and belonging, and at least some level of spiritual elation. Developing countries may undergo at least some development by taking predatory loans, and individuals who manage to repay their inflated mortgages end up owning a home. Even the victims of abusive partners gain bouts of affection and stability within the relationship.

Nonetheless, when resentful Cone revolutionaries come up with a new Solution, they have no appetite for anything that will even remotely resemble the old one, including the things that worked well. This absolutism creates irrefutable Core Certainties and generates the kind of arrogance that dooms the new Solution to re-Coning. More than enough well-intended counter-Solutions had fallen into the re-Coning trap. Fidel Castro, who led the Cuban Revolution in 1959, started by advocating for social justice and equality—the opposite to the presiding dictatorship of Fulgencio Batista. Castro's communist regime ended up a repressive, one-party dictatorship, quashing political pluralism, and denying his people basic freedoms. The Iranian Revolution of 1979 aimed to overthrow the Shah's corrupt secular regime and establish a pure-hearted Islamic

Republic. Soon after, Ayatollah Khomeini, who was seen as a liberator, established a highly corrupt theocracy.

This counter re-Coning happens not only in large, structured Cones but also in smaller or more diffuse Cones. In my youth, punk emerged as an influential counterculture movement, defying rigid, conservative norms and advocating for individuality and freedom of expression. Soon enough, it had become a counter-Cone with very clear rules of engagement, a nearly uniform appearance, and group penalties for transgressors. When the mid-twentieth-century boomers became infamous for their authoritarian, hyper-individualistic, homophobic, and sexist culture, younger generations grew to carry the flag of inclusion, gender equality, and hyper-connectedness. All wonderful and promising values for a better society. However, in being driven by anger, hatred, and vengeance, a large portion of the young generation is already showing all the signs of counter re-Coning. The movement toward long-awaited gender equality is being snatched by angry, radical feminism that cultivates a sweeping hatred and mistrust of men. The leaders claim that since it is impossible to tell the good men from the bad, we should condemn them all. Though originally well meaning, this movement not only aims to suppress men for being men, but it also shames any woman who stands for a more balanced and inclusive stance on gender. These are typical behaviours of Cone othering and the persecution of Internal Traitors.

Many groups that aim to liberate people from religious oppression promise freedom of thought and faith. However, some are quickly growing into an oppressive Dogma by which anyone who dares speak of religious enlightenment vs. a secular-spiritual one is being shamed and excluded. The movement against anti-racial discrimination, which promises the ultimate equality every progressive individual desires, is being derailed by old hatred and vengeance into counter re-Coning where simply being white is an innate flaw and an insult against racial equality.

The movement that fights hyper-individualism and capitalism promises a new dawn of equality, community, and connectedness. What could possibly go wrong with something so enlightened? Anger and vengeance lead to a sense of superiority, and what is supposed to be a positive woke culture is slowly devolving into a punitive cancel culture driven by herd mentality. In this counter re-Coning, anyone may find themselves on a cruel social chopping block for even implying or being misinterpreted as saying "the wrong thing." The cancelling tool that was supposed to be the people's power move against "the man" becomes the new silencing tool typical to Cones.

Each of these rebellious goals and many others are truly noble, progressive, and well meaning, and they fill us with hope for a better future. A better us. But so long as they remain rooted in unhealed, poisonous emotional ground, they will almost inevitably spiral into the same old oppressive Coning pattern. When we lift ourselves up with fury, we grow to feel high and mighty and start pushing others down. When fighting racism leads to, "All white people are...," when leaving a religion leads to, "All religious people are...," and when fighting misogynism leads to, "All men are...," we can tell a counter Cone is on the rise. These types of statements eerily mirror the previous Cones that claimed, "All black people are...," "All heretics are...," and "All women are..."

Counter re-Coning is a childish response to a complex situation led by people who are too angry to be thinking things through. The only difference between the first and the second batch of statements is whose turn it is to have the power to silence or harm the other.

Pendulum and spiral re-Coning

When I was a young dietitian in the 1980s, the prevailing knowledge on nutritional fats boiled down to this: polyunsaturated fatty acids[48] are good, saturated[49] fatty acids are bad. Based on this scientific assertion, monounsaturated fats such as avocado, olive, and coconut oils were close enough to the saturated category to become a nutritional no-no, as opposed to their highly unsaturated counterparts such as canola and corn oils that ruled the day. Everyone was strongly cautioned against consuming these sources of fat lest they develop a cardiovascular disease. Anyone who pointed out the low risk of cardiovascular mortality in Mediterranean countries, where coffee is the only food that doesn't contain olive oil, was ignored or dismissed—a typical response of a Cone faced with contradictory evidence.

Years later, ample new research showed that monounsaturated fats are actually wonderful for our health. The scientific pendulum swung in the other direction, and olive oil and avocado became all the rage, while polyunsaturated fats were bumped down to a category of harmful-if-exceeded. Anyone in the late 1990s who was still holding on to badmouthing olive oil was ridiculed as being out of touch with science. There is nothing wrong with new findings and discoveries that debunk previous knowledge. This is the essence and the beauty of pure science. It is when people treat scientific findings as irrefutable Dogma that we get into the Cone zone.

The pendulum re-Coning is an extension of the counter re-Coning. It operates on the same principle of going the opposite way from the old Solution while denying and discarding everything good about it, but after

---

[48] Fats made of molecules where fatty acid chains have more than one double carbon bond. These fats are typically liquid at room temperature.
[49] Fats made of molecules where fatty acid chains have single bonds. These fats are typically solid at room temperature or become solid when refrigerated.

the shift went from one polarity to the other, it swings back to the previous one. The pendulum doesn't always return to the exact previous point, but it comes close enough to be considered "generally the same thing." We find this pendulum re-Coning pattern on every societal level.

As children, we believe our parents know everything and no one can convince us otherwise. We will fight our sandbox friends over our parents' truths should they dare challenge the teachings of our wise sages. Hitting adolescence, we realize our parents are flawed human beings. Some of us lose all respect for their wisdom and grow to believe we are much wiser than those foolish, backward adults. Anything they say and everything they stand for will be irritating and wrong by default. As we mature and have children of our own, we find ourselves in our parents' shoes. We grow to realize that, though flawed, our parents possess wisdom we can now appreciate and learn from. We will not become our parents' carbon copies because we have our individual takes on life, but the phrase "sometimes I open my mouth and my mother comes out" is quite universal. At first, our children will adore us. Then they grow into adolescents, and so goes the pendulum.

In the political arena, we often see a pendulum re-Coning from one ideological end to the next and back again, as illustrated in Figure 43. Countries rife with wars and political unrest usually vote for the more militant and conservative leaders—those who promise to restore the good old days through strong and decisive governance. Once elected, this government will start making good on its promise, but the "good old days" will have an addendum of "only for the wealthy and powerful." The "strong and decisive" will spiral into "controlling and oppressive." The promise for safety and stability will heighten aggression against minorities, and resort to scapegoating to hide failures and to war mongering. Rising conflicts will mean further investment in enforcement and military, slowly draining "less critical" funds such as education, healthcare, and social supports.

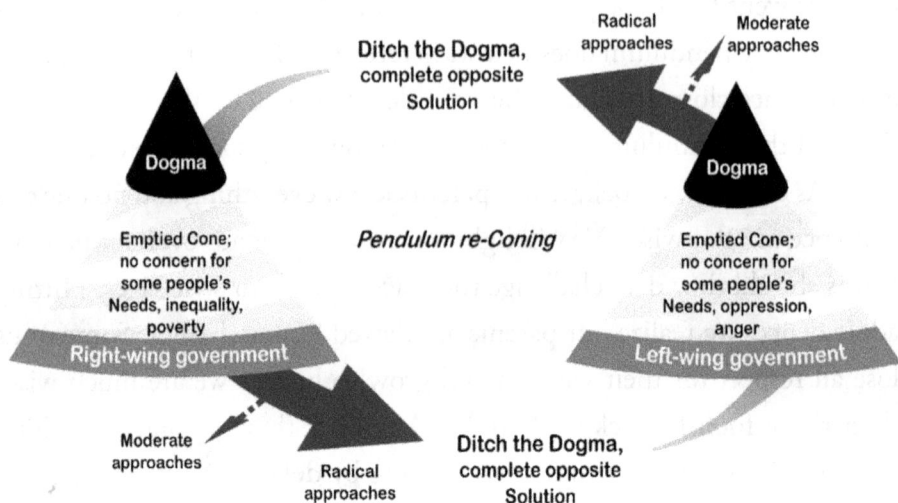

Figure 43: Example of a political pendulum re-Coning

As time goes by, dissent against the right-wing government will reach a tipping point, and the more liberal representatives will win the elections by promising their voters a better, more peaceful, and fairer society. Once elected, the left-wing government will start making good on its promises, but they, too, will have Cone-like pitfalls that will eventually topple their governance. For one, their lax approach to those previously regarded as state enemies will enrage right-wing voters, who will claim their government is compromising their safety. The adherence to existing, rigid Systems will upset the far-left who will accuse the government of being a performative sell-out. On the other political spectrum, the government's progressive approach to equality and minority rights will enrage the entitled and wannabes, who will feel their high status is being threatened by "those inferior others." Anti-democratic groups will gain ground because liberal, democratic leaders often confuse human rights with ultimate tolerance, therefore allowing hate speeches and inciting violence. This unlimited tolerance will play into the hands of anti-democratic factions, who will slowly erode democracy and gain political ground.

In many cases, left-wing governments will be led and supported by the country's intellectual elite, who will snub and ignore the fears and frustrations of "intellectually inferior" right-wing supporters. This will suppress the voices of the disgruntled, in effect oppressing them and adding to the pressure cooker of conflict. Being typical Cone Masters, these elites will ignore and dismiss the swelling opposition. In time, dissent against the liberal, democratic government will reach a tipping point, and the more militant, right-wing, and/or anti-democratic representatives will win the next elections. And so goes the pendulum.

Another example for pendulum re-Coning is related to our approach to health management. Our ancestors, and still many indigenous peoples around the world based their healing on a connection with nature and spirit, on their local plants and herbs, and our ability to self-heal. Once modern medicine started gaining ground, all spiritual and natural healing methods were thrown away and dismissed as useless practices of primitive people. Modern medicine has grown into a powerful Cone that assumes that whatever it can't fix by cutting or medicating is either incurable or "all in the patient's head." In recent years, we are seeing the rise of natural healing methods, and a growing number of both medical practitioners and patients becoming more emboldened in defying the System. Marijuana and psychedelic mushrooms that were used for millennia by aboriginal peoples and have been outlawed by "modern" Systems, are coming back in full swing, supported by the rebels of the medical establishment. The same goes for many herbal substances, and even energy, magnetic, and sound therapies. All the signs are there for the return of natural healing. Unfortunately, this "new age" of healing is already showing the first signs of Coning. We see growing instances where fervent supporters are starting to dismiss everything that has to do with modern medicine, including surgeries, helpful drug therapies, and anything that has to do with vaccines.

We see the same pendulum re-Coning in old agricultural practices that have been abandoned in favour of modern agriculture that depletes the land, exploits farmers, and poisons us with pesticides. A growing number of farmers, consumers, and environmental activists around the world are now advocating and practicing a return to natural and more sustainable and environmental ways of farming while demonizing everything good about modern agriculture. Slow cooking and communal meals used to be the only way to feed ourselves. Then we became too busy and took a hard turn to processed fast foods that are consumed individually, often at our desks. Cooking meals from scratch has become the domain of "unemployed housewives." Now we are seeing a thriving movement of returning to slow cooking and communal meals while feeling superior about it and shaming those who are still consuming fast foods all on their lonesome "like the uneducated fools that they are."

Sometimes the pendulum re-Coning takes a detour into a spiral. Coned Solutions counter one another in a sequence that ends up circling back to square one, albeit as a slightly modified version, as described in Figure 44. Long ago, and still in many regions in the world, many of our societies believed in the spirit world and multiple deities, and knew that everything is alive and connected. We believed to be an integral part of our planet and the universe. Most of us (though not all) knew that harming other humans, animals, or plants, was no different from harming ourselves. As time went by, monotheistic philosophies and myths took hold in some parts of the world, evolving into large-scale organized religions. The old beliefs were ridiculed and branded as primitive. Pagans were colonized, and all but irradicated by organized religion Cones.

Some more time went by, and a new movement of anti-religion rebels abandoned everything that even remotely reminded them of religion and spirituality for the pursuit of science. Everything became physical, mechanical, and measurable, or as we like to call it "evidence based." As of the early twenty-first century, the mainstream Cone of scientism mocks anything that our existing tools cannot see, measure, or prove under our existing Core Certainties. Nowadays, we are witnessing the rise of the next stage. A growing number of courageous scientists are stepping out of the scientism Dogma and exploring the existence of what until now was considered "completely out there." Physicists and mathematicians are coming together with philosophers and spiritual thought leaders to find evidence of multiple dimensions, universal consciousness that connects us all, and an afterlife unrelated to heaven and hell. Slowly but surely, we are circling back to recognizing what our ancestors already knew.

What is interesting about the spiral re-Coning is that even though a Solution ends up circling back to the one used previously, we rarely admit to this "regression." Instead, we consider it to be our own new genius Solution. Have you ever shared with a friend a brilliant idea you came up with only to be reminded it was their idea to begin with? The one they had shared with you a while ago. In some individual cases, a person may intentionally take credit for another's idea. Most times, though, it is a simple case of cryptomnesia—where we forget that we heard something before, and then repackage that memory as our own idea. Usually, it is an innocent mistake. But when it happens in societies, it is much less innocent because societies can access past events through collective knowledge or historic records.

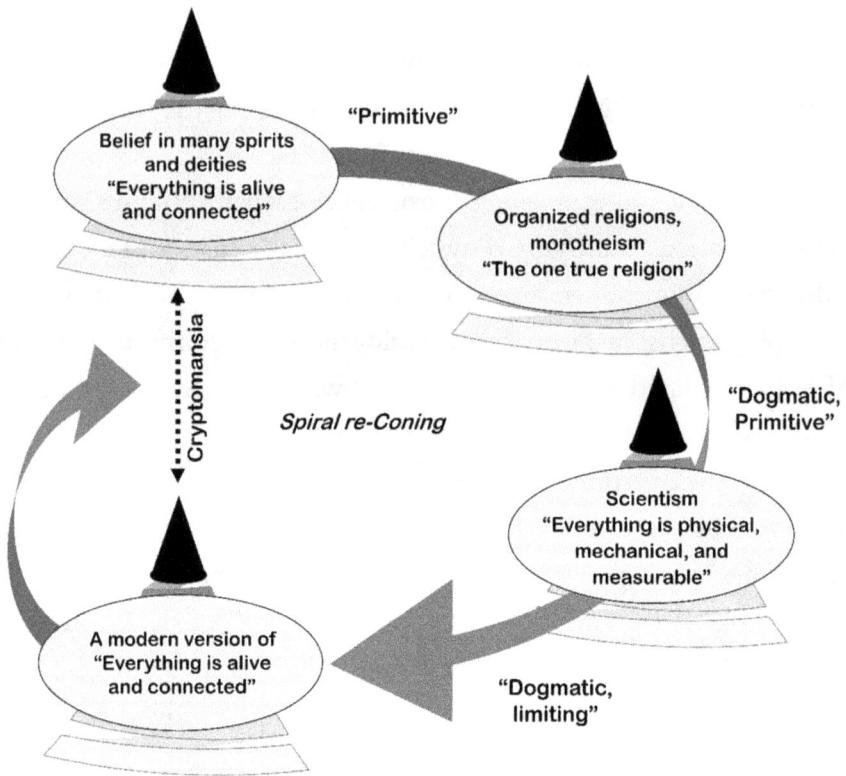

Figure 44: Example of spiral re-Coning

Social cryptomnesia is when whole groups and societies appropriate old concepts and claim them to be new and revolutionary. Millenia-old Solutions that Western scholars have ridiculed for ages are now being presented as brand-new, evidence-based research outcomes. These unsurprising findings that our ancestors considered "every child knows," are being renamed and rebranded as innovative breakthroughs. Meditation was renamed into mindfulness. Yoga has been rebranded into the science of stretching, breathing, and deep relaxation. The ancient practice of Upavaas was appropriated as the modern science of intermittent fasting. To cite another example, biologists have recently discovered that trees are social beings. They nurse sick members by sending them more nutrients, warn each other of upcoming danger by sending electrical signals via a fungal network, and can feel, count, and remember. If you are a member of one of the native peoples on this planet, you are probably saying, "no shit." Seeing trees as living beings was, and still is, a basic understanding of most aboriginal peoples. And yet scientists are now publishing it as a novel discovery, all while either ignoring ancient wisdom or insisting the old ways are mere superstitions held by ignorant people.

Social cryptomnesia is a common practice in spiral re-Coning. New Cone Masters refuse to give credit to current or historic minorities for their ancient wisdom or their role in provoking social change. In his article "Social cryptomnesia: How societies steal ideas" (3), Richard Fisher describes the many ways we rob our minorities of their knowledge and heritage, and then appropriate those as our own. Studies on "minority influence" show that people report positive attitudes toward issues such as equal rights or respect for the environment until they are told that these concepts were first campaigned by unpopular minorities. That's when their appreciation of these causes drops dramatically. Somehow, we just don't want to be associated with those primitives and troublemakers, or openly admit they were right, and we were wrong. Many of the privileges we enjoy today, such as human rights, free education, women's voting rights, democracy, pensions, workplace safety, and more, only happened because an unpopular minority stood up to their Cones. And yet most modern societies will intentionally forget and deny their contribution. Fisher writes: "The dark side of social cryptomnesia is that it allows established power to endure, and discrimination against minority groups to carry on."

What have we learned?

Every Cone, from the smallest (ourselves) to the mega-powers, is rooted in the way we see the world—our beliefs, values, experiences, and personal traits. These are the Core Certainties we never question because "every child should know this." These are the worldviews that inform what we perceive to be Problems and, in turn, the ways we define our Needs. Not only do we view our Problems and Needs through subjective and predefined lenses, but we are also manipulated by a myriad of exploitive profiteers who warp our reality, manufacture, or augment our Problems and Needs, and then offer us their Solutions, as described in Figure 45.

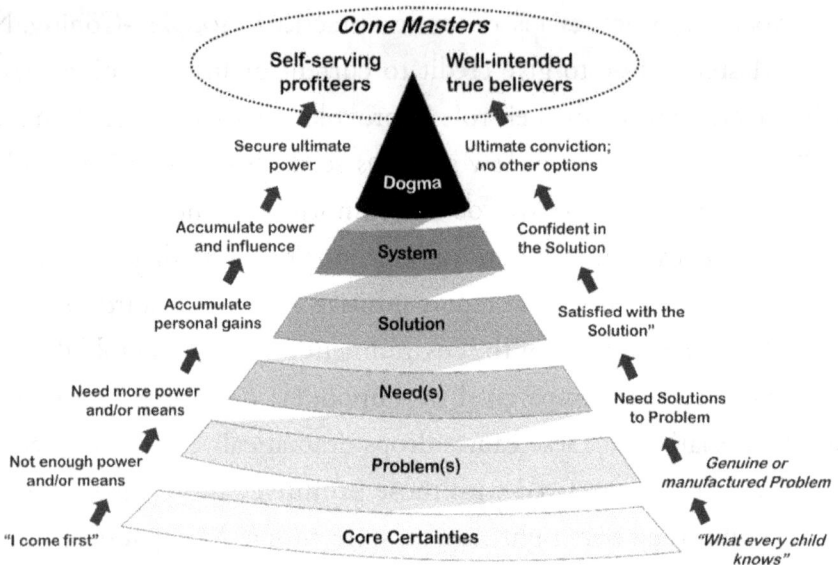

Figure 45: The five stages of a growing Cone

In the early stage, we know the Solutions we come up with (or those pushed on us by profiteers) might not be perfect, but we acknowledge they address at least some of our Problems and Needs. In the months, years, or generations to come, we narrow our selection, sometimes to a single Solution, that becomes part of our lives and regular operations. We come to rely on it, speak its praise, and distribute it outside our immediate circle. Once it becomes widespread and deeply rooted in our daily lives, we develop structures to support its distribution, access, and delivery, which further narrows the Solution through tighter control and implementation.

This is the System stage, where we no longer ask too many troublesome questions about our Solution or justify its use. Some time later, Solution zealots and cynical, self-serving individuals will crown themselves as the uncontested leaders and announce it to be "The One True Solution." At the Dogma stage, the System's self-preservation becomes more important than our Problems and Needs. This is where our freedom dies, and oppression and exploitation thrive.

The plethora of Cones that govern our private and public lives prove that not only naïve idiots buy into these oppressive systems. The reality is that we all experience the same basic fears, needs, fragilities, pains, desires, hopes, and joys, and we are all vulnerable to unhealthy coping mechanisms and shrewd propaganda. Moreover, we all grow up inside many pervasive Cone Systems that are invisible to us and therefore never doubt them.

The Cone pattern doesn't exist because we love it or because it's good for us, but because we fail to recognize it and therefore never learn from our mistakes. When one Cone collapses, we are quick to build the next Cone in line, though most of us don't intend to. When we bring anger and vengeance from our old Cones into our new Solutions, we end up using our old Masters' tools and build the same types of Dogmatic Systems under new management, as described in Figure 46.

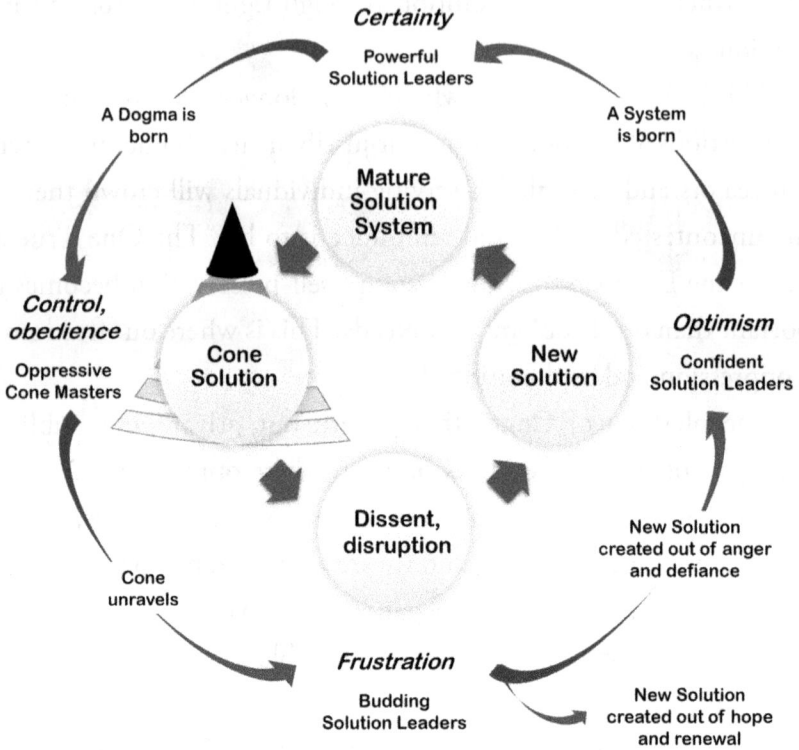

Figure 46: A typical life cycle of Cones

The good news is that once we understand how Cones work, we can no longer unsee them. Understanding the bowels of the Cone beast can help us seek alternative ways to come up with sustainable, inclusive, and non-exploitive Solutions. Martin Luther King Jr. once said, "Darkness cannot drive out darkness; only light can do that. Hate cannot drive out hate; only love can do that." Positivity and love for all is the only mindset that can bring us hope, and our only way out of the cursed Cone reincarnation cycle. And it is perfectly doable. Genuinely good Solutions are not utopian or unrealistic. They already exist. All we have to do is open our eyes and hearts to different ways of doing things and different ways of being.

Part 1:
The answers to our problems

↓

Part 2:
How Cones are built

↓

Part 3:
How Cones gain control

↓

Part 4:
How Cones operate

↓

Part 5:
How Cones fall… and come back

↓

Part 6:
A better future within our reach

CHAPTER 20:

The light at the end of this tunnel

... where we expose the BS of "there's no other way," agree we can't continue this way, and reclaim our freedom. It's also where we explore better alternatives and our role in shaping the future.

The BS of "there's no other way"

s it even possible to change? Aren't all Systems and Solutions doomed to grow into oppressive Cones? The short answer is no. Sometimes we get so bogged down by our troubles, disappointments, and heartbreaks that all we can see is the negative and hopeless. Our politicians, profiteers, and mega-controllers do everything in their power to conceal good and wholesome Solutions. They use influential figures, educational systems, economic constraints, artificial scarcity, and propaganda in ways that emphasize everything scary and evil because they need us horrified and hopeless. This is the surest way to keep us compliant with every insane and harmful Dogma they impose on us.

When you have been wading your whole life in deep mud and taught to keep your head down, you grow to believe mud is all there is; that life is about making sure you don't drown in it. You are so busy pushing your way through the muck that you don't notice the people standing on solid ground beside the pit, pouring water in to keep the mud going. To keep you in a survival mode. Once you recognize at least one major Cone in your life, you can no longer unsee it. The more you raise your head, the more Cones you will spot wherever you look. Suddenly you realize that some people or Systems you thought were your saviours and supporters are the ones deepening your mud pool while enjoying the fruits of your labour. The realization of just how profoundly Cones govern your life might have a demoralizing effect. If it's everywhere, what are your chances of climbing out of this muck?

With a little intentional effort, you will discover there are people who have built whole lives and communities on the fertile lands outside the mud pit. The beauty, awakening, and positive renewal is already here. Great, constructive Solutions are already with us and among us. They simply aren't as loud and visible as our Cones and their zealots. Our oppressors intentionally silence many of these promising Solutions so that we don't develop hope, start thinking for ourselves, realize we don't need them, and step out.

Unlike the preachings of our Cone Masters, human ferociousness and animosity are not inevitable. Oppressing others and harming our planet for our own survival are not necessities, as Cone Masters would have you believe. The first step to your liberation is to stop buying into the most common lie that sustains Cones: "Yeah, what we have isn't great, but there's no other way. That's just how we are." Cones survive by infusing us with a Core Certainty that theirs is the only way to be or do things. They assure us that everything else is foolish, sinful, or unthinkable. Here's how it goes: You think our dictatorship is bad for you? Perhaps, but the alternative is so much worse. Is our cult or religion choking you? Suck it up or you will end up in hell. Is our education system failing you? Too bad, so sad; it's the only way for you to have a future. Your employer exploits you? Yes, but that's just how the world operates, so stop complaining and be thankful you have a job. Your spouse abuses you? Yes, but it's because you deserve it, so stop whining and do better.

And therein lies the bullshit.

Contrary to what Cone Masters are telling us, humanity is not made up of a bunch of lone, hungry wolves that can only survive by being at each other's throats. Though competition exists, we are fundamentally group- and collaboration-oriented beings. A healthy competitive spirit can drive new collective Solutions and opportunities instead of throwing us into zero-sum, mutual destruction. When there is no intervention of malicious, greedy forces, such as colonizers and exploiters, large groups of people prefer to live in peaceful collaboration. We do it not only with each other but also with our mother planet and all her creatures. All it takes is a good, sober look to see the beauty embedded within humanity. Numerous acts of kindness, both on the individual and on the group level. Numerous organized initiatives in times of crisis led by individuals who have never met to help others they have never met. So many people tend to our planet without ever expecting personal gains.

Solutions can and are being designed and delivered in ways that solve Problems and address Needs without causing harm. It isn't only beneficial to develop Solutions that do not succumb to Cones, it is also perfectly doable. The question, "Is it possible to change?" is important, but not as important as, "What if we don't?" At this stage, we no longer have the luxury of twiddling our thumbs and looking away, hoping the Cones will disappear and our Problems will solve themselves. Not unless we wish to collectively reenact the boiling frog experiment. Right now, the only valid question is not whether, but how we can change our ways of doing things.

We can do better

Considering our Cone-riddled world, is there even hope for us? Absolutely. It won't be easy and it won't be quick, but it can be done. We have already managed it many times before. In his book, *The Better Angels of Our Nature* (1), Steven Pinker presents overwhelming evidence that we live in the best time in history. Though our Cone Masters wish us to believe this world is wickeder and scarier than ever, comparing our lives today to a hundred or even as little as fifty years ago, we will find this isn't true. We are seeing a significant decrease in violence and crime, increase in health and prosperity, an expanding reach of human rights for marginalized populations, overall reduced racism and sexism, reduced over-population, reduced poverty and malnutrition, exponential growth of environmentally friendly Solutions, and an ever-growing global awareness of our connectedness. Ironically, we fail to acknowledge and celebrate any of these positive changes. Instead, many of us lean into the sentimental illusion of "the good old days" when everything was allegedly so much better.

Yes, we have immense challenges ahead, but even major endeavours such as stopping climate change and curbing the power of mega-controllers are already underway. Innovations in renewable energy-generating technologies that will replace fossil fuels are already here and are rapidly improving. Swelling public awareness of the ills of predatory capitalism is already fuelling new, regenerative economic systems. A wave of radical anti-democratic governments is already awakening youth to the ills of tyranny and mobilizes new political movements. Growing consciousness of the ills of oppressive religions on one hand, and rigid scientism on the other, is already helping millions of people to seek a non-oppressive, reasoned, spiritual-scientific middle ground. Our growing collective awareness of all forms of repressive constructs—from food production, housing, medicine, mega-media, to educational systems—is already supported by thousands of enterprises that build better, more sustainable foundations for our future.

In his book, *Birthing the Symbiotic Age* (2), Richard Flyer lays out a blueprint for a symbiotic, collaborative society where everyone both contributes and gains without exploiting, oppressing, or harming anyone. In Symbiotic Cultures, maintaining mutually beneficial relationships and collaborations amongst diverse groups of people, from family to neighbourhood, community, nation, and planet, is the norm. Flyer stresses that this blueprint of a Symbiotic Culture is not a modern invention. It is as old as our species and is still practiced in many indigenous groups around the world where colonization had failed to eliminate or corrupt ancient teachings. Flyer's four-step model is based on many current, real-life examples of both small and large groups around the world. Each has successfully transitioned from living under oppressive Cones into healthy, supportive, and sustainable societies.

In their book, *Ideology of Decentralized Civilization and Egalitarian Community* (3), Reed Kinney and Mark Kinney provide a most detailed roadmap for building independent communities. Together, these communities create a collaborative, decentralized civilization where mega-controllers and Cone Masters will play no role. Like Flyer, Kinneys's model builds on ancient roots, such as the Iroquois Six Nation Constitution, countering the current narrative of separation and exploitation. It begins with the creation of small, cohesive groups that establish civic, mutualistic, and sovereign communities. Following the principles of a high-trust culture, these communities contain all the required components for dialogue- and consensus-based decision-making. Together, these communities form highly functional confederations that don't require centralized governments, or a centralized economy. Both the Symbiotic Culture and the Decentralized Civilization models detail the ways communal organizations can actualize a unified civilization. A society where we can all live in peace and in symbiosis with each other and with our planet.

Another excellent model that is fully aligned with these two is the Syntropic Enterprise taught and promoted by Syntropic World (4) and led by Christine McDougall. This model is based mostly on the life works of Buckminster Fuller (5) and the ongoing inputs of the Syntropic community. Like the other two models, Syntropic Enterprise holds life as sacred,[50] and relationships between people and Earth as the sacred thread of all actions and being. Syntropic societies, products, and services are designed to increase the well-being of all life. Syntropy does not exploit, extract, or colonize. It uses models and tools to enable people to come together in ways that help us work well as a community.

None of these models are about making monetary profit or accumulating power. "Profit" is redefined into the gain of well-being, vitality, knowledge, and fair access. Profit of money is merely a side effect; a means to achieving prioritized community goals and doing great work for a world with a future. In all these models, the role of leaders is to be the stewards who serve their community's Needs and hold space for symbiosis and synergy rather than dominating. The economy is local and collaborative. It includes a healthy balance of giving and receiving based on value for all life. Success is measured by the increased well-being in all domains of all who are engaged and affected. These principles embody what Dr. Martin Luther King Jr. called the Beloved Community. This new way of existing as a society cannot emerge from a place of anger, hatred, and defiance because the mindset of "tearing down the System" and "eating the rich" leads to the formation of the next Cones in line. It also cannot emerge from reforming or fixing the existing Cones because it just doesn't work. Instead, we should tap into an ancient approach with a modern slant.

We start by transforming society one person, one group, one community at a time.

In the words of Flyer: "The paradox of our time is that we can't solve global issues globally—we can only solve them locally. The world system, with its top-down economic and political control, is too vast to take on directly. And, since politics AND economics are both

---

[50] The use of the word "sacred" in this context describes an unbreakable and non-negotiable value, rather than a religious term.

downstream from culture, we need a cultural change strategy. But, changing global culture is too formidable to take on directly, so we must break down the challenge to something more manageable—creating a positive cultural movement in each local region... And, we don't have to wait for outside 'experts' in social activism, community building, or even established networkers to start."

We start by stepping away from divisive Cone Masters who tell us, "It can't be done." Once we are out, we can start reconnecting, heart-to-heart, person-to-person, neighbour-to-neighbour, community-to-community, nation-to-nation, and human-to-nature. From tiny, renewed communities, we multiply using this easily scalable model. Collectively, we regain our sovereignty over all major life systems, such as education, banking, production and distribution of food and essential goods, healthcare, information sharing, and all the rest. We flip Maslow's Hierarchy of Needs on its head and use the aboriginal model that reveres art, community, and fulfillment. We practice authentic democracy and let go of class and dominance. We reclaim our sovereignty over our individual spirituality. We work toward a great binding peace amongst ourselves and with our Mother Planet. To many of us who have developed cynicism about this world, this may sound ridiculously utopian. Yet these societies already exist in this very format, though they are still flying low under the global radar.

One of these little-known transformations happened in Sri Lanka. In the last few years, there has been great unrest with civil uprising against government corruption and shortages of both food and fuel, eventually forcing the president to flee. Beyond these sensational headlines, there is an untold story of how the people of Sri Lanka have managed during this crisis. Flyer describes in his book how a unique non-government organization called Sarvodaya[51] has quietly and behind the scenes mobilized a national network of thousands of self-sufficient villages. These micro-communities succeeded where their "official" Systems could not. Founded over sixty years ago by Dr. A.T. Ariyaratne, Sarvodaya grew into a self-governance movement that seeks a no-poverty, no-hyper-affluence society through community-based efforts and volunteerism.

Being a developing country in crisis, many would expect Sri Lankans to struggle to survive by ripping each other off for scraps. At least that's what our Cone Masters taught us. And yet this is where the quiet revolution has been at play for years. Since its inception, Sarvodaya has grown to include over fifteen thousand villages that had built over five thousand preschools, community health centres, libraries, and cottage industries.[52] They developed thousands of village-owned banks and over one hundred thousand small businesses—all with no government support. Their slogan characterizes the relationship between spiritual and economic development: "We build the road, and the road builds us."

Like the Stone Soup story,[53] there are many initiatives worldwide where communities share food. "The matchbox" campaign, started by a Sarvodaya founder, had each family, even the poorest, fill a small matchbox with whatever rice and dal they had and bring it to a local preschool. There, the collected food would be prepared and shared with all. This radical collaboration gave even the poorest the sense of personal power, belonging, and contribution. They could see for themselves how shared food could provide enough for everyone. It also increased their

---

[51] Sarvodaya Shramadana translates to "the Awakening of All through the sharing of energy." The term Sarvodaya was first used by Gandhi to describe his own political philosophy: "Universal uplift."

[52] Cottage industry is a business or manufacturing activity that is done in a person's home.

[53] Stone Soup is a European folk story in which hungry strangers who pretend to cook soup with a stone, convince the town's people to each add a small amount of their food into the soup, until they have a rich meal that everyone ends up enjoying. The moral of the story is that sharing resources, no matter how limited, benefits everyone.

motivation to send their children to school, where they would ultimately have a more consistent food supply. Sri Lanka isn't the only place where change is happening. Many other communities around the world create community kitchens, home and community gardens, communal cooking, and food-sharing systems. This initiative has already reached millions of people around the world, and it keeps growing because it speaks to our basic humanity.

Dr. Ariyaratne of the Sarvodaya movement was once asked, "How have you accomplished what few in world history have achieved—created a thriving network for mutual benefit where many millions of people have learned to empower themselves?" He responded by saying it was very simple. Treat everyone as equals and as human beings. Nurture leaders that hold a sacred space within the community with no personal agenda other than the community's awakening and thriving. The people of the Sarvodaya movement didn't go for toppling their government and its institutions. Instead, they built bioregional ecosystem networks. They created a new society amid the old.

What we need, then, is an alternative path that doesn't involve fighting Cones. Instead, we must build a parallel societal culture that will eventually supersede the old one and render it useless.

Starting with ourselves

Let's start with the basic Cone: ourselves. Though it is an unsavoury thought, each of us has at least a few embedded Cones that govern the way we view and live in this world. Most of these Cones, such as our cultural beliefs, nationality, concept of family, or religious beliefs, are deeply buried in our subconscious. One obstacle to setting ourselves free is our disbelief that we are Subjects of oppressive Cones. Surely, we are too smart for that. Surely, this is something that happens to others, not me. Most of us will require some aggressive mental excavation and great intellectual and emotional courage to pull out our Cones from the shadows into the light. If you feel you are ready, the following exercise may help you start this excavation.

A quick self-diagnostic

This exercise consists of two parts. In the first, you will self-assess your vulnerabilities to Cones. In the second, you will be guided to identify Cones that may already govern your life.

Step 1: What are my vulnerabilities?

Go on my website (www.navainc.ca) to complete the first part of your self-assessment. Start by scoring each of the statements provided as honestly as you can. For best results, ask other people who know you well to fill out this questionnaire about you and then compare notes. Sometimes others see us clearer than we see ourselves. Note that this self-assessment is not a validated scientific tool, and it should in no way be used to make clinical or psychological diagnoses of any sort. This tool is based on the Cone Model principles and is meant to help initiate and guide your self-reflection.

Step 2: Identifying Cones that may govern my life

Once you have completed and reflected on your list of vulnerabilities, proceed with the following self-reflective questions. As in Step 1, it will take ultimate honesty to make this a worthwhile self-diagnostic. If, throughout this part of the exercise, you feel emotionally triggered, just skip to the next section. However, this response should raise a red flag for you. The questions will only trigger you if they make you acknowledge exploitation, oppression, and abuse that you may not have been aware of or refuse to admit.

1. Whom do I look up to, feel aligned with, or idolize?

Make a list of every person or group that meet this description (e.g., family members, friends, peers, co-workers, mentors, supervisors, elders, celebrities, influencers, leaders, etc.)

2. Which social constructs, systems, or institutions do I hold in the highest regard?

(e.g., a traditional family structure or a binary gender system you strongly believe in, your religion, a particular political and/or economic model you support, a group or a movement you belong with, your racial or ethnic identity, your citizenship or nationality, the legal system, the educational system, the healthcare system, the agricultural system, the media, science, technology, particular economic model, etc.). If you come up with a long list, rank them by their level of importance to you, and then focus on the top five to ten for the remaining questions.

3. Which of the individuals and systems I have listed in questions 1 and 2 will I always defend from any form of questioning, criticism, or change?

Try thinking back to times where the credibility or the virtue of your chosen individuals/systems were challenged in some way. A few red flags to consider:

- How willing were you to listen to the critics and disruptors? How quickly did you block out their voices from your mind?
- How willing were you to examine the data or evidence they were providing or searched for evidence on your own?
- How open were you to giving this information serious consideration (vs. finding all the reasons it is wrong)?

- How open were you to considering actual change?
- How open were you to re-examining your opinion of the people/constructs you hold dearly?
- Have you ever had your own doubts about them? If so, why are they still at the top of your list?

4. Who might be taking advantage of my vulnerabilities?

Based on your answers in Step 1 of this exercise, here are a few red flags to consider:

- Who has the power to pressure or make you do things you wouldn't normally do, or that go against your personal beliefs and values?
- Who has the power to make you feel worthless, unloved, ashamed, guilty, scared, anxious, excluded, etc.?
- Will any of your top-ranking individuals or systems make you feel this way if you decide to defy, question, criticize, or leave them?
- How comfortable are you being your true self with these individuals or within these systems? (Being your true self means not having to put on masks and make efforts to please or fit in.)

5. What losses might I experience from following or engaging with these individuals or Solutions?

Almost everything we do in life has pluses and minuses. Hardly anything is perfect or utopian, and there will always be some "loss." The tell of a Cone is when these losses are substantial and avoidable. Here are some ways you may experience losses:

- Physical (deteriorating health, physical risk or harm, food shortage, housing shortage, etc.)

- Financial (loss, debt, poverty, reduced access to financial opportunities, unemployment, underemployment[54], etc.)
- Professional (career stagnation, reduced work benefits, work in silos, job discrimination, poor work conditions, toxic environment, etc.)
- Social (isolation, loss of social status, sense of inferiority, loss of power, pressure to conform, etc.)
- Societal (no social justice, loss of comradery, decreased knowledge and information, worsened governance systems, etc.)
- Global (stifled innovation, environmental damage, unsustainable resource extraction, animosity, division, etc.)
- Emotional (lower morale, reduced personal growth, depression, anxiety, fear, anger, shame, guilt, emptiness, dependency, etc.)
- Spiritual (feeling spiritually lost, loss of connectedness with the universe/deity, a sense of futility, etc.).

6. Whom am I not allowed to question, negotiate with, or critique?

A few things to consider:
- Don't think only about yourself; consider others you know or have heard of who had paid a price for questioning, trying to negotiate, or criticizing your chosen individuals/systems.
- Sometimes, people or systems don't forbid questioning or critique; some even claim to encourage it. But when it happens, they ignore, silence, or quietly punish those who do it.

---

[54] Underemployment is when a person doesn't have enough paid work or is underpaid for their work, or when their job isn't utilizing their skills and abilities.

7. Who rewards me for my devotion?

Enjoying praise for doing well is natural. But the greater the need for praise or for that feeling of "I'm a good person," the more likely it is that you're in a punitive Cone. A few red flags to consider:

- Do you feel you must be unconditionally loyal and devoted to an individual or a system?
- Do you feel guilty or ashamed when you "stray from the path" set by that individual or system?
- Do you feel the only way for you to truly belong is by conforming or obeying?

8. Who has the power to harm or punish me?

A few things to consider:
- "Punishments" may vary depending on the person or system, such as denying love, giving the silent treatment, silencing, shaming, discrediting, demoting, harassing, excluding, cancelling, isolating, firing, enacting financial penalties, beating, incarceration, etc.
- Think about your top-ranking people and systems—would any of them have the power to punish you (and might actually do it)?
- What would you have to do to justify punishment? How serious are these behaviours? What is the most meaningless thing that triggers punishments?
- Are there other environments/Solutions where the same behaviours would not be punishable?

9. Whom do I hate, fear, ridicule, or dismiss?

- You don't have to like everyone, and some people and ideas will naturally rub you the wrong way. In this question, consider:

- How powerful are my emotions toward this person, group, or concept?
- Why do they make me feel this way? Try to really dig deep, beyond "just because."
- Do they truly pose a risk to me to warrant strong emotions?
- Who else feels like me about this person, group, or concept? Who/what may be influencing us to think that way?

What have you found? Before you draw conclusions, consider the following caveats:

If you are deeply immersed in a Cone (e.g., a zealot or an unconditionally loyal Subject), your responses might not reflect reality. One of the strongest indications of being governed by one or more Cones is the level of your discomfort with these questions. The stronger your negative emotions to a certain question (anger, contempt) and the faster you dismiss these statements—feeling the very thought of it is ridiculous—the deeper you sit within this Cone.

Think about it this way: If a member of an extreme cult was to answer these questions, how would they feel about these "accusations" on their revered cult? Probably angry or scornful. How quickly would they resent and dismiss each of these prompts? Probably immediately. How truthful or realistic would their answers be? Probably not so much. That's why it helps to conduct this exercise with other people who know you, and who may have different and possibly more objective perspectives than your own. When you engage others, make sure they aren't members of your "echo chamber" (e.g., other members of the same cult).

Claiming our voice, owning our freedom

The phrase "Change begins with us" has become a cliché, but it doesn't make it any less true. We cannot wait for the Cones in our lives to wisen up and change their ways into syntropic, civic, symbiotic systems that support all and harm none. We also can no longer afford to sit on the sidelines and distract ourselves with nonsense while our planet is spiralling. But what can a single person do?

Understanding power

Though Cone Masters will have you believe you are powerless, no one can truly take your power away. Not even a tyrant or an abuser. Most of us are taught that power is force. Intimidation, violence, emotional abuse, and financial exploitation may all come across as power when they are nothing but brute force. It is the weapon of bullies and Cone Masters who can only control us if they succeed in scaring and subduing us. Genuine power is harmless, and it comes from within. It has a calm quality about it, and it doesn't require us to use force. Why is it important to distinguish between the two? Because when we understand how each concept works, we can reclaim the power Cone Masters took from us. It is the profound difference between seeing ourselves as a casualty versus a victim.

The term "victim" has been in the headlines for a while, heatedly debated, and often misunderstood or misrepresented. To better understand it, we need to separate the legal term from its emotional and mental implications. Legally speaking, a "victim of crime" is a person who has been harmed by a criminal offence. This definition has a major caveat, as we have already seen that laws aren't always objective or fair, and therefore not every abusive practice will be considered a crime. You can be abused by a person or a system that acts "under the law" and therefore not be formally recognized as a victim of crime. Even in highly equitable societies with a strong rule of law, a child may be the victim of bad parenting or bullying without being defined as such by the justice system.

The other side of the same coin is our feeling of victimhood. Even when we face brutality, we can comply with our abuser to survive while maintaining our power by refusing to become victims in our own mind.

When we consider our abuser as more powerful than us, we develop a victim mindset. We stop believing in our inner strength and let go of hope. The truth is, no one can take our power away; only *we* can give it away. And giving up our power is never a good choice.

This is not about diminishing realities of abuse or blaming victims for their condition. Our world is full of victims everywhere we look because it is infested with oppressive Cones. People subjected to abusive parenting and domestic violence. Threatened and displaced by war. Sexually attacked or molested. Economically exploited and locked into poverty. Persecuted for the colour of their skin, ethnicity, religion, or gender identity. And yet, when we create an inner narrative of being a victim, we lose our power, our choice, and our dreams. When we internalize our victimhood as part of our identity, we cannot see a way out of the Cone, which is exactly what Cone Masters are striving for.

We can only start making better choices for ourselves once we stop seeing ourselves as Cone victims and start realizing we are Cone casualties. No matter the circumstances, no matter the horror, it is still up to us to choose how to feel about it and how we respond. This is our true power. Once we realize this, we can use our inner strength to walk away from our Cones. If walking away isn't a viable option, we can internally disengage from them. We can reclaim our inner power by terminating our victim narrative and finding quiet ways to live in peace with ourselves.

The truth and nothing but the truth

Sometimes it will be difficult for us to believe we live in an oppressive environment or society, because our Cones teach us to be proud of our in-group's values and beliefs. I hope this book and the self-reflective exercise helped shed some light on at least a few of the Cones that control your life against your best interest. The first meaningful step is dismantling the false assumption that the teachings and the Systems of our Cones are eternally true and cannot be questioned. It is important we acknowledge that no single Solution, no matter how brilliant, works for everyone all the time. Since each of us has different Problems and Needs, we should be able to tap into a variety of Solutions rather than being locked into the "One True Dogma." Even the best of Solutions become obsolete, either for a particular individual or for the entire group.

For these reasons, you should always be allowed to question absolutely everything, be it your relationships, family members, cultural and religious moral directives, country, leaders, elders, idols, and all other life Systems. When you see that something doesn't work or make sense, don't doubt your instincts because "the leaders/Systems know better" or because "everyone says it's good and true." When things don't feel right, it is usually because corrupt and powerful Cone Masters are lying and manipulating you. If this isn't the case, you should be allowed to question everything and everyone without them feeling threatened and finding ways to silence you.

If you've never been the critical or rebellious type, you may not believe you are controlled by Cones because you never experienced their push-back. Try stepping out of your normal groove, even as an exercise, and see what happens. If your inquiry or controversial opinions on a particular matter start a healthy dialogue with your peers and people in power, it is probably a free-range Solution. But if it invokes public outrage, if you are being silenced or punished in some way, there should be no doubt in your mind you are dealing with a Cone and its loyal Subjects.

A good place to start is re-examining the foundations upon which the Systems you subscribe to are built (their Core Certainties). We have tons and tons of them lurking in our subconscious. Do you believe men are naturally superior to women, or that men and women are different but equally valuable and capable? Do people have a moral duty to respect, obey, and care for their parents no matter what, or is our first duty to ourselves and our own prosperity and well-being? Are doctors and scientists the most trustworthy people in society or are they as fallible and corruptible as the next person? Do you believe it isn't the responsibility of the rich to care for the poor, or that it is their responsibility to eliminate poverty? Do you believe success comes from ultimate competition, or that collaboration is the key to everyone's success? Is a good employee the one who obeys their managers, or the one asking the difficult questions?

All these, and so many other Core Certainties, guide the way you see the world and carry yourself. Some will be inconsequential, whereas others will lead to harm—to you, others, or the planet. Remember that none of these are "God given." They were all codes that were written by people at particular moments in history, with particular agendas in mind. These are all human inventions that we mistake for the conditions of nature or the decree of the divine.

Once you recognize the flaws, irrelevance, and lies in some of the Core Certainties you take for granted, you can start believing in your ability to rewrite these codes to reflect your own values. The key here is for you to stay away from the traps of "but it's always been this way," "this is the way of the world," or "this is human nature." Jobs, rent, prisons, policing, money, national identities, religions, money, borders, schools, gender identities, and monogamous marriage are all Systems invented by us. Some may still be relevant and beneficial to some extent, but they must all be open to reinvention once they become harmful, even if only to some of us.

Stepping out, bravely and wisely

Once you have acknowledged the Cones in your life, you will have to find the courage to get out. Walking away from a Cone will never be easy. In some rare cases, people experience a flash of clarity and a profound change of heart; some sort of unforeseen enlightenment that illuminates their lives and reveals hard truths and new paths. We have seen warlords turning to peacemaking, millionaires relinquishing their possessions to benefit their community, and criminals changing their lives to pursue social justice. But these are the anecdotal exceptions. Nevertheless, even without sudden divine intervention, we are all capable of change, but it is rarely a short and simple journey. It will take time and require at least some form of support.

Even when you are resolved to step out of a Cone, you might have a hard time admitting your past beliefs and behaviours were wrong and perhaps even harmful. It might be necessary for you to take time to deprogram your Cone-controlled mind, heal from personal and generational trauma, or recover from abuse. You may fear punishment and retaliation. You might think that you're the only one crazy enough to defy an indisputable Cone doctrine. The unknown that awaits you out there might scare you. You might dread the thought of having to leave "your people" behind and becoming isolated from everything and everyone you knew and relied on. You might feel guilty for betraying your peers and loved ones, even if only ideologically.

These are all natural and valid concerns. Nonetheless, once you awaken from your Cone-induced stupor, sticking with it becomes intolerable. Walking away—either physically, mentally, or ideologically—becomes nearly inevitable. If you are a fan of The Matrix (at least the first one), once you have chosen the red pill, there is no going back into the illusory matrix. The only way is forward.

That said, it doesn't always have to be all or nothing. Sometimes smaller steps are more viable and sustainable than big leaps. When Edison invented the lightbulb, he still used candles to illuminate his evenings until the use of electricity became widespread. Horse-drawn delivery wagons remained in use long after the automobile was invented, especially in smaller towns where horses could negotiate poor roads better than cars. People embracing a more natural and holistic medicine will be wise to also rely on the benefits of modern medicine. Often going "all out and away" from Coned Solutions will not only be difficult, but also unwise. Remember—going to the extreme is how re-Coning happens.

Be that as it may, once you are ready to consider this journey, try to savour the benefits of the change. You can start by making a list of gains and losses. For every loss you fear, find an equivalent gain that will offset it. You may have lost a connection with family members, but gained emotional freedom, self-worth, and a family of choice that makes you happy. Losing your faith may cost you your community affiliation, but have led you to deeper realities that finally speak your truth. Your new support system may make you feel truly seen and valued, compensating for your feeling of betrayal by those who were supposed to be your allies and protectors. You may have walked out on a high-earning job, but regained joy, a sense of well-being, and a path to a more meaningful life. You may have lost your popularity and reputation within your old circles, but have gained authenticity. Sometimes we need to write things down to actually see them.

You are not an island

Trees in a forest seem to grow separately from one another, but underneath the surface they are all bound and connected. Humans are no different. Our Cone Masters do everything in their power to make us forget who we are at our core and cut us from one another, but no one can truly cut our roots, and our natural networks can always be restored. Speaking your mind might be difficult (and sometimes unsafe), but it will help you pull yourself away from a harmful Cone and put you on your path to your true community. Seek like-minded people who share your dream or vision; people who are also looking for people like you. Create or join a group or a community that strives to build something better from a place of optimism and renewal, not from anger and revenge. It is easier to dream up a better life with others that have similar dreams. It will also

make you feel less ousted and isolated, and more hopeful about new opportunities. You may even realize that you are already a part of local social
networks to which you can contribute and be supported by.

Beyond likeminded folks, you may need deeper, more individualized supports. Contrary to the popular phrase, not everything that breaks
you makes you stronger. Sometimes the things that break us leave us broken. There is no shame in asking for help. Even the smallest change, let
alone de-Coning, can throw your emotional state into disarray. Being isolated and trying to go it alone might end up making you feel you're
fighting windmills and throw you back into your Cones' suffocating embrace. At the very least, join a group of people who are on the same journey and struggle with the same daemons. This kind of support may provide you with great relief from your fears and anxieties, because this shared
journey will make you realize there is nothing abnormal about you. You
may also consider reading self-help books if it's your thing or talking to
professional or spiritual guides.

Change takes grit and time

In our fast-paced lives, patience comes in short supply. We grow up to
believe in quick fixes: Five steps to changing your life, three tips for a
happy relationship, seven secrets of eternal success. Long and nuanced
Solutions are daunting for our minds that have been conditioned for ever
shorter attention spans. Three tips may be tempting, but these are usually
shallow and, following a momentary sense of excitement, perish from our
minds. These snippets of wisdom are both useless and damaging. By accepting the illusion of simplicity, we set ourselves up for failure when we
can't build a relationship, lose weight, or become an overnight success
using the quick-and-easy advice. Eventually, we might develop chronic
pessimism about our ability to make even the smallest change. Some in-
terventions aim to be more thorough than a three-tips article. But even
then, we fall into the trap of quick fixes.

One commonly used quick fix is the brief intervention. Following an increase in police brutality against people of colour in the United States (or more precisely an increase in the long-awaited media coverage and public outcry), there were calls for greater investment in diversity training for law enforcement. This spurred the development and delivery of interactive day-long diversity training. Hundreds of training sessions were delivered to nearly four thousand police officers between 2019 and 2022. The researchers who evaluated this program found that, while the training was well designed and delivered, it wasn't about to change police behaviour for longer than one month post-training (1). In what way was this surprising? Most of our attitudes and Core Certainties are infused into our subconscious from early childhood and we never question or revisit them. Our habits and behaviours take years to develop. We can't change any of these by reading a nifty article or by attending a brief training, no matter how well these are written and delivered. The more the behaviour is tied to our very identities, the harder it is and the longer it will take to internalize it.

Beyond basic awareness building, the more realistic way to achieve a lasting change is to start with small and manageable goals that will help us build confidence in our ability to change. Going from nothing to everything is a sure recipe for failure. There's a reason our old habits are called "comfort zone." Trying to change our behaviours can feel like switching our writing hand from right to left (or the other way). It is better to take it slow and steady to make sure our discomfort doesn't overwhelm and despair us. When we achieve small goals, we start believing we have the power to achieve greater changes. There is a reason why support groups for people with addictions keep the "one day at a time" approach.

Even when we've managed to change our behaviour, it requires upkeep lest we fall back into old comfort zones. Just like a relationship, maintenance of new behaviours requires continuous intention and effort.

To maintain change, most of us need constant supports and encourage-ment, because old habits are like an addiction of sorts. That's why so many of us revert to bad habits like smoking, drinking, overeating, or discriminating against minorities. It will happen to most of us, at least once in a while. It takes determination and continuous reinforcements to keep rising above our failures and trying again. All that to say, change takes grit and time.

Some more pointers for a better future

Though it is neither easy nor quick, releasing ourselves from our preda-tory, exploitive Cones is worth our effort and patience. You may find the following suggestions useful for your personal de-Coning journey. These are NOT the "ten tips for ultimate success." They are merely a few direc-tional arrows on a goalpost showing the many paths you can choose to take on your journey.

Dare to imagine a better future.

You can start with your own future, but you don't have to stop there. When you try to imagine a different world, unshackle your mind from old paradigms where you were made to believe "there are no other ways." Every thought that pops in your head starting with "this could never work" is usually the inner voice of your many Cones. Ignore them and keep imagining. There are always other, better ways, and deep down you know it.

No person or System is flawless or sacred.

If you grew up believing in idols, saints, heroes, and the righteousness of "your people," this will be a difficult transition. Proverbial holy cows are the most powerful anchors Cone Masters sink into our minds, and the hardest ones to walk away from. Most of us are taught to revere something that is beyond reproach. Yet, if you wish to build a new future outside the Cone, it is imperative for you to start questioning every Dogma and person you currently aren't allowed to doubt. This doesn't mean dumping everything you value. It simply means unveiling and shedding unrealistic beliefs.

Let go of cynicism and sarcasm.

Being a funny doomsayer may reward you with a few minutes of glory at office parties, but in the long run, it will keep you dwelling in misery and hopelessness. Worse yet, it will make you a downer and a spreader of gloom.

Misery loves company.

Try not to waste your time dwelling on your suffering and complaining about the Cone with people who love doing the same. The only thing it will get you is aggravated despair about "those horrible people/Systems and the change that will never come." Chronic pessimism is a terrible hindrance to change and a difficult state of mind from which to heal.

Beware of toxic positivity.

When times are hard and your emotional wounds are raw, denying your reality and plastering a smile on your face will not boost your resilience. The same goes for those around you. People in pain don't need to be preached to about thinking positively and sticking with good vibes. They need a helping hand and sometimes a shoulder to cry on. Strength comes from feeling supported, not from forcing positivity. True happiness blooms naturally from within; it cannot be force-fed.

Step out of your comfort zone and make time to act on your vision.

Having to make changes may add to your already busy or stressful life, but it is worth the effort. There are many wonderful caricatures depicting people who insist on pushing square-wheeled carts while ignoring those who offer them round wheels because they are "too busy to be trying something new." Don't be that square-wheeled person. It may take time to get used to something new, but the more you do it, the easier it becomes until it grows into your new comfort zone.

Try bringing friends and family with you or let go.

Help the people you care about awaken from the Cone, but don't be mad if they are not ready. We all have our different starting points, and our individual paths. This is where you will have to make difficult decisions about the people in your life, because leaving a Cone often means leaving people behind. Painful as it may be, sometimes it's the only way forward.

Don't give up on yourself.

Every big change in our lives, especially liberation from an oppressive Cone that used to be our "normal" and "one and only," will take its toll. You will have days when you feel completely confident of your decision, and others when you will ask yourself, "What the hell was I thinking?" Some days you will take a step forward, and on others you will take two steps back. That's when you might start beating yourself up and losing hope. That's when you should be extra compassionate with yourself. Lean into your new support system and forgive yourself if you stumbled or relapsed. Breathe, take a break, and try again.

Be kind to yourself.

Stepping out of a Cone is likely to have you face past behaviours you might not be proud of. You may have mistreated yourself or others. You may have caused harm "in the name of the Cone." It is natural to feel regret and even shame, but these emotions are unhelpful to your journey. There is a reason the saying "hindsight is twenty-twenty" describes a pointless and even a condescending sentiment. We can't know what we were never taught, shown, or experienced until we learn it. Your freedom from Cones relies on you not beating yourself up or putting yourself down for a time in your life when you didn't know any better. Finding ways to make up for the things you have done in the past may help you move forward. Dwelling in shame and regret most definitely will not.

Be compassionate with hard-core followers of Cone Solutions.

Understand and be compassionate with people who support an oppressive Cone, but don't waste your time and energy trying to convert Cone zealots. Use your inner resources on those who show greater promise of opening their minds. That said, don't get despaired when the "almost ready ones" don't believe or listen to you, even when you come prepared with facts and logic. Even open-minded people aren't always ready and willing to "betray" their Cones. Sometimes what feels like a futile attempt can work like a slow-release medication. You may be planting seeds of change in their minds that will sprout and grow once they are ready. When they finally decide to make a change, most won't even remember it was you who had planted those seeds and won't credit you for their evolution. Let go of your ego and take it as a gift that pays itself forward.

Do not tolerate Cone enforcement tactics and don't use them yourself.

Understanding the mental limitations of zealots and having compassion for them doesn't mean you should tolerate abuse. When you encounter bigotry, hate, name-calling, bullying, silencing, intimidation, or violence—even if they are not directed at you—call them out and resist if you feel you can. If you can't stand up to the oppressive Cone, at least don't take part in these acts. Even more importantly, don't practice them yourself against "Cone villains." Nothing good ever comes out of counterviolence. Or, as Mark Twain once said, "Never argue with an idiot. They will drag you down to their level and beat you with experience." Just do your best to help vulnerable people, and then walk away and focus on building your own healthy, symbiotic, and syntropic environment outside the Cone.

Don't let the media distract you.

The latest sensationalist post or story is usually nothing more than manufactured noise to make you forget or look away from the bigger issues. Remember that even wars, with everything terrible they bring, are mostly Cone-devised distractors to keep you fearful and loyal. Every minute you waste on bickering with someone over inflammatory news and postings, is precious time you could have used to focus on your journey away from the Cone.

Counter lies with truth.

When you hear someone repeating Cone propaganda, you can choose to stand up for the truth. If this is something you are passionate about, and you have the inner strength to deal with conflict, go for it. Consider acting against the Cone if you believe it will open minds to possibilities, but don't delude yourself into thinking you will change the System. You can equally decide to stay out of public discourse. Not everyone is destined or built to be an activist, and activism isn't the only way to create change. You can find small, quiet ways to support activists, or you can focus on your own journey. Trust that true evolution begins with each of us until it swells and reaches a tipping point.

Current Cone Masters are not your hope for the future.

Cone Masters are very talented and shameless liars. They make us believe they are our allies, shepherds, and saviors, but they are nothing of the sort. *Ever.* They are our enslavers, and we will never be anything else to them but their Subjects. Whenever you hear billionaires speak of their blessed initiatives to save this world, think again. There may be a handful of them who have seen the light, but these are the odd cases. Even Cone Masters of the smallest Cones, such as narcissistic partners, will never change no matter how many promises these abusers will make to their victims. If there is one thing you will take away from this book, let it be this: **The only way to build a better future is out and away from Cone Masters and their Systems.**

Watch for re-Coning traps

Once you are mentally prepared to walk away from your Cones, you have to keep in mind the rules of re-Coning lest you end up recreating the very thing you have left. Don't leave all hot and bothered; do your very best to let go of fury and vengeance because they are the seeds of the next Cone in line. "Privilege," for example, has recently become the favourite bad word of radical social justice movements. Of course, some privileges are destructive, like the ability to harm, discriminate, and exploit others without personal consequences, but there is absolutely nothing wrong with privilege, per se. We should all have the privilege of being treated well, having decent housing, accessing healthy food, feeling safe, getting medical care, enjoying art, being loved, or going out to nature. It is only when some people are denied these privileges, while others have them in abundance, that this term becomes negative. When we come from a place of anger and vengeance, we start considering all privileges as something negative, thus missing the point and risk going astray. This was one reason the humanitarian concept of socialism had devolved into oppressive communism. Once any form of privilege became synonymous with elitism and corruption, instead of pulling everyone up to enjoy privileges, everyone was pushed down to be equally underprivileged. Finding balance post-Cone can be difficult, but without it you will soon find yourself trapped in the next Cone of your own making.

Learn how to do better and then do it.

There are thousands of wonderful, innovative initiatives out there that are already implementing symbiotic and synergistic Solutions. Many native peoples have been doing it since time immemorial. Respect their ancient wisdom and learn from them. There are countless thought leaders, visionaries, and communities that can show you more sustainable ways to live and build enterprises with a more promising and sustainable future. There are better ways to live with each other and with Mother Earth. It's been done for thousands of years, and it's happening right now, even if still on a small scale. There's no reason you shouldn't be part of it. All you have to do is start seeking them out. They are not hiding or difficult to find. They simply aren't as loud as Cones.

Being used to life-under-Cones, it can be truly difficult for us to imagine achieving a consensus in a world of cut-throat, separatist, and warring cultures where we can't even agree on facts. And yet we have seen that change is possible even in the poorest communities. The world is open to disruption of Cone Systems. We can reimagine and redesign absolutely every life aspect, even if our Cone Systems claim we can't. If you aren't sure where to start, check out the list of such initiatives and enterprises I'm continuously updating on my website and go from there (www.navainc.ca).

A few final words

I believe that, at our core, we all want to live in peace with each other and with our Mother Earth, and that "world peace" isn't an empty answer given at a beauty pageant. If we are not "there" yet, it is not because people prefer hardship and oppression, or because no one thought of building a more harmonious life on this planet. We simply keep falling into the same traps. We keep being duped by profiteers, divided from one another to be easily controlled, played to lose in rigged zero-sum games, and then indoctrinated into crab mentality where we pull each other back into our Cones.

This book is not a call for a bloody revolution. It is a call for awakening and reclaiming our inner power.

Our hope doesn't hinge on tearing down the existing Coned Systems. It hinges on restoring our individual and communal power to build new and better systems. This is a reminder that we are the ones in charge, not our Cones. What most of us find despairing is that the change we need is global. Who among us can take up such a Sisyphean task? No one can, and no one should. True and long-lasting change can only happen locally, by having many small initiatives multiply and grow into a global mosaic.

We already have the foundation for a new society—it is both ancient and modern and it works beautifully. All we need is to believe we can grow it by dissolving fragmented, competing, tribalized silos. In the words of Richard Flyer: "Imagine thousands of communities, each building multiple, vibrant Symbiotic Networks, bringing together their leaders who are already doing good in their local area, with each community strengthening its own capacity for social and economic cooperation and self-sufficiency. Our local communities have both the resources and the needs to make this a reality."

It is up to us to help these new and renewed systems sprout and grow. We can create a new syntropic economic power where no one is exploited and marginalized. We can transform top-down power structures into a commonwealth of local communities and economies. It is not only possible; it is necessary for our collective survival. All that remains is for each of us to believe in it. In doing so, we will build the new world we all wish to live in.

Though I'm not much of a poet, here goes my heartfelt wish for us all.

Wishes and Blessings

May we all walk with humble bearing,
With minds wide open, enduring hearts,
Away from traps of senseless tenets
Where Cones are lurking in the dark.

May we shed shackles of false hatred,
Embrace our inner light instead,
May we remember our true beauty,
No terms, conditions, expiration dates.

May we disrupt with grace and courage,
Without destruction on our path,
May we renew without our dogmas,
That push us back into the muck.

May we be one with those unlike us,
As surely as with those like us,
May we shed fear that isn't ours,
And walk with love no matter what.

May we all soar without restrictions,
May we all heal without the shame,
May we forgive without the vengeance,
And build anew without regret.

May we sojourn with every creature,
May we move gently on this earth,
Walk hand in hand with Mother Gaia,
And tap the Source for all its light.

References

Chapter 1: The things we know to be true

1. *The 6 dimensions model of national culture by Geert Hofstede* (2021) *Geert Hofstede*. Available at: https://geerthofstede.com/culture-geert-hofstede-gert-jan-hofstede/6d-model-of-national-culture/ (Accessed: 15 January 2022).
2. McLeod S., (2024) *Maslow's hierarchy of needs, Simply Psychology*. Available at: https://www.simplypsychology.org/maslow.html (Accessed: 13 April 2021).
3. Brown, S.S., (2014). *Transformation Beyond Greed: Native Self-actualization*. Sidney Stone Brown.
4. American Psychological Association Convention, Denver CO (2016). *It's so old it is new: Native Self Actualization Placement Assessment*. Available at: https://zbook.org/read/900deb_it-s-so-old-it-is-new-native-self-actualization-place-ment-pdf.html (Accessed: 15 January 2022).
5. Crook, P. (2003) *Darwinism, war and history: The debate over the Biology of War from the 'Origin of Species' to the first World War*. Cambridge: Cambridge University Press.
6. Wilson, M.L., et al (2014) 'Lethal aggression in pan is better explained by adaptive strategies than human impacts', *Nature*, 513(7518), pp. 414–417. doi:10.1038/nature13727.

Chapter 2: From Problems to Needs

1. Little, A.C., Jones, B.C. and DeBruine, L.M. (2011) 'Facial attractiveness: Evolutionary Based Research', *Philosophical Transactions of the Royal Society B: Biological Sciences*, 366(1571), pp. 1638–1659. doi:10.1098/rstb.2010.0404.
2. Fothergill, E., et al (2016) 'Persistent metabolic adaptation 6 years after "The biggest loser" competition', *Obesity*, 24(8), pp. 1612–1619. doi:10.1002/oby.21538.
3. Vedel-Larsen, E., et al (2016) 'Major rapid weight loss induces changes in cardiac repolarization', *Journal of Electrocardiology*, 49(3), pp. 467–472. doi:10.1016/j.jelectrocard.2016.02.005.
4. Memon, A.N., et al (2020) 'Have our attempts to curb obesity done more harm than good?', *Cureus* [Preprint]. doi:10.7759/cureus.10275.
5. *Promotion of Baby Formula Threatens Progress on child nutrition* (2014) *Cambodia | World Vision International*. Available at: https://www.wvi.org/cambodia/article/promotion-baby-formula-threatens-progress-child-nutrition (Accessed: 23 August 2020).
6. Prak, S., Dahl, M. and Oeurn, S. (2014) 'Breastfeeding trends in Cambodia, and the increased use of breast-milk substitute—why is it a Danger?', *Nutrients*, 6(7), pp. 2920–2930. doi:10.3390/nu6072920.

7. Petersen, A.H. (2021) *Is it a resolution or is it capitalism, is it a resolution or is it capitalism.* Available at: https://annehelen.substack.com/p/is-it-a-resolution-or-is-it-capitalism (Accessed: 11 February 2022).

8. Wu, T. (2014) *Why airlines want to make you suffer, The New Yorker.* Available at: https://www.newyorker.com/business/currency/airlines-want-you-to-suffer (Accessed: 15 February 2024).

9. *Assigned seating fees are big business with estimated revenue of $4.2 billion for 8 US Airlines - press release* (no date) *IdeaWorksCompany.* Available at: https://ideaworkscompany.com/assigned-seating-fees-are-big-business-with-estimated-revenue-of-4-2-billion-for-8-us-airlines-press-release/ (Accessed: 1 January 2024).

10. *Global baggage fee revenue leaps to $29 billion - press release* (no date) *IdeaWorksCompany.* Available at: https://ideaworkscompany.com/global-baggage-fee-revenue-leaps-to-29-billion-press-release/ (Accessed: 01 January 2024).

11. Clayton, J. (2020) *Apple to pay $113m to settle iPhone 'Batterygate', BBC News.* Available at: https://www.bbc.com/news/technology-54996601 (Accessed: 15 February 2022).

12. Plc, G. (no date) *Annual sales of Apple's iphone (2007 – 2021), GlobalData.* Available at: https://www.globaldata.com/data-insights/technology--media-and-telecom/annual-sales-of-apples-iphone/ (Accessed: 15 April 2023).

Chapter 3: From Needs to Solutions

1. Harari, Y.N. (2015) *Sapiens: A brief history of mankind.* London: Vintage Books.

Chapter 4: Obstacles to great Solutions

1. Bechara, A., Damasio H., Damasio A.R. (2000) 'Emotion, decision-making and the Orbitofrontal Cortex', *Cerebral Cortex*, 10(3), pp. 295–307. doi:10.1093/cercor/10.3.295.

2. Bandes, S.A. and Salerno, J.M. (2014a) *Emotion, proof and prejudice: The cognitive science of gruesome photos and victim impact statements, SSRN.* Available at: https://papers.ssrn.com/sol3/papers.cfm?abstract_id=2416818 (Accessed: 1 May 2023).

3. Dörner, D. (2022) *The logic of failure: Recognizing and avoiding error in complex situations.* New York: Basic Books.

4. Energy.Gov, Department of Energy (2014) *The History of the Electric Car.* Available at: https://www.energy.gov/articles/history-electric-car (Accessed: 5 May 2021)

5. Norton, P.D. (2014) *Fighting traffic the dawn of the Motor Age in the American city.* Cambridge: MIT Press.

6. Huber, M.T. (2013) *Lifeblood: Oil, freedom, and the forces of Capital.* Minneapolis: University of Minnesota Press.

7. Toews, O. (2018) *Stolen city: Racial capitalism and the making of Winnipeg.* Winnipeg, Manitoba: ARP Books.

Chapter 7: The Cone Master emerges

1. Slater, A. *et al.* (2000) 'Newborn infants' preference for attractive faces: The role of internal and external facial features', *Infancy*, 1(2), pp. 265–274. doi:10.1207/s15327078in0102_8.
2. McCutcheon, L.E., Aruguete, M.S. (2021). 'Is Celebrity Worship Increasing Over Time?' *Journal of Studies in Social Sciences and Humanities*, 7(1), pp. 66-75 JSSSH. ISSN: 2413-9270

Chapter 8: Picking the low hanging fruits

1. Paul Slovic, P. (2004) 'What's Fear Got to Do with It – It's Affect We Need to Worry About.' *Missouri Law Review*, 69(4). Available at: https://scholarship.law.missouri.edu/mlr/vol69/iss4/5/
2. *Impact of fear and anxiety. Taking Charge of Your Wellbeing.* Available at: https://www.takingcharge.csh.umn.edu/impact-fear-and-anxiety#:~:text=Fear%20can%20interrupt%20processes%20in,intense%20emotions%20and%20impulsive%20reactions (Accessed: 15 August 2022).
3. Cialdini, R.B. (2021) *Influence, new and expanded: The psychology of persuasion.* New York: HarperCollins.
4. Sharot, T. (2011) 'The optimism bias', *Current Biology*, 21(23). doi:10.1016/j.cub.2011.10.030.
5. Gladwell, M. (2021) *Talking to strangers what we should know about the people we don't know.* New York: Back Bay Books.
6. Strunk, D.R., Lopez, H. and DeRubeis, R.J. (2006) 'Depressive symptoms are associated with unrealistic negative predictions of future life events', *Behaviour Research and Therapy*, 44(6), pp. 861–882. doi:10.1016/j.brat.2005.07.001.
7. Kantor, M. (2006). *The Psychopathology of Everyday Life: How Antisocial Personality Disorder Affects All of Us.* Praeger.
8. Simon, G.K. (2016) *In sheep's clothing: Understanding and dealing with manipulative people.* Marion, MI: Parkhurst Brothers, Inc., Publishers.
9. *How certainty transforms persuasion* (2015) *Harvard Business Review.* Available at: https://hbr.org/2015/09/how-certainty-transforms-persuasion#:~:text=and%20other%20stakeholders).-,Certainty%20profoundly%20shapes%20our%20behavior.,influence%20on%20what%20we%20do. (Accessed: 27 June 2022).
10. Stephan, W. G., and Stephan, C. W. (2000) *An integrated threat theory of prejudice* in *Reducing prejudice and discrimination.* ed. S. Oskamp, Hillsdale, NJ: Lawrence Erlbaum, pp. 23–46.
11. DiGiuseppe, R., and Tafrate, C. R. (2010). *Understanding anger disorders.* Oxford, UK: Oxford University Press.
12. Hoffer, E. (1951) *The True Believer: Thoughts on the Nature of Mass Movements.* New York: Harper & Row.

13. Boyle, M.H. *et al.* (2004) 'Differential-Maternal parenting behavior: Estimating within- and between-family effects on children', *Child Development*, 75(5), pp. 1457–1476. doi:10.1111/j.1467-8624.2004.00751.x.

14. Gabay, R. *et al.* (2020) 'The tendency for interpersonal victimhood: The personality construct and its consequences', *Personality and Individual Differences*, 165, p. 110134. doi:10.1016/j.paid.2020.110134.

15. Lustig, C., Hasher, L. and Zacks, R.T. (no date) 'Inhibitory deficit theory: Recent developments in a "new view"', *Inhibition in cognition.*, pp. 145–162. doi:10.1037/11587-008.

16. Hooghe, M., Marien, S. and de Vroome, T. (2012) 'The cognitive basis of trust. the relation between education, cognitive ability, and generalized and Political Trust', *Intelligence*, 40(6), pp. 604–613. doi:10.1016/j.intell.2012.08.006.

Chapter 9: Building Cone foundations

1. Christie, R. (1984) *Studies in machiavellianism.* New York u.a: Academic Press.
2. Patrick, C.J. (2019) *Handbook of Psychopathy.* New York: The Guilford Press.
3. Boddy, C.R. (2011) 'Corporate psychopaths, bullying, conflict and unfair supervision in the Workplace', *Corporate Psychopaths*, pp. 44–62. doi:10.1057/9780230307551_3.
4. *Share of global population affiliated with major religious groups in 2022, by religion. (2022)* Statista. Available at: https://www.statista.com/statistics/374704/share-of-global-population-by-religion/ (Accessed April 30, 2024).

Chapter 10: Stupefying us

1. Bonhoeffer, D. (2021) *Bonhoeffer: On stupidity: The North State Journal, The North State Journal | Elevate the conversation.* Available at: https://nsjonline.com/article/2021/12/bonhoeffer-on-stupidity/ (Accessed: 23 August 2023).
2. Cipolla, C.M. (2020) *The basic laws of human stupidity.* Doubleday Books.
3. Postman, N. (2006) *Amusing ourselves to death: Public discourse in the age of show business.* New York, NY: Penguin Books.

Chapter 11: Dividing and isolating

1. Glassner, B. (1999) *The culture of fear: Why Americans are afraid of the wrong things: Crime, drugs, minorities, Teen Moms, killer kids, mutant microbes, plane crashes, road rage, & so much more.* New York: Basic Books.
2. Stahl L. (2018): *Trump admitted mission to "discredit" press. CBS News.* https://www.cbsnews.com/news/lesley-stahl-donald-trump-said-attacking-press-to-discredit-negative-stories/ (Accessed: 15 February 2024).

3. Haque, U. (2023) *How do we take our societies back from the lunatics, Fanatics, and morons?, Medium.* Available at: https://eand.co/how-do-we-take-our-societies-back-from-the-lunatics-fanatics-and-morons-a5f3829eba24 (Accessed: 15 February 2024).

4. Schaller, M., Duncan, L.A. (2007). *The behavioral immune system: Its evolution and social psychological implications.* In Forgas, J.P., Haselton, M.G., von Hippel, W. (eds). *Evolution and the social mind: Evolutionary psychology and social cognition.* New York: Psychology Press. pp. 293–307.

5. Taifa, N. (2021). *Race, Mass Incarceration, and the Disastrous War on Drugs. Brennan Center for Justice.* Available at: https://www.brennancenter.org/our-work/analysis-opinion/race-mass-incarceration-and-disastrous-war-drugs (Accessed: 15 February 2024).

6. Webster, R.J. and Saucier, D.A. (2015) 'Demons are everywhere: The effects of belief in pure evil, demonization, and retribution on punishing criminal perpetrators', *Personality and Individual Differences,* 74, pp. 72–77. doi:10.1016/j.paid.2014.09.041.

Chapter 12: Mind control by a thousand cuts

1. Vale, G. (2018). 'Cubs in the Lions' Den: Indoctrination and Recruitment of Children Within Islamic State Territory'. King's College London, Strand UK. Available at: https://icsr.info/wp-content/uploads/2018/07/Cubs-in-the-Lions-Den-Indoctrination-and-Recruitment-of-Children-Within-Islamic-State-Territory.pdf (Accessed: 1 March 2024).

2. Herman, E.S. and Chomsky, N. (1988) *Manufacturing consent: The Political Economy of Mass Media.* New York: Vintage.

3. *The 6 companies that own (almost) all media [infographic], WebFX.* (2017) Available at: https://www.webfx.com/blog/internet/the-6-companies-that-own-almost-all-media-infographic/ (Accessed: 1 June 2021).

4. *Covid-19 in schoolchildren: A comparison between Finland and Sweden* (2020) Public Health Agency of Sweden, Article number: 20108-1. Available at: https://www.folkhalsomyndigheten.se/contentassets/c1b78bff-bfde4a7899eb0d8ffdb57b09/covid-19-school-aged-children.pdf (accessed on March 21, 2024))

5. Modan, N. (2023) *Half of students start school year behind—again. K-12Dive.* Available at: https://www.k12dive.com/news/NCES-school-pulse-panel-december-2022-students-behind-grade-level/642421/ (Accessed on March 22, 2024)

6. Vorhies, Z., and Heckenlively, K. (2021) *Google Leaks: A whistleblower's expose of big tech censorship.* Skyhorse Publishing.

7. Paulhus, D.L. (1984) 'Two-component models of socially desirable responding.', *Journal of Personality and Social Psychology,* 46(3), pp. 598–609. doi:10.1037//0022-3514.46.3.598.

8. *Truth and Reconciliation Commission of Canada (TRC)* (2015) Available at: https://nctr.ca/records/reports/

9. Richmond, V.P., Wrench, J.S. and McCroskey, J.C. (2013) *Communication apprehension, avoidance, and effectiveness.* Boston: Pearson.
10. Turner, M.E. *et al.* (1992) 'Threat, cohesion, and group effectiveness: Testing a social identity maintenance perspective on groupthink.', *Journal of Personality and Social Psychology*, 63(5), pp. 781–796. doi:10.1037//0022-3514.63.5.781.
11. Postmes, T. and Spears, R. (1998) 'Deindividuation and antinormative behavior: A meta-analysis.', *Psychological Bulletin*, 123(3), pp. 238–259. doi:10.1037//0033-2909.123.3.238.

Chapter 13: A Cone by any other name

1. Gladwell, M. (2015) *David and Goliath: Underdogs, misfits, and the Art of Battling Giants.* New York: Back Bay Books.
2. Hunt, D., Ana-Christina Ramón, A.C., and Tran, M. (2020). 'The Hollywood Diversity Report: Five Years of Progress and Missed Opportunities.' *UCLA College, Social Sciences.*
3. McMahon, J. (2015). *What makes Hollywood run? Capitalist power, risk and the control of social creativity.* PhD dissertation, York University, Toronto, Ontario.
4. Ali, H.A. (2013) *Infidel.* New York: Atria Paperback.
5. Crenshaw, K. (1991) 'Mapping the margins: Intersectionality, identity politics, and violence against women of color', *Stanford Law Review*, 43(6), p. 1241. doi:10.2307/1229039.

Chapter 14: The corrupting power of power

1. Devonis, D.C. (2020) 'Stanford Prison Experiment (SPE): Icon and controversy', *Psychology* [Preprint]. doi:10.1093/obo/9780199828340-0269.
2. Piff, P.K. *et al.* (2012) 'Higher social class predicts increased unethical behavior', *Proceedings of the National Academy of Sciences*, 109(11), pp. 4086–4091. doi:10.1073/pnas.1118373109.
3. Piff, P. (2013) *Does money make you mean? TED Talk.* Available at: https://www.ted.com/talks/paul_piff_does_money_make_you_mean?hasSummary=true&language=eo (Accessed: 17 February 2020).
4. Dubois, D., *The two big ways power transforms a person* (2016) *Harvard Business Review.* Available at: https://hbr.org/2016/02/the-two-big-ways-power-transforms-a-person (Accessed: 22 July 2022).
5. Genschow, O. *et al.* (2019) 'The effect of money priming on self-focus in the imitation-inhibition task', *Experimental Psychology*, 66(6), pp. 423–436. doi:10.1027/1618-3169/a000466.
6. Snyder, B. *et al.* (2007) *Dictatorships often survive with local support, Stanford Graduate School of Business.* Available at: https://www.gsb.stanford.edu/insights/dictatorships-often-survive-local-support (Accessed: 16 February 2024).

7. Padro i Miquel, G. (2007) *The control of politicians in divided societies: The Politics of Fear*, OUP Academic. Available at: https://academic.oup.com/restud/article/74/4/1259/1553658 (Accessed: 16 February 2024).
8. Lexchin, J. (2017) *Doctors in Denial: Why Big Pharma and the Canadian medical profession are too close for comfort*. Lorimer.
9. Anderson, T.S. *et al.* (2014) 'Academic Medical Center leadership on pharmaceutical company Boards of Directors', *JAMA*, 311(13), p. 1353. doi:10.1001/jama.2013.284925.

Chapter 15: Cone legalities and enforcement

1. Rosenthal, R., and Jacobson, L. (1968) 'Pygmalion in the classroom.' *The Urban Review*, 3(1), 16-20.
2. McNatt, D.B. (2000) 'Ancient pygmalion joins contemporary management: A meta-analysis of the result.', *Journal of Applied Psychology*, 85(2), pp. 314–322. doi:10.1037/0021-9010.85.2.314.
3. Babad, E.Y., and Inbar, J. (1982) 'Pygmalion, Galatea, and the Golem: Investigations of Biased and Unbiased Teachers' *Journal of Educational Psychology* 1982, 74(4), pp. 469-474

Chapter 16: Belly of the beast

1. Dalrymple, W. and Fraser, O. (2021) *The anarchy: The relentless rise of the East India Company*. New York: Bloomsbury Publishing.
2. Perkins, J. (2020) *The New Confessions of an Economic Hit Man*. Vancouver, B.C.: Langara College, pp. 1.
3. Perkins, J., (2016) *An economic hit man confesses and calls to action tedxtraversecity YouTube*. Available at: https://www.youtube.com/watch?v=btF6nKHo2i0 (Accessed: 1 February 2022).
4. Literary Life, October 13 (2022) *Cory Doctorow: Why our current tech monopolies is all thanks to Ronald Reagan and Robert Bork*, *Literary Hub*. Available at: https://lithub.com/cory-doctorow-why-our-current-tech-monopolies-is-all-thanks-to-ronald-reagan-and-robert-bork/ (Accessed: 14 November 2022).
5. *Monsanto vs. United States farmers*. (2005) Available at: https://www.centerforfoodsafety.org/files/cfsmonsantovsfarmerreport11305.pdf (Accessed: 15 December 2023).
6. *Behind the brands: Food Justice and the 'big 10' food and beverage companies* (no date) *Oxfam Policy & Practice*. Available at: https://policy-practice.oxfam.org/resources/behind-the-brands-food-justice-and-the-big-10-food-and-beverage-companies-270393/ (Accessed: 17 February 2024).
7. Friedman, R.E. (1997) *Who Wrote the Bible?* HarperOne; Reprint edition.
8. Graeber, D. and Wengrow, D. (2023) *The dawn of everything: A new history of humanity*. New York: Picador/Farrar, Straus and Giroux, pp. 276-327.

9. Jorge, V.O. (2017) 'Ian Hodder - Studies in human-thing entanglement', *Midas*, (8). doi:10.4000/midas.1163.
10. Cain, B. (2023) *Are monopolies evil geniuses or blundering fools? Medium.* Available at: https://aninjusticemag.com/are-monopolies-evil-geniuses-or-blundering-fools-af9f6315dbe3 (Accessed: 05 December 2023).
11. Arendt, H. (2022) *Eichmann in Jerusalem: A report on the banality of evil.* London: Penguin Books.

Chapter 17: Trouble in paradise

1. Bardon, A. (2020) *The truth about denial: Bias and self-deception in science, politics, and religion.* New York, NY: Oxford University Press.
2. Tooze, J.A. (2019) *Crashed: How a decade of financial crises changed the world.* London: Penguin Books.
3. Aspen (2016) *Anand Giridharadas: The thriving world, the Wilting World, & You, The Aspen Institute.* Available at: https://www.aspeninstitute.org/videos/anand-giridharadas-thriving-world-wilting-world-you/ (Accessed: 1 January 2021).
4. Greenpeace in partnership with Canadian Association of Physicians for the Environment (CAPE) (2023). *Greenwashing big oil & gas: The fossil fuel deception playbook.* Available at: https://cape.ca/wp-content/uploads/2023/12/Greenwashing-Toolkit-Part-1.pdf (Accessed: 17 December 2023).
5. Greenpeace International, 21 September (2022) *Harvard investigation reveals social media as the new frontier of climate deception and delay.* Available at: https://www.greenpeace.org/international/press-release/55714/harvard-investigation-reveals-social-media-as-the-new-frontier-of-climate-deception-and-delay/ (Accessed:17 December 2023).
6. Li, M., Trencher, G. and Asuka, J. (2022) 'The clean energy claims of BP, Chevron, ExxonMobil and Shell: A mismatch between discourse, actions and Investments', *PLOS ONE*, 17(2). doi:10.1371/journal.pone.0263596.
7. Stern, F. (1961) *The Politics of Cultural Despair: A study in the rise of the Germanic ideology.* University of California Press.
8. Oluo, I. (2020) *Mediocre: The dangerous legacy of white male america.* London, UK: John Murray.
9. Illing, S. (2020) *'flood the zone with shit': How misinformation overwhelmed our democracy, Vox.* Available at: https://www.vox.com/policy-and-politics/2020/1/16/20991816/impeachment-trial-trump-bannon-misinformation (Accessed: 1 March 2021).

Chapter 18: The emptying Cone

1. Light, D.W., Lexchin, J. and Darrow, J.J. (2013) 'Institutional corruption of pharmaceuticals and the myth of safe and effective drugs', *Journal of Law, Medicine & Ethics*, 41(3), pp. 590–600. doi:10.1111/jlme.12068.
2. Haque, U. (2021) *Why don't societies see their own collapse coming?*, *Medium*. Available at: https://eand.co/why-dont-societies-see-their-own-collapse-coming-4484d0b226d2 (Accessed: 18 February 2024).
3. Rushkoff, D. (2023) *Survival of the richest: Escape fantasies of the tech billionaires*. New York: WW Norton et Company.
4. Gladwell, M. (2002) *The Tipping Point: How Little Things Can Make a Big Difference*. Back Bay Books.

Chapter 19: Cones die…and reincarnate

1. Zurich Open Repository and Archive Research Report, University of Zurich (2019). *Trapped by misperceptions: Women, work and social norms in Saudi Arabia*. Available at: https://www.ubscenter.uzh.ch/en/publications/policy_briefs/trapped-by-misperceptions.html (Accessed: 1 March 2021).
2. Collins, C.M. (2018) *Tethered: Technology, faith & the illusion of self-sufficiency*. Walnut Creek, CA: Winds in the Reeds, pp. 4.
3. Fisher, R. (2020) '*Social Cryptomnesia*': How societies steal ideas, *BBC News*. Available at: https://www.bbc.com/future/article/20200827-social-cryptomnesia-how-society-steals-ideas?utm_medium=10today.media.20200901.436.1&utm_source=email&utm_content=article&utm_campaign=10-for-today%E2%80%944.0-styling (Accessed: 18 February 2021).

Chapter 20: The light at the end of this tunnel

1. Pinker, S. (2012) *The better angels of our nature: Why violence has declined*. Penguin Group USA.
2. Flyer, R. (2024) *Birthing the Symbiotic Age: An Ancient Blueprint for a New Creation*. Available at: https://richardflyer.substack.com/ (Accessed on February 7, 2024).
3. Kinney, R.C., and Kinney, M.C., II (2022) *Ideology of Decentralized Civilization and Egalitarian Community: Handbook for independence*. Poems For Parliament. Available at: https://poemsforparliament.uk/book-kinney/ (Accessed: 18 April 2023).
4. *Syntropic world - Re-design business for a world with a future* (2024). Available at: https://syntropic.world/.
5. Fuller, R.B. and Kuromiya, K. (2002) *Critical path*. Londres: Saint Martin's Press.
6. Lai, C.K. and Lisnek, J.A. (2023) 'The impact of implicit bias-oriented diversity training on police officers' beliefs, motivations, and actions.' *Psychological Science* [Preprint]. doi:10.31234/osf.io/dxfq6.

Index

80/20 Pareto principle, 157

A

Ableism, 18
   Mental health stigma, 18
Aboriginal, 123, 277, 395, 399, 410
   Indigenous, 18, 28, 39, 41, 109, 224,
      228, 263, 274, 289, 305, 326, 333,
      335, 395, 408
   Native, 263, 333, 399, 433
Abott, Jennifer, 349
Absolutism, 174, 389
Abuse, 18, 27, 62, 65, 66, 183, 189, 196,
   204, 226, 230, 264, 278, 283, 284, 299,
   318, 324, 361, 376, 381, 413, 419, 420,
   423, 431
Abusive relationship, 134, 196, 272, 332
Acid rain, 109
Africa, 290, 336
Agricultural revolution, 74
Alcoholic drinks, 79
Ali, Ayaan Hirsi, 276
American Doctrine of Discovery, 304
American National Security Agency (see
   NSA), 311
Amish community, 33
Amoeba, 58
Amusing Ourselves to Death, 205
Amygdala (see emotional place), 203
Analyzed Risk, 162
Andersen, Hans Christian, 159
Anderson, Robert, 110
Animal Farm, 37, 198, 303
Antidepressant, 115
Anti-racial discrimination, 390
Antisemitism, 10, 18, 276
   Jews, 11, 38, 231, 233, 276, 356
Antiseptics, 93
Anti-union legislation, 305
Anti-vagrancy legislation, 306
Apes, 89

Apocalypse, 372
   Apocalypse insurance, 372
   Apocalyptic scenarios, 169
Arendt, Hannah, 330
Aristocracy and intellectuals, 233
Ariyaratne, A.T., 411
Army, 117
   Military, 95, 97, 105, 154, 162, 179,
      291, 319, 321, 333, 336, 337, 338,
      340, 346, 368, 372, 378, 384, 393
Artificial human prosthetics, 98
Artificial Intelligence (see AI), 113
Asimov, Isaac, 57
Assault, 18, 143, 265, 295
   Violence, 18, 43, 153, 162, 177, 227,
      229, 235, 236, 244, 284, 336, 346,
      354, 360, 394, 407, 419, 420, 431
Assertiveness, 165
Atheists, 277, 317
Atrocity, 262, 263, 266
   Little atrocities, 263
Augmenter, 75
Authoritarian, 32, 134, 144, 226, 254, 258,
   288, 289, 304, 310, 317, 332, 345, 378,
   390
Authoritarian families, 32
Autocratic, 92, 280
Autonomy, 34, 212
Awakening, 204, 360, 405, 407, 412, 434

B

Bakan, Joel, 349
Bandwagon, 53
Bangladesh, 336, 346
Bannon, Steve, 359
Bardon, Adrian, 347
Basic needs, 171
Basic Needs, 71
Bate dogs, 213
Batista, Fulgencio, 389
Beauty industry, 9, 15, 75, 77, 81

Beauvoir, Simone de, 316
Behavioural patterns, 10
Belonging, 40, 83, 132, 140, 175, 216, 234, 239, 244, 300, 315, 388, 389, 411
Bhattacharya, Jay, 256
Bias, 17, 51, 63, 143, 168, 174, 250, 258, 259, 261, 353, 354
  Black and white cognitive bias, 174
  Cognitive Bias, 47, 143, 201, 353
  Cognitive dissonance, 51, 53, 129, 369
  Confirmation Bias, 250
  Good-old-days Bias, 168
  Halo effect, 143
  Optimism (optimistic) Bias, 168
  Pessimism (pessimistic) bias, 168
  Reporting Bias, 258, 259
  Self-enhancement bias, 261
Bible
  Holy scriptures, 323
Big Agro, 138
Big Oil, 337
Big pharma, 138, 292
Bigotry, 226, 431
Billionaires, 149, 150, 343, 372, 381, 432
Binary gender system, 414
Bio-system, 108
Birthing the Symbiotic Age, 407
Black people, 208, 277, 391
Blackfoot Nation (Siksika), 41
Blackfoot Nation motivational model, 41
Blame-shifting, 354, 355
Blasphemous, 92
Blind spots, 68, 140
Blueprint, 407, 408
Bonhoeffer, Dietrich, 201, 351
Boomers, 168, 390
BP (oil), 355
Brain-wiring, 43
Bread and games, 205
Brexit, 209, 251, 355
Brisket, 20
British Empire, 263, 375
Bronze Age, 104
Brothers Grimm, 323
Brute-force approach, 193
Bunkers, 372
Bureaucracy, 320, 329, 330, 370

Burglary, 284
Burma, 336
Bush Jr., George, 150

C

Caesar, Julius, 212
Cain, Benjamin, 330
Calculated misery, 76, 85
Caliphate, 243
Callous and coercive, 167, 188, 189, 261, 264
  Psychopaths, 262, 282
Cambodia, 77
Canada, 11, 103, 112, 275, 309
  Canadian anthropological expedition, 41
Cancer treatment, 237, 255
Capitalism, 162, 179, 238, 241, 247, 338, 371, 381, 391, 407
Capitalistic societies, 42, 306
Capone, Al (see American mafia), 290
Caribbean, 336
Castro, Fidel, 389
CBS 60 Minutes, 221
CBS News, 355
CDC, 255
Ceaușescu, Nicolae, 146, 289
Celebrity worship, 149, 150
Censorship, 251, 258, 260, 261, 318
Certainty, 21, 23, 24, 25, 26, 34, 35, 41, 44, 45, 51, 52, 74, 253, 325, 348, 405
Chaplin, Charlie, 72
Charity, 44, 89, 128, 129, 287
Chávez, Hugo, 144
Cheap grace, 351
Child, 12, 16, 18, 25, 27, 28, 34, 38, 47, 66, 76, 116, 126, 153, 156, 177, 192, 232, 244, 247, 254, 255, 263, 300, 303, 307, 310, 345, 357, 371, 398, 400, 419
  Child abuse, 147
China, 42, 103, 247, 337
Chinese agriculture, 103
Chomsky, Noam, 247
Christian, 91, 159, 319, 335
Chronic pessimism, 425, 428
Church, 107, 151, 179, 279
Cialdini, Robert, 164

Cigarette, 81
Cinematography, 274
Cipolla, Carlo, 201
Cis heterosexual man, 304
Civilization, 94, 408
Civilized systems, 326
Class, 74, 112, 179, 215, 229, 230, 255,
    257, 259, 265, 280, 306, 410
    Classism, 18
Climate change, 108, 109, 202, 209, 348,
    351, 370, 407
    Global warming, 108, 209, 370
Climate leader, 351
CNN, 256
Cognitive ability, 181, 182, 202
Cognitive ability factors, 181
    Environmental, 181
    Physiological, 181
Cognitive Revolution, 87
Cold War rivals, 96
Collapse, 170, 264, 326, 340, 349, 354,
    355, 359, 361, 362, 370, 371, 372, 374,
    375, 376, 377, 379, 382
Collins, C.M., 387
Colonization, 18, 262, 325, 333, 334, 336,
    338, 339, 343, 408
Columbia University, 85
Combustion engine, 94
Comfort zone, 17, 42, 105, 426, 429
Commercial, 73, 75, 124, 158, 196, 213,
    249, 250, 252, 260, 272, 289, 292, 324,
    333, 336, 338, 349
    Commercial conglomerate, 196, 272
Commodity market, 135
Common othering mechanism, 219
    Bully, 9, 62, 135, 153, 179, 183, 188,
        216, 223, 224, 264, 265, 266, 267,
        278
    Dehumanize, 259, 330
    Demonize(d), 162, 172, 230, 231
    Discredit, 129, 143, 221, 222, 293, 347
    Objectifying, 23, 228
Communal groups, 32
Communism, 9, 15, 37, 162, 433
Community, 33, 34, 37, 41, 45, 46, 121,
    124, 134, 157, 225, 244, 245, 248, 256,
    281, 313, 315, 319, 332, 375, 388, 389,

391, 407, 408, 409, 410, 411, 412, 423,
    424, 435
Companies, 73, 77, 84, 85, 111, 159, 225,
    248, 290, 292, 293, 341, 342, 343, 352,
    355, 368, 372
    De Beers diamonds, 341
    Five big publishers, 341
    Monsanto, 341, 342
    Nestle, 341
    Rockefeller's Standard Oil Company,
        341
Concealed Cone, 273
Conditioning, 165
    Indoctrination, 18, 53, 133, 139, 180,
        184, 206, 241, 242, 243, 245, 381
Cone Builder(s), 135, 136, 137, 138, 139,
    140, 142, 143, 144, 145, 146, 147, 148,
    149, 151, 152, 153, 154, 155, 156, 157,
    161, 162, 163, 164, 165, 166, 167, 168,
    170, 172, 173, 174, 175, 176, 178, 179,
    180, 181, 182, 183, 184, 185, 186, 187,
    188, 189, 191, 192, 193, 195, 203, 204,
    205, 208, 209, 210, 214, 215, 216, 217,
    218, 219, 223, 225, 231, 232, 233, 252,
    261, 388
Cone Dogma, 132, 197
Cone heretics (see Internal Traitors), 234
Cone indoctrination, 241
Cone legalities, 320
Cone Master(s), 131, 132, 133, 134, 135,
    138, 139, 146, 157, 162, 186, 188, 192,
    195, 196, 197, 198, 199, 201, 202, 203,
    205, 206, 207, 209, 210, 213, 214, 215,
    217, 220, 222, 223, 224, 225, 226, 227,
    228, 229, 231, 233, 234, 237, 238, 239,
    243, 244, 245, 246, 248, 249, 252, 253,
    254, 258, 260, 261, 263, 266, 267, 268,
    269, 275, 276, 282, 283, 287, 288, 289,
    290, 291, 292, 293, 294, 295, 296, 298,
    303, 304, 311, 313, 315, 316, 318, 319,
    320, 324, 329, 330, 333, 336, 338, 343,
    345, 346, 347, 348, 353, 354, 355, 356,
    357, 358, 359, 360, 361, 369, 370, 371,
    372, 374, 376, 377, 378, 379, 380, 381,
    384, 386, 395, 399, 405, 406, 408, 410,
    411, 419, 420, 421, 424, 427, 432
Cone Model, 12, 15, 16, 17, 54, 413

Cone penalties, 310
Cone reincarnation, 402
Cone self-enforcement, 318, 319
   Self-flagellation, 318
   Self-mutilation, 318
Cone topples, 15
Cone zealots, 373, 379, 380, 430
Conglomerates, 248, 367, 368
Conspiracy, 16, 46, 157, 158, 188, 206,
   224, 225, 239, 240, 347
   Conspiracy theory, 188, 224
Consumerism, 79, 115
Cookie-cutter solution, 117
Cordal, Isaac, 370
Core Certainty, 21, 23, 24, 25, 34, 41, 44,
   45, 51, 74, 253, 325, 348, 405
Corporate, 10, 188, 248, 272, 279, 335,
   336, 337, 339, 357, 360, 369
Corporatocracy, 340
Corrupt, 37, 38, 105, 125, 142, 246, 283,
   289, 298, 302, 307, 348, 372, 384, 386,
   389, 390, 408, 421
   Corruption, 35, 36, 37, 248, 288, 290,
   296, 302, 336, 354, 361, 370, 384,
   387, 410, 433
Cosby, Bill, 143
Coup, 192, 294, 356, 384
Coverly, Dave, 212
COVID-19, 209, 229, 251, 255
Cox, Palmer, 371
Crab mentality, 316, 434
Crashed, 349, 351
Creativity, 88, 89, 91, 92, 93, 94, 95, 98,
   118, 125, 130, 274, 327
Crenshaw, Kimberlé, 278
   Intersectionality, 278
Crime, 9, 10, 15, 36, 135, 139, 258, 264,
   280, 281, 290, 295, 296, 297, 298, 300,
   302, 303, 307, 308, 309, 310, 319, 326,
   388, 407, 419
   Crime Organization, 280, 281, 290
   Criminal activity, 140, 158, 280, 299,
   300, 308
   Organized Crime, 9, 15, 280
Critical race theory, 259
Critical thinking, 118, 206, 209, 237, 385
Cross-cultural communication, 29

Cryptomnesia, 397, 399
Cuban Revolution, 389
Cult, 14, 32, 135, 151, 188, 198, 202, 215,
   245, 273, 296, 332, 358, 405, 418
   Cult Leader, 198
Cultural Core Certainties, 29, 105
Cultural Dimensions, 29, 30, 32, 39, 42
Cultural Stereotyping, 30
Culture of oppression, 139
   Fostering Stockholm Syndrome, 139

D

Daesh, 243
Dalrymple, William, 336
Damasio, Antonio, 100
Dark-skinned women, 74
Darwin, Charles, 52
David and Goliath, 273
Dávila, Nicolás Gómez, 356
Death camps, 10
Debt, 204, 339, 340, 357, 370, 416
Decentralized Civilization, 408
Deflection, 354
Demigod, 80, 154
Democracy, 248, 290, 340, 346, 394, 399,
   410
   Anti-democratic, 340, 350, 394, 395,
   407
Dependency, 137, 416
Depression, 67, 150, 168, 175, 254, 372,
   416
Detroit, 350, 351
Devout believers, 52, 161, 195, 206
Dictatorship, 213, 251, 290, 330, 384, 389,
   405
Dieting, 74, 75, 81
   Dieting industry, 74
Discrimination, 11, 66, 67, 181, 229, 259,
   274, 298, 303, 318, 346, 399, 416
Disgust, 76, 176, 228, 229, 231, 232, 237,
   244
Distraction, 162, 205, 206, 358, 360
Divergent Solutions, 127, 133
Diversity hires, 349
Divide-and-conquer, 212, 213, 214, 215,
   216, 217, 219, 222
Doctorow, Cory, 341

Doctors in Denial, 292
Dogfighting, 18
Dogmatic patterns, 16
Domineering, 164, 167, 173, 184
Domino effect, 101, 233
Dörner, Dietrich, 101
Dostoyevsky, Fyodor, 193
Double-slits experiment, 50
Drag queens, 356, 358
Dualistic thinkers, 174
Dutch East India Company, 337

E

Easy prey, 216, 332
Economic Hit Men (see EHMs), 338, 339
Economy, 40, 79, 280, 338, 349, 351, 368,
    375, 376, 408, 409
Ecuador, 338
Education, 11, 21, 48, 53, 66, 67, 73, 114,
    123, 137, 139, 179, 181, 182, 183, 202,
    233, 245, 255, 257, 260, 273, 275, 297,
    298, 299, 305, 318, 324, 389, 393, 399,
    405, 410
    Curriculum, 226, 244, 259
Ego-driven, 25
Egotism, 172
Ehrlichman, John, 230
Electric vehicles, 111
Elite, 32, 171, 213, 395
Embezzling funds, 289
Emotional Marketing, 100
Emotional responses, 28, 58
Empathy, 177, 178, 188, 206, 217, 228,
    254, 262, 266, 285, 286, 298, 310, 386
Enforcement, 14, 133, 140, 188, 280, 295,
    298, 311, 312, 313, 314, 315, 316, 317,
    318, 319, 320, 326, 328, 330, 332, 345,
    356, 357, 360, 379, 393, 426
    Control, 13, 14, 43, 44, 67, 81, 97, 102,
    125, 126, 133, 135, 139, 148, 153,
    154, 164, 166, 167, 173, 174, 200,
    203, 204, 212, 213, 214, 217, 220,
    229, 232, 234, 243, 245, 246, 250,
    254, 258, 259, 261, 266, 271, 274,
    275, 277, 278, 284, 287, 288, 289,
    292, 294, 299, 300, 308, 310, 313,
    317, 320, 324, 327, 328, 329, 330,
    332, 333, 335, 336, 338, 342, 346,
    356, 357, 360, 369, 370, 377, 401,
    409, 419, 420
    Peer enforcement, 313, 315, 316
    Propaganda, 139, 146, 156, 158
    Self-enforcement, 318
Enforcement vectors, 314
Entitlement, 63, 150, 154, 163, 170, 286,
    386
Envious, 180, 187, 189, 190, 216, 311
Environment, 72, 109, 110, 162, 166, 213,
    250, 283, 291, 318, 327, 328, 331, 351,
    359, 360, 372, 399, 416, 420, 431
Epidemiology, 10, 255, 373
Erdoğan, Tayyip, 356
Escobar, Pablo, 290
Espionage act, 312
Ethnic, 21, 228, 346, 414
Ethnocentric, 30, 386
Evil, 43, 75, 102, 105, 142, 151, 152, 201,
    230, 231, 243, 262, 264, 267, 277, 283,
    330, 331, 378, 404
Evolution, 52, 78, 87, 114, 123, 130, 327,
    348, 430, 432
Exploit, 138, 147, 171, 173, 188, 190, 194,
    218, 266, 290, 291, 305, 324, 327, 331,
    335, 360, 409, 432

F

Fallacies, 129
    Ad hominem fallacy, 347
    Sunk cost, 129
Family, 10, 21, 29, 31, 34, 37, 38, 45, 49,
    65, 66, 80, 118, 120, 134, 135, 150,
    157, 186, 188, 196, 216, 217, 222, 224,
    226, 232, 235, 244, 245, 246, 248, 265,
    272, 276, 281, 299, 304, 310, 317, 318,
    319, 332, 353, 357, 378, 380, 388, 389,
    407, 411, 412, 414, 421, 424
Fandoms, 278
Fantasy-building, 76, 78, 81
Fawn response, 266
    Fawning, 165, 266
FDA, 255

Fear, 12, 16, 28, 44, 56, 57, 75, 82, 83, 95, 100, 115, 138, 139, 140, 161, 162, 163, 166, 167, 169, 171, 172, 173, 178, 198, 199, 204, 208, 214, 215, 216, 217, 223, 226, 228, 231, 232, 244, 260, 264, 265, 267, 268, 276, 287, 291, 296, 310, 311, 318, 319, 320, 329, 340, 354, 356, 380, 381, 383, 386, 416, 417, 423, 424, 436

Fedak, Marina, 9

Federal Aid Highway Act, 112

Feedback loop, 22, 165

Feeling of Risk, 162, 163

Feminism, 390

Fig, 362
    Strangler fig tree, 362

Fighting Traffic, 111

Film industry, 247, 274, 275, 349

Fine Arts, 273

Fisher, Richard, 399

Fit to print, 248

Fitting in, 216, 268

Five senses, 22, 23, 24, 48

Flag, 90, 97, 146, 212, 235, 236, 237, 239, 241, 390, 413

Fleming, Alexander, 93

Flight response, 264

Flyer, Richard, 407

Formal enforcers, 198, 319

Fossil fuel, 111, 339, 352, 355

Fougner, Emine, 229

Fragilities, 12, 14, 401

Freeze response, 265

French East India Company, 337

Frog, 132, 366, 370, 386, 406
    Boiling frog syndrome, 366

Fuller, Buckminster, 408

Fungal network, 399

Future, 16, 102, 109, 168, 170, 237, 291, 309, 352, 372, 386, 391, 403, 405, 407, 409, 427, 428, 432, 433

G

Gallic tribes, 212

Gandhi, Mahatma, 375

Gang, 29, 140, 295, 384, 389

Gaul (today's France), 212

Gay, 356

Gen Z, 168

Gender, 21, 27, 29, 48, 52, 66, 202, 228, 269, 276, 279, 318, 389, 390, 414, 420, 422

Genocide, 18, 243, 259, 262, 263, 277, 305, 334, 346

German, 201, 231, 353

Germany, 33, 153, 201, 209, 231, 353, 359

Giridharadas, Anand, 351

Gladwell, Malcolm, 168, 273, 374

Glassner, Barry, 218

GMO, 307, 342

Golem effect, 301

Gonorrhea, 76

Google, 113, 259, 341

Governance, 29, 32, 105, 196, 238, 239, 265, 272, 280, 282, 325, 375, 393, 394, 411, 416
    Government, 11, 37, 38, 77, 90, 102, 112, 124, 129, 135, 205, 235, 246, 248, 255, 273, 280, 289, 296, 311, 325, 336, 338, 340, 346, 350, 351, 356, 357, 360, 361, 393, 394, 395, 410, 411, 412

Graeber, David, 325

Great Barrington Declaration, 256

Great Depression, 103

Greed, 38, 98, 111, 167, 290, 291

Greenpeace, 352

Greenwashing, 352

Gregory IX, Pope, 102

Guantanamo Bay, 361

Guilt, 49, 82, 100, 153, 173, 174, 178, 217, 229, 260, 262, 272, 416

Gupta, Sunetra, 256

H

Halitosis appeal, 76

Hallucinogenic drugs, 47

Hand-waving, 346

Happiness, 78, 79, 100, 176, 178, 179, 180, 218, 428

Haque, Umair, 225, 370

Harari, Yuval Noah, 87

Harvard University, 257, 352

Hatred, 16, 28, 140, 153, 214, 231, 263, 276, 319, 354, 386, 388, 390, 409, 436

Hate crimes, 18
Heckenlively, Kent, 259
Herman, Edward, 247
Herron, Peter John, 224
Heterosexual, 304
Hierarchy, 30, 39
Historical events, 21, 247
Hitler, 208, 231, 247
Hodder, Ian, 330
Hoffer, Eric, 176
Hofstede, Geert, 29
Holocaust, 202
 Homelessness, 18, 66, 299, 306
Homophobia, 18, 36
 Transphobia, 18
Honour killing, 304
Hope, 16, 17, 32, 57, 81, 106, 176, 195,
 339, 340, 384, 386, 391, 402, 405, 406,
 420, 429, 434
Hopeless, 169, 184, 297, 340, 357, 404
Household appliances companies, 84
 Amazon, 84
 Apple, 84, 85, 148, 438
 General Electric, 84
 Google, 84
 Microsoft, 84
 Tesla, 84
Huber, Matt, 112
Human trafficking, 38, 290, 295, 335
Humanitarian crisis, 346
 The Rohingya Crisis in Myanmar, 346
Human-Thing Entanglement, 330
Hush money payments, 311
Hussein, Saddam, 289
Huxley, Thomas Henry, 43
Hyper-individualism, 238, 391
Hyper-sexuality, 376

I

I Miquel, Gerard Padró, 290
Ibrahim, Dawood, 290
Iceberg, 297, 300
Idi Amin, Dada, 384
Ignorant, 109, 183, 184, 197, 399
Illing, Sean, 359

Illusion, 48, 67, 96, 125, 202, 234, 248,
 300, 349, 407, 425
Illusory matrix, 423
Immigrants, 11, 80, 228, 233
Impressionism, 273
Incarnation, 102
India, 31, 42, 229, 305, 336, 337, 375
Inequity Aversion, 177
Infidel, 276
Influencers, 81, 149, 205, 222, 225, 375,
 414
In-group, 178, 216, 220, 231, 244, 274,
 298, 311, 420
Injustice, 10, 138, 139, 140, 156, 157, 163,
 170, 175, 176, 177, 180, 190, 230, 238,
 277, 285
Inner circle, 175, 186, 187, 188, 189, 289,
 291, 311
Innovation, 91, 92, 94, 96, 98, 104, 113,
 118, 125, 132, 148, 195, 416
Insecure, 10, 53, 64, 165, 167, 189, 216,
 268
Internal Traitors (see transgressors), 132,
 133, 198, 199, 207, 234, 275, 316, 340,
 354, 375, 390
Intersecting Cones, 279, 280
Intersectionality, 281
Ionesco, Eugène, 268
Iran, 281, 305, 338
Iraq, 243, 289, 327
Iron Curtain (see USSR), 11, 37
Iroquois Six Nation Constitution, 408
ISIL, 243
ISIS (ISIL, Daesh), 244
Israel, 1, ii, 11

J

Jacobson, Lenore, 300
Jaywalking, 160
Jew, 275
Jigsaw puzzle, 48
Jim Crow laws, 305
Jobs, Steve, 92, 148, 155
Jomo Kenyatta, Charles, 375
Jones, Jim, 151

K

Kaplan, Mitchell, 341
Keeling, Charles, 109
Khan, Genghis, 193
Khomeini, Ayatollah, 390
Kinney, Mark, 408
Kinney, Reed, 408
KKK, 313, 314, 315, 319
Kleptocracies, 289
Kosher, 322, 323, 324, 330
Kulldorff, Martin, 255

L

Land degradation, 108
Law, 35, 36, 38, 160, 168, 203, 233, 265,
    275, 280, 298, 299, 302, 303, 304, 305,
    306, 307, 308, 312, 314, 325, 327, 360,
    361, 419, 426
    Law-abiding, 281, 307
Leader, 14, 41, 80, 103, 138, 140, 146, 147,
    151, 153, 181, 182, 186, 187, 188, 189,
    190, 215, 278, 323, 328, 346, 354, 380,
    384, 386
Lenin, Vladimir, 234
Lexchin, Joel, 292
Liberation, 382, 405, 429
Life choices, 65, 67, 376
Liquor Master, 242, 243
Listerine, 76
Loan, 289, 339, 349, 389
    Debt, 339, 357
Lobbyists, 100, 251
Locust, 103
Love-bombing, 166
Low self-esteem, 73, 83, 166
Low-hanging fruit, 155, 157, 216
Luntz, Frank, 209
Luther King Jr., Martin, 402, 409

M

Machiavelli, Nicholas, 184
Magician, 75, 341
Malaysia, 337
Malignant, 222, 232
Man as a machine, 240

Manufactured Problems and Needs, 86
Manufacturing Consent, 247
Marcos, Ferdinand and Imelda, 289
Marginalized, 144, 183, 209, 212, 249,
    306, 407, 435
Margulis, Lynn, 52
Marriage, 21, 33, 34, 38, 134, 137, 212
Martin, Lockheed, 337
Marx, Karl, 153
Maslach, Christina, 285
Maslow, Abraham
    Maslow's Hierarchy of Needs, 39, 410
Matchbox campaign, 411
McCain, John, 222
McDougall, Christine, 408
Media, 73, 116, 130, 134, 138, 139, 149,
    158, 169, 191, 205, 207, 210, 223, 225,
    226, 227, 245, 246, 247, 248, 249, 250,
    251, 252, 256, 257, 259, 260, 261, 273,
    277, 292, 293, 340, 346, 352, 354, 356,
    357, 358, 359, 370, 376, 407, 414, 426,
    438
    Independent media, 247
    Mainstream media, 169, 226, 249
    Mass media, 205, 248
    Social media, 56, 249
Medicine, 11, 65, 67, 98, 206, 240, 241,
    368, 395, 407, 423
    *Healing, 10, 22, 95, 107, 108, 236, 241,
    308, 309, 395*
    Modern medicine, 9, 15
Mega-cities, 325
Mental clutter, 182
Mental health, 74, 163, 171, 255, 257, 299,
    306, 376
    Mental health stigma, 18
Mental immune system, 156
Mental workspace, 182
Mental zombie, 210
Messiah, 154
Michelangelo, 88
Middle East, 111, 214, 275
Military radar, 97
Mind control, 273
    Brainwash, 385
    Thought-terminating, 208

Minorities, 80, 228, 233, 235, 259, 393, 399, 427

Minority influence, 399

Misogynism, 221, 391

Mob mentality, 268

Mogilevich, Semion, 290

Money, 21, 27, 77, 84, 85, 86, 89, 111, 118, 129, 135, 139, 148, 162, 172, 182, 186, 187, 237, 257, 273, 285, 287, 289, 290, 291, 292, 294, 311, 327, 336, 338, 339, 352, 356, 368, 384, 409, 422

Wealth, 18, 83, 119

Moneylending, 233

Monogamous marriage, 241, 422

Monopolizing, 294, 342

Monopoly, 341, 386

Monopoly game, 285

Monotheistic philosophies, 396

Monounsaturated fats, 392

Monsanto (Bayer), 341

Monster, 262

Moral, 148, 156, 171, 172, 176, 178, 190, 227, 229, 230, 232, 235, 315, 318, 358, 421

Immoral, 172, 175, 182, 184, 188, 190, 223, 227, 235, 238, 298, 299, 307

Morality, 150, 163, 171, 172, 188, 227, 245, 261, 319

Mother Gaia, 436

Motherland, 11, 90

Motivational model of indigenous people, 39

Muslim, 90, 276, 346, 360

Islam, 305

Mussolini, Benito, 153

Myanmar, 346

Myths, 89, 90, 91, 245, 276, 323, 396

Creation stories, 89

Invisible gods, 89

Tribal spirit, 89

N

Nader, Ralph, 111

Naïve, 14, 134, 180, 181, 183, 184, 190, 233, 401

Narcissist, 143

Narcissistic injury, 372

Narcissistic partners, 432

Narcissistic Seduction, 143

Nationalism, 239

Natural selection, 52

Nazi, 209, 303, 330, 359

Anti-Nazi rebel, 201

Need (capitalized), 13, 17, 21, 25, 27, 34, 38, 46, 58, 59, 60, 61, 62, 63, 65, 68, 69, 70, 71, 73, 74, 75, 78, 81, 82, 83, 86, 93, 94, 96, 98, 100, 104, 106, 107, 112, 113, 121, 131, 132, 136, 158, 159, 161, 167, 173, 174, 178, 179, 197, 224, 253, 282, 291, 315, 316, 318, 348

Need-generating fantasies, 81

Neurotic, 42

Neuroticism, 150

New Year's Resolution, 81

New Zealand, 372

Newton's third law of motion, 233

Neznayka, 371

Nixon, Richard, 230

Nkrumah, Kwame, 375

Noble savage, 43

Non-white, 319

Non-white ethnicities, 73

Norms, 36, 50, 53, 171, 267, 390

North Korea, 247

Norton, Peter, 111

Nosov, Nikolay, 371

NSA, 312, 338

O

Obedience, 16, 153, 165, 175, 192, 208, 246

Objectifying, 227

Objective truth and reality, 24

Obote, Milton, 384

Obsolescence, 84

Oil and gas companies, 337, 352

BP (oil), 352

Chevron (oil), 352

ExxonMobil, 337, 352

Saudi Aramco, 337

Shell, 352

Standard Oil Company, 341

Oil and gas companiies
  PetroChina, 337
Oil drilling, 209
Oluo, Ijeoma, 355
Operational system, 49
Opportunist, 187, 213
Oppression, 10, 13, 67, 193, 254, 278, 349,
    354, 382, 390, 401, 413, 434
  Oppressive cones, 16, 202, 241, 298,
      300, 327, 404, 408, 412, 420
  Oppressive regime, 37, 225, 327
Optimism, 44, 45, 46, 424
Orthodox, 118, 193, 258, 317, 381
Orwell, George, 37, 198, 249, 303
  Orwellian, 360
Other-blaming, 354
Out-group, 298
Oxfam, 342, 343

P

Pakistan, 281, 305, 336
Panama, 338
Paranoia, 268
Parent, 34, 79, 146, 147, 192, 232, 254,
    310, 345, 348, 363, 378
Partner, 52, 62, 71, 136, 145, 166, 173,
    190, 202, 215, 222, 232, 295, 348, 360,
    380
Patriarchal societies, 51, 57, 165, 231
Patriarchy, 18
PATRIOT Act, 360
Patriotism, 153, 239, 361
Patronage networks, 291
Patterns, 9, 10, 11, 16, 96, 161, 362
Pear, 241, 242, 243, 273
Peer pressure, 42, 49, 171, 244, 315
Penicillin, 93
People of colour, 221, 356
Peoples Temple, 151
Perceptions, 20, 27, 62, 227
Performance throttling, 85
Performative tokenism, 348, 349, 351
Perkins, John, 338
Perpetual victims, 184
Persona, 96, 136, 143, 146, 147, 148, 151,
    152, 153, 154, 155, 185, 190, 332, 348,
    354, 384

Partner persona, 145
Rebel persona, 151
Saviour persona, 154
Shepherd Persona, 146
Superstar persona, 150
Personality, 20, 30, 42, 44, 152, 177, 178,
    187, 227, 264
Peter the Hermit, 169
Petersen, Anne Helen, 81
Petri dish, 93, 101
Pharaoh, 159
Pharmaceuticals, 368
  Big pharma, 368
Philanthropic donations, 292
Philanthropist(sm), 148
  Philanthropy, 351
Philippines, 289
Physical punishment, 139
Piff, Paul, 285
Pinker, Steven, 406
Pinocchio, 247
Planned obsolescence, 83
Plastic, 81, 85, 95, 115, 285, 296, 359, 360
  Plastic straws, 359
Plato, 42, 169
Pluralistic ignorance, 381
Police, 18, 37, 210, 233, 235, 236, 265,
    280, 284, 294, 319, 346, 368, 426
  Police brutality, 426
Polyunsaturated fatty acids, 392
Ponzi scheme, 202, 313
Pope, 102
Postman, Andrew, 205
Post-perestroika, 327
Poverty, 37, 144, 162, 255, 285, 297, 298,
    299, 305, 326, 350, 407, 411, 416, 420,
    422
Power vector, 313
Prepubescent, 73, 157
Primitive savages, 224
Privilege, 170, 274, 286, 432, 433
Problem (capitalized), 13, 16, 21, 34, 36,
    38, 54, 56, 58, 59, 60, 61, 62, 63, 64,
    65, 68, 72, 75, 76, 77, 78, 82, 83, 86,
    94, 95, 101, 104, 112, 113, 114, 115,
    116, 124, 125, 132, 136, 253, 311, 385,
    387

Professional attire, 154
  Lab coats, 154
Profit, 409
  Profiteer, 80, 81, 83, 100, 279
Programming, 50, 88, 143, 235, 276
  Indoctrinating, 193, 243, 313
Propaganda, 14, 53, 73, 83, 113, 133, 137,
  169, 180, 184, 223, 225, 243, 246, 247,
  248, 250, 252, 319, 332, 348, 359, 401,
  404, 431
Psychedelic, 47, 50, 235, 395
PTSD, 265
Puddle sculpture, 370
Punishment, 139, 216, 242, 309, 311, 318,
  329, 417, 423
Punitive, 49, 53, 175, 213, 238, 310, 318,
  320, 327, 328, 357, 391, 417
Puppeteer, 223
Putin, Vladimir, 356
Pygmalion effect, 300, 301

Q

Queer, 17, 306, 358
Quick fix, 118, 127, 204, 426

R

Rabbinic scholars, 324
Racial discrimination, 66
Racism, 18, 36, 55, 67, 162, 208, 221, 263,
  276, 278, 298, 348, 387, 391, 407
Radical, 192, 203, 243, 244, 277, 278, 347,
  370, 390, 407, 411, 432
Reagan, Ronald, 150
Rebels, 151, 198, 269, 274, 379, 382, 387,
  388, 395, 396
Rebound effect, 104
Re-coning, 383, 385, 386, 388, 389, 390,
  391, 392, 393, 394, 395, 396, 397, 398,
  399, 424, 432
Recruit, 138, 155, 157, 168, 170, 175, 190,
  216, 319
Red flags, 414, 415, 417
Rednecks, 208, 224
Reebok's campaign, 252
Refugees, 162, 228

Relentless optimist, 45
Religion, 9, 15, 33, 92, 135, 176, 179, 190,
  193, 194, 196, 206, 260, 275, 277, 279,
  281, 305, 306, 323, 324, 335, 362, 391,
  396, 405, 414, 420, 440
Religious congregations, 52, 183
Repeats, 158, 161, 184, 189, 216, 330
Residential schools, 263
Revenge, 175, 176, 178, 180, 187, 218,
  244, 300, 316, 424
Rhinoceros, 268
Rigged game, 285
Righteous, 14, 43, 153, 172, 173, 175, 184,
  199, 232, 258, 259, 262, 316, 323, 376
  Righteous indignation, 263
Robespierre, 384
Roddenberry, Gene, 96
Rohingya, 346
Role reversal, 193, 199
Roman Empire, 325
Romania, 146, 289
Rules, 15, 21, 36, 42, 156, 160, 176, 177,
  186, 193, 203, 285, 302, 303, 305, 307,
  308, 309, 310, 313, 315, 318, 319, 321,
  322, 323, 324, 325, 327, 328, 329, 330,
  332, 335, 357, 390, 432
Russia, 290, 312, 356

S

Salem Witch Trials, 229
San Suu Kyi, Aung, 346
Sapiens, 72, 87
Sarvodaya, 411, 412
Saudi Arabia, 305, 338, 381
Scapegoat, 231, 354
  Scapegoating, 219, 230, 231, 232, 393
Scarcity mindset, 44, 139, 163
Scholl, Sophie, 303
School, 18, 31, 65, 90, 116, 120, 150, 191,
  216, 226, 244, 256, 260, 278, 300, 301,
  373, 375, 412
Schrödinger's cat, 50
Schwarzman, Stephen, 290
Science, 10, 23, 25, 40, 50, 52, 65, 105,
  126, 150, 206, 209, 276, 348, 392, 396,
  398, 414

Scientist, 43, 50, 52, 95, 103, 124, 149, 183, 225, 256, 257, 331, 397, 399, 422
  Scientism, 397
Secular regime, 389
Self preservation, 57, 121
Self-aggrandizement, 151, 283
Self-assuredness, 154
Self-confidence, 81, 96, 217, 291, 357
Self-deception, 64
Self-denial, 34, 172, 272
Self-diagnostic, 413
Self-hate, 175
Self-healing, 368
Self-image, 51
Self-indulgent, 172
Self-inflicted naivete, 183
Self-justification, 286
Self-preservation, 36, 371, 372, 401
Self-sabotage, 272
Self-serving, 13, 14, 36, 71, 105, 107, 112, 194, 196, 249, 282, 401
Self-sufficiency, 41, 435
Sese Seko, Mobutu, 289
Sex, 27, 40, 71, 228, 278, 338
Sexual abuse, 66
Sexual deviants, 231
Shame, 49, 77, 79, 82, 100, 115, 138, 153, 161, 170, 173, 217, 223, 238, 260, 262, 272, 416, 425, 430, 436
  Shaming, 73, 74, 76, 77, 80, 119, 136, 139, 173, 216, 277, 396, 417
Shaw, George Bernard, 300
Siblings, 183
Silence, 129, 143, 209, 226, 246, 251, 254, 256, 257, 259, 349, 369, 391, 405, 416, 421
  silencing, 119, 254, 258, 260, 261, 391, 417, 431
Simon, George, 173
Skewed perception, 47
Slavery, 38, 202
  Enslaving, 262, 340
  Slavery-free zones, 38
Sluggish bureaucarcies, 329
Smoot–Hawley Tariff Act, 102
Snakes and Ladders, 101
Snowden, Edward, 311

Snowflakes, 208, 224, 359
Social construct, 355
Social cryptomnesia, 398
Social Determinants of Health, 64, 65, 67, 300
Social isolation, 56, 67, 82, 83, 181, 266, 298
  Marginalized groups, 181
Social justice, 37, 151, 277, 389, 416, 423, 432
Social media platforms, 249
  Facebook, 249
  MySpace, 249
  Twitter (X), 256
  YouTube, 252
Social narrative, 31
Social norm, 287, 302
Societal crises, 162
Sociopathy, 156
Soft spots, 100, 138, 145
Solution (capitalized), 13, 14, 15, 21, 22, 23, 25, 27, 30, 32, 33, 36, 38, 39, 45, 46, 47, 54, 59, 60, 61, 62, 63, 64, 65, 67, 75, 77, 80, 82, 83, 87, 88, 91, 93, 94, 95, 96, 97, 98, 99, 100, 101, 102, 103, 104, 105, 107, 108, 110, 112, 113, 114, 115, 116, 117, 118, 119, 120, 121, 122, 123, 124, 125, 126, 127, 128, 129, 130, 131, 132, 133, 134, 135, 136, 137, 138, 139, 142, 143, 144, 151, 162, 170, 172, 174, 175, 178, 179, 185, 186, 187, 189, 190, 191, 195, 196, 197, 198, 204, 225, 240, 249, 252, 253, 275, 277, 288, 291, 292, 294, 315, 321, 328, 329, 330, 333, 341, 362, 368, 369, 373, 374, 375, 377, 379, 382, 384, 385, 386, 387, 388, 389, 392, 396, 397, 398, 400, 401, 402, 404, 405, 406, 407, 415, 417, 421, 424, 425, 433
Solution Users, 122, 328, 329
South Africa, 305, 337, 354
Soviet Union, 11, 96, 103, 225, 246, 247, 326
Space Race, 96
Sparrowcide campaign, 103
Spectrum of autism, 161

Spiritual, 11, 22, 23, 25, 89, 107, 123, 149, 323, 388, 389, 390, 395, 397, 407, 411, 425
Spiritual practices, 22
Sports club, 239
Sports fandom, 269, 277
Sri Lanka, 337, 410, 412
Stahl, Lesley, 221
Stanford Prison Experiment, 283
Star Wars, 331
Star Wars fandom, 278
State-sanctioned violence, 18
State-sponsored actors, 251
Statistics, 253, 440
Steam engine, 103, 104
Stereotyping, 30, 181
Stern, Fritz, 353
Stolen City, 112
Stone Age, 102
Stone Soup story, 411
Stupefy, 205
Stupidity, 201, 202, 203, 209, 210, 240
Subconscious, 203, 267, 347, 412, 421, 426
Sub-human, 32, 227, 229
Subject (capitalized), 14, 16, 131, 134, 136, 138, 139, 190, 196, 198, 225, 232, 234, 235, 238, 267, 279, 288, 319, 379, 418, 421, 432
Sub-oppressors, 316, 317
Suharto, 289
Suicide, 18, 109, 151, 372
Super-controllers, 340, 361, 382
Superior, 22, 41, 51, 77, 126, 170, 171, 174, 216, 243, 244, 262, 286, 380, 396, 421
Sweden, 255, 257
Switzerland, 372
Symbiogenesis, 52
Symbiotic, 366, 407, 419, 431, 433
Symbiotic cultures, 407
Symbiotic system, 366
Symptom, 60, 61, 62, 65, 166, 387
Synergies, 35, 282, 336
Syntropy, 409
Syntropic Enterprise, 408
Syntropic World, 408

T

Taljanky, 325
Talking to Strangers, 168
Tax, 102, 193, 290, 292, 294, 306, 350
Tax loopholes, 290
Tech moguls, 149
Technology, 43, 95, 259, 280, 368, 414
Tendency for Interpersonal Victimhood (*see* TIV), 177
Tethered, 387
Texas, 111, 372
The Anarchy, 336
The Better Angels of Our Nature, 406
The Culture of Fear, 218
The Dawn of Everything, 325
The Democratic Republic of Congo, 289
The Emperor's New Clothes, 159
The Indian Penal Code, 305
The Iranian Revolution, 389
The Keeling Curve, 109
The Laws of Stupidity, 202
The Logic of Failure, 101
The Ministry of the Imperial House, 273
The Natives Land Act, 305
The New Confessions of an Economic Hit Man, 338
The One True Solution, 333
The Prophet, 151
The Republic of Indonesia, 289
The tipping point, 373, 375, 376
The Tora (Old Testament), 322
The Truth About Denial, 347
The Wild West, 326
The Wise Men of Chelm, 60
Theocracy, 390
Theocratic society, 305
Thinking things through, 100, 391
Thought-terminating, 208, 209
Toews, Owen, 112
Tooze, Adam, 349
Toxic waste, 58
Traitor, 194
Trauma, 18, 21, 83, 158, 171, 181, 265, 266, 299, 309, 388, 423
Trauma response, 264
Trickle down, 313

Trickle down enforcement, 313
Trudeau, Justin, 150
True believers, 14, 261, 267, 379
Trump, Donald, 311
Trust, 16, 30, 33, 35, 36, 37, 38, 46, 67, 72,
    82, 83, 139, 142, 143, 144, 153, 156,
    166, 176, 177, 182, 186, 187, 189, 191,
    210, 220, 221, 229, 230, 237, 238, 244,
    266, 267, 298, 299, 302, 310, 323, 324,
    325, 326, 327, 328, 329, 330, 331, 345,
    365, 386, 408
    High-trust, 326
    Low-trust, 324
Truth teller, 136, 310
Turkey, 356
Twain, Mark, 143, 431
Types of Cones, 277, 315, 354, 376
    Ad hoc Cones, 102, 277, 278, 376
    Diffused Cone, 276
    Embedded Cones, 275, 412
    Emptying Cones, 362, 363, 366, 367,
        369, 370
    Mega-cones, 257, 259, 272, 279, 282,
        330, 331, 338, 340, 367, 368, 382
    Mini-cones, 272
    Obvious cones, 198, 273
    Reactionary cones, 277
Tyrannical leader, 147
Tyrannical societies, 36
Tyrant, 151, 154, 192, 331, 384, 419
    Tyranny, 153, 157, 407
Tzu, Sun, 378

U

Uganda, 384
Ukraine, 11, 150, 246, 290, 325, 342
UN (United Nations), 346
Underground Railroad, 38
Unhoused, 235, 237, 238
    Homelessness, 236
Union, 215, 293, 355
    Anti-union, 305
Unsustainable system, 15
Upavaas, 398
US Patent and Trademark Office see
    (USPTO), 342
USAID, 338

Useful idiots, 225
User (capitalized), 16
USSR, 37, 97, 246
Utopia, 16
U-turn, 366

V

Vader, Darth, 330, 331
Vegans, 234
Venezuelan, 144
Vengeance, 163, 264, 386, 390, 391, 401,
    432, 433, 436
    Vengeful, 152, 180, 184, 187, 190, 212,
        382
Vicious cycle, 189
Victims, 143, 148, 178, 180, 215, 218, 224,
    264, 265, 304, 309, 326, 389, 419, 420,
    432
    Victim of crime, 419
    Victimhood, 139, 140, 178, 419, 420
Vietnam War, 230
Voice of reason, 204, 215, 387
Volcano, 68
Voluptuous, 73
Vorhies, Zach, 259
Vulnerability, 134, 165, 176, 178, 182, 260,
    261
    Vulnerabilities, 14, 135, 138, 143, 165,
        185, 190, 217, 413, 415

W

Wannabes, 171, 184, 189, 216, 319, 394
War
    War on Drugs, 230
Water pollution, 108
Watson-Watt, Robert, 95
Wealth, 244, 248, 285, 286, 287, 288, 289,
    290, 291, 292, 293, 294, 335, 343
Wealth inquality, 248
Weaponized, 355
Web search engine, 113
Well-intended, 14, 194, 195, 196, 250,
    277, 389
Wengrow, David, 325
Westerveld, Jay, 351
Whistleblower, 224, 296, 312

White supremacy, 18, 355
Winnipeg, 112
Wokeness, 359
Women, 47, 52, 57, 73, 77, 81, 143, 147,
    158, 165, 180, 227, 228, 231, 233, 260,
    277, 278, 358, 381, 391, 399, 421
Workaholism, 272
World Bank, 338, 339, 340
World building, 155
World War I, 93
World War II, 38, 95, 97, 112, 176, 337,
    353, 375
Wu, Tim, 85

X

Xenophobia, 18, 163, 348
Xinjiang region, 360

Y

Yachts, 228, 291
Yardstick, 27, 176, 271
Yea-sayers, 165
YouGov poll, 355
YouTube, 249, 259, 341

Z

Zealots, 13, 14, 186, 187, 195, 303, 319,
    376, 377, 379, 382, 401, 405, 431
Zedong, Mao, 103
Zelensky, Volodymyr, 150
Zero-sum game, 163, 164
Zimbardo, Philip, 283
Zionist, 275
Zoo, 193
Zookeeper dynamic, 196
Zuma, Jacob, 354